THE ARYAN ORIGIN

OF THE

GAELIC RACE AND LANGUAGE

THE ARYAN ORIGIN

OF THE

GAELIC RACE AND LANGUAGE

SHOWING THE PRESENT AND PAST LITERARY POSITION OF IRISH GAELIC ITS PHONESIS, THE FOUNTAIN OF CLASSIC PRONUNCTATION; ITS LAWS ACCORD WITH GRIMM'S LAWS; ITS BARDIC BEAUTIES THE SOURCE OF RHYME; THE CIVILISATION OF PAGAN IRELAND

U. J. BOURKE

GYAN

Published by

Gyan Publishing House
5, Ansari Road
Daryaganj, New Delhi-110002
Phone: 011-47034999, 9811692060
E-mail: books@gyanbooks.com

Distribution Network
gyanbooks.com
India, USA, Canada, UK, Australia

ISBN: 978-93-6780-805-4 (PB)

First Published, 1875

2nd Impression 2024

Printed at: Gyan Press, Delhi.

THE ARYAN ORIGIN OF THE GAELIC RACE AND LANGUAGE
Author: U. J. BOURKE

THE ARYAN ORIGIN

OF THE

Gaelic Race and Language,

SHOWING THE PRESENT AND PAST LITERARY POSITION OF IRISH GAELIC; ITS PHONESIS, THE FOUNTAIN OF CLASSIC PRONUNCIATION; ITS LAWS ACCORD WITH GRIMM'S LAWS; ITS BARDIC BEAUTIES THE SOURCE OF RHYME; THE CIVILISATION OF PAGAN IRELAND; EARLY KNOWLEDGE OF LETTERS; THE ART OF ILLUMINATING, ANCIENT ARCHITECTURE.

THE ROUND TOWERS.

THE BREHON LAW.

TRUTH OF THE PENTATEUCH.

KNOWLEDGE IN PAGAN TIMES RETROGRESSIVE, NOT PROGRESSIVE; THE INDUCTIVE SCIENCES; PHILOLOGY AND ETHNOLOGY CONFIRM THE TRUTH OF IRISH HISTORY; GAELIC NAMES OF PERSONS AND PLACES FULL OF HISTORIC SUGGESTIVENESS; IN THIS RESPECT AND IN POETIC POWER

IRISH GAELIC SUPERIOR TO SANSKRIT.

ONE THOUSAND UNPUBLISHED IRISH MANUSCRIPTS

BY THE

VERY REV. U. J. BOURKE, M.R.I.A.

Canon of Tuam Cathedral, and President of St. Jarlath's College; Author of the "College Irish Grammar," Easy Lessons in Irish, &c.

LONDON.
LONGMANS, GREEN AND CO., PATERNOSTER ROW.

1875.

TO HIS GRACE

THE ARCHBISHOP OF TUAM,

METROPOLITAN, AND PRIMATE OF THE PROVINCE,

FIDEI ET PATRIÆ,
DECUS ET TUTAMEN,

THE FIRMEST CITADEL OF THE IRISH-GAELIC TONGUE,

THIS WORK

ON THE ARYAN ORIGIN OF THE GAELIC RACE

AND LANGUAGE,

IS, AS A MEMORIAL OF THE

CELEBRATION ON THE 8th JUNE, 1875,

OF THE

FIFTIETH ANNIVERSARY OF HIS CONSECRATION

BY PERMISSION AFFECTIONATELY DEDICATED;

FOR, IN HONORING

"THE GREAT ARCHBISHOP OF THE WEST,"

MARKED WITH A BLESSING OF LENGTH OF YEARS,

NOT GRANTED TO THE PRESENT TIME

TO ANY OTHER BISHOP OF THE GAEL

IRELAND'S GLORIOUS PRIESTHOOD

IS HONORED,

THE SHIELD OF THE POOR AND THE PERSECUTED,

THE DEFENDER OF A NEGLECTED RACE

IS HONORED,

AND THE HAPPY UNION WHICH SHOULD REPRESENT

LOVE OF CREED AND COUNTRY.

IS COMMEMORATED.

September, 8th, 1875.

PREFACE.

A mere accident has given the first impulse to the composition of the annexed work.

In the spring of 1874 a few clerical friends and the author formed, at the same festive board in the college, a social meeting, not unusual on solemn feast days; and the subject of conversation turned on the language and antiquities of Ireland.

Ever since the publication of *Easy Lessons in Irish*, and the *College Irish Grammar*, the author has, time after time, received from amateur scientists, and occasionally from scholars—all differing in position, or in country, —letters in which questions like the following were put: "What was the character of the Irish race before the "coming of St. Patrick? How far had a knowledge "of the Christian religion spread through Ireland before "the Apostle preached the faith from Tara hill? Had "the pagan Irish any knowledge of literature? If so, "what kind of alphabet did they use?—was it Roman, "Grecian, Ogham, or some form of letter now unknown? "The phonesis of the Irish-Gaelic language? The law "of slender and broad vowel sounds? On what does it "rest? The correct sounds of the consonants in their "natural and aspirated state? The number of letters in "Irish? in Greek? How many did the supposed "Cadmus introduce into Greece? Did the Greeks really "loose F (Vau)? The lost F preserved in Irish Gaelic

"The Round Towers. Which opinion—that of Dr. "Petrie or Thomas Moore—is correct? Were the Etrus- "cans Gaels? Were the children of the Gael of Aryan "origin, and not Cuthite or Phenician?"

From these letters it was plain, that from a scientific point of view, the field of Irish Antiquities and of the Irish-Gaelic language lay fallow; and it seemed right that some one should aim at cultivating it. The present volume is the author's attempt.

U. J. BOURKE,
PRESIDENT.

St. Jarlath's College,
Feast of the
Nativity of the B.V.M., 1875.

PREFACE TO THE SECOND EDITION.

A PREFACE is to a book what a porch is to a house; or it is to the body of the book what a miniature photograph is to the full living form.

A preface to the second edition should superadd some new feature, and tell how the first issue of the work has been received by the literary public.

The opinions of the press are, as a rule—particularly when coming from quarters opposed in political and religious interests and views—a fair criterion by which the value of a new work may be estimated. Regarding the "Aryan Origin of the Gaelic Race and Language," there has been from all quarters—from the press in England, Scotland, Ireland, America, and in a remarkable degree from the "Athens of the North," from Derry, Omagh; from Cork, Limerick and Dublin, a pæan in praise of it poured forth with a ready and cheerful willingness, not alone by the proprietors and editors of Catholic journals, but by those who have been, from education and early training, opposed to the religion of the writer.

One must, however, like a wise sea-captain, be prepared for adverse blasts.

Diversity of interests, of knowledge, and even of tastes, begets diversity of thought; and hence reviewers will often find fault, where, in the judgment of others equally learned, no fault is to be found.

All critics, it must be remembered, are not scholars, nor men of large and enlightened views. There are many persons who prefer class interests and pride of party to all the learning in the world.

The first edition of this work has received far less hostile criticism than the author had expected. Although the book was written and printed in the short period of eighteen months, the views presented in its pages are not the effect of haste; they had been formed and matured over a decade of years, from reading, observation, and thought. The friendly Scot reviewing the volume in the *Keltic Magazine*, Inverness, sees with a kindred perceptive power the facts regarding the writer: "The work," he says, "is a Keltic repository—the writer's Keltic reading for many years being apparently thrown into a crucible, and having undergone a certain process there, are forged into the handsome volume before us."

The book has been written for the reading public generally, at home and in America; for students in colleges; for young ladies in educational establishments and convent schools, and on this account the style is clear, lively, and attractive.

The writer's aim has been to trace the Gaels to the original habitat of their race and language. His duty, then, had been not unlike that of an explorer in a territory not much known—sailing up one of its great rivers, to note on the right bank and on the left the footprints of a by-gone race still traceable in the language they spoke; in the names which they gave to the places through which they passed ; in the monumental remains; in the style of architecture, which still outlives the ravages of age ; in other abiding signs of civilised life, to be seen in their poetry, love of rhyme, knowledge of colours and of musical sound. Their laws, still extant, like the pillar-towers of the land, bring, at a bound, the archæologist back three thousand years.

These jottings along the stream of time up to the highest and earliest source are varied ; but they all tend to point to the Origin of the Gaelic Race and Language.

The varied lines of proof, tending all to one point, present in their collected force a most convincing argument that the Gaels were the first who came westward from the ancient Aryan region in Asia.

St. Jarlath's College, Tuam,
15th Sept., 1876.

(To the Editor of the *Athenæum.*)

St. Jarlath's College, Tuam, Ireland.
March 30th, 1876.

SIR—In the world of letters and in the walks of literary criticism, "fair play" ought to be a maxim dear to the sons of Britain and Ireland. Even on the turf, or at the target, and in other circles of international social life, this maxim is not ignored. Men, professedly of intellectual culture—sons of science who, we suppose, aim at the acquisition of truth—should cherish truth and honour with a fidelity equal, at least, to that shown by persons less highly educated.

The circulation and influence of the *Athenæum*, as a literary organ, is acknowledged by all. Were it a provincial or a party journal, or a literary weekly less favourably known, a place in its pages would not, on the present occasion, be claimed for the following correction.

The new work lately published by Longmans, London —"Aryan Origin of the Gaelic Race and Language"— has, in your columns, No. 2525, issued March 18th, been reviewed. In that review, sent to me by some friend, there is one leading untrue statement (p. 393) which I wish to set right before the readers of the *Athenæum*. The following is the passage—a summary framed by the critic, and put forth as if made by the author of the work in support of his theory on the Pillar Towers of Ireland:—

" Canon Bourke's arguments may be regarded as a sort of very lengthened sorites: 'The pagan Irish were Aryans, therefore Easterns; the Easterns were great builders; Noah built the Ark; his sons must also have been good builders; some of his descendants were certainly such, *e.g.*, the builders of the Tower of Babel and the hanging gardens of Babylon, &c.; the sons of Japhet must have been as clever as their cousins: the pagan Irish were descendants of Japhet; they must have inherited the family talents; they *could* accordingly have built the Round Towers; they *did* build them; *ergo*, these structures are of pagan origin.' "

Allow me to refer your readers who have the work, to pages 381, 382, in which is read the contradictory to the foregoing; and to quote, for the sake of those who have it not, the words of the text which the author did really pen:—

" The argument can be put in this way: All the Aryan nations were skilled in the sciences and arts, especially those of architecture, sculpture, dyeing, and painting. But the early natives were, as their language proves, Aryan. Therefore, the inhabitants of ancient Ireland were skilled in the sciences and arts, and they possessed a knowledge of architecture, sculpture, dyeing, and painting. Does this argument prove that the pagan Irish built the Towers? *Not at all.* It only proves that they had knowledge and power sufficient to erect those perennial piles which are a source of wonder to succeeding generations."

Observe the words, " not at all." The writer of the notice in the *Athenæum* ignores their existence, and states, as the author's own, the very contradictory of that found in the text. That is strange! The book was in his hands, it is supposed, and the sentence before his eyes, and yet he writes, as the author's words, the very contradictory of what he had seen and what he had read! One is amazed at assertions such as this—made coolly and not uncommonly by men "of more than ordinary grasp and depth of intellect or of general scholarship." A scholar from Oxford, or Cambridge, or one of our brethren of the Highlands, who are well-educated gentlemen, would not write after that fashion. The literary critic had heard something about a sorites, and thought it would be a capital hit to "do" Lord Macaulay, and to give a counter-touch of dispraise, in order to heighten the colouring, as he thought, of the literary picture, for his philo-Anglican readers.

He writes with the air of the greatest scholar of the day; and strives to make his readers believe that he not only knows everything about which he writes, but that he alone is right. This air of assumed infallibility puts me in mind of a strange amateur Irish writer who made an appearance some years ago before the Irish-Gaelic public, and whose acquaintance, very likely, the critic on the present occasion has made. This wonderful scholar was (according to himself) the only centre of literary and philosophical orthodoxy. How did he show it? In this wise:—He argued: His own views are right! This was invariably the major proposition of the syllogism; and the minor: The views of his opponent were quite different! Therefore his opponent's views were wrong. In this handy, happy fashion he settled all difficulties.

The only supposition that can be made favourable to the reviewer is, that he wrote from a vague recollection of what he had read in the work given him to notice; or that he had formed some notion of it from a hurried glance at the summary of the chapters. This appears plain from another untrue statement—but one of less importance—found in the review. He says Canon Bourke derives the term Gael, or Gaedhal, from "Cath" (pr. *Kah*), a battle, and "oilte," trained, educated. The derivation of the term Gael is nowhere found in the work—that of *Keltoi*, or *Keltos*, is.

The explanation which he give of the days of the week in Irish-Gaelic is phantastic and quite harmless, if it was only less dogmatic. This is not the place nor the time to prove that the meaning and origin of the Irish names of the days of the week, shown by me at p. 474, are quite in accord with (1) correct radical spelling of the terms in Gaelic; (2) with sense; (3) correct phonesis; (4) analogy with other dialects of Aryan origin; (5) with history and authority; and that the reviewer's notions are, at least, conjectural, and are not supported by radical spelling; nay, are opposed to it—opposed to sense, to phonesis, to the pronunciation of the terms in the present and in the past—opposed to history and to authoity. If "aoıne," (Friday) was derived from *Jejunium*, it should be (like "Iosa," from *Jesus*, "Ion," from *Joannes*), written "Ieıuné," and pronounced quite differently from that by which "Dıa aoıne" (Friday) at present is known. "Dıa cedéın" (Wednesday)—"cedéın" (in two syllables) should be written "Dıa ceud-ıeıuné," and pronounced, not "Dıa-cedeín, as it is at present, but "dra-ceud-ɪeʀuné" (in four syllables), as it never yet has been written or pronounced, and never will be.

As the views of the critic on the subject of the derivation of Gaelic, and on the meaning of the Irish names for the days of the week, have been formed merely by haphazard, so, too, is his guess at the logical reasoning presented in my arguments against Dr. Petrie.

The sorites, as a form of argument, is not employed at all in the work. The arguments consist of distinct syllogisms, or of epichiremata. Dr. Petrie makes use of three kinds of argument—1, negative; 2, positive; and 3, that it was impossible for the Pagan Irish to build such perennial pillars, as they were a people barbarous and ignorant. It was necessary in establishing the truth of the new theory to prove how valueless were Dr. Petrie's arguments; nay, more, to show that the Pagan Irish were, as a fact, well skilled in the knowledge of architecture.

This last was a kind of "*retorqueo argumentum*" directly against Petrie's statement. They did not know how to build, therefore they did not build, is his argument. I answer—they were as an Aryan race skilled in architecture—therefore it is not true to state that they did not know how to build; and, therefore, the argument founded on their supposed want of knowledge is valueless. Let me quote from p. 381 of the "Aryan Origin," one passage.

"The great objection hitherto against the opinion that the Round Towers are of Pagan origin is, that our Pagan progenitors had not, they say, as far as can be known, knowledge or skill and practical power to erect such superstructures. 'Hitherto,' says Petrie (p. 2), 'we have had little on the subject but speculation, growing out of a mistaken and unphilosophical zeal in support of the claims of our country to an early civilisation; and even the truth having been advocated only hypothetically, has failed to be established, from the absence of that evidence which facts alone could supply.' This objection fades away under the increased knowledge which the light derived from the science of comparative philology sheds on the early history of the Irish race. The early Irish were Aryan, therefore they were a race possessed of skill and power to erect those Towers."

The reviewer tells his readers that the work is written "in a style vigorous, exact, and clear;" that the book "brings within the reach of the general reader, and of the tyro in philology many of the most striking results achieved by the comparatively new science of language."

He adds, however: "It contains nothing new to scholars."

If this statement is true, then every new work, in which are embodied theories and dogmata of philosophy already known to a few, must be, by a parity of reasoning, pronounced a work "containing nothing new to scholars."

Sir William Hamilton wrote nothing new to scholars, for almost all he has written on logic and metaphysics are found in the writings of the Angelic Doctor, and of the schoolmen of the fourteenth century, of the fifteenth, and sixteenth. Euclid wrote nothing new to scholars, for mathematics as a science was most certainly known and put into practice ages before he was born. Aristotle wrote nothing original, for logic, natural and technical, had been known long before Stagyra was honoured by his birth; and ages before he wrote his treatise on politics, on physics, and metaphysics, these sciences were known to the learned of those remote times.

As a matter of fact, however, several new subjects are treated in the work:—"(1) The phonesis of the Irish language; (2) the principles on which it rests; (3) those principles in accord with the mother Aryan tongue; (4) comparison between the early pronunciation of the Latin and Greek and Irish-Gaelic; (5) Hymnology; (6) origin of Rhyme; (7) a new view regarding the Round Towers—that they were first built in the early Pagan period, and that, after the gospel had been preached in Ireland, St. Patrick turned the Round Towers, as he did the Pagan fountains, to the service of Christian rites, and hallowed them by Christian practices and religious associations."

These views and opinions are supported by arguments which cannot fail to convince any fairly unprejudiced mind. The arguments furnished in the book are sustained by the written views and opinions of distinguished scholars of the present time quite unknown to the reader.

The best writers support their own views by the authoritative statements of able scholars. This practice ought not to displease "men of more than ordinary grasp and depth of intellect or of general scholarship." Neither ought it to excite their anger that the book is written, not as a purely scientific work but one which the general reader can peruse with pleasure. Not a few have expressed themselves delighted in perusing its pages. One thousand copies have been sold off. That is a good sign of the appreciation in which the book is held by the people. The work is making way amongst all unbiassed readers. A certain distinguished scholar has written to me to say: That he admits the arguments in favour of the pre-Christian theory regarding the Round Towers, but he prefers still to believe that these ancient piles had been erected by Christian hands.

One cannot expect to convince people against their will. The will must be convinced calmly and gradually. Are arguments faulty because "intellectual graspers" are not convinced? By no means. Were his Eminence Cardinal Manning to preach with the tongue of an angel, or with the convincing logic of St. Thomas, he would not convert a Whalley or a Newdegate to believe in the truth of the Church of Rome. Is it that the arguments are not convincing? Not at all. With prejudiced minds, and men moved by spleen or spite, as with unbelievers, miracles would not, as with the Jews of old, be proofs convincing.

I have the honour to be your faithful servant,

U. J. CANON BOURKE.

CORRIGENDA.

The name *England* is in one instance put for *Ireland;* and *Ireland* for *England*; *Gaelic* is written for *Greek*; in another the word *vertu* is, notwithstanding great care, printed *virtue;* palæontology is found in two instances for palæology. The "literal" errors are such as can be corrected by any intelligent reader: "mistry" for misty, owing to a type-slip. Those trained to literary labour know that a book cannot be completely free from errors of press.

CONTENTS.

CHAPTER I.

CHAPTER II.

2F

Page

CHAPTER III.

CHAPTER IV.

CHAPTER V.

CHAPTER VI.

CHAPTER VII.

CHAPTER VIII.

CHAPTER IX.

GRIMM'S LAW.

CHAPTER X.

CHAPTER XI.

CHAPTER XII.

CHAPTER XIII.

CHAPTER XIV.

CHAPTER XV.

CHAPTER XVI.

CHAPTER I.

INTRODUCTORY.

The *Dublin Review*, in the summer of 1865. The lack of literary zeal at present amongst Irishmen. Matthew Arnold, John Stuart Blackie. Dawn of a new day. New forms of thought brought forth under the light of inductive science. Englishmen affected by this intellectual action. Irishmen are not to them aliens in race. The *Science des Origines*. Keltic studies a portion of philology. The study of language supports the truth of history and of the writings of Moses. If Englishmen and Germans study Irish-Gaelic, why should not the children of the Gael ? Example. The Catholic University. Trinity College. Learned men who have not had a University training. O'Donovan. Work to be done. The past gone; the present our own. The future new. Ireland's inward world of thought and knowledge that must win. The genius of Ireland should turn to Irish-Gaelic. The language—its phonesis, relation to cognate tongues. Irish Literateurs. Learned Ecclesiastics should not overlook it, because it is a medium of higher scholarship; because the language is at their doors; because the rising age, as one of science, demands it; because priests and people should be one in national advancement. Religion should be to science what science is to art. Motives for study. Activity of modern scholarship. The stream of Greek mythology turned to a Christian channel. Irish mythology; "fairy notions." Result of the study of the language and literature of Ireland.

Just ten years ago the following words appeared in the pages of the summer quarter of the *Dublin Review:* "It is disgraceful to the whole of us, Saxons and Kelts alike, that we leave the real work of Keltic research to continental schools. With Irish-Gaelic—the Keltic root-tongue—and three dialects spoken in the very midst of us, with stores of documents of all kinds accessible to enquirers, with every means at command, we supinely permit the German and the Frenchman to take the honors that ought to rest with ourselves."

However much Irishmen can plead the want of facilities at present, and a crushing legislation in the past, in justification, it must be admitted that there is a great deal of truth in the words of the Reviewer regarding the supineness or apathy of natives of Eire on the great question with which their existence as a distinct people is vitally connected.

A French critic in the *Revue Celtique*, Mons. H. Gaidoz, commenting on the important question of Ireland's ancient speech, observes that the great and decidedly important national questions amongst Irishmen—the Franchise, Education, Religious Equality, Home Rule, or Repeal—have, throughout the country and in the assembly of the nation, their respective advocates, but that the great question in which the existence of Ireland, as a distinct nationality, is centered, has no one to advocate its merits, or to represent it in the Press or in Parliament.

The spirit, however, which, ten years ago, animated the breast of the writer in the *Dublin Review*, has not breathed in vain over the still waters of past apathy or indifference.

ENGLAND TO THE RESCUE.

A move has been made in a quarter, in which, as usual, it had been least expected—England.

With no slight pleasure the lovers of Gaelic literature read in the *Cornhill Magazine*, issued in the summer succeeding 1865, *Essays on the Study of Keltic Literature*, from the pen of Matthew Arnold, professor of poetry in the University of Oxford. About the same time, John Stuart Blackie, professor of Greek in the University of Edinburgh, became the zealous apostle of the Gaelic cause in North Britain. The honest native pluck and power of the Anglo-Saxon element had been now brought for the first time into play. This was encouraging. It was a source of gratification to the lovers of literary progress in the Gaelic school of research. It was an omen of hope for all devoted sons of Ireland.

The grey line of incipient dawn on the social horizon shot suddenly up in the East before the eyes of Irishmen who lay looking listlessly on. This was the first gleam of genuine day that broke through the darkness in which Ireland had for centuries lain enshrouded.

Under the new light of the inductive sciences, a change in the aspect of thought, regarding our language amongst Englishmen, has manifestly set in. English scholars have begun to admit that some good can come from the *Nazareth* of the sister-land. If Englishmen could only learn to know more about Ireland and her sons than they had known, they would, we feel assured study, even for the sake of knowledge, her annals, her history, her language.

THE SCIENCE OF LANGUAGES SHOWS THAT ENGLISHMEN AND IRISHMEN ARE NOT ALIEN.

Irishmen are not all that Lord Lyndhurst declared they were "Aliens in speech, in religion, in blood." Science shows that they are with Englishmen and Scothmen brethern of the one great Aryan family, who, thousands of years ago emigrated from Persia in the East to the most western portion of Europe, and made island homes of Eire and Britain. *

At this moment, as Matthew Arnold observes, "there exists in the mind of many Englishmen, yea, and of many Irishmen in Ireland, such a sense of mutual repulsion, such a feeling of incompatibility, of radical antagonism between the two races that the Jew seemed, at least not long ago, nearer than the Gael to Englishmen; "Puritanism had so assimilated Bible ideas and phraseology,—names like Ebenezer, and notions like that of hewing Agag in pieces—came so natural to the lovers of England, that the sense of affinity between the Teutonic and the Hebrew nature was quite strong; a steady middle-class Anglo-Saxon much more imagined himself Ehud's cousin than Ossian's.

"I remember when I was young," says the Professor of Poetry, Oxford University, "I was taught to think of Kelt as separated by an impassable gulf from Teuton; my father in particular was never weary of contrasting them; he insisted much oftener on the separation between us (English) and them, than on the separation between us and any other race in the world."

Political and religious differences doubled the estrangement. The sneers and insults of writers in the *Times*, assuring the Gaels that everything of theirs not English

---

* Linguæ quæ inter cognatas linguas ab India per Asiam et Europam dilatatas extrema est in occidente, naturam, verietatam formasque exponere aggredior.—*Zeuss—Præfatio.*

Primus (Zeuss) ariano semini evidenti vindicavit Celticam gentem, antiquam, late olim patentem, numero, virtute, institutionibus, rebus gestis inlustrem, quæ fatali quadam instabilitate jactata, postquam fere tota Europæ litora vestigiis suis signavit, prævalentibus et tenacioribus stirpibus affinibus Latinis et Germanicis, non tamen sine obstinato, diuturno nec inglorioso certamine, patriam, nomen, linguam aut jam cessit aut mox cessura est."—*Nigra, p. iv, Glossæ Hibernicæ*

is "simply a foolish interference with the national progress of civilisation and prosperity" tended to make this estrangement immense, incurable, fatal.

There have been no greater enemies to the English nation and people than ignorant, conceited writers who decry everything Irish, Gaelic, Keltic, and who can find nothing of good even in virtue or knowledge, unless tinged with the yellow beams that radiate from some golden focus, or with the mellow light of imperial favor.

All that is gradually being changed under the influence of increased knowledge. The science of origins—as the French call it—enables scholars to ascend to early times and to first principles, and thence trace the kinship that exists between all the Indo-European nations. What effect has this study already produced? "The sense of apathy to the Irish people, of radical estrangement from them has visibly abated amongst all the better part of us," says Matthew Arnold. "I am inclined to think that the march of science—science insisting that there is no such original chasm between us—has had an appreciable share in producing this changed state of feeling." It is not one but a host of learned Englishmen who testify to this fact at the present time.

WORK TO BE DONE THAT IRISHMEN CAN DO.

We must leave the "dead past to bury its dead," and strive, we who are alive, to advance in the way of perfection. Let each one consider that the appeal to advance, and to do good for country and kin, is addressed to himself. Son of Eire, indifferent hitherto, strive now to be earnest; if good, aim at becoming better. There is much to be done. The past is now a matter of history. Ireland cannot live the past over again. Her future is new. The whole social and civil world has put on a fresh form of life. Steam and Electricity have brought the far off families and races of mankind together. The earth is now simply a large stage. At present, rivalry exists between nations; between clans no longer. Witness the international competitions between England, Scotland and Ireland; and between Ireland and America. It is brain and intellect and knowledge that come off first in the fight of races. The high hand of mere material power can no longer conquer; the clear head, and the power of thought gain the prize. "It is not in the outward and visible world of material life" says Matthew Arnold, "that the Keltic genius of Wales, or of Ireland, can at this day hope to count for much, it is in the inward world of thought and science . . . . If the genius of Ireland can get itself thoroughly known, as an object of science, it may count for a good deal far more than most of us, Saxons, imagine." It is a power in a way.

IF ENGLISHMEN STUDY GAELIC LITERATURE, WHY SHOULD NOT IRISHMEN?

Men of Saxon mind and tone have sat down to study the history, the language, the laws, and the poetry of the Gael; why do not the children of the Gael do as much for themselves? Students from London and Oxford have, within the past five years, come to Tuam to learn Irish Gaelic; how many students in Ireland have turned their attention to that branch of study? The Oxford professor of poetry states that the comparative study of languages and literature gains every day more followers; how many natives of Ireland could be found amongst students of this class? They are easily numbered.

MOTIVES.

To all—French, and Germans, and Americans—the

language and literature of the Gael are, as an object of study, full of interest and profit; to Englishmen they present a two-fold advantage—first, as a new field of science, and secondly, as a medium calculated to reconcile the Anglo-Saxon with the Gael, by pointing out the identity of their Aryan origin, and thus helping to break down that wall of separation between the two races, which had been built up by ignorance, prejudice, and religious hate. The language and literature of our race ought to have a threefold interest for Irishmen—those just named, and in addition, the fact that our language and our literature are a national inheritance. The inhabitants of every nation love and cherish their own national existence. Our language and our literature constitute our special national life. Let them perish—then, the life of the Irish nation, as such, has existence no longer.

EXAMPLE.

The present writer wishes to do a man's share of the national work. In the midst of important duties as priest, and professor in the College over which he presides, he has devoted snatched moments of time to the study of his country's language, its philologic value, its orthography and phonesis, its Aryan origin, its relation with kindred dialects of Europe. The literature of ancient Eire has claimed and received attention; and this subject has led to the study of the Brehon Law, to the early poetry of pagan and Christian Ireland, to her architecture—Round Towers; to a knowledge of the arts as known at the remotest period.

With that certainty which arises from science, and with that correctness of detail, the result of authentic research, the writer presents his views to the public on those interesting and important national subjects, with a fair-grounded confidence that he is performing a work agreeable and useful to scholars in England, Scotland, France, Germany, and America. He is aware that for Irishmen the subjects are too homely, and that most of our countrymen lack training sufficient to enable them to appreciate studies which men of research alone can value.

KNOWLEDGE A SOURCE OF HAPPINESS.

Knowledge, according to Epictetus, contributes largely to make man's life happy. Knowledge of ancient records and of the inductive sciences, forms a great source of pleasure to those who make them a study. The Rev. George W. Cox writes in the preface to his great work, *Aryan Mythology:* "The delight which this investigation has never ceased to impart is strictly the satisfaction which the astronomer or the geologist feels in the ascertainment of new facts."

Another source of pleasure to the writer of any new work on subjects of a scientific character is to know that his efforts are not for his own benefit alone, but that, whatever new facts may be brought to light, whatever good may be achieved they are a gain to the brotherhood of scholars all the world over. Whenever an astronomer in the west of Ireland makes any discovery like that, for instance, made a few years ago by John Bermingham, Esq., of Millbrook, it is deemed by the whole body of science men as so much gain to the school of astronomical knowledge. In like manner, any new discovery in geology is regarded as so much added to the stock of information respecting that science. The same holds good in this department of knowledge in which the Keltic dialects, and therefore the Irish-Gaelic language, are investigated. Amongst literateurs, scientists, scholars, there exists onl y one nationality, the entire earth; only one sun, knowledge; one atmosphere, social brotherhood.

Many sons of Ireland will cry out and say, with much truth, no doubt: We have had no university education; we are not prepared for these higher studies; the Catholic University is only in its infancy; and Trinity College had been for the great body of the youth of Ireland a hidden garden. Scientific and historic knowledge was there, if you will, for the past three centuries; but the Catholic youth of Ireland—that is, eight out of every ten of the nation, could not even glance at it. The golden apples had not been guarded with so much jealous care as had been the treasures of Trinity from the Catholic youth of Ireland.

That excuse is certainly well founded; nevertheless, men who are willing and in earnest can do much. Dr. O'Donovan and Professor O'Curry had never enjoyed the advantages of a University education; yet, behold the splendid works which they achieved for Ireland, her language, and her history.

There are many who are pondering on the past, and forget to act in the living present. A writer in the *Dublin Review* says: "Dwelling intensely on the past is neglect of the present, and deadly sin against the future."

THE PRESENT—ITS WORK.

The great questions of the hour—questions in which princes and statesmen, prelates and peasant parents are concerned, are—education, science, knowledge.

"The bent of our time," says the author of *Study of Keltic Literature*, "is towards science, towards knowing things as they are. So the Kelt's claims towards having his genius and its works fairly treated as objects of scientific investigation, the Saxon can hardly reject when these claims are urged simply on their own merits, and are not mixed up with extraneous views which jeopardise them. What the French call the *science des origines*—a science which is at the bottom of all real knowledge of the actual world, and which is every day growing in interest and importance is very incomplete without a thorough critical account of the Kelts, their genius, language, and literature."

The object and aim of the present work is to give a thorough critical account of the language of the Gael, to show its early origin; that it is Aryan, and comes to us down the great stream of migration that had begun to flow westward from the high country between the Tigris and the Indus, even before Abraham went forth out of his country, and from his kindred, and out of his father's house, and came into the land which the Lord did show him.

Through the eastern origin of the language, one reaches the habitat of the people who spoke a common mother tongue in the hilly country of Persia and Armenia, and all along the fertile valleys watered by the Oxus, the Araxes, and Euphrates once, as many learned men suppose the blissful site of Paradise. The phonesis of this primitive Aryan tongue did not rest on chance, but had been wedded, like music, to principles of science. These principles were handed down to the eldest daughter of the mother tongue—Gaelic—the phonetic developments of which show forth, at this day, the truth of Jakob Grimm's law. Gaelic is the twin sister of Sanskrit, and like it, is the oldest of the Indo-European family. At the present time it is useful in many ways for students to know the position of the literature of the Irish-Gael; the orthography, the phonetic force of the language in the present and in the past; the correct pronunciation of the classic languages—Latin and Greek, taking as standards the ancient Gaelic and the oldest forms of the tongues spoken in southern Europe; the growth of human speech, its grammatical developements; the Pentateuch, its truth; and that man in pagan times was not progressive. These are questions full of interest, and of knowledge as exciting, as if one were writing the history of a lost race or of a newly disentombed city.

In times now past, the study of philology had not been much known save to a few amongst the great body of European scholars. It is not so at present. The lectures of Professor Max Muller; of Mathew Arnold at Oxford; of Geddes, Professor of Greek at Aberdeen; and of John Stuart Blackie, Professor of Greek at the University of Edinburgh; the published works of Prichard and Pictet; of Cox and Nigra; of Sir Henry Sumner Maine and of Monsieur H. Gaidoz in the *Revue Celtique*; the publication at home of O'Curry's Lectures, or *MS. Materials of Irish History;* the Essays and learned works on philology by W. K. Sullivan, have given the science in this country a public status which it had never before the present time enjoyed. The German host of Gaelic lovers are found in the van of this wonderful movement. Next in order come the French scholars; and after them British scientists; but last of all, the natives of Ireland. The talented and energetic sons of Caledonia are far ahead of Irishmen in this new literary movement. Blackie and Geddes and Mackenzie, and Mackay, Lord Neaves, and others, are quite in earnest in their efforts to do all that possibly can be done to re-establish the Gaelic in the Highlands. Very soon Professor Blackie will have collected the amount of money necessary to found a Keltic chair in the University of Edinburgh. All this time Ireland's sons are looking supinely on. They have no Blackie; they have no Professor of pluck or patriotism fitted for the task; and the odds are directly against such a one, even if he had the courage to venture on a duty of the kind. Some one like the President of the Royal Irish Academy alone could effect a result so desirable, for he alone is the centre around whom gather men of mind—Catholics and non-Catholics; philo-Kelts and philo-Saxons. It must be admitted that the Royal Irish Academy has done much—it could do more—for the advancement of Keltic literature. The prizes which it offers are not calculated to effect any practical good. The amount proffered is too little to stimulate for money's sake the industry of the learned; and no one but scholars of deep erudition can effect anything worthy the name in favor of Keltic literature. The field of reading is very extensive; the amount of research, and the knowledge of Comparative Grammar necessary to enable one to form a correct opinion on points of history and of etymology are very considerable; and when a scholar sits down to write, he ought to receive for his services such remuneration as the proprietor of the *Edinburgh Review*, or the rich owner of the *New York Herald* has been accustomed to bestow.

IRISH GAELIC NECESSARY FOR PHILOLOGISTS.

All who aim at acquiring a scholarly knowledge of the science of Comparative Grammar cannot at the present day well overlook this branch of philologic study—Irish Gaelic. In order to obtain anything like a correct notion of philology, and to be skilled in any fair way in Comparative Grammar, the student must learn either Sanskrit or Irish Gaelic. He must learn some primitive language, one of those two. And the writer, to support his view of this point, quotes the words of Geddes, Professor of Greek in the Aberdeen University, who maintains that Gaelic is as good a medium as Sanskrit for the philologist: "And why should Gaelic have been overlooked? Because till a very recent period scholars have uniformly and systematically neglected in a culpable, short-sighted manner the Keltic speech. The blame of this must be shared by the Highlanders—say Irishmen, instead—who have, with rare exceptions, done very little to render their tongue philologically appreciated. Professor Blackie is indignant with Highlanders themselves for the neglect of their own tongue. He complains that they have no Gaelic newspapers; no Gaelic sign boards on their shops." Neither have the Irish people.

Men of all nationalities are making philology the object of their study. And when scholars of every other nationality in Europe makes philology a study, and that through the medium of Irish-Gaelic, it ill becomes Irishmen to neglect so useful a branch of knowledge.

It is useful to the worldly scientist and to the learned ecclesiastic. In the early ages of Ireland's history her clerical sons won first honors in every place of learning throughout Europe—from Asia-Minor to Spain, and from the coast of Greenland to Greece. It would ill become noble successors of a noble race to neglect a study which at present is much needed, not alone by ecclesiastics, but by Christians of all classes, to combat infidelity and to show plainly and readily the beauty, clearness, and strength of the arguments that tend to support the truths of the Christian religion.

Persons professing infidel views, who follow the teaching of Darwin and Huxley, reviving in the nineteenth century of the Christian era the untenable theories of Democritus, who profess to think that matter came into being without a cause; that the harmony of the spheres is the result of atomic confusion, free from all intelligent control; that there is no spiritual power except the higher forces of material development; no soul, no free will, no hereafter, no God, are to be met in public and in private, in the saloon and railway carriage, on board a steamer, at lecture-halls, and private meetings. They are not afraid nor ashamed to put forward their views, for they have devoted years of study to the subject of their belief, or rather absence of all belief.

Irish clergymen, constituted masters in the schools of knowledge, ought to be skilled in the inductive sciences; and therefore, in philology, palaeontology, in ethnology, too, as well as in geology, in order to be able to shew clearly that the views of the disciples of the modern Leucippus and Democritus have no foundation in fact and in the laws of nature; and that at best the light streaming from such sciences is grossly overrated, or as far as it is the expression of truth that, like artificial light mingling with the sun's effulgence, it harmonises with other well-known truths.

The literary and scientific worth of new books and periodicals on the subject of the inductive sciences ought not to be overlooked by those who in Ireland have the reputation and position of learned men. Take an instance—Greek Mythology. Even in this plainly wild and at first sight incoherent system, Mr. Gladstone, the late Premier of the British Parliament, shows in his learned work, *Homer and the Homeric Age*, that it presents under "corrupted forms the old Theistic and Messianic traditions; that by a primitive tradition, if not by a direct command, it upheld the ordinance of sacrifice; that its course was from light to darkness, from purity to uncleanliness, from knowledge to ignorance." The starting point, however, of this varied and corrupt mythology was "the idea of a Being infinite in power and intelligence, perfectly good by an unchangeable internal determination of character, and not by the constraint of an external law." The knowledge of the Divine existence roused the desire to know where He dwelt, and as Cox observes, in the mighty agencies and sublime objects of creation, in which they fancied that they saw Him, Mr. Gladstone discerns the germs of that nature-worship which was ingrafted on the true religion originally imparted to mankind. This religion involved the Unity and Supremacy of a Godhead; with this Unity of essence, a trinity of personal existence; a Redeemer invested with humanity, who as God-man should finally establish his kingdom; a Wisdom—the holy Spirit—personal, eternal, divine. With this view was joined the revelation of the Evil One, as the tempter of men and the leader of rebellious angels, who had for disobedience been hurled from their thrones in heaven."

As a writer so ably wielding his pen against infidel theories, Mr. Gladstone has done good work; as a scholar he has with a strong array of proofs in favor of the existence of God and the divinity of Christ, met the infidel writers of the day, in the very fighting-ground which they had themselves selected. So far he is worthy of imitation. Honest home scholars should be prepared to act a similar part.

All the fairy legends told by the peasantry in Ireland to this very hour is traceable to a similar source. The early pagan progenitors of the Irish race had, like the Hellenes before Homer's time and Hesiod's, lost all knowledge of the true God; and then in their blindness they ascribed to Nature and to great men the attributes which belonged to God. The sun represented the brightness and glory, and the light material and intellectual of the invisible God; and hence they worshipped the sun as the symbol of the divine eternal Light, which is the life of all things that are. This subject shall be fully discussed in the closing chapter of this work. The Irish people, like the Greeks, had their heroes—Fergus, Oisin, and Fionn; and heroines like Madḃ (Mauv), Maud or Mab, whom they venerated during life, and placed when dead amongst the Immortals in the land of perpetual youth.

The "Caisils," "Duns," raths, or forts, became to the simple people the abode of these unseen demigods. All this strange fairy mythology is quite familiar to every peasant in Connacht.

The same causes that gave rise to these fairy fancies continue still to keep the delusion amongst the uneducated, or amongst those who are only partially educated. First, everyone naturally believes, even Pagans have always held to it, that there is a supernatural state in which beings of superior power, knowledge, and happiness dwell; secondly, that the children of men if they merit it are destined for that state. The human mind dwells on these thoughts so natural and so common to all mankind, and, as philosophy teaches, man's mind cannot form a thought without, at the same time, clothing it with a fancied objectivity; therefore the living peasant race naturally people the abode with blessed creatures of their own fancy, and call them fairies; they call the land in which these good people dwell "the land of youth." Oral traditions tell each succeeding generation that a strange race, the Danaan, lived in the caisels; and others, the Firbolgs, in the raths; hence, from their imperfect knowledge of history, they assign those abodes to the fairy heroes. If any bold peasant opens a "fort" or rath, the mesmeric effect of the confined air of the cave is ascribed to supernatural agency, and in this way the poetic folly is perpetuated.

There is another class of writers and thinkers whom Irish scholars should combat,—those who maintain that the early ancestors of the children of the Gael were *Cuthites*, that is, descendants of Cush, the eldest son of Cham or Ham; neither were they Phenicians or Carthagenians.

The primary result of the study of the language of ancient Ireland as a branch of the science of philology, is to lead the student to the conviction, that the first immigrants who made Eire their home had come from the East; and that the language which they spoke was Aryan, identical at that early period with the tongue known and spoken in the valleys of Persia, and eastward to the banks of the Indus. A knowledge of this lost language has been obtained by the labours of men of science, much in the same way, as one could form a new Latin speech from the six living romance dialects, if it were possible that Latin, like Cornish, or the Etruscan, or the Aryan, had died out. The newly efformated Latin tongue would, like a broken vase remoulded, be similar in every respect to the original defunct Latin language. In this way, the lost primitive Aryan tongue has been reconstructed, a grammar written, a dictionary compiled. This revived language could well be styled Japhetic, or, the tongue spoken by the descendants of Japhet, in contradistinction to the Semitic spoken by the children of Sem, and which is the mother tongue of Hebrew, Chaldaic, Syriac, Arabic, Samaritan, Ethiopic, and old Phenician; while the Aryan or Japhetic is the parent tongue of Sanskrit, Keltic, Greek, Latin, Gothic, Slavonic—nigh every dialect in Europe, and in parts of Asia, where the descendants of Japhet took up their abode.

CHAPTER II.

MEANING OF ARYAN.

Aryan. What does it mean? The language: the race. High value of Irish-Gaelic. The Four Masters. Brother Michael O'Cleary. What the brave friar did without help. The Civil War. Writers in the present age must know the sciences, and possess aesthetic and logical skill. Discoveries: (1) Language; (2) The Brehon Law; (3) the Cities of the Dead. A parallel. The Cities of the Dead in Etruria tell the tale of Etruria's civilisation. The Language and the Laws of Eire are an undying proof of Ireland's ancient social state. Monasteries of Donegal and Ros-Errily. In order to obtain a knowledge of antiquities it is necessary to learn the language. Hence, Irish-Gaelic, as it is at present spoken and written, must be studied. The position of the language from 1650 to 1874. Irish then the only tongue; now it is nigh gone. Causes of its decay.

Why call the language and the race Aryan?—what does it mean? The answer will be given the reader in the words of Rev. George W. Cox, M.A., in the preface to the *Mythology of the Aryan Nations, Vol. I.*; *London, Longmans, Green and Co.*, 1870: "I have retained the word *Aryan*, which is a name for the tribes or races akin to Greeks and Teutons in Europe and in Asia.

"Objections have been lately urged against its use on the ground that only Hindoos and Persians spoke of themselves as Aryans. And the tracing of this name to Ireland Mr. Peile regards as very uncertain. To him the word appears to mean, not 'ploughman,' but *fitting, worthy, noble.* If it is so, the title becomes the more suitable as a designation for the peoples who certainly have never called themselves Indo-Germanic."

Pictet shows plainly the word means *high*, *illustrious*, *noble*, of the *highest rank*, *primitive.* He devotes several pages to the explanation of the word; and in his wake follow Max Muller and most English writers.

"Arya is a Sanskrit word, and in the later Sanskrit, it means *noble*, *of a good family*. Max Muller devotes fifteen pages (*vol. i., p.* 275, *Lectures on the Science of Languages*) to the explanation of the term. "I can only state," he says, "that the ethnological signification of Aryan seems to be one who ploughs or tills, and that it is connected with the Latin root *arare*, (root, Irish "ar," ploughing.) *Airya*, in Zend, means *venerable*, and is, at the same time, the name of the people."—p. 277. Again, that "*Aryan* was a title of honour in the Persian empire, is clearly shown by the cuneiform inscriptions of Darius."

Max Muller closes the dissertation with the following judicious remarks:

"As comparative philology has thus traced the ancient name of *Aryan* from India to Europe, as the original title assumed by the *Aryans* before they left their common home, it is but natural that it should have been chosen as the technical term for the family of languages which was formerly designated as Indo-Germanic, Indo-European, Caucasian, or Japhetic."—*Lecture vi.*

The scholars of Europe and the East, and of America, have, in German, French, and English, within the past twenty years, adopted the term.

Who were the Aryans? Pictet and Max Muller answer the question:

"It can be proved by the evidence of language, that before their separation, the Aryans led the life of agricultural nomads—a life such as Tacitus describes that of the Germans. They knew the arts of ploughing, of making roads, of building ships, of weaving and sewing, of dying and painting, of erecting houses; they had counted at least as far as one hundred. They had domesticated the most important animals—the cow, the horse, the sheep, the dog. They were acquainted with the most useful metals. They had recognised the bonds of blood, and laws of marriage; they followed their leader and kings; and the distinction between right and wrong was fixed by customs and laws. They adored a God and invoked him under various names." All this is proved by the evidence of language. It is proved further that they were a powerful, an intellectual race, their language wonderful in its fecundity and plastic potency. Their descendants came from their country to Europe, by two roads—"one through Chorasan to the north, through Russia, and thence to the shores of the Black Sea, and through Thrace; another from Armenia, across the Caucasus, or across the Black Sea to Northern Greece, and along the Danube to Germany." The first branch who came to Europe were Kelts. Those who came by the south-western route settled in Greece, Thessaly, Pannonia, Etruria, Tyrol, Helvetia, Spain, Gallia, Hibernia. Those who came by the northern course were also Kelts. To this hour ethnology points to two distinct races.

HIGH VALUE OF IRISH-GAELIC.

How does Irish-Gaelic, as a branch of philology, prove more clearly than historic records, the civilization of the ancient Keltic race in Ireland?

This question is answered by an illustration.

One well ascertained fact, the expression of a physical law, tells the sons of science a great deal more than could be written in a hundred pages. The falling of the apple read, while touching the earth, a great lesson to Newton. The oscillation of a slight steel magnet opened up a world of latent knowledge to Oersted. Cause and effect are correlative; every great effect must have had a cause, and that must be proportionate to the greatness of the results. Scholars analyze the linquistic facts of philology and trace them to an efficient cause, as Paley traces the workings of the "human eye," on principles laid down by the intellect of the schools—Aristotle. The whole panorama of the past rises up before the vision with an apparent objective reality not unlike the sight which presented itself to the mind of St. Peter, when he beheld "the heavens opened and a great linen sheet let down by the four corners from heaven to earth—wherein were all manner of four-footed beasts and creeping things of the earth, and the birds of the air." Even so, the human mind builds anew a past age, from its reflex seen in history, or from its impress stamped on a language.

Further still, it is well known that not alone havè new powerful and practical sciences been brought, within the past half century, to the aid of man, but there have been discoveries made of buried cities, which once belonged to the living, and of cities properly called "of the dead;" specimens of art and of science; ornamented works in bronze, in iron, and gold, in metals of all kinds, and in glass, have been found in profusion; secret writings and hierographical paintings have been brought to light; and most fortunate discovery of all, the art of deciphering and of correctly reading and understanding these antique specimens of ideography has, after much labor and persevering skill, been attained.

Two centuries and a half ago—1632, and earlier—Brother Michael and his associates, the masters Conary O'Clery, Peregrine O'Clery, and Fearfassa O'Mulconry had not the advantages of modern science, or the aids which large libraries and new published records supply those who dwell in Dublin, Edinburgh, or London.

This intrepid leader of that historic band, the poor Friar, Michael O'Clery, had, with infinite labor for the space of eleven years, gathered together from the various libraries of Europe, and from the four shores of Eire, a splendid collection of Irish and Latin M.SS., and from these, with the aid of his fellow-laborers, supported by the hospitality of the Friars and sustained by the patronage of Farrell O'Gara, Lord of Moy O'Gara and Chief of Coolavin, who gave the rewards of their labors to the four chroniclers, had "transcribed, collated, and com-compiled," in huts or cottages near the famous monastery of Donegal, then for thirty years in ruins, *The Annals of the Kingdom of Ireland*, from the earliest times to the year 1616.

Under difficulties which might have deterred others less earnest and devoted to the future fame of their native land, these simple men, with a zeal like that which animated the prophets of old, devoted themselves on the eve of the long night of war and bloodshed through which Eire was about to pass, to the herculean task of recording everything worthy of note in the new compilation, *The Annals of the Kingdom of Ireland*, thus preserving as in a sacred shrine, the glory of the past, that in the morning of peace and prosperity its golden beams, like the sacred fire of the Holy Temple, might serve once again to enlighten and gladden the sons of Inisfail.

The fierce tornado of civil war swept, nine years later, over Ireland and destroyed the possessions, crushed the rights and even the hopes of the ancient sons of the Clanna Gael. The cloud of which O'Clery spoke when writing to the Lord of Moy O'Gara burst like a cataract and drowned the nation in its destructive waters. This sad state of things did not end with the sad death of Charles I., nor in 1659 with the fatal end of Oliver Cromwell.

The baneful effects of civil war and religious strife in Ireland were felt even in the days of the Second Charles and the Second James.

At the present time, any "master" of archaeology, or any truthful Irish annalist, must bring to bear on the past not only a knowledge of a few languages—Latin, Greek, Irish, French, or Spanish—but he must be familiar with the sciences; he must be so skilled as to form a correct logical and æsthetical view from the data presented regarding the varied important subjects which arise in discussing the truth of Ireland's ancient annals.

When Lord O'Gara patronized the Four Masters, Irish scholars knew nothing of, and could know nothing of (1) philological developments of languages, and especially of Irish-Gaelic; (2) the Brehon Law was then known, but its publication is an event of the past ten years; (3) and within the past fifty years the literary world and the sons of science and of art have been amazed at the grand and valuable discoveries of whole "cities of the dead" in Tuscany, and in the Papal States, the buried glory of a lost dynasty or autonomy in ancient Etruria. And first a word regarding the buried cities.

Cities of tombs have been discovered at Vulci, at Norchia, at Castel d'Asso, at Bomazo, Faleria, Bieda, Sutri, Orte, and at Savona—places of little note in modern Italy; but occupying the sites of cities which held a high rank in the history of Etruria. The tombs of Vulci which have furnished the prince of Canino with the means of forming a very splendid collection of Etruscan antiquities, and have enriched many of the museums of

Europe, were unknown until 1825, and even then were discovered by chance. The tombs of Norchia and Castel d'Asso, which are remarkable for their beautiful sculptured façades, were brought to light, only in 1835; those at Bomarzo and at Orte in 1837. The cemeteries and town of the dead at Savona became known in 1843, and even to the present time discoveries of important Etrurian remains are being brought to light,—cemeteries containing innumerable tombs.

What is the character of these cemeteries? They are simply underground cities. They are laid out in streets and squares; the façades of the tombs occupy the place which the houses in the city of the living would have held.

Every Necropolis in Tuscany has its own special style; but each tomb has its portico, and pediment, and house-like roof; and the whole internal arrangement recalls to mind the habitations of the living. The houses of the dead are elegantly built, and decorated with much cost and skill; the vases and furniture are rich and elegant.

What lesson do these cemeteries and their treasures of art read?

First, it is plain, although not a word of their history is recorded, that a powerful people had lived in Etruria some ten hundred years before the period that Rome was first founded; that the people had been immensely wealthy, wonderfully intelligent, skilled in the knowledge of building to a degree that has not since been equalled. This is proved by the fact that not only had they magnificent palaces for themselves, while living, but for their dead also. That they possessed wonderful knowledge in the arts of painting, sculpture, glass-making, enamelling, dyeing, of working in brass, and in silver, and gold, and iron; that they had a knowledge of writing and reading; that they had schools not only for boys, but for girls, as is seen by representations on the rich vases—maidens with scrolls of parchment in their hands, like those made use of by children at schools; that woman was held in respect; that their social manners and habits were superior to those of Rome in after times; that they had a government, partly republican and partly kingly. All this and much more is gleaned from the disentombed remains of art from the Etrurian cemeteries.

In like manner, the ancient laws and the ancient language of Ireland tell that the early inhabitants of Ireland had a knowledge of the arts and sciences; of the laws of social life; that woman was held in respect, and marriage declared honorable; that they had a government, partly monarchical and partly republican.

In order to obtain a knowledge of the antiquities, it is necessary to learn the language of Ireland.

In the opinion of the writer, the best way to learn the ancient language is to commence to study the modern. The phonesis at present is the same as that in the past. The orthography is improved.

IRISH MONASTERIES—GAELIC NURSERIES.

Monasteries were the great centres of learning in the middle ages, up to the rise, in the thirteenth century and in the fourteenth, of University education. It was at Monte Casino St. Thomas Aquinas laid the foundation of the massive temple of learning, of which he became the living exponent and the ornament, and in his *Summæ*, a miracle of knowledge during all coming time. The Irish monasteries were the centres of Irish-Gaelic lore and learning. The Franciscan monastery at Donegal has been already put before the notice of the learned reader. When and by whom was that monastery at the head of the lovely bay of Donegal founded?

"In the year 1474, when the Franciscans were holding provincial chapter in the monastery of Ross-Triall," says the author of *Rise and Fall of the Franciscan Monasteries*, Edited by Rev. C. P. Meehan, M.R.I.A., "Nuala O'Connor, daughter of O'Connor Faly, wife of Hugh Roe O'Donnell, came, accompanied by a brilliant following of noble ladies and a company of kerne and gallowglass, to present an humble memorial to the assembled fathers. When the latter had duly considrred the prayer of the Lady Nuala's memorial, they deputed the provincial to inform her that they could not comply with her request at that moment, but that at some future time they would cheerfully send a colony of Franciscans to the principality of Tirconnell. 'What!' replied the princess, sorely pained by the refusal, 'I have journeyed a hundred miles to attain the object that has long been dearest to my heart, and will you venture to deny my prayer? If you do, beware of God's wrath; for I will appeal to his throne, and charge you with the loss of all the souls which your reluctance may cause to perish in the territory of Tirconnell!' "

She succeeded. She returned to Tir-Hugh, followed by a goodly number of Franciscans. The site was selected. The monastery soon raised its architectural form over the waters at Donegal bay.

The parent house, Ros-Errily, in the county of Galway, is described by Sir William R. Wilde in his able and erudite treatise on "Lough Corrib."

"Looking north-eastward from Killursa church into the fertile valley through which Owenduff flows, the eye rests on the picturesque ruins of Ros-Errily. Upon a slight elevation on the Galway bank of the river, surrounded by fat pasture lands and approached by a long avenue, or causeway, on the south, stand the extensive ruins of this Franciscan convent and church, and which are thus referred to by the Donegal Annalists: 'A.D. 1351, the Monastery of Ros-Òirḃealaig (afterwards called Ros-Errily), in the diocese of Tuam, was erected for Franciscans.' "

Oliver J. Burke, A.B., T.C.D., Barrister-at-Law, in a small volume on the ABBEY OF ROSS, writes regarding its origin. In A.D. 1351, the Monastry of Ross was founded. "The great Fraciscan chronicler, Luke Wadding, states that it was in this year the Monastery of Ross was built. He describes it as a lonely spot surrounded on all sides with water, and that it was approachable only by one path paved with heavy stones. This account by Wadding agrees with that given in the 'Annals of the Four Masters under the year 1351, and also with the Louvain manuscript. In the year 1470 the monastery of Ross adopted the rigid rules of the strict observance."

The name is formed from the Gaelic "Ros," a peninsula; "oir," eastern, elevated; and "bealaċ," a way.

MODERN IRISH GAELIC.

When the mother-Abbey, Roserrily, and its far-famed daughter, the Abbey of Donegal, had flourished; when that humble, self-sacrificing lay brother, Michael O'Clery, with the able, erudite men who laboured during the darkest hour of Ireland's night of suffering and sorrow, had been for years collecting authentic materials from which the grandest monument of Ireland's historic genius was to be erected; when an Englishman, William Bedell, Anglican Bishop of Kilmore, was emulating the zeal of O'Clery in his efforts to have the Irish language patronised by the crown; when O'Neill had ruled in Tyrone and O'Donnell in Tirconnell; when James the First of the Stuart dynasty had succeeded to the throne of the Tudor line of sovereigns, and long anterior to that period, the Irish-Keltic tongue was the only one spoken in all its purity throughout the length and breadth of Ireland, even within the territory known as the English pale.

The student of Irish history is assured by Leland, that within the English Pale the Irish language had been in the sixteenth century "predominant;" and it is a well-known fact that in those portions of Irish territory which intersected some of the English settlements, no other language had been ever thought of. The real truth is, that at that time the Irish had been a highly cultivated literary language; while at the same period the English had been only in its infancy.

In the seventeenth century, the Irish tongue was the only speech in use through the length and breadth of this land. In every county, cantred, or "cluan" where a native Kelt had made for himself a home, there the Irish language was spoken; Latin, if you will, and Norman French, were heard amongst the Irish ecclesiastics and the literary men of the period.

The seventeenth century was a time of trial and tribulation for Irishmen, like the period of the captivity in days of old for the Hebrew race. Language like love of country, or the religious love of a nation for the faith of their fathers, has its exponents and representatives. And amongst those of the seventeenth century the Chief of the Four Masters, 1632, with his faithful co-labourers rise up before the vision of the student who investigates the subject of the language and history of that eventful time. What beacon-lights in the darkness are to a tempest-tossed ship, enabling those on board to view the angry sea and the foaming billows, and to note at the time the direction in which the vessel is sailing, men like O'Clery and the Four Masters—men like Bedell and Ussher—are in the ship which steered through the stormy period of the seventeenth century, carrying on board the language of the Irish race. Rosserily, Donegal, Armagh, and the Irish Monasteries are the luminous spots which shed rays of lurid lustre over the vessel of literary Keltic Ireland.

From the year 1649 to 1749 a century rolled by and no change took place in the language of the Irish people. Up to the first quarter of the present ninteenth century, the peasant population spoke their native tongue with the same sweetness and grammatical excellence with which it was spoken in 1631, when the Four Masters penned the annals of Ireland. For the past fifty years the language is fading fast. The "coarse *bodach* almost alone," says the writer in the *Dublin Review*, "retains it as the language of common life, and he insensibly mingles the destroying dialect with it."

And in reference to the sorrowful yet beautiful poem by Father Michael Mullens, Clonfert, the writer in the *Review* remarks: "And this mourner, too, must wail his plaint in Saxon words and Saxon idiom, lest his lamentation should fall meaningless on the ears of Ireland.

It is fading! it is fading! like the leaves upon the trees,
It is dying! it is dying! like the western ocean breeze,
It is fastly disappearing, as footsteps on the shore,
Where the Barrow and the Erne, and Lough Swilly's water roar;
Where the parting sunbeam kisses the Corrib in the west,
And the ocean, like a mother, clasps the Shannon to its breast.
The language of Old Eire, of her history and name,
Of her monarchs and her heroes, of her glory and her fame;
The sacred shrine where rested through her sunshine and her gloom,
The spirit of her martyrs as their bodies in the tomb!
The time-wrought shell, where murmured through centuries of wrong,
The secret voice of freedom in annal and in song,
Is surely fastly sinking into silent death at last,
To live but in the memories and relics of the past.

CHAPTER III.

What are the Causes of this Decay?

Anglo-Norman Invasion. No books printed in Irish. Prohibition of the Irish Language by statute under Edward III. Prohibition by statute under Henry VIII. Penal Enactments against Catholics. Væ Victis: the Irish Language the Language of the Conquered. The hostile spirit engendered by those enactments. Use of scores. Social inferiority. Total exclusion of the Irish Language from National Schools. Neglect of Irish in family circles. Phonetic antagonism, opposition in the sounds of Vowels as pronounced in Irish and English. Passive neglect on the part of the hereditary fosterers of the Irish Language. Much could be done by Maynooth College. Want of encouragement on the part of Government. What Trinity College did not do for Irish Gaelic. What the Catholic University could do. Absence of Home Legislation. Professor Blackie. Natural desire to excel. Anecdotes. Most Rev. Dr. Moriarty's views.

The causes are manifold. In the moral world as well as in the physical, one cause seldom acts alone. It works in concert with many others which tend all to the production of some great and general effect. In order, for instance, that the crops in harvest time may ripen and "be gathered into the barn," what a variety of causes, general, special, and individual, must conspire to bring about the effect? It is necessary that the ground be well prepared for the reception of the seed. This process alone claims the attention and the labor of the husbandman. Any serious neglect will prove a source of failure in the growth and development of the coming crop. The seed sown must be good in its kind; and care and labor must be expended in committing the seed to the soil. God's blessing must accompany all this attention and labor of the husbandman, for, though man may sow the seed, it is God alone who is to bestow a plentiful increase. Hence, the sun must bestow its fostering warmth on the sown grain; the rains must necessarily fall; the air contribute, even as it sustains animal life, its share of gaseous nutritive support; the earth must, like a nursing mother, feed the young roots which, with so many sucking mouths, drink in that which supports the growing plant. The summer weather must be favourable, nay, propitious to the proper development of the ear, and warm ripening breezes must come to crown all the forgone labors. Man, too, must all this time not neglect that special line of duty which the growing crops require at his hands. In the moral world philosophers have put the question, what was the cause of the French revolution of 1793, which ended in the destruction of monarchy, and the uprooting of religion throughout Catholic France. Sir Archibald Alison, Bart., F.R.S.E., in his history of Europe, gives the answer; and he shows that the general destruction of political power—which is in fact the exponent at once and preserver of social order, and the final banishing of every form of religion from the State, did not spring from any single cause, but that a number of concurrent causes, remote and proximate, general and special, had combined to produce that terrible upheaving of French society against the social and moral order of Christendom.

In the same way the decay or destruction of a language, like that spoken by the Irish people, is not owing to any one cause, it is the result of a series of concurrent causes tending to produce the same effect.

First—The writer prefers to give the words of another rather than his own, when the proof presented is well told, and when it is sure to derive additional force from the authority cited. In the first of the series of lectures published by professor O'Curry, *MS. materials of Irish History*, p 6, the learned author, after describing all the evils which the Danes had committed in burning and drowning Irish manuscripts, says, the chief cause (of the loss of early writings) was the occurrence of the Anglo-Norman invasion so soon after the expulsion of the Danes and the sinister results which it produced upon the literary as well as upon all the other interests of the country. The protracted conflicts between the natives and their invaders were fatal not only to the vigerous *resumption of the study of our language*, but also to the *very existence* of a great part of our ancient literature. The old practice of reproducing our ancient books, and adding to them a record of such events as had occurred from the period of their first compilation, as well as the composition of new and independent works, was almost altogether suspended. And thus our national literature received a fatal check at the most important period of its development, and at a time when the mind of Europe was beginning to expand under the influence of new impulses.

SECOND—Again, the discovery of printing at a subsequent period made works in other languages so much more easy of access than those transcribed by hand in the Irish tongue, and this cause also may have contributed to the further neglect of native compositions. So far, O'Curry's views.

THIRD—Every student reading Irish History now-a-days, when there are abundant facilities for knowing the past—school histories and large volumes in quarto and folio—knows that during the reign of Edward III., and while Lionel Duke of Clarence, Edward's second son, was viceroy, a statute was passed at Kilkenny, by which every person of English descent, or of Anglo-Norman extraction, had been forbidden, under pain of forfeiture of his lands and possessions, to use the Irish language.

That unwise and impolitic statute soon produced, not directly and immediately, its effect in every part of Ireland in which the power of the crown and the policy of the English court prevailed. The spirit, too, of that law survived long after the letter of the act had ceased to be effective.

O'Curry had this statute and its results before his mind's vision when he wrote: "aided by the new political rule under which the country, after a long and gallant resistance, was at length brought, these and similar influences banished at last, almost the possibility of cultivating the Gaelic literature and learning."*

The Irish chiefs and the Irish people still clung to their own tongue in preference to any other. In good truth the English settlers had no speech worthy the name to offer in its stead. The Kings of England and the Nobles at the time, and all connected with the King's household and with the administration of the laws, spoke Norman French. English had not yet been formed. The Irish language continued, therefore, to be spoken, not alone in that portion of the land possessed and ruled by Irish chiefs and governed by Irish laws, but as a fact it was spoken in the "pale" itself, the territory set apart for the Saxon settlers. In the year 1483 an Archbishop of Dublin presented to Parliament a petition written in Norman-French, to relieve him in his own diocese from the inconvenience brought about by the statute of Kilkenny in proscribing the Irish tongue. And the Archbishop stated as his reason that, owing to the out-lawry exercised on the language of the people, even in Dublin, "the cure

*Stat. 2, Richard iii., c. x, and v, Edward iv., Anno 1485.

of souls was piteously neglected—*pitieusement neclecte.*" A statute was then passed, and by it, liberty granted to present natives who, of course, spoke Irish, to livings in the diocese of Dublin and Glendalough—a thing which, during the early reign of Richard III., and long before, was contrary to statute law.

Again, O'Curry's views on this point are in accord with the views expressed in these pages:

"Not only the old Irish nobility, gentry and people in general were lovers of their native language and literature, and patrons of literary men, but even the great Anglo-Norman nobles themselves who effected a permanent settlement among us, appear from the first to have adopted what, doubtless, must have seemed to them the better manners, customs, language and literature of the natives; and not only did they munificently patronize their professors, but became themselves proficients in these studies; so that the Geraldines, the Butlers, the Bourkes, the Keatings and others thought, spoke, and wrote in the Gaelic, and stored their libraries with choice and expensive volumes in that language; and they were reproached by their own compatriots with having become —'*ipsis Hibernis Hiberniores*'—more Irish than the Irish themselves. So great, indeed, was the value in those days set on literary and historical documents by chiefs and princes, that it has more than once happened, that a much prized manuscript was the stipulated ransom of a captive noble, and became the object of a tedious warfare. And that state of things continued for several centuries, even after the whole frame-work of Irish society was shaken to pieces by the successive invasions of the Danes, the Norsemen and Anglo-Normans, followed by the Elizabethan, Cromwellian, and Williamite wars and confiscations, and accompanied by the ever-increasing dissensions of the native princes among themselves, disunited as they were after the fall of the supreme monarchy at the close of the twelfth century."*

The intercourse of the native Irish by fostering, by inter-marriage and alliances was quite common in the reign of Henry VIII. The Lord Deputy himself at the time set the example. Thus the statute enacted for the purpose of retarding the growth and of preventing the use of the Irish language, apparently effected little. The prevailing power of the native speech, and the absence of any other tongue more ready or elegant, enabled it to hold its sway over every inch of territory in Ireland. But the spirit of the statute, and the subtle active policy that dictated it, were not dead.

FOURTH—In the year 1537, the 28th year of Henry VIII., another parliamentary statute against the Irish tongue was framed and passed. No person using the Irish tongue could obtain patronage in the new church of which the King had been recognised supreme head.

This policy was in some measure reversed in the reign of Edward and of Elizabeth. The greatest of England's Queens made use of every means that tended in any way to advance the spread of her own spiritual supremacy and of the new regal religion. In her reign Sir Henry Sydney was for a period Lord Deputy of Ireland. For six months he journeyed around the four provinces and visited every county from sea to sea. In a letter to the Queen, dated 28th April, 1576,—nigh three hundred years ago—he presented to her Majesty his views regarding Ireland and the Irish people, and especially their language, setting forth his opinion, that "none should be recommended as ministers for places where the English tongue is not understood, but those who can speak Irish

*O'Curry—MS. materials, p. 7.

for which searche should be made first and speedylie in your own universitie." Lord Bacon recommended (A.D. 1601) the same course of conciliatory policy to Secretary Cecil. Nineteen years later, 1620, his Majesty James I. wrote to the Lord Deputy recommending that "whenever any livings, *not of any great value*, fall void among the meere Irish, *these men who know the Irish tongue be thought of before others.*"

This, indeed, was right royal encouragement! "when any livings, not of any great value," fall void, then those who knew the Irish tongue should have the preference. Of course when a "living" of any value—a living worth the having—fell void, it is not an Irishman who would then be preferred. Such remiss encouragement on the part of the Crown, even amongst those who followed the English interest in Ireland, and who, after their own fashion, were solicitous for the salvation of the benighted natives—all to a man Catholic—was as damning to the native language as the statute of Edward III., or the law passed in the reign of Henry VIII. Contempt oftentimes works with mankind more effectually towards the end aimed at than legal censures.

Honor, however, ought to be bestowed where honor is due. The most earnest and by far the most energetic and practical in favor of the cultivation of the Irish language and its adoption, although they regarded it only as a means to promote the English interest in Ireland, and for the advance of the cause of Anglican teaching amongst the natives, were his Grace Archbishop Ussher, of Armagh; Bedell, at first provost of Trinity College, and next Anglican Bishop of Kilmore, and the Most Rev. Dr. William O'Donnell of Tuam. These scholars were the only men animated with an intelligent perception of what was right to be done. It is a striking fact that amongst all the Anglicans in Ireland at the time, those men were the most learned in every branch of knowledge, and at the same time the most liberal in their treatment of the history, of the language, and of the manners and antiquities of the people of Ireland. Ignorance and selfishness are the parents of bigotry and oppression; knowledge and enlightenment, of liberalism and legitimate liberty. With these few noble exceptions Sir Henry Sydney, Lord Bacon, Archbishop Ussher and O'Donnell, and the energetic Bedell, the spirit that first dictated the statute against the Irish language, and revived it in the time of Henry VIII., animated the breasts of every man in this country who at that period, and subsequently, represented the English interest. At that time, just before the Irish war, when the Four Masters were engaged at their labor of love in the huts hard by the shores of Donegal Bay, the Irish language was spoken in every county and parish in Ireland—in the English territory as well as that still ruled by Irish chieftains.

FIFTH.—A further development of this spirit so hostile to the people and to their language was, in all its fulness, sadly seen, after the terrible wars of the seventeenth century, in the penal enactments against Catholics who were, be it known, all Irish-speaking natives. Every Catholic was at the time an Irish speaker; and in passing penal enactments against Catholics and the religion they professed, the language, too, in which they prayed and in which alone they could receive instruction, was proscribed.

The soldiery and the yeomen of that fearful period were well aware of the twofold hostility of an anti-Catholic government against the religion of the Irish, and against the language in which that religion was propagated.

It is well known even to this day amongst the Irish peasants and native Catholics that at the close of the century just passed, the possession of an Irish manuscript, would have been quite enough to make the owner a suspected person; and that such a national literary remain had frequently been the cause of the ruin of a native Irish family. Professor W. K. Sullivan, now President of the Queen's College, Cork, in his learned introduction to the *Manners and Customs of the Native Irish*, confirms this view, for he says that the tradition of the danger incurred by having Irish manuscripts, has come down to his own days, and that he has seen Irish manuscripts which have been buried until the writing had almost faded, and their margins had rotted away. And why had these manuscripts of the Irish language been buried? In order that those people, whose property they were, might avoid the danger which the discovery of such forbidden literature was sure to entail, if the local yeomanry of the penal days had heard that such national relics had survived. An Irish manuscript in the reigns of Queen Anne or of George I. and George II. was, if found, much more dangerous for an Irishman than the posseesion at the present day of a revolver or a rifle without license in a proclaimed district. Thus the spirit that had first awakened, four centuries before, opposition to the Irish language, now breathed the burning breath of hot hate and brutal tyranny into the bosom of every man who sought either favor, patronage, or pay from the ruling powers. The yeomen were the worst enemies of the Catholics of this country; the bitterest foes of the language and the religion of the people, and yet they were natives of Ireland. They became the willing instruments in the hands of a destroying power; nay, like all men acting from an evil impulse, they found pleasure in their work of blood, and even outdid their masters.

Many Irish manuscripts were stowed away in the cottages of the peasantry behind what are called the rafters of the house. The present writer has in his possession, at this moment, two such manuscripts that had lain for years hid behind rafters in the cottages of respectable peasants named, the one Bodkin, the other Bourke.

Sixth.—The Irish language is the language of the vanquished. The word is here employed in its widest acceptation. *Vae victis* is true of the language when it succumbs, as of the people who speak it. The language pines with the pining unnational life of the vanquished.

> The Russian bear ne'er stood secure o'er Poland's shattered frame,
> Until he trampled from her breast the tongue that bore her name.

In connexion with this view, the writer quotes from the introduction to the *Manners and Customs of the Ancient Irish*, the words of Professor W. K. Sullivan, p. 69 :—

"When a struggle of languages takes place after a conquest, and that the language of the subject race wins (as that of the Saxons under the Normans) the effect of the language of the dominant race upon that of the subject race during the struggle for mastery, is far greater than that of the subject race (the Irish under the rule of England) upon that of the dominant one, when the language of the latter wins. The case of the Norman-French and English is an example of the first, while the gradual suppression of the Irish language by the English is an example of the second. These effects are such as we might anticipate *a priori*, and they have nothing, or at least very little, to do, one way or another, with the original superiority of one language over another. The use of such words as 'beef,' 'mutton,' 'pork,' 'veal,' &c., which are only Anglicised forms of the French names of the animals that yield them—*boeuf, mouton, porc, veau*—instead of the corresponding Saxon terms, 'ox,' 'sheep,' 'hog,' 'calf,' does not imply any original superiority of the Norman language over the Saxon; nor is it of itself a proof of the higher civilization of the Norman people over the English, but only that the Normans were those who made the laws, and consequently enforced the legal nomenclature of the several articles of commerce, besides which *they were those who chiefly constituted* the classes who led the fashion in language as well as in dress."

Again he remarks, "Races fuse, but languages do not. . . . . When two races mix, one language must, therefore, ultimately suppress the other; sometimes it is that of the dominant race, but not necessarily that of the most numerous one." The Cambro-Britons are an exception to this general deduction; and the French element in Switzerland.

Seventh.—Though slowly yet surely at last the prohibitions against the Irish language, the contempt, the deterrent action of the yeomen, the knowledge that no step could be taken upwards in the social scale without a knowledge of the tongue of those in power, made the Irish peasant feel the necessity not only of learning English, but also, as he thought, of despising and ignoring the language of his fathers. He seemed to think that he could not learn English without unlearning Irish. This false notion in his untrained mind was just what in the circumstances it should be. From this view, forced on the Irish peasant by the necessity of the position in which he had been placed for centuries, resulted the following barbarous practice:—

It was usual, until recently, for parents living in the country districts to have what were called *scores* or a small tablet tied to a string and suspended from the necks of their children. On this tablet the parents were in the habit of cutting a notch or a mark each time the growing boy or girl spoke Irish at home, so that the heartless anti-Irish pedagogue should inflict an equal number of stripes next day at school on the innocent delinquent.

The author of the College Irish Grammar writes: (p. 4. 5th edition) "There are hundreds of persons still living who, in boyhood's days, had scores or tablets suspended from their necks. The number of incisions on those scores showed how often the prohibition to speak Irish had been violated, and accordingly the schoolmaster inflicted on the innocent delinquent a proportionate number of stripes. Verily that was beating the language out of the country with a vengeance! yet depart it would not till the lash of fashion and corruption was employed against it."

That this barbarous custom prevailed is certain. The writer has seen within the past eight years several children, one a young girl from the village called Garrda Mór, within eight miles of the town of Tuam, who had been beaten by a pedagogue named Corcoran, because the guileless Irish girl composed in her native tongue. I have seen and spoken to several ecclesiastics who, while boys suffered this inhuman and unnatural punishment for opening their lips in the language which nature herself taught them to articulate. His Grace the Archbishop of Tuam has, several times, assured the writer that he had in the days of his youth suffered for speaking his mother tongue. Could any system more horrible be conceived? The fathers and mothers at home speak Irish, and yet they mercilessly beat their own offspring for uttering the language which they by example teach them to speak!! The sad result of this torturing system has been ruinously felt to this day.

Eighth.—Even in districts where this foul fashion of banishing the language did not exist, yet the spirit that dictated it prevailed; and the result has led slowly but surely to bring about the destruction of the speech of the Keltic race.

Ninth.—The humbler classes of the people naturally feel a desire to speak and to use as a medium of thought that language which is spoken by their more enlightened countrymen; and as they rise in the social scale to despise the speech of the peasant. This effect is the natural result of that human though foolish desire which all, in some measure, feel of following those who lead the fashion in language and pronunciation, as well as in dress. Irish-speaking natives who wish to advance their prospects in life must certainly learn English. But while they acquire a knowledge of English as Welshmen do, let them at the same time, like the same Kymric scholars, retain their own speech.

Tenth.—Another cause, and a very efficient one, of the fast decline of the Irish language is the total exclusion of Gaelic from the national schools. This cause at the present moment is silently effecting the greatest amount of destruction to the language amid Irish-speaking quarters. The punishment of the score has ceased. The penal power of the law has ceased. Fashion even has turned a favorable countenance to the Gaelic speech; but exclusion of Irish from the national schools of Ireland destroys the language in the cradle of our national hopes.

Eleventh.—From the habit of speaking nothing but English at school, the children of Irish-speaking people become, of necessity, and in time, so familiar with that language, that the children meeting at play on their return from school naturally lisp in the tongue they had been speaking during school hours. This baneful result to the language, produced by the total exclusion of Irish from school, could be remedied by insisting on reading or speaking in the native tongue for half an hour each day, and committing to memory proverbs or old sayings, or reading Irish songs and stories in the evenings at home. It is in this way, but with much energy, the Kelts of Wales act, in order to sustain and transmit to their children the language of their forefathers.

TWELFTH.—Between the sounds of the same vowels and consonants, as spoken in English and in Irish, there seems to be a kind of natural antagonism. Take, for instance, the sounds of the vowels "*a, i, u*"—*a* is sounded *aw*; *i* is always *ee*; and *u* in Gaelic is *oo*. The sound of each of these three vowels in English is quite the contrary of the phonetic power of the same vowels in Gaelic. The same holds true in regard to the consonants. Take *s*, for example, *before* the slender vowels *e* or *i*, or *after e, i*, its sound is invariably that of *sh* in shine; while its sound is that of *s* simply, as in sun, before the broad vowels *a, o, u*.

THIRTEENTH.—In those provinces in which Irish-Keltic is still spoken, much could be done by the Catholic Clergy in promoting the spread of the language. The fact that their effective power in this matter is not brought into action is at least a negative cause of the decline of the national tongue. Non-action, when one should act, assumes a positive value, and must be termed real neglect, and perhaps positive injury. Much can be said, certainly, as a palliative for this great omission. Many young levites wish to learn their native tongue, and they find that, for them, it is not as easy a matter as they at first had thought. At home they do not, while young, learn to speak Irish, even in those districts in which boys hear the language spoken; nay, even in many instances, where it is the household speech. During their college course, say at Maynooth, their young and growing taste for the language of their fathers is not satisfied by the superficial instruction in Gaelic usually imparted there. In Maynooth, not one student out of a hundred learns during his course to spell, to speak, and write Irish as a language, so that, having finished his college course, he could write to a fellow-clergyman in Irish, just as he writes in English, in French, or in Latin. There is an Irish class, but the language of the Gael is treated as the language of the Hebrew race—as something foreign—not the language of thought, of the country, of life, of business. Young Irish priests, entering on their missionary career, have no zeal, therefore, either to preserve the language, or to see it propagated. Whatever early ardor they had felt has grown cold. And from this fatal indifference on the part of young clergymen, the Irish people under their pastoral care adopt the language spoken in the schools and patronised by their own priests, and in this way neglect the language of their fathers, which they seldom hear.

If young ecclesiastical students were taught in their youthful days to speak their native tongue, and if they had learned while in Maynooth to read it, as well as to write it, and to preach in it, a great change from the present state of apathy would soon be effected.

While the printed sheets now before the reader were passing through the press, the writer received the following letter from a Parish Priest living in the county Kilkenny:—

"April 22nd, 1874.

"My dear Canon Bourke,—Your "College Grammar and Easy Lessons in Irish" have come to hand. The language has not died out yet. The good old seed of the speech of our fathers is still in the country. I am having it propagated in my parish. I have employed a teacher from Kerry. Even here the old people say the Rosary in Irish. The young generation answer, it is true, in English. At Confession they say the Confiteor, and the Act of Contrition in Irish. Many prefer to speak to the priest in the tribunal of penance in the old language, if a *Maynooth Priest* could hear them. I learned, and others like me learned, almost nothing during our time in Maynooth.—Hoping to be excused, I am your faithful servant,

"D. B."

Soon after the receipt of this letter, the present writer replied, and again he received another, from which the following excerpt is taken :—

"Ask his Grace the Most Rev. Dr. MacHale to get the Board of Maynooth to require of all candidates for entrance to that College to know some Irish—say a knowledge of the Catechism, Grammar, and of the "Easy Lessons," at least. The Diocesan Colleges should then teach it. And next the parochial schools, which are preparatory training establishments to Diocesan Colleges; and thus at once and for ever the whole machinery of Ireland is set to work to promote the study of the national language. His Grace the Archbishop of Tuam will have no objection to do that much. He has done much already. This act of his will crown all. If he think that he will meet opposition, as he is likely to meet, then we could get up in the South, sign petitions, and present a memorial to the Board of Maynooth to adopt the motion of his Grace, namely, that candidates for Maynooth be required in future to know some Irish. If he succeed, as succeed he must, he will have done a good work.

"D. B."

There is no doubt but the proposition as suggested is one worthy of the consideration of the learned Board who hold in their hands the destiny of the Irish Catholic Church and of the Irish tongue as far as it is possible to save it from utter decay. The scheme, however, will appear to their lordships quite chimerical and relatively impracticable. As the writer had been asked to communicate the views here given to his Grace the Most Rev. John MacHale, he has done so. His Grace says, that such a proposition would not, he is quite sure, find favor with the Board; that for him to propose such a scheme without a hope—even a remote one—of success would be beating the air. Some of their lordships entertain the opinion, which in some dioceses is founded on fact, that the national language is now a dead language for the rising generation of Irishmen.

The next reason in this list of causes that seem to the writer to have remotely or proximately, directly or indirectly, contributed to the decay of the Irish-Keltic language is—WANT OF ENCOURAGEMENT.

In truth there is no encouragement of a practical kind held out from any quarter in the past or in the present to Irishmen to learn or to cultivate their native tongue. Formerly they required no encouragement; now they do. Really, instead of encouragement, there is positive discouragement staring every man in the face who moves his pen, either in defence of the language or to help in some way the malingering cause which publications in that tongue represent and symbolize. The people feel that injustice of the grossest kind has been done regarding their own speech, and yet no one knows precisely who is in the wrong. The causes just assigned have at length produced their sad effect. The language has fallen from the lips of the children of mother Eire, whilst the people all the time felt full sure that they were in secure possession for ever of their mother tongue. Who is to restore it to the lips of these children? The growing youths do not know a word of it. The language, like a mother, never beheld by infant eyes, seems to the full-grown girl or boy quite foreign—not motherly at all. To effect any kind of practical change much must be done. There is no encouragement. Sentiment is not enough; nor speech-making; nor writing platitudes in the press. Men there are who write letters in the press praising the excellence of Ireland's ancient tongue, but will not, at the same time spend ten minutes to acquire a knowledge of its beauties. Two of the moving moral agents which incite mankind to act are: a sense of self-interest, and hope of reward, direct or indirect; direct, seeking to obtain the boon offered; indirect, by aiming at the many advantages resulting from the acquisition of a knowledge of the language. These moral forces should be brought into play, first, by forming societies and offering rewards, as the Cambro-Britons do; secondly, by speaking the language and insisting on its being spoken, if possible, among the household.

The reader has in some measure seen now with what neglect, contempt, and persecuting policy the language of the Irish race had been treated from the days of Edward III., to those of Henry VIII., who passed an act prohibiting all alliances with the *wild* Irish. From the death of Henry VIII. to the accession of George III. the language never received even one solitary ray of the sunshine of encouragement or of fostering care from those in power.

At the close, however, of the past century and the opening of the present, the minds of English statesmen took an enlightened view of this country, of its language, and its antiquities. The opinions of able statesmen and great scholars like the Right Hon. Edmund Burke, Dr. Johnson; the publications and the learned works of the Royal Irish Academy in the field of Irish antiquities and of philology; the researches of erudite Englishmen like Dr. Prichard have given the reading public a favorable opinion of the utility and worth of Ireland's ancient records, and of the language in which they were written. The growing enlightenment in secular science of all kinds peculiar to the present period is favorable, indeed, to the antiquities and the language of Ireland, and much more than has been done will, it is hoped, yet be accomplished favorable to the language, to the people, and to the country.

This chapter has furnished the reader with the fullest view yet written of the causes which have tended to the extinction of the Keltic tongue in Ireland. The British Government is awaking to a sense of justice in this matter of the language of Ireland. Yet how little may be expected from that government compared with the efforts of the people themselves, the history of the past forty years sufficiently attests.

From the year 1829, when the Emancipation Bill, granting freedom to Catholics in England, Scotland, Ireland, and the Colonies was passed, English statesmen appeared to look favorably to the public interests of the sister country—Ireland. A national system for educating the people was established. The Ordnance Survey, which, in its kind, the most perfect that had ever been planned was commenced. The work was committed to Lieutenant Drummond, to Captain Larcom, aided by the learned Dr. Petrie. Drummond guided the geodesical and the engineering department, and would, if encouraged, have laid the foundation of an Irish school of geodesy and geology, and perhaps of meteorology. Captain Larcom ably directed the topographical department.

Dr. Petrie, it is certain, did not forget his share of the duties, for to him they were a labour of love; he worked with zeal and success in the antiquarian and Keltic department. Hear Dr. Stokes's opinion on the labors of Dr. Petrie, copied from a singularly interesting memoir of the gifted antiquarian:

"He saw that, however valuable the accurate surveying and mapping of each county, as well as the description of its geological features, might be, the work would be deficient if it did not embrace all attainable knowledge of its topography, including its natural products, its history and antiquities, economic state, and social condition. This great and comprehensive thought, this truly imperial idea, he lost no time in putting into effect. A staff of civil assistants was organised, to some of whom the duty of making social and statistical inquiries was entrusted; while to others, who were Irish scholars, the more difficult task of orthographical research, with a view to obtaining the correct names of the baronies, townlands, and parishes throughout the country, was allotted. The investigation of all existing remains, whether Pagan or Christian—the cahirs, raths, tumuli, cromleachs, and other monuments of primitive times; the lowly bee-hive houses of the early saints of Ireland, their oratories, churches, towers, crosses, and monumental stones; and, to come to a later period, the description and history of the Keltic and Norman castles, and of the later monasteries and abbeys, were required. A memoir embracing all these subjects was to accompany the map of each county; so that, when completed, the work of the Ordnance Survey would embrace, not the geographical features of the country alone, but also the geology, natural history, ancient and modern records, antiquities, economic state, and social condition of each and every barony, townland, and parish throughout the length and breadth of the land."

To carry out this work so auspiciously begun, Dr. Petrie secured the services of such men as Dr. John O'Donovan, Eugene O'Curry. Besides these able men, he had on his staff Mr. O'Connor, Messrs. O'Keeffe, Wakeman, and that gifted but unfortunate poet and linguist, Clarence Mangan. These men laboured at their great undertaking from 1834 to 1839; sometimes at office work, sometimes travelling through the country, accompanied by some members of the Ordnance staff, gathering local information; at times making researches in Irish manuscripts in the Library of Trinity College and that of the Royal Irish Academy.*

In 1839, the first volume of the Ordnance labors—the Memoir of Londonderry—was published. The appearance of the first volume was hailed by learned men at home and abroad. By order of the government, the Topographical department of the Survey was immediately suspended. The Treasury, so lavish of money in other matters of State policy, demurred at the cost of a few thousand pounds. A parliamentary enquiry was instituted. Proofs in favor of the continuation of the work were put forward; proofs that could not fail to convince every man of mind and intelligence, but all in vain. The staff was discharged. The vast amount of materials even then collected—it is said four hundred quarto volumes of letters and documents relating to the topography, language, history, antiquities, productions, the social state of Ireland in the past and in the present—were stowed away into the Library of the Phœnix Park, and were subsequently, at least some, handed over to the guardian care of the Royal Irish Academy.

As a matter now publicly known, the British Government discouraged the publication, and do still discourage, the publication of those manuscript volumes. In putting the text and translation of the Brehon Laws before

* While the writer had been a divinity student in Maynooth College, in '56-57, he heard much that he has here recorded, from the lips of Dr. John O'Donovan, in whose house he was a guest.

the public, the spirit of British statesmen displayed the same illiberal tone. They were not, as far as one can form a judgment from the published reports, seemingly in earnest, or as liberally enlightened as they should be, and as the public of the present day expect and demand.

Men holding high positions under the British Government naturally, and from motives of policy, partake of this kindred spirit of their masters. They do not appear to be in earnest about anything relating to Ireland, or her past history. Although they do not certainly act in the spirit and in the letter peculiar to ages past; yet it is plain that in all they do regarding the history, language, and antiquities of Ireland, they would for the present, much rather let the past perish.

FIFTEENTH.—Without wishing to classify the action, or rather the non-action of the two Universities—namely, the Dublin University, as represented by Trinity College, and the Catholic University of Ireland, as a separate and a distinct cause from those already presented to the reader in the foregoing pages, to show why it happens that the Irish language is fading in Ireland, the writer feels that he would not be acting with honor or with truth as known to him in this matter, if he should, in enumerating fully the various causes that have combined in the past, and are combining in the present, to obliterate the spoken language of Ireland, shirk the question which is patent to every body—"What *have* Irish Universities done? what are they doing for the Irish language?"

Whilst this page was being put to press, the writer has been honored with a visit from the world-famed John Stuart Blackie. The name of John Stuart Blackie is a household word, not only in Scotland and, to no small extent, in England. Wherever a native of Scotland has, in any part of the habitable globe, taken up his abode, he looks up to John Stuart Blackie as one of the lights of his nation, one of the stars in the firmament of literature and science; one to whom Scotchmen can, from every part of the world, point with pride as a man of learning, a man of profound thought, great common sense, and unflagging energy. He views the world just as it is, with the eye of a historian and a philosopher, familiar with the pages of the past, yet valuing the present, and making the most of it, for the improvement of his fellow-countrymen, and for the rising generation of Scotch students. John Stuart Blackie is Professor of Greek in the University of Edinburgh, and the best linguist in Scotland. In his critical knowledge of languages he is not inferior to Frederick Max Müller, Taylorian professor at Oxford, who at present is deemed by Englishmen to be the greatest linguist of the day. He has published a translation in verse of Goethe's "Faust," and an edition of Plato; he published several volumes of poems and ballads, in which the spirit of Scotch nationality breathes freely and healthfully. When the late Earl of Derby had just sent his poetic version of Homer's "Iliad" to the press, the professor in Edinburgh university was publishing his translation of the "Iliad" in four volumes. The translation is excellent, and it has received the highest commendation from every critic who is known amongst writers of the day for scholarly skill on linguistic lore. In 1872, the learned professor visited Germany; last year he made Denmark, Sweden, and Norway the theatre of his rambles and literary research. He has never been in Ireland until the present summer. Anxious to see his Grace, the Archbishop, he has paid a visit to Tuam. He spent an evening with the professors and the President of Saint Jarlath's College.

He is a great lover of the Gaelic, just as he is a great lover of mankind. He is an honest man, and he wishes to see Keltic take the place which all the great scholars of Germany, and those who in England and France have written on the subject of philology, say it should by right hold. He does not join in the cry of despising Gaelic, because it is not the language of the lordly and the noble. He takes it for what it is worth, and in the family of the Aryan tongues he gives it its proper place, next in order to Greek. He has studied it, and although not a Kelt, yet he speaks the language of the Gaels of the Highlands. In his tour through the south of Ireland he has made his observations on the spoken Irish language in order to learn the extent to which it is employed as a vehicle of thought amongst the people. He had been astonished, he said, to witness how few in Ireland, as far as he could see, spoke the language of the Gael. He says that in the Highlands of Scotland a traveller could hear Gaelic spoken more commonly than one could at present hear Irish spoken in Ireland. He ascribes the comparative readiness of the Gaels of Scotland in using their own language to the fact that in their Sunday services, and in their devotional exercises, they make use of the Gaelic Bible and of the Gaelic book of Common Prayer, and that they have a certain share of religious literature in Gaelic.

The learned professor is perfectly correct in his views. For the writer knows that in every parish in Connaught in which the pastor of the people makes use of the Irish language in teaching his flock and in offering the ordinary prayers of the Catholic Church, and that wherever the peasants recite the Rosary and other prayers in the vernacular language, there Irish Gaelic flourishes; but in the parish in which this attention is not paid to

Gaelic, the Irish language is fastly fading. Even those who know it, cease, as a fact, to speak it. Professor Blackie hopes soon to have a Keltic chair established in the University of Edinburgh. When shall one be established in the Catholic University of Ireland? What have the Universities in Ireland done hitherto for the language of Ireland?

And first, as to the University of Dublin. To answer the question fully, let the reader accompany in thought the writer while he runs along the historic road of university education in the past, when Trinity had been first founded, and let him cast his eye quickly along that narrow pathway of literary patronage leading to the present, and then he will see at a glance all that has been done for the Irish language. In founding Trinity College near Dublin, one of the motives that "principallie" influenced Queen Elizabeth, it is said, was, that the people could have "ministers who could speak the Irish language," educated in Home University.

King James I., in his letter to the Lord Deputy in Ireland in 1690, publicly declares that this was the object for which, in the quaint language of the period, "our colledge of Dublin was first founded by our late sister of happie memorie, Queen Elizabeth, and hath been since plentifullie endowed by us, *principallie for breeding upp natives of that kingdom.* And he commands "that choise be made of some competent number of towardlie younge men alredie fitted with the knowledge of the Irish tongue, and be placed in the Universitie, and maintained there for two or three years; and that these men be thought on *before others.*"

Christopher Anderson, a native of Scotland, writing in the year 1846, on this subject, says in his work, "The Native Irish," p. 74. "That he is not aware of any approach to a conformity with those instructions, 'till the days of Bedell," who, when Provost in 1627 and 1628, established an Irish lecture in Trinity College. All this died away, says Mr. Anderson, and again an attempt was made thirty years later. (in 1656), under Dr. Winter, the Provost of Trinity College, in the time of the Protectorate. And this effort of Dr. Winters failed. The eloquent Dr. Jeremy Taylor knew, as he states, when Vice-Provost of Trinity, "The University near the City of Dublin, founded by Queen Elizabeth, was principally intended for the *natives* of this kingdom." And yet the learned and the earnest Jeremy did nothing for the language while Vice-Provost, or subsequently, while he ruled the Protestant Episcopal See of Down and Connor.

The author of the "Institutiones Logicæ," Dr. Narcissus Marsh, did during his provostship in 1680, all that an earnest and a learned man could do. He appointed an Irish lecturer, a Mr. Higgins, who, at one time, had eighty students in his Irish class. During his time, an Irish sermon was delivered each month in the College Chapel. But all these efforts met with much opposition. Mr. Anderson observes: "It is melancholy to contemplate the withering of such a seed-plot as this before the breath of blind political expediency." The truth is, that with the removal of Dr. Marsh, who was nominated to the Protestant Episcopal See of Leighlin and Ferns, and on the decease of Dr. Jones of Meath, "the whole cause was finally relinquished."

In the year 1711, the Rev. Dr. Hall, then Vice-Provost, supported for a few years at his own expense an Irish lecturer named Denny, to teach Irish privately to such scholars of the University as had a desire to learn that language. A Mr. Lyniger, too, was employed by Dr. King, Archbishop of Dublin. "But," says Anderson, "there is no proof of his continuance after that period" (1713). However, all such efforts were in vain. The writer must quote once more Mr. Anderson, who, the reader should know, is not an Irishman, or a Catholic, and therefore must be held naturally as an impartial writer of public facts relating to an Irish non-Catholic College. What does he say? Writing before the publication of his work in 1846: "All suggestions were in vain; and from that time (1713) to the present day (1846), *if the Irish language has been cultivated in schools of learning*, it is to *foreign countries* far from the native soil and the seat of the language we must look to for that fostering care, and not to home Universities" (p. 76). And our zealous Gaelic friend from Scotia Minor observes in a note: "Within some years past there is one professor of Irish, where the language is at least professedly taught on Irish ground. This is at Maynooth. But in Trinity College to the present hour (when Mr. Anderson wrote his book, "Schools of Learning in Ireland"), nothing of the kind exists!

Read the following:—

Before, however, dismissing the subject, it is of importance to record one most noble *intention*. It is worthy of special notice, as a substantial and standing proof of what one eminent man conceived to be a desideratum in Ireland. The late Henry Flood, Esq., of Farmly, in the county of Kilkenny, by his will, dated 27th May, 1790, had constituted Trinity College residuary legatee to a considerable part of his property, valued, in 1795, by Sir James Laurence Parsons, afterwards Earl of Ross, at £1,500 per annum, but since that period at about £1,700 annually. "I will," said Mr. Flood, "that on their coming into possession of this my bequest, on the death of my said wife, they do institute and maintain, as a perpetual establisment, a professorship of and for the Native Irish or Erse language,—with a salary of not less than three hundred pounds sterling a year." "And I do will and appoint, that they do grant one annual and liberal premium for the best and another for the next best composition in prose and verse, in the said Native Irish language, upon some point of ancient history, government, religion, literature, or situation of Ireland; and also one other annual premium for the best and another for the next best composition in Greek or Latin prose or verse, on any general subject by them assigned,"—and I will that the rents and profits, &c., shall be further applied by the said University to the purchase of all printed books and manuscripts in the said Native Irish or Erse language, wheresoever to be obtained; and next, to the purchase of all printed books and manuscripts of the dialects and languages that are akin to the Irish language; and then to the purchase of all valuable books and editions of books, in the learned and in the modern polished languages."

Yet, notwithstanding this distinctness of this last will and testament, there seems to have been some defect or informality. The validity of the bequest was questioned. The College instituted a suit for the purpose of establishing their claim; but, in the end, failed of success. After a trial at bar, the will has been broken, and at the present moment, nothing approaching to any of its provisions exists in Ireland.

A Professorship of Irish has been established in Trinity College, Dublin, since 1840. The Rev. Thomas De Vere Coneys, was the first professor, and he held the Irish chair for twelve years, up to the time of his death. He was succeeded by Dr. Foley, who was professor up to the spring of 1861. Since that period the Irish chair has been filled by Rev. T. O'Mahony, M.A., M.R.I.A. Each of the professors has contributed a little to the stock of Irish Keltic literature.

In Trinity College lectures are given for twelve days in each of three college terms—a lecture of one hour to the junior class, and a lecture of one hour to the pupils who have made some progress in the study of the language. The average number in the Irish class is seven. For this information I am indebted to the present distinguished professor, Rev. T. O'Mahony, M.A., M.R.I.A.

The learned French savant, Monsieur Gaidoz, editor

of *La Revue Celtique*, (published by A. Franck, 67, rue de Richelieu, Paris: and by Trübner & Co., Ludgate-hill, London) who has learned to speak and read and write Irish, visited Ireland some seven years ago. He did the present writer the honour of staying a few days at St. Jarlath's College. He spent some weeks in the Irish Metropolis, and while there, he did not neglect his Irish studies. He attended lectures given by Rev. Professor O'Mahony; and he states that on those occasions, when he was present, only one pupil had been in attendance .Possibly Mons. Gaidoz attended the junior class, or that some portion only of that class had been present, or that the professor wished to give the benefit of the entire lecture to the distinguished French visitor.

SIXTEENTH.—The Catholic University, the youngest public national institution for the education of the great body of the rising youth of Ireland—the latest in date—rises before the writer's view and comes to close this line of causes—which directly or indirectly affect the growth or decay of the nation's language.

It cannot be denied that some twenty years ago, the Catholic youth of Ireland entertained high hopes of what the then infant Catholic University was likely, in days to come, to effect for country and creed, and for the country's cause—the venerable Gaelic tongue. At all events, the writer, while a student in Maynoth, felt very confident in the future success of that hopeful seat of Catholic teaching; nor could he then understand how it could possibly be anything but the fruitful mother of myriad children devoted to religion and learning. He had fondly hoped that the second spring had at length come, when Ireland was destined to be in her renewed life once again, what the Venerable Bede said she had been—*Insula Sanctorum et Doctorum*,—" the island home of saints and learned men." The eagerness with which Irishmen, in the first age of Christianity, in the fifth century and in the sixth, rushed to retreats of learning, to slake, at these Christian fountains, their thirst for knowledge, was, in some way, a pledge that the sons of such lovers of learning would now aim at rivalling their heroic fathers. In this spirit the writer each summer for several years attended the lectures delivered at the University during the final month of each session in summer by Professors O'Curry and Hennessy. In the year 1856 he penned, while yet a student, and published without any pecuniary profit, "The College Irish Grammar," chiefly with a view to aid the students of St. Patrick's College, Maynooth, and those of the Catholic University of Ireland in the study of the national language." The high hopes, which in his youthful years he had entertained of the future of the Catholic University, have, as far as they relate to the study or the advance of the people's language, sadly subsided. A score of years and more have passed by, and during that time not a single scholar has left the halls of the Catholic University capable of uttering a sentence of the national language; nay, more, not a single word of the speech of the nation, as spoken at present, has been taught. The writer has been zealously enthusiastic regarding the University; the Grammar which he had written, he intended for the use of the students, who, as he then thought, were likely to study the language of their native country. he attended the lectures on Irish Antiquities delivered by Professor O'Curry, with whom he had become acquainted. He must not, however, hesitate to declare what all Irishmen, with whom he has spoken, or whom he has met in society, appear to feel, that in a University intended for the education of the sons of nine-tenths of the Irish people—the old language of that people ought not to be forgotten.

The lamented Professor O'Curry and his successor, Mr. Brian O'Loony, the present professor, no doubt merit just praise for ability, and knowledge of Irish. But, antiquities are not language, and teaching Irish antiquities is not teaching the Irish language. To neglect to teach the language of a people, or silently to overlook its literary existence, to ignore its name in the cradle of their national literary life, as a Catholic people, is dooming it quietly, but surely, to decay and death.

On this particular view of the subject, his Grace the Archbishop of Tuam—the Most Rev. John MacHale—wrote, some twenty years ago, a letter, of which the following paragraph merits particular attention:—

"Those antiquarians who devote so much time to the remains of the language of the early past, and at the same time neglect the living, breathing forms of our beautiful language, are like preservers of Egyptian mummies, wholly devoted to the decoration of the remains out of which life has just departed. Were their zeal for our olden literature accompanied with an anxiety for its perpetuation, then it would be entitled to the praise of a laudable devotion to the fame and glory of ancient Ireland. It is not one of the least strange anomalies of our country to find so many entirely sentimental about the old language, whose ears are at the same time so fastidious as not to endure the continuance of what has been ever deemed the moral striking characteristic of every nation."

That man performs his part in the drama of life well and nobly for God and his country, who attends to the faithful fulfillment of all the duties and social obligations which his office and position impose. The lamented

Eugene O'Curry may well be addressed, then, in the words recorded in the Gospel text, as spoken by the master of the faithful servant—"*Euge! serve bone et fidelis.*"—"Well done! thou good and faithful servant." He did well all that had been entrusted him to do. It is a historic fact, however, and, as such, cannot be concealed, that in a University intended for the sons of the people of this country, the people's language has not been taught. No scholar knowing a single word of acquired Irish has issued from its walls. In all our colleges at home and abroad, every possible encouragement is given, and rightly, for the sake of the growing youth, to the study of that tongue which is driving before it the speech of the Gael. Of this no one complains. In truth, young men must know that language in which commerce and mercantile business are carried on over, at least, half the world. Irishmen, to be merchants—men of business, men of public life, men of the time—must acquire a knowledge of English, and acquire it correctly. It is well to encourage the study of English; but the study of Irish, by Irishmen, ought not to be forgotten.

The Welsh have a firm faith in the truth of the saying—"Oes y byd i'r iaith Gymraeg!—as long as the world lasts the Kymric tongue will be spoken." As long, say we, as the world lasts, the Irish Keltic must be appreciated by men of learning. Why, then, should not the present living tongue be appreciated by a body of learned Irishmen, who are the lights and intellectual guides of the Irish people. As a fact, the language of Ireland, that lies like a piece of sculpture or a painting in a buried Roman Basilica, crushed in the debris of the past, and is found entombed in tomes of antiquity, is prized; why should not the living language of the present meet equal favour from learned patrons and lovers of our people and nation? Why this anomaly exists seems, indeed, passing strange.

SEVENTEENTH—To the reasons already assigned for the growing decay of the Irish language in Ireland, may be added another, namely—the absence of Home Legislation.

It has been already stated in this chapter, on the authority of O'Curry—and as a publicly-known historic fact—that not only the Milesian nobility, the old gentry and people of Ireland were lovers of their native language and literature, and patrons of literary men, but the Anglo-Norman nobles also, who had come as strangers to Ireland, adopted the language and patronized the literature of their new country. This natural and ready preference for the Irish tongue lasted as long as the native chieftains or Anglo-Norman nobles continued to exercise a sort of sovereign sway in their respective domains, and the native Irish language and literature were patronized and held in favor as long as Irishmen had been entrusted with the legislative control of the affairs of Ireland. This view of the subject urges many to believe that a home government for Ireland would certainly encourage and patronize the language and literature of Ireland, just in proportion as the absence of "Home Rule," has aided, not a little, the decay of our home language.

EIGHTEENTH.—On the occasion of the recent visit of Professor Blackie to Tuam, he did not see, as he had expected, owing to absence from home, the Archbishop, whose opinion on several subjects of interest the Professor was anxious to obtain. Accordingly, on his return to Scotland, he wrote from Edinburgh to the Archbishop, wishing to know why (1) the Irish language was fading in Ireland; and (2) why it has so very much disappeared as a spoken language amongst the masses of the people;

and (3) why—compared with the Highlands—there is not a strong pervading literature in the Irish Gaelic through this country? The writer has heard from the Archbishop the substance of his reply to the learned Professor of Greek in the University of Edinburgh.

The decay of the Irish language, and especially the lack of literary culture, are, in his opinion, due very much to the action, in the past, of the penal laws on the Irish speaking natives. That statute especially which made it penal for a priest or a schoolmaster to teach, effected the greatest amount of evil on the people and their speech. The priest and teacher were obliged, at the peril of their lives, to fly, or to be concealed in some cave or glen; and the lamp of learning, like the sacred fire of old, was hid in a mountain gorge, unseen by public eye. All open literary culture had to be suspended for over one hundred years. Those who knew how to read and write the Irish language had passed away. The generations of native Irishmen who arose in those days, could not, except by stealth, acquire knowledge. The children asked for literary food and there was no one found to supply it. When at length brighter days dawned over Ireland—when the Catholic natives were allowed the privilege of acquiring learning, if they could—then very few, like the true prophets of Israel, in the days of Achab and Jesabel—were found capable of teaching. This dearth of teachers of Irish has continued for the past century. The Irish people, unaccustomed, as a nation, to literary training in their native tongue, have forgotten its literary existence; and, owing to their poverty and down-trodden spirit, have not been able of themselves, and against great odds, to create a new one, or foster that which had even still not ceased to exist.

The following is a copy of the letter referred to. Professor Blackie did the writer the favor of transmitting a copy of the Archbishop's views. Many of those who read these pages will be glad to learn the opinions on this subject, of the decay of the Irish language, from the only living Irish scholar who connects the present century with the past; who has been for four score years, and longer, a witness to the sufferings endured by Ireland, in the heroic struggle of the ancient language and the ancient faith against the foreign tongue of a foreign power, and a creed which the people abhorred :—

" St. Jarlath's, Tuam, July 3rd, 1874.

" DEAR SIR,—I beg to acknowledge the receipt of your kind letter of the 29th ultimo. and to express my regret at being in Dublin when you did me the honour of a visit here.

" Besides the personal compliment, I appreciate much the influential motive of your visit in connexion with our old Celtic language—common to an extraordinary degree, to both our countries. Near a half century ago, one of your countrymen and I discoursed together in Celtic, mutually understanding each other, as well as if each were conversing with one of his own countrymen: and a few years ago, in an excursion to your Highlands, I was quite at home in the Gaelic with the oldest natives of the place, for, as in Ireland, the language is not, I regret, so familiar to the younger generation.

" Now, to come to what appears so anomalous to you, viz :— Our books in English and Latin rather than in Irish, and that amongst an Irish-speaking people! No doubt, it must appear strange to any one not sufficiently versed in our history. As to the Latin books, there are none in general use save our missals or mass books and breviaries, or office-books, exclusively by the clergy, with the exception of some nuns who read their office in Latin.

" Your countrymen possess Gaelic books, as well as retain the Gaelic tongue; ours retain the latter in despite of penal enactments, under which the former disappeared. When you reflect that under every form, whether written or oral, the Irish language was banned under the severest penalties, and all Irish and Catholic teachers doomed as felons to transportation, you will not be surprised that the Irish youth could not then read or write their own language. Nay, I well recollect when at hedge schools, some unfortunate urchins were whipped by the cruel teachers for the great crime of speaking Irish at home to their parents—who could speak no other language—the parents being the informers, by cutting a notch in a small piece of wood which the boy had carried in attestation of the cruel efforts to extinguish the Irish language.

"You can no longer be surprised that we have no Irish printed books; nor would we have even the language, but that tyranny itself cannot succeed in interdicting all oral communication. The knowledge of Irish, as a learned and written language, having been thus extinguished, the English was substituted and encouraged, and its schools frequented by the children of the native Irish, as well as by those of the English settlers. Outside the schools, the speech of the former was still Irish, when conversing with the people; but as they learned to read and write, their reading and writing, as a matter of necessity, was in the English language, so zealously and so exclusively patronized by the Government.

"I fear I have tired you by those tedious observations, founded, as they are, on undoubted facts. In a word, *your* Gaelic has never been banned or proscribed in any hostile manner—and it is no wonder that its Gaelic books should abound and be continued,—whereas *our* Irish having been interdicted and persecuted to the death, the wonder is, that in the cultivated form of school language, it should have survived.

"Towards the beginning of the present century, there were not, I understand, more than two founts of clumsy Irish type in all Ireland; now, you can find several of elegant form.

"Hoping that you may deem the length of my letter a sufficient apology for the length of the delay in acknowledging yours,

I am, my dear Sir,

Your faithful servant,

✠ JOHN MACHALE,

Archbishop of Tuam.

John S. Blackie, Esq., Professor,
Edinburgh.

NINETEENTH.—As a race, the Irish people appear to have a strong natural desire to excel others and to scorn the very notion of being inferior to any race. Nay, this feeling is increased by the knowledge which pervades the masses in Ireland, that their Milesian progenitors had been either princes or nobles in the land before the Norman King Henry II., had set foot on the soil of Eire. It is quite true that feelings such as these are not in themselves wrong. A strong innate desire to excel and to be superior to others, becomes either a virtue or a vice, according as the object aimed at, and according as the end in view is good and worthy, or, on the other hand, is bad and unworthy. A certain father of the Church, St. Bonaventure, says, "*Ex fine dicitur actus vel bonus vel malus*," the act is good or bad, according to the end in view. If the internal eye—the intention of the mind—be simple, the whole body of the act will be lightsome; if the eye—the intention, be evil, the whole body of the act will be darksome, is the teaching of our Blessed Lord. If a person wish to excel in virtue and in knowledge, and to do so for the glory of God and the good of holy Church, or even of his country and of his fellow-men, the desire is praiseworthy. Ambition in this sense is laudable; and reasonable pride of dignity and just power, commendable. Pride and ambition of this sort are continuously stimulated in every college in the world. The hearts of men of fame must foster the feeling. The ambition of military glory, for instance, sought for in defending the cause of honor, justice, truth, or country, finds a place in the breast of every distinguished soldier or every daring general. Only yesterday or the day before, the Spanish Republican General, Marshal Concha, was urged by this feeling to deeds of valour and daring before the heights of Estella, not less than his opponent, the Carlist Commander-in-Chief, General Dorregary, who gained the victory. Irishmen have at all times been ambitious of glory and of honour, and hence have, for military prowess, won renown in every country, except their own. During the period from the fifth to the ninth century, the children of Ireland were the most learned, as Venerable Bede records, of all the children in the world.

In this way, when the end aimed at is worthy, or when the motive is good, the action or pursuit is, in fact, morally as well as socially, and at times, materially good. And of course, when the end is bad or the motive bad, the action becomes morally bad, even though the material work done, or the social effect resulting from it is, in reality, good. If a person give an alms, like the Pharisees of old, for the sake of show, or to have one's name blazoned in the newspapers; the alms bestowed may help the poor, or may aid in building a church, but, for all that, the moral act is vicious before God, who sees the heart, and judges not according to the work done before men. This is the teaching of our Blessed Lord, who told the Hebrew people that the Pharisees, who fasted twice a week and gave tithes of all they possessessed, who gave large alms to the poor, and were zealous for the law far above others, had, in their vain glory, received " their reward." Unless our just acts exceed in purity of intention, the external justice of those Jewish zealots, we cannot merit the promised reward of the kingdom of Heaven. In this way, it is plain, that if the object aimed at is one of vanity or of pride, or if the motive that prompts our action is bad or unworthy, the action is of the same complexion as the motive. It happens, then, that the natural impulse of man—and, of course, of a high-minded, intellectual race, whose temperament is warm and prone to emulation, like the Kelts of Ireland—can readily be turned either to good or to evil. Irishmen bear privations, hardship, want, misery, hard labor, loss of friends and of fortune, with patience and even with equanimity, while they cannot bear the idea of being regarded as a race inferior to the Saxons, or to be of those who are slaves or helots in their native land. Individuals feel this national pride, and often care not to conceal it. As it has no available channel in which to flow, it manifests itself, at the present day, in a desire to rival the dominant race in the use of their own language, their habits, manners, material refinement, elegance, pronunciation, tone, advance in the arts and sciences. The rich portion of the middle classes are not content with the loss of the Irish tongue, but they send their sons and daughters to England to learn, in colleges and schools, the English accent—often from Irish masters ; whilst the humbler classes, who can speak Irish, conceal their knowledge of their own native tongue lest they be considered uneducated.

In their untrained and often uneducated views, they fancy that one cannot acquire a correct English accent at home ; and those who speak Gaelic seem to think that they cannot acquire a knowledge of English without losing their knowledge of Irish.

Many others, too, even amongst those considered learned in Church and State, despise Irish, simply because they are ignorant of the language, with the vain and foolish notion, that as they do not know the language, therefore it is not worth knowing, and the sooner it ceases to exist the better for the country and the people. The writer has met many of this class, particularly amongst young professional gentlemen, especially those who have received marks of honour or distinction in some special branch of knowledge.

The writer has seen and spoken to the son of a merchant from the city of Cork—a man of middle class position, whose income was barely sufficient to meet the requirements of a growing family of five children—two sons and three daughters; and has learned from the young gentleman that he had been, at the earnest desire of his own mother, sent during three years to an English college, for no other reason than that he might acquire what was called a correct English accent. It happened that there were two Irishmen professors in the college at which the young Hibernian had been a pupil. His accent —fortunately for the boy—was not a bit changed. The grandmother of the young gentleman knew Irish, but the mother did not know a word of it; and she was determined, like a great many foolish mothers of the present day in Ireland, that her son should not have, even as an ornament to the English speech, the fine *ore rotundo* accent which he had inherited from his fathers.

This section closes with an anecdote, which, like the foregoing, rests for its truth on facts. The writer has heard it told by the Very Rev. Thomas MacHale, S.T.D., Professor of Sacred Scriptures and Hebrew in the College des Irlandais, Paris. On one occasion, about the year 1861, on coming from Paris, for the summer vacation, to Tuam, the Very Rev. Professor was detained for a short time at the Euston Station, London, waiting till the North Western train to Holyhead should start.

While leisurely walking along the stand or piazza, he observed a young girl, over twenty years of age, manifestly waiting, like himself, for the train to Holyhead. The maid was of midd'e size, elegantly dressed, for one in her position, yet modest'y; her fresh, full, and slightly ruddy complexion showed that she had not been long living in London. There was a tinge of bashful simplicity playing over her features, with a slight expression of deferential regard for the priest as he passed, although she wished to assume, as she thought, the high tone of London fashion, and to do the elegant in the presence of a dignified stranger. Notwithstanding her dress and her airs, there hung around her, like the freshness of morning, a *naivète* and a homeliness of bearing in which any discerning eye, much less that of a priest and professor, could not be mistaken. Accordingly the Very Rev. Doctor said to himself that the young girl who stood on the platform before him, was a daughter of Eire, and that she was, as is said, from the country. She must be a Catholic, too; this he immediately conjectured from the satisfied glance with which she had occasionally viewed the strange priest. He thought it well to speak to her; and as she was, as he had thought, a Catholic and the daughter of a peasant, she must necessarily know Gaelic; and, therefore, he spoke in the Irish tongue, and saluted her in those well-known, familiar words, in which the Catholic peasantry are wont to salute each other at home—"Go m-beannuige Dia duit, a cailín óig—God save you, my young woman," said he. The maid looked quite surprised at the strange Reverend Father:—he thought with himself for a moment that, perhaps, she did not hear the words that had just fallen from his lips, and accordingly he repeated the salutation, in Irish—"Go m-beannuige Dia duit a cailín óig." There was no doubt remaining on his mind this time that she had heard his words. So, she looked again with the same expression of surprise at the Very Rev. Professor, and after a slight pause, assuming in the meantime the grandest tone she could command, replied, with a slight touch of a London accent, "Sir, I do not understand what you say." "Is it true that you do not understand what I have said to you ?" said the priest. "Yes, Rev. Father," was the reply. Dr. MacHale then began to suspect that he had been mistaken in supposing the young girl was from Ireland. So he moved on, and came up after a moment's walk to an elderly man who had seen some three score and five summers, and who, while the learned professor and the young girl were, for the moment, apparently conversing, had stood some fifteen yards off, looking anxiously and with enquiring gaze at the dignified stranger and the maid, to see what was the conversation about. The mien and manner of the elderly unknown were unmistakably Hibernian. But, to remove all doubt as to the country to which he belonged, he carried a stick, and on the ferule projecting over the left shoulder, a small parcel tied up in the usual red handkerchief. From the watchful eye and anxious glance directed towards the young girl, Dr. MacHale divined that some tie of consanguinity or affinity must needs exist between the maid and the man. The latter was, beyond all doubt, of Irish origin. As the priest drew near, the stranger put on a pleasing expression of countenance, such as one cannot avoid assuming in presence of an esteemed friend, though at the time there is not on his part an equally ready mutual recognition. A priest is a kind of familiar friend to every Irishman, and especially to every Irish Catholic, even though it happen that he is not an acquaintance. It was so in this instance. There had already existed positive proof that the man was from the sister isle. He is a Catholic, too, for he salutes the priest. This act is seldom performed in London by any one except an Irish Catholic. If he is a Catholic, and from the sister isle, he must, therefore, speak Irish. Accordingly, Dr. MacHale addressed him in Irish—"Go m-beannuiġe Dia duit a duine cóir—God save you, my good man." With a bright flush of light beaming from his eye, and a smile playing on his lips, fully assured that he stood face to face with one of his own countrymen, with one who spoke his own language, with one of the priests of his country who had, for over two centuries, been the guardians and the fostering and spiritual fathers of the race to which he belonged, he replied, "Go m-beannuige Dia agus Muire duit fein"—God and Mary save yourself. "An as Eirinn tusa?"—Are you from Ireland. "Seadh go deimin, a athair"—Yes, indeed, father. "B-fuil eolas agat air an mhnaoi oig so?"—Do you know this young woman? "An b-fuil eolas agam air an mhnaoi óig sin?" "Nach í si m' inghion í"—Do I know that young woman? Why, sure she is my daughter. By this time the young girl came up, blushing, to where her father stood speaking to Dr. MacHale; and then the professor said, in presence of the maid—"Is iongantach nach b-fuil gaodhailge aici"—It is surprising that she does not understand Irish. "Well," said he, in reply, and with great vehemence of expression, "si an ceud teanga a labhair si; ta gaodhailge aice co maith a's ta agam-sa"—Irish is the first tongue she spoke; and she knows Irish just as well as I know it. The young maid appeared now to feel ashamed of the part she had played, and of the answer she had given the Very Rev. Professor of the College des Irlandais, Paris; and when he asked her, in Irish, why she had denied that she knew her native language, she modestly looked to the ground, and replied, "Bi náire orm"—I was ashamed.

Smoke is a sign of fire, or of heat, though it may be unperceived heat. The blush on the cheek is a sign of the stirring of the feelings of the soul within, and of the struggle between pride and principle. The shame of the Irish girl to speak her native language is a sign of the state of feelings by which she had been actuated at the time—wishing to appear somebody, and for that purpose trampling on the principle that told her she ought to love Ireland and the language of her fathers, and not to be ashamed to speak it before princes. It will be said that the anecdote records only one single instance of false shame, and that from a single case, and in a matter not essential, but merely accidental, it is not logical to draw a conclusion quite universal regarding the whole population of Ireland. This objection is quite correct:—it is illogical to draw a universal from a particular proposition, unless the particular enunciates a truth founded on the nature or in the essential qualities of the subject of which there is question, or in the accidental relations which produce in the same circumstances, always the same effect. It is true that there are thousands of Irishmen in America and in Ireland who are not ashamed, even before the stranger or the lordly, to speak the language of their fathers; but it is equally true that with a class of no high social standing, and who are devoid of sufficient enlightenment as linguists or historians, and especially with those who are lovers of fashion and who aim at that which is held in honor for the hour—it is deemed a sign of ignorance and lowliness of position to speak Irish. The growing maidens of Connacht who have been for any time attending school, either religious or secular, blush if spoken to in Irish. They reply: "Oh, I know how to speak English, your Reverence; I am not so ignorant as you seem to think me to be." This very summer the writer met more than one instance plainly shown, not in the case of a girl, but of a woman who had seen some fifty summers. The incident occurred at Lios-dun-varna, near the sulphur spa. He addressed a woman whom he had heard speaking in Irish to those of her own class—in the language of the people. Her reply, directly and with the expression of surprise, was:—"Sir, I do not know Irish." The anecdote then puts before the reader a state of feeling and a dislike for speaking Irish that actuates a large class. And this state of mind and of feeling arises from a perversion of an innate desire "to excel and to scorn the very notion of being inferior to any one," as was shewn in the opening passage of this nineteenth section. All that is required, in order to correct this, is to make the speech itself of the Irish people, and the study of it honorable and worthy of their ambition.

Do what the Welsh are doing.—Offer prizes; hold Eisteddfodan; make the spoken speech of the Gael appreciable and honorable.

TWENTIETH—His Lordship the Most Rev. Dr. Moriarty, Bishop of Ardfert and Raphoe, county Kerry, and the Very Rev Dr. O'Brien, Dean of Limerick, author of "Ailey Moore," "Jack Hazlitt," and other able literary works, have been visiting Tuam and the western coast of their native island.

Each of the two is eminently distinguished as a churchman, as an ecclesiastical scholar and theologian —each has left, already, footprints impressed on the literary landmarks of their country's history, and of her social advancement; each holds a high place in the walks of English literature; each is thoroughly conversant with the condition of Ireland, past and present—with the causes of her decay in commerce, material and social development; in education, too, and enlightenment, if the present period be compared with the times of St. Columba and St. Columbanus, Sedulius and Scotus; St. Fursey and Fiacre; Saints Benignus, Jarlath, Alcuin, Malachy, and Laurence O'Toole. Each of the two is thoroughly conversant with the language of the people. They speak and preach to their flocks in Irish. His Lordship, accompanied by the Dean, visited St. Jarlath's College. In the course of conversation, his Lordship, Dr. Moriarty, told the present writer that Professor Blackie of the Edinburg University, had written to him, too, regarding the decay of the Gaelic language in Ireland, and the causes of that decay. His Lordship enumerated as causes of this fading away of our national speech, some of those just enumerated—such as the fact that our national language is not taught in our National Scnools. "I remarked, also," said his lordship, "that landlords and their agents, and gentlemen of the legal profession, attorneys and barristers, and all who represent the dominant interest, have helped to bring about the decadence of the speech of the Irish people. I often asked the peasants of my diocese why they essayed so often to speak English, omitting the use of the vernacular speech. And they invariably answered that the agents and landlords would listen to no Irish, and that, therefore, they were forced to speak as best they could in the English tongue. The same is true of the intercourse of the poor people with lawyers of all conditions from the Chancellor to the attorney's clerk.

A Catholic farmer, a subject of his Lordship's diocese, came some years ago to the Bishop and told him that he was about to "go to law," and that all the money he had then to carry on the suit was only two ponnds. His lordship advised the poor man not to go to law; to settle the matter by arbitration; to keep his money, and not to lose the two pounds, and seven times more, by appealing to lawyers. The good simple man went his way. Some time afterwards the bishop met the same farmer. His lordship asked him what did he do with the two pounds, whether he had expended that moderate sum in fair arbitration? The poor man, in a tone of regret, assured the Bishop, that he did go to law; that he lost the case; and that he had expended the two pounds on the interpreter alone, or as he called that legal functionary, the "tetherpreter," in order that his sworn examinations in Irish should be fully and to the point translated for council and judge, and by that means that success might attend the suit. Knowledge of Irish alone was, in the case of that poor peasant, a twofold loss. In Wales, judges and lawyers of all degrees are obliged to know the Welsh language. Nay, some of the Judges who go on circuit in the North of England must know the Yorkshire dialects. Why not in Ireland? Why?

Dr. Connop Thorlwall, an Englishman, was not appointed to the Bishopric of St. David's until he had acquired a thorough knowledge of the Kymric tongue; neither did Dr. Campbell, a Scotchman, receive his appointment to the Episcopal See of Bangor until he had been able to preach in the Welsh tongue.

How differently we act in Ireland. Ignorance of the people's language and habits has been the best passport to places of position and emolument.

CHAPTER IV.

In what counties of the West of Ireland is the language fading? It is fading, but not in an equal degree, in Galway and Mayo. The statement rests for its truth on the personal knowledge and experience which the writer has acquired of the people and of the places. In the counties of Mayo and Galway nine out of every ten of the inhabitants dwelling in the rural districts speak their country's language. The educated classes do not speak it. This was not the case thirty years ago. Numberless cases arise, in which magistrates who administer the law in Galway and Mayo, treat the natives who speak Irish as criminals. A case in point. In Roscommon, Leitrim, and Sligo, peasants and people in business, who are of the middle age, know to speak the Irish language; but from its gradual disuse, prefer to speak English. The growing youth in these counties know nothing of the speech of their forefathers.

The views which naturally come next in order, regard those districts, in which, throughout the west of Ireland, the Irish language is fading. And the question which directly starts to the mind of every man is—if the language is fading, is it worth the while of Irishmen to stop this decay—is it worth their while to go farther, and not only to keep it in existence, but to foster it, and to strive to make it grow into literary life?

The scope of the present work regards the living Gaelic language of Connacht. In its topographical bearing it does not reach to—

"Where the Barrow and the Erne and Lough Swilly's waters roar."

The writer has to deal with the ancient tongue spoken

at present within the territory lying east and west between the Shannon and the sea; and north and south between Bundoran and the borders of Banagher—

> "Where the parting sunbeam kisses the Corrib in the West,
> And the ocean, like a mother, clasps the Shannon to her breast."

Each of the five counties in the province has been, for the past twenty years, visited, from time to time, by the writer, and, therefore, whatever is stated in these pages respecting them, is the expression of those thoughts, which, from personal observation, since the days of his boyhood to the present hour, have been moulded in his mind—taking their rise from acquaintance with the districts and their inhabitants, and expanding with the train of his experience and his knowledge of the people.

In Connacht there are five counties—Sligo, Leitrim, Roscommon, Mayo, and Galway: the two latter are washed by the waters of the Atlantic, and they extend to the west and south of the province. Roscommon, Leitrim, and Sligo, border on the provinces of Leinster and Ulster. A distinction must, in the question regarding the spoken Gaelic language, be drawn between the three counties bordering on Ulster and Leinster, and the two counties, Mayo and Galway, situate to the west and south of the province.

Such is Connacht in its leading topographical outlines. Now for the language spoken within its borders.

The Irish language is fastly fading in Sligo, Leitrim, and Roscommon; fading in Mayo and in Galway, but not with that rapidity with which it is being swept away from the face of the three counties bordering on Leinster and Ulster. In each of the two counties beaten by the waters of the Atlantic, the language of their fathers is still spoken by nine out of every ten of the inhabitants dwelling in the rural districts.

In every country village within the Metropolitan Diocese of Tuam, except that portion of it which lies near Athlone, namely—the parish of Moore—there is no language, save Gaelic, spoken or heard by the peasant portion of the native Irish population. It is true that in towns the tongue of the Keltic race is not generally employed as largely as it is in the rural villages. However, it is certain, that at present, Irish is the only language made use of in Mayo and Galway, in buying and selling at fairs and at markets, by the inhabitants of towns as well as by the peasant proprietors who dwell in country districts.

The educated classes who have been trained in English colleges, or in colleges at home in Ireland, are all quite ignorant of the speech of their Keltic sires. This was not the case some twenty years ago amongst the immediate progenitors of living Irish gentlemen. The lord of the soil and the middle-man, with their sons and daughters, spoke, in days now past, the language of the people. At present the same classes are not only ignorant of the language themselves, but they wish to crush it out of life. Gentlemen of the legal profession and magistrates who, by right ought not to have a place on the bench of justice without a knowledge of the people's language, are the most hostile classes against the speech of their Hibernian progenitors.

Thr writer has witnessed, in small sessional courts, at Tuam, Ballinrobe, Castlebar, and other towns of the West, the simple peasants treated with the greatest display of harshness because they could not give evidence in the English tongue. It must be said that, as a rule, the magistrates who have treated, and do treat, the people so, are ignorant themselves of law, of language, and of those polite and considerate manners that become gentlemen.

The writer has been amused and pained to see, on one occasion within the past year, a legal functionary, who himself speaks Irish, assume a high tone and brow-beat an unfortunate peasant by putting trying questions in English. The following, from the *Tuam News* of August 21, deserves to be recorded. The facts as reported are truthful, and the treatment recorded is only one instance out of hundreds like it:

TUAM PETTY SESSIONS—MONDAY, AUGUST 17, 1874.

A. N. Blake, Esq., J.P. chairman; Captain Ball, R.M.; H. Kirwan, Esq., J.P.; and W. Gannon, Esq., J.P.

Sally Ryan next came upon the table. She said in Irish that she was an Irish-speaking witness.

Captain Ball said (in English) that she should try and give her evidence in English; and ordered Mr. Gannon, C.P.S., to interpret that to her. Not waiting for the interpretation, Sally replied (in Irish) that she could not speak English.

Captain Ball—Oh! I see now you know English; and I must tell you that it is loss of time for you to go on. I know what credibility to attach to your evidence.

Mr. Gannon, addressing her in Irish, said that she should speak in English.

Sally Ryan then protested (in Irish) that she could not tell what she knew to be the truth to her satisfaction in English.

Captain Ball—Constable, remove that woman off the table.

Sally Ryan then offered to do her best.

Captain Ball—No. She has got her chance.

John Ryan was then examined. He explained that what brought the woman there was to draw water from a well.

On cross-examination, he said that he was a cousin of James Murphy's.

Lawrence Ryan, an Irish-speaking witness, was then examined through Mr. P. J. Gannon, as interpreter.

Commenting on the foregoing, the Editor of the *Tuam News*, Edward Byrne, Esq., makes the following judicious remarks:

IRISH MAGISTRATES AND "IRISH WITNESSES."

Any person who frequents the Courts of Justice in Ireland

cannot fail to have observed the objection which is in nearly every instance entertained to a witness giving evidence in the Irish language. Strange and anomalous as this statement may sound it can hardly be gainsaid. The case on which comment is made at present is only a solitary instance of a truth general to the whole country. A witness comes upon the table, and avers that he or she can give evidence only in Irish. Immediately the thought of the trouble and the delay of interpretation involuntarily enters the magisterial mind. Immediately it occurs to this thesaurus of nature and art that the witness is shamming. These irrepressible Irish are like the noble Redskins—prodigious liars. The witness wants to prepare his answers, and the repetition of the questions by the counsel and the interpreter gives the knave the necessary time to forge his prevarication or evasion. Too, did I not hear him, this very instant, say "no," with just as perfect enunciation and accent as I could say it myself? Thus thinks and speaks the Bench. The counsel against whose case the witness is summoned starts up and tells his worship that he has just been told by a most respectable person that the fellow on the table is quite a professor of English, in fact, competent to take a prize in Belles Lettres. Then the poor fellow on the table, or the poor woman (in the particular case referred to the witness was a woman) is pressed, and badgered and coerced to give evidence in English. He is admonished in English by the Bench, and advised in Irish by the Interpreter. At last he answers in Irish a question put to him in English. "Thou hast said it: out of your own mouth you have condemned yourself. Is it not so, my brethren?" "Constable, remove that person." Such is the magisterial fiat—hot, hasty; but irrevocable as the laws of the Medes and Persians. The poor fellow is then taken, collared, and cast into the outer courts as an unconvicted criminal. Or, perhaps, he tries to testify in English. The bench attaches great weight to his evidence then. Then there is no measurement of credibility. But we know what amount of trust to place in his words,—just not an iota. They may be correct; but ten to one they are all a mistake. We place just the same amount of confidence in his depositions as we would place in our own if we were forced to give evidence in German; because we understood some sentences addressed to us in that languag-, Every little word has a distinct meaning for every collocation. No just bench that reflects upon it; no man of educated intelligence, valuing his words on oath, would dream of attaching credibility, sufficient to turn the most delicate balance of evidence, to the testimony of any man in any language except that to which he is accustomed as his own, or to which be has naturalised himself by thought, training, association, and use. Let it even be admitted that Irish peasants are disingenuous. Years of persecution, during which they had to breathe almost by stealth, made them so; and it is not laws made by the descendants of those who legislated to debase them that ought to be their first accusers. In Wales, a portion of the British Empire, about the size of Connaught, judges must qualify for their judicial seats by a knowledge of the Kymbric tongue. Nay, the advocates themselves are not admitted to practice until they learn the language. Indeed, it would be an empty honour if they were; for they could get nothing to do from the Welsh. In India the English Judges and Counsel, and in fact, officials in general must pass a competitive examination in Hindostanee before they are eligible for office. In Ireland alone is the programme of WILLIAM, the Conqueror of the Saxons, studiously copied; and the language of the country banished from its courts of law. In practice, the laws against speaking Irish are at this day just as intolerant as they were at the worst period of the penal code. Salaried magistrates are appointed, as honorary magistrates are, through family favour, or services on flood or field, rather than because of any qualification of intellect or peculiar fitness.

The case which occasions comment at this time is only one of many, and almost every magistrate seems to require a mnemonic to the effect that, as the law presumes the innocence of every man until he is duly pronounced guilty, so the good faith of the Irish witness must remain unimpeached and unimpeachable until he clearly demonstrates his Anglican acquirements.

(From the *Irishman* of June 13, 1874.)

OUR NEGLECTED MOTHER TONGUE.

The neglect of the Irish tongue is one of the saddest, if not the very saddest phase of Irish national decay, and Irish national shortsightedness and stupidity. This is strong language, but the case is so monstrous that no form of human speech could supply words too strong for its condemnation. No nation having a refined, cultivated, and ancient language, ever let it go to ruin as we have let ours. It was, to be sure, banned by the stranger, but the barrier has long ago been removed. There is now no fine for learning Irish, and the fact of its having been banned and proscribed ought only to make it more dear to us. No conqueror ever yet destroyed a language without destroying root and branch the nation that spoke it. If we know nothing of the language of Carthage, it is because the Carthagenian nation was utterly exterminated. Russian and Prussian persecution have not succeeded in destroying the Polish language, and never will, although every threat and artifice are used for that purpose. Polish may be banned by Russia and Prussia; books and newspapers may not be allowed to be published in it; it may be a crime even to speak it in Posen and Warsaw; but as long as the Polish nation lasts so long will the Polish language be spoken. If the Poles are forbidden to print books in it, they will at least continue to pray to God in it, and to curse the Czar in it to the end of time.

Politicians may laugh at the idea that the Irish national cause has suffered by the neglect of our language; but it could be easily proved that this neglect has done it more harm than all the finest orations of our best patriots have done it good; for just in proportion as we adopt the manners, dress, customs, and, above all, the language of our conquerors—just in proportion do we appear to others to resign our claims to a distinct nationality.

In all ages and in all countries similarity of language was considered the great bond between peoples; and the first effort of every conqueror was to force his speech on the vanquished; when this was done, resistance to his yoke generally closed. This idea is as prevalent to-day as ever it was. One proof out of the thousand that could be given will be enough, and we give from the great popular German national hymn—*Des Deutschen Vaterland*:—

Was ist des Deutschen Vaterland?
So weit die deutsche Zunge klingt,
Und Gott im Himmel Lieder singt;
Das soll es sein, das soll es sein!

What is the German Fatherland?
Wherever the German language sounds,

And sings praises to God in heaven—
That shall it be, that shall it be'

To come nearer home let us look at Wales. There is probably not a pure Welshman in existence that cannot speak his own language. A Welshman can be in every sense of the word an educated man without knowing English, for he has books, newspapers, and periodicals in his own language, and has most of the popular English educational works translated into Welsh. A hundred years ago Welsh was nearly dead; there were only a few books and no newspapers in it; *but the Welsh clergy were patriotic;* they preached to their flocks in it and it only. So the Welsh have a sort of Home Rule, and we have no sort.

The neglect of our language has worked evil to Ireland in every possible way in which the question can be regarded. The most serious evil it has done is the undeniable distaste for literature which it has caused amongst our poorer classes.

The great question now is; can anything be done to revive the culture of our almost dead language; the language of those who fought, and worked, and suffered most for Ireland, the language of the Seanachus Mor, of Ossian, of O'Dugan, and of the Four Masters? We answer yes—emphatically yes. Have it taught in the National Schools first in all districts where it is yet spoken. This is the first step that can be taken; and this can be done within twelve months if the Irish people go about the matter in earnest. The Government will not throw any obstacle in the way; in fact they could not, for Welsh is taught in the National Schools in Wales, and Gaelic is taught, or about being taught in Scotland. There might be some difficulty in getting a sufficient number of teachers at first, but in a year or two the difficulty would disappear, for there are still a million of people in the country who are acquainted with the language. The hopes of being able to earn even a small salary as an Irish teacher would soon call into existence a larger number of competent teachers than there might be employment for. Let the question be agitated at once. It will be a proper accompaniment for Home Rule, for the one never can be perfect without the other.

If we allow our native language to die we shall have committed the blackest crime that was ever recorded in the history of nations.

In the three counties—Roscommon, Leitrim, and Sligo

—the language of their fathers is not spoken by those who at present are in the years of adolescence, nor by those who have reached the full term of manhood or womanhood. The vast body of the people, even the poorest class, speak English. The writer has, in many villages, conversed with the country people living in these counties—Roscommon, Leitrim, and Sligo—and the result of his experience is, that all who at present have attained the age of thirty or forty and upwards, *can*, and sometimes *do speak* Irish. On the other hand, the youth of the present generation, from the age of three to that of thirty, are, as a rule, unacquainted with the tongue spoken by their forefathers. Hence, amongst all that class and their descendants in Sligo, Leitrim, and Roscommon, Irish Gaelic will, it is believed, become, in fifty years from the present period, a dead language.

In Galway and in Mayo, however, the speech of the Gael will—come what may—live for one century longer. It will flourish for many centuries to come, as the Welsh language flourishes in Wales and wherever Welshmen make for themselves a home—provided only our people wish, really, like the Welsh, to see it live.

CHAPTER V.

Opinions and Enactments of the Catholic Prelates of the Province of Connacht regarding Gaelic. Are they Enforced? Is Gaelic, as a spoken language, worth retaining? The answer may be given by a native of Eire. Reasons for the affirmative—special and general reasons. Vous êtes Anglais? Anecdotes: Natives of Ireland should act towards their National speech as the natives of other countries, the Welsh, the Poles, the Hebrew race act with their respective National languages. Thoughts of material profit and worldly advantage are unworthy of enlightened, cultivated minds. Contrast between painting and linguistic studies. What does the art of painting profit one. Prodigious prices for rare paintings. Prices paid for rare books; for manuscripts. Instances of how Irish-Americans love the language of old Ireland. It is not by bread alone man lives. The life of the intellect is not material. Other reasons—The literary character of the language. Its literary relations. Its native worth. It is not a sign of filial devotedness to drive away one's grandmother; so, children of Ireland ought, at least, to allow the language of Ireland to die in peace, and not to forestal its decay or death.

"*Maximopere dedeceret, si nostro ævo oblivioni consignaretur lingua illa in qua, beatissimi apostoli nostri, eorum sancti successores verbum fidei patribus nostris prædicaverunt, et per quam, sæviente inaudita persecutione, eadem fides sine ruga et sine macula ad nos usque transmissa fuit.*" —*Decreta Conciliorum Provinciæ Tuamensis, c. ix., s.* 4, *p.* 68.

Although the writer knows full well that the statements made in this chapter rest on the truth of facts which he himself "has seen with his eyes," as it is said, and heard with his ears;" yet for those who read these pages the testimony of at least more than one witness to afford sufficient proof of the truths put forward is necessary. The written words of the Catholic Prelates of the ecclesiastical province of Tuam, assembled in council at St. Jarlath's College, Tuam, in the 15th August, 1859, are on record in the copy of the decrees which have been by them promulgated to direct and regulate the ecclesiastical discipline of the western ecclesiastical province of the Catholic Church in Ireland. At that synod—the latest that has been to the present period held for the province of Tuam—were assembled his Grace, the Most Rev. John MacHale, Archbishop of Tuam, Metropolitan and Primate of Connaught; his Lordship the Most Rev. Thomas Feeny, Bishop of Killala; the Most Rev. George Joseph Browne, Lord Bishop of Elphin, and his co-adjutor, the Most Rev. Dr. Gillooly, at present Lord Bishop of Elphin; the Most Rev. John Derry, Lord Bishop of Clonfert; the Most Rev. Patrick Durkan, Lord Bishop of Achonry; the Most Rev. Patrick Fallon, Lord Bishop of Kilmacduagh and Kilfenora; and the Most Rev. John MacEvilly, Lord Bishop of Galway. Of these venerable prelates three have passed away to receive the reward promised to all those who teach others unto justice, to shine like stars amongst the blessed, even as they had shone here by the light of their superior learning and virtues. The learned prelate the Most Rev. Hugh Conway, who is successor to the Most Rev. Dr. Feeny in the see of Killala, is a most distinguished Irish scholar. Irish is his mother tongue, and that which to him is the language of his heart.

The Lord Bishop of Clonfert—the Most Rev. Dr. Duggan, successor to the Most Rev. Dr. Derry in the see of Clonfert—had acquired fame as an Irish preacher decades of years ago, long before he had been selected to govern the diocese of Clonfert. All the venerable prelates who rule and guide the Catholics of Connaught and of county Clare are Irish in heart and tongue. The moral paradox then which cannot be comprehended is, how it happens that the language of the people, so much prized and appreciated both by people and venerable and learned prelates is fading!

In the year 1859, the illustrious prelates of the province, in synod assembled, published the following well-known facts:

"Juventus sola patriæ linguæ ignorare incipit." The youth alone are beginning to have no knowledge of their country's language.

And they express their feelings on this subject in those words:

"Vehementer angebamur cum videremus ex scholis parochialibus excludi, vel saltem leviter et non nisi per transennam attingi studium linguæ nostræ nationalis." We felt very much annoyed when we saw that the study of our national language was banished from the parochial schools, or that its cultivation was only lightly, and as it were occasionally, attended to.

An important truth propounded by the assembled prelates:—

"In manibus sacerdotum est sors antiquæ et pluribus nominibus reverandæ linguæ nostræ." In the hands of the priests and of the hierarchy is placed the destiny of our ancient language—a speech rendered venerable by a long roll of illustrious names."

The venerable prelates then exhort the Catholic Clergy of the province to encourage the study and culture of the national language, and to offer premiums to those who excel in their knowledge of its spoken and written forms:

"Agite, itaque vos, O sacerdotes nostri, bonoque animo contendite ut in parochiis, ubi lingua hibernica viget, in singulis scholis, classis in ea instituatur, cui juvenes omnes interesse debent. Præmiis quibusdam cohonestandi erunt juvenes, diligentia cæteris præcellentes ut alacriore usque animo in hoc studio proficiant, et æqualibus suis exemplar præfulgentes, eosdem post se, in eadem jucunda contentione abducant."

Bestir yourselves, priests of this province, and strive with earnest and sincere zeal, that in the parishes where the Irish language flourishes a class be established in each school for the purpose of teaching the language to the youth, and that the rising generation be all made to attend these classes. Those young people who excel others in diligence ought to be fairly encouraged by rewards of merit, so that they may, with a greater degree of cheerful spirit, make progress in this kind of study, and that, by giving a bright example to their own equals they may influence them to join in the same promising pursuit.

Men have asked—and the writer has heard them say—"Is Gaelic, as a spoken language, worth retaining in life?"

A fair common-sense answer to this question—taking it for what it is worth—can be given (1) either by a child of Eire or (2) by one who is not a native of Eire, yet, who cherishes a love of learning and knowledge.

First—*For a child of Eire* there is only one befitting answer to this question, and that is—"Yes." And if it is asked "Why?"—convincing reasons in number are at hand; for, Irish Gaelic is (1) the language of his fathers; (2) of St. Patrick; (3) of the saints and sages who, for fourteen hundred years and longer, have cherished the speech of the sons of the Gael. (4) It is a natural inheritance. It is the sign or stamp of our Keltic descent. For a child of Eire, the foregoing are reasons enough. If one wish to appeal to patriotism he can add (5) that a distinct language is the exponent of a distinct and a separate nationality, or at least, of a distinct race of the human family.

At the present day Irishmen are not regarded, on the Continent of Europe or of Asia, for instance in Calcutta, or of Australia, by foreigners, as belonging to a nationality distinct from that of Englishmen. Irishmen speaking English must bear to be told by foreigners—"Vous étes Anglais" —*You are English*. The Most Rev. Dr. MacHale, Archbishop of Tuam, tells an anecdote regarding himself, which fully illustrates this point. When travelling to Rome on one occasion, in the year 1834, he presented himself at Calais before the French official, whose duty it was to see the passports of the various passengers from England. The Frenchman looked at the Archbishop, and said quietly—'Vous étes Anglais?" His Grace, unwilling to pass for what he was not, and to represent a nationality with which he disclaimed all connexion, at least, of race or kindred, replied, "Non." Well, then, said the official, in French, you are a German.—'Non," was the reply. An Austrian?—No. A Dane?—No. A Spaniard?—No. You must be an Italian, then, or a Greek? His Grace, answered—"Je ne le suis pas"—I am not. Perhaps, said the polite Frenchman, you are a native of Poland, or of Hungary? I am not a native of either, was the reply of his Grace. The politeness of the Frenchman could hold out no longer; and in a fit of puzzled indignation, he cried out—Qu' est ce que le diable que vous étes?—What the d—— are you. The Archbishop, quite amused at the bewilderment of the fiery Frenchman, and satisfied at having maintained that he did not belong to any of these nationalities, calmly said, "Je suis Irlandais"—I am an Irishman. "Oh," said our Gallic cousin, with a half polite smile, wishing to insinuate there was no such distinct nation as Ireland—"C'est la même chose"—It is the same thing. In the mind and the view of his Grace the Archbishop, it was not the same thing. But the anecdote illustrates the opinion entertained by foreigners respecting Irishmen from home. Irishmen from home are everywhere regarded as English (Anglais). Every Irishman who has travelled through Europe is well aware that the statement is, unfortunately, too true. Frenchmen and Germans cannot respect, as native Irish, those Gaels who do not speak the language of Ireland. To speak our native tongue, is to foreigners the only exponent of our distinct Irish nationality. Do we wish to be regarded as Irishmen abroad as well as at home? Then let us learn the language of Ireland.

On another occasion his Grace the Archbishop of Tuam, in company with the Most Rev. Dr. Derry, Lord Bishop of Clonfert, and the Very Rev. Thomas MacHale, D.D., Professor in the Irish College, Paris, travelled together through France, Germany, and Italy. They had agreed, for their own social satisfaction, in order to be, while in a foreign clime, as much at home as possible, to speak in no other tongue than in the language dear to the hearts of the three—the language of the learned and saintly ecclesiastics of Ireland in the past. It happened that a certain English gentleman, a man of learning and position, staying at Paris for a day or two, selected the same hotel that the three ecclesiastical dignitaries had made choice of for the evening. He heard them convers at dinner; he listened, looked at them wistfully, seemed anxious to know what kind of language these strange gentlemen were speaking. It was not French, nor German, for he understood both; neither was it Latin or Greek, for he could, from his University training at Cambridge, distinguish a few words, even though the pronunciation were new to him. There were Russians at the hotel, and Polish exiles, too; he understood from them that the language spoken by the unknown three was not Russian nor Polish nor any of the Sclavonic dialects. Neither was it Hebrew or Syriac, for the style of features of these strangers was manifestly of European type. At length the good man resolved to remain no longer in doubt about a matter which, he thought, could be easily set at rest, and which, insignificant as it seemed, gave him no slight uneasiness. Accordingly, he addressed himself, in the English tongue, to the youngest of the three strangers, wishing to know what nationality they represented, and what language was that in which he had heard them converse. The younger, Dr. MacHale, with every mark of apparent desire to satisfy his inquiries, courteously replied, but still in a tongue which the English gentleman could not understand. They seemed like two of the leading architects at the tower of Babel—the one wishing to give all the information in his power to the other, but in utterance which, to the latter, was quite unintelligible. During the evening, the Archbishop and his nephew, with the Bishop of Clonfert, felt amused at the episode, and seemed quite pleased with the robe of complete *incognito* which a knowledge of their mother tongue had thrown around them, and at the advantage gained on that occasion from its possession.

Next day all four travelled by the same train and in the same railway carriage. The three strangers continued, as often as required, to converse in their own native tongue. The English gentleman did not forget to look and to listen. Still he felt anxious to know to what country they belonged, and what language they were speaking. His Grace the Archbishop, without advertence, soon gave him the wished for opportunity of prosecuting his desire to gain some satisfactory information on the point. His Grace took up Murray's or Bradshaw's continental guide to tourists. He read the book for some time. This was an opportunity not to be lost. "Sir," said the English gentleman to the Archbishop, "although you are not a native of England, I perceive from your reading Murray's Guide, that you understand English?" His Grace could not deny the fact that he had read the guide-book, or that he could read English; so, he said directly in reply:—"It is true that I am not an Englishman; yet, I have prosecuted my studies in the English tongue to such a degree that I can read, and even speak that language. "Oh! well, how glad I feel to meet a gentleman who can speak with me in my own tongue," observed the delighted English tourist, greatly relieved from the weight of anxious thought that had for two days preyed upon his mind; or, moved, most likely, with a sudden thrill kindred to that which one feels who has unexpectedly found out a way to the solution of a difficult problem, like Archimedes in the bath, pondering over the proposition of Hiero, startled by the sudden opening of intellectual light that burst on his view, scattering what had appeared before dark and hidden—became suddenly excited and nervously wild.

The Archbishop and his English acquaintance conversed for some time. They spoke on the subject of the different mother-tongues known throughout Europe—the Romance languages, the Sclavonic dialects, the different branches of the Semitic speech. After a time, the astonished Cambridge scholar could not help exclaiming, "I declare to you I never heard in all my life any foreigner speak the English tongue, sir, so well as you do; for one who is not a native, you speak it astonishingly well." His Grace bowed the expression of his thanks for the compliment, and continued the conversation with his new courteous companion, while the Most Rev. Dr. Derry and the younger Dr. MacHale seemed the while, as though, bewildered at the prolonged unknown conversation between the Archbishop and his foreign friend.

At length they touched on the politics of England, and on her treatment of Ireland. The views which the London *Times* gives the British people of the sister isle were those of this learned and social scholar. He praised Ireland, as a fine fertile land; that its people were discontented he did not deny; but their discontent arose, he said, from a restlessness inherent in the Keltic character. His Grace asked him who were the leaders of the people, who their political guides, and their religious teachers. He said that the people were led astray for a long time by O'Connell; that the peasantry were, as he styled them, Roman Catholics; that they were foolishly devoted to their priests, and that the most remarkable firebrand amongst the Irish Hierarchy was the Archbishop of Tuam, the Most Rev. Dr. MacHale.

Having spent that evening at the same hotel, the three dignitaries and their English acquaintance, took different lines of route—the one party for Civita Vecchia, the other for Geneva.

His Grace the Archbishop of Tuam, the Most Rev. John MacHale, and his Lordship the Bishop of Clonfert, the Most Rev. Dr. Derry, and the Very Rev. Dr. MacHale, plainly proved, on this occasion, even to the satisfaction of an English gentleman and scholar, that Irishmen were of a nationality quite distinct from that of Englishmen. If other Irishmen could act in the same way, the admission would soon be made by Frenchmen and Englishmen that we are "a people in ourselves, and not English."

A native of Ireland, possessing a knowledge of the Irish speech as it is spoken and written, possesses a passport and proof the most convincing, that he is, in truth, an Irishman.

It does not follow, however, that the contrary propoposition is not true—namely, that natives of Ireland, not knowing the native language, are not Irish and national in their love of country, of kind, and of creed. Unfortunately, over sixty per cent. of the population do not know Irish; yet, they are, let us hope, good Irishmen. All that is here asserted is, that a knowledge of the language as it is spoken, is proof positive just now, that one possessing such knowledge, must be Irish in all that represents his Irish character to the world—Irish in word and in deed.

Within the past two months a distinguished Irish Catholic priest, a native of Leinster, visited Bonn. He was introduced to learned and distinguished German scholars. One of these was a great student of the Keltic speech—a disciple and a perfect follower in literary research of Professor Zeuss. When this simple savant had learned that the clerical gentleman to whom he had been introduced, was a native of Ireland, and a clergyman, his joy became intense. "Just the very thing, I have been," said he, "so long hoping for. Here is a real living Irishman and a scholar." Before many hours had passed, the German consulted his Irish friend on the proper pronunciation of the present spoken Irish language, and wished to acquire some clearer views than those he had learned from books regarding the orthography and pronunciation of certain forms of Irish speech. To his utter astonishment he found that the savant from Ireland did not only not know one word of it, but that the latter had not ever heard a word of Irish. Quite annoyed at this discovery he took very little trouble to consult him a second time on the subject of home and foreign antiquities or languages.

Every person has heard of another very distinguished Irish ecclesiastic who in his own native Gaelic had been addressed by the world-famed Cardinal Mezzofanti—"A duıne cόır," said the Cardinal, "cıannos a b-fu.l tu? Na: d-tu geann tu gaoda.lge?" And the strange reply of the Irish gentleman was, that "really he did not know German." "It is not in German," said the illustrious Italian, "that I am addressing you; it is in your own language." The youthful ecclesiastic blushed. He profited by the telling remark. On his return to Ireland he learned to read, write, and speak the language of his Irish forefathers.

His Eminence, Cardinal Mezzofanti, knew how to speak the Irish language fairly. For in the year 1831, he—then only Monsignore—was for nigh three weeks, occasionally in the company of the present Archbishop of Tuam, at that time Bishop of Maronia, who in the winter of 1831, and the spring of 1832, had visited the City of the Seven Hills.* (*See Letters of his Grace the Archbishop of Tuam. Dublin: Duffy, pp.* 222-300.)

* His Grace told the present writer that he conversed in Irish with Monsignore Mezzofanti. Giuseppe Cardinal Mezzofanti was, as early as 1820, pronounced by Lord Byron "a walking polyglott, a master of languages, and a Briareus of parts of speech." His Eminence was a native Bologna; he was born in that city 17th September, 1774, just one hundred years September, 1874. In 1831 he settled in Rome, and was advanced to the dignity of Monsignore. In 1833 he was appointed Secretary to the College De Propaganda Fide, and keeper of the Vatican Library. In 1838 he was raised to that

Natives of Ireland should act like the Cambro-Britons; they should acquire a knowledge of English, and cultivate, at the same time, their native speech. The Swiss learn two languages—nay, three, and speak them. The Poles do the same. The children of the Hebrew race are remarkable for their devotion to their own tongue; yet, they avail themselves of the European languages for purposes of trade, commerce, and social intercourse. An accession of knowledge is no weight to the mind. It does not oppress, nay, it elevates the soul. It is its light, its life. This is true of all kinds of earthly knowledge, as far as it extends, but it is especially true when that knowledge relates to the soul, to Divine revelation, to the end of man and his duties to God.

"I cannot see," says Professor Blackie, "that the academic claims of Greek and Latin, however highly allowed, can justify us in the habitual neglect of that most venerable member of the Aryan family—Gaelic, which lies at our own doors. Lecture—the Gaelic language, page 2. Published at Edinburgh, 1861.

But some one will ask, as certain Irishmen have asked, what will a knowledge of Irish profit me after I shall have left the Irish shore? What shall I gain by it? It is of no use then to learn it?

Answer—1. Well, that materialism which measures greatness and worth by the standard of money and of private advantage, is certainly selfish and sordid. It is very common amongst people who live to make money, and who look only to the present; its passions, its fashions, its gains. But it is in no way intellectual, elevated, springing from the nobler impulses and the

---

dignity of Prince of the Church, and created Cardinal. He died at Rome 15th March, 1819.

directing intelligent influences of our nature. That man, indeed, will do little for creed or country, or for kith or kin, who first puts himself the question before he undertakes anything noble or lasting :—" What profit is this to me? What can I gain by it."

2. The appreciation of a language is an act of the mind arising from an intelligent knowledge of its worth. In this view, a language must be appreciated, although not commercially useful.

Let us see the value of the argument by contrasting language with painting as an intellectual study apart from pecuniary profits. What material benefit does one gain by the mere possession of beautiful paintings, works of virtue and of art? Nothing; and yet, the art of painting, and the taste which preserves specimens of past civilization—pictures in oil, in water-color, in encaustic—are highly valued, not alone at the present time, but they have ever been appreciated highly, even by civilized Pagans. The works of good artists have been valued beyond all ordinary calculation. For a painting from the pencil of Apelles, Alexander the Great is said to have given the fabulous sum of £50,000. The drawing represented, it is true, the Conqueror of Darius, as Jupiter in the act of hurling thunderbolts. It was an enormous sum for one picture. The gain resulting from its purchase was an intellectual gain. The beauty and value of works of art, like that purchased by the princely pupil of the philosopher of Stagyra, could not have been appreciated by any save by intelligent and educated minds. Pliny records that Mnason, tyrant of Elatea, paid Aristides of Thebes, the sum of three thousand six hundred pounds for a single easel picture of the battle of the Persians. And Attalus III., King of Pergamus, offered, after the siege of Corinth, the sum of five thousand three hun dred pounds for a painting of Bacchus and Ariadne, by the same artist; and he was refused.

The Emperor Augustus gave a hundred talents for a picture by Apelles—a fabulous sum, if one bear in mind the relative value of money in those days, compared with the present. For one shilling then, an amount of value could have been purchased, which, at the present day, costs one pound sterling. The painting purchased by Augustus, or taken from the inhabitants of the island of Cos, in lieu of one hundred talents tribute, was the celebrated *Venus Anadyomene*, or Venus rising out of the ocean, which was so highly prized by the Romans that Ovid declared, in terms of praise, that, were it not for that painting by Appelles, Venus would have still remained buried under the waters of the sea. The British Government, in modern times, has paid large sums for grand paintings. But the French Government has been, to the thinking of mere materially minded men, lavish beyond measure in the enormous sum, £23,600, which it gave for the famous "Soult Murillo," or, *Our Lady of the Immaculate Conception*, painted in 1678 by Murillo of Seville.

The paintings of the Spaniard, in the seventeenth century, are as much prized as those of the Ionian, in the fourth, or Zeuxis, or Parrhasius, in the fifth, before the Christian era.

The Governments of England and France, in modern days, have rivalled the generous appreciation of the kings of Macedon, and of Pergamus, and of the first Emperor of Rome in days of old, by the fabulous sums at which they valued pictures painted by celebrated artists.

And yet painting is an art which has charms only for the intelligent and the learned. They alone can see the power of mind which is capable of conceiving the image, and of placing it in its objective fulness before the eye. The fowl in the fable did not see the value of a gem. He declared he would rather have one grain of barley than the most precious and valuable of gems. Gems to him were things he could not eat. He had no power of head to soar higher than the notion of eating and drinking. A gem to a bird was certainly useless. There are men who prefer the possession of material value, which contributes to their gross animal life, to all the precious paintings ever pencilled in ancient or modern times by Grecian, Dutch, Italian, or Spanish artists. A man who values money and material riches for what they bring of earthly enjoyment, of civic honor, social state, or sensual living, cannot appreciate the possession of precious pictures as creations of intellect and works of genius. Of course he may value them as he values bank notes ; but that is not intellectual appreciation. Painting as well as music, does not satiate animal cravings, or satisfy mere earthly tastes. Persons of mind, of thought, of intelligence, alone can understand those works of intellectual creation. And how very highly they are valued is plain from the fact that kings and emperors and governments, in modern and ancient times, prefer to have them to the possession of hundreds of thousands of pounds.

The value of a language, too, must not be estimated by its commercial worth. Men of mind and of linguistic knowledge alone are capable of estimating it at its real value.

3. Every one knows how highly rare books are prized by the learned. Above all the manuscript works of renowned writers, such as the Bard of Stratford-upon-Avon, whose house, even as a natural heirloom, has been purchased (in 1847) by the British Government.

The manuscript by Dante of the *Divina Commedia* would

be purchased, not alone by the Florentines, but by every nation in Europe, at a great price. The manuscript of the *Canterbury Tales* would make a fortune for their possessor. Every people of civilization and intelligence throughout the world appreciate, in the highest degree, the creations of gifted genius, far above all the material splendour of Eastern monarchs.

It is in this way, too, that literary men value a language. One cannot argue or reason with persons of gross views regarding a subject which is intellectual, which has nothing material about it—the value of which does not present itself to the view under the appearance of bulk, or material profit, or social rank. On this point the words of Professor Blackie are pertinent: "People whose low ambition does not soar above what is called 'getting on in the world,' that is to say, whose whole anxiety is expended on planting laboriously, one above another, a series of steps, by which they may mount to the highest possible platform in the merely material world, without the slightest regard to moral or intellectual considerations, may well question the utility of Gaelic; for no Gael, I imagine, in these latter days, ever gained a penny by any remarkable proficiency in the knowledge of his mother tongue; but those who believe with Plato and St. Paul, that money is not the one thing needful, may be allowed to think otherwise."

If a manuscript of some great writer of the past is valued exceedingly; if paintings are highly prized; if an heirloom, bequeathed by a dear friend, is carefully preserved—why not the language of our fathers? The language of the Irish people is a precious heirloom transmitted to the present generation of Irishmén through a period of over two thousand years.

"Whose youthhood saw the Tyrian on our Irish coast a guest,

Ere the Saxon or the Roman, ere the Norman or the Dane
Had first set foot on Britain, or the Visigoth in Spain;
Whose manhood saw the Druid rite at forest, tree, and rock,
The savage tribes of Britain round the shrines of Zernebock;
And for generations witnessed all the glories of the Gael,
Since our Keltic sires sung war-songs round the warrior fires of Baal!

The tongues that saw its infancy are ranked among the dead;
And from their graves have risen those now spoken in their stead.
All the glories of old Erin, with her liberty, have gone,
Yet, their halo lingered round her while her olden Tongue lived on;
For, 'mid the desert of her woe, a monument more vast
Than all her pillar-towers, it stood—that old Tongue of the past."

Is not an heirloom so precious worth preserving? Surely yes.

Any Irishman who says that his nation's language—one of such antiquity, so rich and valuable in the eyes of scholars—is not worth retrieving, is sordid, selfish, and at heart he is not divested of those traits of character which belong to the uncivilized and the barbarian—a lack of that faculty which appreciates learning, knowledge, intelligence. The writer has heard several Irishmen—educated men—repeat that the Irish language is not worth preserving. These men regarded the language from a material point of view, from its productive value in the money market, or in society. He could understand how one could be so blinded by the love of England that he would, following the fashion of people in position, see nothing good in the Nazareth of mother-land; but for an Irishman and a Catholic priest to say that the national heirloom bequeathed him by his Irish Catholic forefathers not worth keeping, is expressing a proposition which is simply revolting to every sense of our intelligent nature, as a civilized and enlightened people, which is subversive of the national character of the Keltic race,* that for thousands of years have been, with a force strong and enduring as if it sprung from nature, devoted to the traditions and the historic glories of the past.

4. In the opinion of men of thought, the acquisition of knowledge is better than the possession of money, particularly the knowledge of a language, ignorance of which is deemed a shame—ignorance of one's mother tongue.

The writer has before him a letter received while this page is passing through press, from an Irish gentleman at present dwelling in Sumter, South Carolina—a Mr. Barrett. He states that the Most Rev. Bishop Lynch declared to him: "I would give a thousand dollars to be able to hear confessions in the language of my fathers." A similar statement has been sent by the Rev. John MacNulty, Pastor, Caledonia, Dominion of Canada, that the Bishop of the diocese declared he would rather than the possession of thousands of pounds, have a knowledge of even a little of the speech of the sages and saints of his own mother Eire."

The writer has met over a score of Irishmen who have, since they emigrated to America, learned to speak, in a foreign land, the language which it was their misfortune not to have learned at home. This fact shows with what ardour Irish-Americans love the language of their forefathers. There are, thank God, at home in Ireland and abroad in America and Australia, many men of mind and of scholarly attainments, who, like those most rev. dignitaries, prefer the acquisition of knowledge to the possession of the mighty dollar. Men of this class will ever value learning and scholarship above silver and gold.

* "Morum priscorum semper tenacissimi fuerunt Celtic populi."—Zeuss Gram. Celtica, p. 916.

5. It is not by bread alone that man doth live. And men of intelligence in every clime will always appreciate that which is stamped with the image of genius, nobility, and historic worth.

If those Irish gentlemen and ladies, too, who do not hold in esteem the language of their fathers, care not for its preservation, the fault cannot at present be helped. Let the language fade away and die in peace, but do not scoff at it, scorn it,—treat it as even its worst persecutors in days past, did not treat it—with contumely and disdain. It is not a sign of filial devotedness to beat one's grandmother, and to turn her out of the house before the term which nature has fixed for the close of her life has arrived. Our mother tongue is still alive. It has a residence in Connacht. It is fading; to be plain, it is dying. Is it a sign of filial devotion to say, "Out—begone!" A sad retribution is threatened against children that act undutifully towards parents. Let us take care that no social retribution is in store for un-Irish Irishmen who despise and hunt to death their mother tongue.

In an appeal, addressed by Professor Blackie, on the 12th September, 1874, to the members of the Argyleshire gathering, requesting Highlanders to contribute the sum of ten thousand pounds to enable him to establish in the University of Edinburgh a Keltic chair, he writes:—

"Yet, somehow or other, by sad neglect and a concurrence of untoward circumstances, the venerable language of the Gael, in whose picturesque phrase the sublime scenery of our country has been so admirably photographed, is systematically neglected by those who should naturally cherish it. This most unreasonable and unnatural neglect is the cause of the sad blank in the department of the Keltic language and literature. There are Professors eminent for their knowledge of Keltic philology in German Universities, but none in Scotland. The existence of this blank is a blot on the fair scutcheon of our national intelligence, which ought to be removed; and I appeal to you, as intelligent Keltic gentlemen, to give me a helping hand in its immediate removal. If you do so, you will at very little expense achieve a five-fold good—you will (1) co-operate with the founder of the Sanscrit Chair, Edinburgh, in the creation of a great school of comparative philology in the metropolis of Scotland; you will (2) elevate the tone of the Highland pulpit, by giving to the native preachers a more masculine hold of the venerable language which they wield; you will (3) advance the teaching of English in the schools of Scotland by that aid which every practical teacher knows can be given only by the apt comparison of the mother tongue; (4) you will enrich the intellect and warm the fancy of the people in the North by cherishing those gallant memories, and fanning those generous sentiments which it is the mistaken policy of some to obliterate and to extinguish; and finally you will (5) gain for yourselves by one stroke the love of the Highland people, and the respect of all the great scholars and the large thinkers of Europe."

CHAPTER VI.

To those not of Irish origin of what use is a knowledge of Irish? Much in every way. The primæval Aryan race. How the science of philology points them out, and shows where they dwelt. Emigration westward: Greek, Latin, Keltic. The Gaelic family of the Aryan race the earliest in their migration to the west of Europe; to Iberia; some to Northern Italy, Helvetia, Gaul, Britain, and Ierné or Eire. Authorities for these statements—Newman, Pictet, Sullivan, Geddes, Pritchard, Bopp, Blackie, Schleicher. Keltic installed in the hierarcy of the Aryan tongues. Though the last installed, the Irish Gaelic branch is the purest, the fullest, the best preserved, the least affected by change of all on account of the insular situation of the Irish Keltic race. (1) Therefore, for all lovers of philological research a knowledge of Irish is as necessary as a knowledge of Sanskrit; nay, more so. (2) It is at the door for European scholars, an El-Dorado which they neglect, while they weary themselves by needless journeying to the East. (3) The lips of a living Gaelic speaker a nobler and a surer source of philological science than the graves of dead Rabbis and mummied Bramins. (4) Philology a sister science to Ethnology: both are in accord with the inspired writings of the author of the Pentateuch. (5) Irish Gaelic being free from phonetic decay in the past, and affected least of all by foreign influence, is of great use in setling the vexed question of classic pronunciation regarding the natural sounds of the consonants *g*, *c*, and the vowels *a*, *e*, *i*, *u*.

The reader now sees the value and interest which natives of Ireland should attach to the vernacular speech of their country.

Regarding those, however, who are not of Irish origin, it will be asked, "Of what use is a knowledge of the Irish tongue to them, for they are not natives of Ireland. Why, then, should they be expected to unite in preserving all that remains of Ireland's language?

To answer this question fully one must ascend the heights of the history of human speech.

The primaeval language of man, called amongst the learned of the present day—the *Aryan*, of which Keltic is a dialect, brings us back to the period before the human family had emigrated from the first home wherein they had settled.

For the sake of those who are not acquainted with the science of comparative philology, by the aid of which scholars can point out clearly and distinctly the connexion as well as the difference between living languages, and, at the same time, trace all to one common origin, it is necessary to state, that by aid of this science and by kindred aids, without direct reference to revelation, men of literary research have found proofs the most convincing, to shew that before the dispersion of the human family, there existed a common language, "admirable in its raciness, in its vigour, its harmony, and the perfection of its forms."

The sciences in connexion with languages are, in this respect, quite in accord with the tradition of every nation on the globe, and with the teaching of history and the inspired writings of Moses and the Prophets.

These linguistic sciences do not deal with any particular language; they take in all modern radical tongues, and like those who sail up separate small rivers, till they reach a common source, they trace the different streams of language up to a primaeval fountain-head, from which all the European dialects have taken their rise.

Thus, it has been discovered that there had been, anterior to the dispersion, one common primaeval speech.

Learned men in England, France, Switzerland, Germany, have, by their labors, within the past half century, contributed to this important result.

It is the same class of scholars in Germany and Switzerland, and not Irishmen, who have shewn that Irish Gaelic is, in origin, one with Sanscrit, Greek, and Latin; and that it is amongst the oldest branches of the one primaeval *Aryan* tongue.

First—The Irish speech is, therefore, for all lovers of languages, and for all who wish to become, like German scholars, acquainted with the first tongue spoken by the human family, equal in value to Sanscrit, Latin, and Greek.

This is not merely the opinion of the writer—it is held by Professor Blackie of Edinburgh, by Monsieur Pictet of Geneva, by Bopp, by Geddes, Professor of Greek in the University of Aberdeen. Geddes says—(Lecture—*the Philologic uses of the Keltic tongue*—published by A. Browne & Co., Aberdeen, 1872) :—" A great field of investigation, as yet comparatively unexplored, lies before you in your (the Gaels of the Highlands) own tongue—it is an El-Dorado for the winning."

Second—Schleicher, a German scholar, shows in his compendium of comparative grammar, the position which Irish holds as a language in the wide field of Aryan speech.

ARYAN.

Eastern.	1. Alt Indisch or Sanscrit.
	2. Baktrisch or Zend.
Classic.	3. Griechisch.
	4. Italisch or Latin.
	5. Irisch or Gaelic.
	6. Bulgarisch.
	7. Litauisch or Lithuanian.
	8. Gothisch.

According to this distinguished linguistic scientist, a foreigner to Ireland in all save her ancient language, Irish holds on the tree of early human speech a position next after the eastern and classic off-shoots of the great Aryan tongue. Fuller investigation shows that Irish, with its 16 or 17 primitive letters, had an earlier start westward than either Greek or Latin from the Aryan region—namely, that high table land around Mount Ararat, whence the four rivers—the Euphrates, and the Tigris, the Araxas and the Oxus, flowing out from the Garden of Eden, took their rise. Professor Geddes does not fail to observe, viewing the linguistic tree framed and developed by German hands, that Schleicher makes, immediately after the separation of Sanscrit or Zend from the common stem, the Keltic keep company with the Greek and Latin in what he calls a common Greco-Italo-Keltic branch, and that there remained the Italo-Keltic which shot far more to the west, after the Greek had sprouted forth to the south, and had attained development. It there found, as history testifies, a congenial clime for further growth in the mountains and valleys of Thessaly, and stretching more southward still in the Peloponnessus and in the isles of Greece, and, above all, in Ionia, where it blossomed and ripened into the highest and the most matured perfection. Under the stylus of the father of Grecian poetry, it had been made the medium of the undying Epics, that tell of the direful wrath of Achilles with the destruction of Troy, and the wanderings of Ithaca's king.

In following the line of march of those amongst the very early emigrants to Europe from the table land in which the primitive Aryan speech had once been spoken, the writer has necessarily accompanied on their way that colony which, at a subsequent period, was known as Hellenic, and was styled, at a still later period, Greek, by Roman historians and by modern writers. This knowledge of the Hellenic colony derived from the light of comparative philology, is, in a certain sense, *a priori*. The primitive mother land and her peoples are first discovered, and then with the light of the knowledge thus obtained, shedding its rays steadily from a settled centre, the different routes eastward and westword become well-tracked and clearly defined. There is onward on the highway another lamp receiving its oil from the facts of history—as far as the events before and immediately after the times of Homer—are certain. In addition, a third light gleams, beaconing *a posteriori*. It comes from aesthetical science and exegetical analysis. All combine in pointing to the same objective reality, and their harmony in this respect leads to that certainty which truth alone presents. The harmonious adaptation of the re-adjusted fragments of a rich vase, producing in their union the fulness and grace of the original unbroken figure, is a sign and a proof that the portions thus coalescing, are not foreign to the elements of the original vessel as it came from the artist's hands; so it is when isolated fragments of history coalesce, and are in harmony with what science teaches. First amongst the foremost of the best writers in modern times is John Stuart Blackie, Professor of Greek in the University of Edinburgh. From his "Homeric dissertations"—Vol. I. (p. p. 80-113) he shows clearly that (1) such a poet as Homer existed; (2) that he was a native of the coast of Asia Minor, between the Propontis and the Hermus, occupied by Æolian and Ionian settlers from Greece; (3) that he followed the profession of a wandering minstrel; (4) that the different cities on the coast of Asia—Smyrna, Chios, Cumæ, Colophon, &c., mentioned in the biographies, if not the actual scene of the actions to which they are attached in the legends, were certainly the principal stage on which he acted, and the atmosphere which he breathed; (5) that he lived about 850 B.C.

And first, as to the colonies from Greece to Asia Minor, and the date of the poet's birth.

Herodotus states that the poet lived about four hundred years before his own time—that is, in round numbers, 850 B.C.

(1) The Roman writers place the poet about a century and a-half before the foundation of Rome; and if (continues the learned Professor Blackie) we take our previous high road of the register of the Spartan Kings, by the help of which we got the year 1100 B.C. for the Trojan war, and allow after this, according to the general tradition of the Greeks, some fifty or sixty years for the Æolic and Ionic migrations, with which the legends of the old Greek families came into Asia Minor; and, further, add to this another half century, to give the colonies time to settle, and to obtain that measure of outward prosperity which is necessary for the growth of the highest poetry, we shall have reached the year 900, when the wicked Achab and the Phenician Jezebel were misruling Israel, which tallies with the date of Herodotus, if we take it for the period of the poet's full and perfect manhood, and the zenith of his poetic powers.

(2) Homer is a real character . . . . A people, like an individual, may forget its great benefactor. But the fact is otherwise. The Greeks did not forget Homer. He was as living in their memory, through their whole history, as the person of Robert Burns is in the heart of every true Scot; he has been a living fact in the intellectual consciousness of the cultivated world everywhere, except in a certain academical atmosphere of Germany, and in some English heads which have received the taint of mistry

negation from that quarter. Beyond this region, there is no more doubt of the existence of a great poet who wrote a great poem called the Iliad, than there is of Alexander the Great, who Hellenized the East, or the great Julius who Romanized the West. The belief in the personality of Homer, which Mr. Grote denies, rests directly and naturally on the double fact that there exists a great poem which demands the existence of a great author, and that this authorship has been constantly recognised by the Greek people, in the person of Homer.

There are no less than nine Homeric biographies. They resolve into two principal varieties, the one of which makes Homer an Æolian Greek; the other, an Ionian.

(3) Seven cities contend for the birth of Homer—Smyrna, Salamis, Ios, and Rhodus, Colophon, Argos, and Athens.

Now, we can happily not have the slightest difficulty, says Blackie, in deciding in favor of the first claimant in the list—that is Smyrna.

According to all the rules of evidence, as understood and acted on in the courts of law, the claim of Smyrna, when contravened by that of Cumæ and Ios, must be held valid.

Proof—From internal evidence.

(1) In Homer the strong tempestuous winds always blow between west and north from Thrace, is perfectly just. . . . . This clearly indicates a minstrel whose habitual residence was the coast of Asia Minor, about Smyrna, precisely where tradition places the author of the Iliad.

(2) The dialect of the Hellenic tongue, used by the author of the Iliad and Odyssey, is precisely such an admixture of Ionic and Æolian Greek, as a poet living in a country of mixed Æolic and Ionian population would

naturally use.—Dissertation III. by Professor Blackie. Summarised from p. 79 to 113. Homer and the Iliad. Edinburgh, Edmonston, and Douglas, 1866.

A thousand years anterior to the days of Homer, and before the Greek was matured in southern Europe and on the coast of Ionia, the second sprout of the Greco-Italo-Keltic branch was planted in the Italian peninsula, and there, like the grain of mustard-seed, grew into a large tree, the branches of which ultimately filled the whole earth. The Keltic branch took root for a time in Northern Italy. It bore fruit, and, like the oak, scattered its seed to the west in Iberia or Spain, to the north-west in Keltic Gaul, along the banks of the Garonne, the Loire, and the Seine. The best part was wafted to our "noble island," Inis Alga, where it sprung up and formed the luxuriant tree of Irish Gaelic, which at this very day presents all the features that mark the primaeval speech of the Aryan race and country.

The views just put before the reader are confirmed by the opinions and arguments of savants famed throughout Europe for their knowledge of philology and ethnology.

The extent of the Latin coast from the mouth of the Tiber to Circeii is about fifty miles; the breadth of Latium from the coast to the Sabine hills is estimated at about thirty miles at most. Within this area before the dawn of history, many Latin cities flourished in more than one confederation; and we are accustomed to think of them as of a pure race, yet there is reason to believe that many mixtures of population had already occurred.

Two nations are mentioned as dwelling in the earliest times to the north and south of Latium—the Umbrians and the Oscans. The Umbrians were regarded by the Romans as a truly primæval Italian race, who at one time held possession of all Lombardy and Tuscany, reaching perhaps into Latium.

The Oscans—under various names, Volseians, Ausones, (Greek Aurunes), Ausonians, Auruncans—appear as a principal people of South Italy. The language of all these seems to have been called Oscan. The Oscan and the Umbrian were sister-tongues. The Oscan has often "r" final in substantives where the Latin has "s"; it begins its interrogatives with "p" instead of "qu," or "c." Oscan sides with Greek and Welsh in this respect; Umbrian with Latin and Gaelic. The Sabine race were a branch of the Umbrians.—*Regal Rome* (*substance of pp.* 2-3-4) *by Francis W. Newman. London: Taylor, Walton, & Maberly.* 1852

In addition to the Umbrian, Oscan, Sabine, and sea-borne population, a nation called Siculians came in. This people had spread along the eastern coast of Italy from north to south. One branch only of them crossed the Apennines and settled in Latium, who seem to have been the true progenitors of those known to us as the Latin Nation. Another portion of this people—the Siculian—had been, as Thucydides testifies, driven by the Oscans into Sicily; and they gave to that island the name it keeps to this day. The whole language of this people was fundamentally Latin. The tongue of Latium itself received further changes from new immigrants. The Siculians were conquered by another people who seem to have descended from the Apennines. Who they were is uncertain. After that immigration a distinction was drawn between the ancient Latins (Prisci Latini), and the other Latins, or the Latins who adhered to Alba Longa as their leader. Though there exists a very great mixture in the ultimate Latin language, it is plain that the Siculian element was the largest in its composition."—(*Pp.* 10, 11, 12, 13, *condensed.*)

Again, one quotation more from pp. 16, 17, 21:—"That the old Latins were at least a double people is implied in every ancient account; and it might be reasonable to think that large masses of words were taken up into the same tongue—whatever it was primatively—from Siculians, Umbrians, Oscans, Sabines, Greeks, Etruscans. So much *à priori.* But on actually comparing the Latin vocabulary with that of Greeks, Germans, and Kelts, a far closer similarity to the Keltic shows itself. This comparison suffices to establish that at least one of the stocks of population out of which the mixed Roman people was made up spoke a tongue so much akin to Welsh and Gaelic that we are justified in extending the term Keltic to embrace this Italian tribe. The only point left uncertain is whether the oldest Latin itself—or only some of its affluents, say the Siculian—was the Keltic influence. He proves that the Sabines used a vocabulary which was akin to the Gaelic. And the argument appears to be unassailable except by admitting a relation so close between the oldest Latin and the Keltic, as to imply a recent divergency from a common stock.'

It is certain that there was a primaeval speech, called at present by scholars the Aryan tongue; that it was once spoken by the people who lived in the high table lands of Armenia and Iran; that it was carried to Europe by the inhabitants who emigrated from the land now ruled by the Shah, that Greek, Latin, Keltic or Irish, Slavonic or Bulgarian, Lithuanian, Gothic, or German, are dialects of that common pre-historic speech.

Listen to the words of Adolphe Pictet, of Geneva, expressed in his famous work—"*Les Origines Indo-Européennes, ou les Aryas Primitifs.*—(p. 2). Paris, 1859:

"A une epoque anterieure a tout temoignage historique, et qui se derobe dans la nuit des temps, une race destinee par la Providence a dominer un jour sur le globe entier grandissait peu a peu dans le berceau primitif, ou elle preludait a son brillant avenir. . . . .

Tout en croissant ainsi joyeusement en nombre et in prospérité, cette race féconde travailla á se creer, comme puissant moyen de dévelopement, une langue admirable par sa richesse, sa vigueur, son harmonie et la perfectiou de ses formes; une langue ou venaient se refléter spontanément touts ses impressions, ses affections douces ses admirations naives, mais aussi ses élans vers un monde supérieur, une langue pleine d'images et d'idées intuitives, portant en germe toutes les richesses futures d'une magnifique expansion de la poésie la plus élevee, comme de la pensee la plus profonde. D'abord une et homogene cette langue, servit d'organe commun à ce peuple primitif tout qu'il ne dèpassa pas les limites de son pays natal."

"At a period anterior to every historic developement, and one which is lost to view in the night of the remote past, a race destined by Providence to be, at a coming day, rulers over the entire globe, were gradually growing great in their ancient cradle, where during their infancy they gave indications of a brilliant future". . . . .

In coming thus with a happy growth to matured fulness, not in prosperity alone, but in numbers, this vigorous race sought to secure for themselves, as a potent agent for the process of development, a language admirable for its richness, its vigour, its harmony, and the perfection of its forms—a language which was likely to foreshadow in its own features naturally and without effort, not alone all the impressions affecting it; its nice shades of form and of thought; its natural expressions of admiration, but also its tendency upwards towards a sphere higher still; a language full of images and of ideas precise, and perceived at a glance; a language bearing in its infant state all the future wealth which was to be developed by a magnificent practical expansion, in the region of poetry the most elevated, as well as of thought the most profound. This language, at first one and of the same stock, served as the common medium of inter-communication among the people of this primitive race, as long as they did not extend beyond the limits of their native country.

Monsieur Pictet for good reasons styles this primitive race Aryan, and calls the language they spoke the Aryan tongue. He says that in course of time they spread from Armenia eastward to India, and westward to the extreme limits of Europe, and that they formed one long chain of parent peoples, one in blood and in kin, yet no longer recognising each other as brothers:

Il faut donc bien se contenter de partir du fait incontestable de cette dispersion déjà accomplie plus de deux mille ans avant notre ère; car à cette époque, la race que nous appelerons Arienne ètendait ses rameaux depuis l' Inde jasqu' aux limites extrêmes de l'Europe à l'occident, et formait d' un bout à l'autre, comme une longue chaine de peuples sortis d'un même sang, mais ne se reconnaisant plus comme frères."

The name—Aryan—has now been accepted by modern philosophers in Europe, as well as in America and in the East. Keltic is Aryan. "The Keltic," says Geddes, (p. 7,) "is now duly installed in what may be called the Hierarcy of Aryan tongues. Pritchard established the affinity; Pictet has done much in the same direction; but the work has been fully performed by four Germans—Bopp, Zeuss, Ebel, and Schleicher."

The root of this remarkable term is "aria," which has been preserved in the two sister-languages, the Sanscrit and the Zend—"ár" and "éré." "Ce que je veux remarquer encore," says this clever scholar, "c'est qu' il en sort un synonyme de *Arya*, le Sanscrit *arta*, en Zend, *areta*, vénéré, illustre, anquel Burnouf a rattaché l'ancien nom de Perses "*Artaioi*." Les Ossetes du Caucase, il est vrai, s'appellent eux-mémes *Iron* du nom de leur pays Ir.

Further the root "ar," and "er," and "her," has been found in many Keltic and German names throughout Europe.

But it is in the ancient name of Ireland Pictet finds the cleverest clue to the connexion between Sanskrit and Irish—between the extreme territories India and Iernè:

"Une analogie mieux fondée á tous égards dans celui des Celto-Gaels de l'Irlande lequel a du *Er* ou *Eri* (pp. 29, 30, 31). Ceci, toute fois, resterait á l'état de simple hypothése si ce nom de *Er* n' avait pas, en Irlandais meme, un sens tout semblable á celui de *Arya*. Il se trouve en effet, que *Er* comme adjectif, signifie *noble*, *bon*, *grand*; et comme substantif, un *guerrier*, un *heròs*. De plus, la racine Sanscrite *ar* est restée vivante en Irlandais avec le sens de *colere* (Latin) *honorare*; car, *air-im*, *orr-im*, *air-igim*, signifie soigner, garder, servir, honorer; et les dèrivès *aire* soin, attention noblesse; *aireach* soigneux, attentif, noble, riche, célebre; homme noble, chef, gardien, &c., se rattachent de près aux acceptions diverses de *arya*, *ariaka*. L' adjectif *arta*, en zend *areta*, *ereta*, illustre, vènèrè, se retrouve de même dans l'Irlandais *aireadha*, excellent fameux, et *art*, noble magnanime, &c. Ces coincidences multipliès laissent peu de doute sur l'affinitè rèelle et primitive de *Er*, avec *Arya*.

This argument of Monsieur Pictet is very clear, connected, and, it seems, valid. He shows plainly the connection between Sanscrit in the far East, and Irish in the far West of the Old World. They are only sister languages, which in the youthful period of the rise of the human family had turned their face to opposite regions of the globe—one, like Lot, taking for its abode the country to the East; and the other, like Abraham, settling down in the West.

Comparative philology plainly points to the truth told by the inspired author of the Pentateuch—that there was one parent race of all mankind, and that they made use of only one original tongue.

In the work lately published "on the manners and customs of the ancient Irish," W. K. Sullivan writes in Vol. I., p. IV., as follows :—

"It is now a recognised fact in science, that from the Indus to the Atlantic Ocean, and thence across the American continent to the shores of the Pacific, the descendants of one primitive, blue-eyed, fair-haired race, divided into several branches, and speaking dialects of what was once a common language, held sway. To determine the common elements in the languages, mythologies, legends, laws, and customs of the several branches of this great Aryan race, and thence inductively rehabilitate the primitive parent race, whence they issued, is one of the most interesting and important problems of historical science. The Irish race, it is confessed, had been the earliest emigrants from the land of Iran, and had led the van in the great army which came westward to people Europe.

" Ce fait que le nom *des Aryas*, le plus ancien sans contredit des branches orientales de la famille, se retrouve aussi chez le peuple (the Irish) qui en forme la limite extrême à l' occident —fait qui me semble ètabli avec toute l' evidence qui comportent de semblables rescherches, est une forte raison de croire, que ce nom a été celui de la race dans son unité primitive. Des indices de plus d' un genre, tirés, soit des langues, soit des données géographiques, tendent a montrer que les Celtes, et en particulier le rameau *Gaëlique, ont été les premiers émigrants vers les contrées lointaines de l' Europe.* Cela peut expliquer comment seuls ils auraient emporté avec eux l'antique dénomination de la race, que d'autres peut-être avaint déjá perdue avant de quitter l'Asie."—Pictet, p. 33.

"Nor in fact, of all the Indo-European tongues has *any* so near a likeness to the Latin as the Gaelic has."

"Keltic words were not introduced into Welsh by the Roman conquest of Britain, for in a large number of instances the words are members of families in Welsh (and Irish), and are nearly isolated in Latin." Again—"Many Latin words retain only secondary meanings where the primary ones are manifest in the Keltic. Thus 'monile,' a necklace, is from Gaelic 'muineal,' a necklace; 'incolumis,' from 'in,' *not*, and 'caill,' *loss* (Irish)."—*Regal Rome, Newman, pp.* 19-25.

On this account the language of Eire should, as a philological medium in arriving at this truth of history, of language, of race, so much in accord with the truth of revelation, be studied.

"The ancient language," say Professor Sullivan, "the laws and traditions of Ireland, are, in truth, among the most valuable, nay, indispensable materials for the solution of the problem above stated."

"The Romans, Kelts, and Germans have so commingled on the continent of Europe and in Britain that it is almost impossible to say what is peculiar to each, and what borrowed. . . . . The only branch of the Keltic race not directly in contact with this highly developed political organization was the Irish. . . Fortunately, we possess in the remains of the Irish language, poetry, laws, &c, such a mine, and in fulness too, greater than is to be found in the other branches of the Aryan race, except the Sanskrit, Greek, and Latin."—*Manners and Customs of the Ancient Irish, Vol. I.*

It is quite plain, therefore, from all that has been shewn, that for all lovers of philological research, a knowledge of the Irish language is as necessary as a knowledge of Sanskrit.

This is the conclusion to which the Professor of Greek in the University of Aberdeen, W. D. Geddes, M.A., has come to. In his lecture—"The Philological Uses of the Keltic Tongue," (published by A. & R. Milne, Aberdeen, 1872), he addresses the members of the Keltic debating society, and says: "A great field of investigation, as yet comparatively unexplored, lies before you in your own tongue; it is an El-Dorada for the winning." "From the systematic neglect of Keltic, it has resulted that our scholars, both Keltic and Saxon, have gone far to find what they could have got nearer home. They have wandered to the extremities of Europe and of Asia in search of philologic facts, digging them out of the graves of dead Rabbis or Aristarcuses, when they might have found them far more easily exemplified on the lips of a living Gaelic speaker—a living Highland shepherd by the side of a Highland burn" (p. 6). "Until these days, British philologists have been for the most part poverty-stricken creatures, clamouring for gold from what they thought classic sources, and stumbling blindly among the jewels that lay around them for the gathering, all upon their own shore and their native hills."

To sum up—From the light which Irish Gaelic throws on the science of linguistic palaiology, the language of Ireland, it must be admitted, is worthy of the attention of students and savants. It opens up, as widely at least as Sanskrit, a field of philological enquiry. In that field its usefulness is admitted to be equal to that of Sanskrit; not only because it is more ready at hand than that ancient eastern tongue, but it once held dominion over the west of Europe, and left, consequently, in the early nomenclature of Continental countries its mark on the face of the western world, which Sanskrit did not, and could not have done. Irish Gaelic is for European savants a very ready, practical, and truthful vehicle for linguistic research in archaic fields of human speech and of history.

FOURTHLY.—The science of comparative philology demands the study of Irish Gaelic and the acquisition of a knowledge of that tongue. In the present day, when the light of science is making vast strides, and when, moreover, it rivals, according to some, the light of revealed truth, nay, as they say, surpasses it in fulness, in splendour, in definiteness of outline; philology, too, like other sciences, claims the attention of men of mind, and of men in colleges, who have the direction and control of the growing youth of the world. The sciences of anthropology and ethnology require for their complete development a knowledge of comparative philology. And this necessity demands a knowledge of Irish Gaelic (or of Sanscrit) if one wish to become a skilled scientist and an efficient laborer in the fields of linguistic studies. "Languages are to the ethnologist what strata are in geology—dead languages have been well called his fossils and petrifactions. By skilful interpretation of their indications, aided by the light of all other available monuments, he is able to spell out with more or less probability, the ethical records of the past, and thus obtain a glimpse, here and there, into the gray cloud that rests over the dawn of ages."—Physical History of man. Chambers, Edinburgh.

The conclusions which ethnology treated rationally and scientifically points to as certain are identical with those which the study of comparative philology proclaim as true; and in all cases, the same as those which the inspired pensman, nigh three thousand years ago, wrote regarding the origin of the world and the creation of man. "In the beginning God created the heavens and the earth."—Genesis, verse I. "So, the heavens and the earth were finished and all the furniture of them."—v. I. "And the earth was of one tongue, and of the same speech."—c. XI., v. I.

FIFTH—CLASSIC PRONUNCIATION.—A knowledge of Irish Gaelic as it is spoken and written at the present time is, as the writer knows, of great advantage in supplying from analogy arguments by means of which a scholar versed in comparative philology, can be certain what had been in the days of the Emperor Augustus, the pronuciation of the Latin tongue. The announcement made in the sentence just read would have been, fifty years ago, met with jeers, laughter, or with an expression of downright contempt. The writer has no doubt that the announcement will be even to-day met by many with laughter. "Can anything of good come from Nazareth," is the expression of a feeling, a partiality, or of a mental bias that lies to-day as deep in the heart of the mere unenlightened man, and of many guileless, plain, blunt men, as it did in the days of Nathanael whom the Saviour of men pronounced to be an Israelite without guile. Can anything good come from Ireland or her language will be the expression of many a reader, and not least of all from many of her own children—well-meaning men, no doubt, but who do not know the facts, regarding their own country speech. And yet the statement made in the leading sentence is true in every particular. It is a fact that a controversy has been for years carried on amongst scholars of the universities in England about the pronunciation of the classic language of Republican Rome. The writer does not now allude to the lengthened and even yet unsettled war amongst the learned which has been for centuries past waged throughout Europe respecting the pronunciation of Greek as it was spoken from the days of Plato to the period of St. Paul's preaching, or of Latin from the days of Plautus to those of Suetonius. He alludes simply to the war of words that has been fought in England, and chiefly to the controversy that has been carried on for the past ten or twenty years, and with such splendid results by Professors H. A. J. Munro and Edwin Palmer. Writing just a few months before success had crowned the efforts of Professor Munro, W. D. Geddes, Professor of Greek in the University of Aberdeen, tells how the voice of the learned combatants had been heard in Scotland: "We hear much at present of a discussion carried on in England as to the mode of pronouncing Latin, and we can hear the low murmur of a confused battle going on against the peculiar, solitary, not to say fantastic pronunciation of Latin that has prevailed so long there. Scotland had begun to be corrupted in this matter of Latin pronunciation from English influence. The Court of Session and the Academies of the South were acquiring the mincing pronunciation from the other side of the Borders; and I was once looking forward to the time when the tide of this English influence should have submerged all the rest of Scotland, and left us in Aberdeen maintaining in its last retreat the old *Ore rotundo* national pronunciation of *Romanos rerum dominos gentemque togatam.*"

The reader will be pleased to observe what has been stated in these words by the learned professor of Greek, himself by birth, education, and position an admirer of England and of her language,—a scholar thoroughly acquainted with the speech of Attica and that of Latium; yet he styles the way in which Englishmen pronounced Latin—*peculiar, solitary, phantastic.* And this peculiar, solitary, phantastic pronunciation was spreading, he says, amongst Scotchmen; so, too, it was in Ireland. The teaching staff of Trinity University, Dublin—more English than the English themselves—have been for the past two centuries and a half spreading this phantastic pronunciation in Ireland. They have failed however. Reform has set in at home in England; and Trinity Latinists must follow on the road of reform.

Observe further, that in the opinion of the learned professor, the Gaels of the Highlands in speaking, use the round, full-toned pronunciation (*ore rotundo*) of the old Romans (*Rerum dominos gentemque togatam.*" Hence, he must admit that Irish Gaels who speak with the same national *ore rotundo*, pronounce the Latin tongue, as the Lords and Masters of the old world pronounced it in the days of Cicero—*Rerum dominos, gentemque togatam.*

On this subject, which refers so intimately to England and the English language in contrast with Ireland and her language, the writer prefers to present to the view of the reader the words and opinions of England's own friends. Geddes continues (the text is from page 9 of his lecture, "The Philologic Uses of the Keltic Tongue," published by Milne, Aberdeen, 1872): "Not that the Scottish pronunciation of Latin is unimpeachable, but it is sound in many points where English is false; and I do not know that the English pronunciation is ever sound where the Scottish happens to be false. It is other wise with the Keltic. *It can be shown to be sound where both are false.*"

That is the FIRST argument which the writer adduces to show the truth of the statement made by him in the leading sentence of this section regarding Gaelic, elucidating classic pronunciation. It is an argument drawn from authority; but it ought to have weight with Englishmen and Scotchmen, with scholars and men of mind, and with those who know the facts of the literary controversy, and who believe that Geddes in an honest, a learned, and an unprejudiced witness. Honest and honourable he undoubtedly is; learned, of that there is no doubt; and certainly he is not a prejudiced witness, for he gives testimony against all that is favorable to his personal and public interests, and national and social leanings. And yet he says: "Keltic pronunciation is sound where Scotch and English are *false*. The proposition is strong; it is true.

Another—The subject of classical pronunciation of the Latin tongue is one on which a large volume of several hundred pages could readily be written, equal in size to that lately penned by Alexander J. Ellis, on "Early English pronunciation." The writer then shall quote only one other author—Henry John Roby, M.A., late Fellow of St. John's College, Cambridge. This very learned classical scholar, writes in his work—"A Grammar of the Latin language, from Plautus to Suetonius, in three books. Published in 1871, by MacMillar & Co.—p. xxx.

"The question—*What was* the Roman pronunciation? is quite distinct from the question—Shall we adopt it? Professor Max Müller's argument tends to confuse these questions, I quite admit that a change in our pronunciation of Latin is inconvenient; but the inconvenience is greater in imagination than in reality, and will be soon overcome, whilst the benefit to any student of philology will be very great. With our (natives of England) English pronunciation of the vowels, a, e, i, o, u—of j of v, c,g, r and others, the development of the language becomes an inextricable riddle, and the student naturally gets into the fatal habit of dissociating letters from sounds.

. . . . We shall approach (the

pronunciation of) the continental nations at once; and if, as seems to me probable, they change their pronunciation eventually, we shall be coincident with them in proportion as we and they respectively have succeeded in ascertaining the truth. Nothing short of that (truth) can or ought to be the common goal and place of meeting. Arguments of some supposed superiority of one sound, as sound, to another, seems to me worthless. The question is one of historical fact, not of aesthetical selection; and we shall do better in speaking Latin as the Romans speak it, if we discover *how*, than in either indulging fancy or being swayed by delusive associations, however habitual."

It is very cheering to read the words of a man anxious to find out the truth in any particular matter which he investigates, and ready, when he finds it, to admit it. There are those—let us say good men—who, even when they see the truth and the right thing, will not wish to admit it, because some pet notion or opinion is in danger from the light of fact, truth, and reason. These English scholars —men of mind and of honor, like them—deserve to succeed.

Roby adds, in a note, page XXXII.—"If the question were one of taste, I should not be afraid of asking—is a sibilant or a buzz a finer sound than that of a mute or a demi-vowel? Are *seas* and *cheese* (sounds of *s* and *ch*) pleasanter than *keys* (sound of *k*); *sin* and *chin* pleasanter than *kin*; or *veal* and *vain*, than *weal* and *wane*?" And the present writer will add, is Selly a pleasanter sound than Kelly, sent than kent, sill than kill, Seltic than Keltic? In the sound, as a mere phonetic impact on the ear, or vibratory sign of thought conveyed, there is no superiority; the notion that there is something in it, viewed objectively, is a matter of custom, habit, or early training.

He continues: "I assume throughout, until the contrary be proved, that a letter has but one sound, except so far as it is necessarily altered by its position as initial, or medial or final. The phenomenon presented by most letters in English, of sound and sign, having but a fortuitous connexion, is nearly *unique*.'

In fully fifty pages small octavo, he discusses the question—what is the correct sound of the consonants—v, c, g, r, s, t, and ss—what the phonetic value of the vowels a, o, u, e, i. Roby wrote, in 1871, when the Latin controversy between Professor Max Müller, of Cambridge, and Professor Munro, was at its height. Even then Mr. Roby, summing up all he had written on the then vexed question of Latin, thus expresses his views: "The following is a summary statement of the probable pronunciation of educated Romans in the period from Cicero to Quintilian, say from 70 A.C. to 90. P.C.

The long and short sounds of a vowel were probably identical in quality. "A, as in Italian, that is, as a in father; o, as in Italian; u, as in Italian; u, in pull, u long, as oo in pool; e, as e in where (middle e); i, as i in machine; (i, anciently, was never dotted); c, always k, as in Kitty; g always hard, as in give, anger, not gin, or ginger; s, always like ss, never like z; r, like r in German or in Irish.

Diphthongs:—"The right rule," he says, p. xxx. "for pronouncing diphthongs is to pronounce the constituent vowels as rapidly as possible in their proper order; hence the diphthongs eu, is in Latin, sounded as eu in Europa; and ei, like ei in foreign or feint. Hence "ai,!' like "ahee" quickly, not eh: and ia is "ee-a," as piano.

The fact is, the sounds here shewn, as illustrating "the

pronunciation of educated Romans in the period from Cicero to Quintilian," are identical with the sounds presented at the present day in the published works regarding Irish Gaelic. The present author, while a student in the College of Maynooth, wrote, in 1856—eighteen years ago,—the first edition of the *College Irish Grammar;* and in that work the sounds of the vowels, and of the consonants, *c*, *g*, *s*, *t*," are explained in the following words :— "*c*, hard like *k*, never pronounced like *s*, or *eh* soft; *g* always *hard*, as in *get*, *give* ; never sounded soft like *g* in *gin* ; *s* like *ss.*, p. 13.

"The vowels have two principal sounds—the one long, the other short."—(p. 15.) "Vowels have two sounds, the accented aud the non-accented"—(p. 16), "There must be two sounds or shades of the same vowel sound, according as the accent is shifted to a leading or to a closing syllable; as in *able* (English) *a* is long; in *ability* the same *a* becomes short. The sound of *a*, then, in Irish is *aw* or *ah*, never *e* ; of *e*, as first *e* in *where* ; of *i*, as *i* in *pique* ; of *o*, as *o* in *told ;* of *u*, as *u* in *rule*, *u* in Italian, or *oo* in *tool.* —College Irish Grammar, p.p. 18, 16.

The diphthongs in Irish are sounded by pronouncing the constituent vowels as rapidly as possible, *ai* like *ah-ee*, not *eh ; ia* like "*ee-ah*, sounded quickly, as pian, *(pee-an* in one syl.) *pain ; eu, always* "*e-u*," *as feur*, *(fey-urh) grass ;* pronounced like *eu* in *Deus*, or *eu* in *meus* ; *geur (gey-urh) sharp.*

This pronunciation of Irish—both in the vowels, consonants, and dipthongs is precisely that correct pronunciation arrived at by Henry J. Roby, He came to the true pronunciation partly from historic data ; partly from philologic data ; partly from comparisons with well-known sounds in languages kindred to the Latin ; partly from analogy and comparing phonetic with written symbolic equivalents. The foregoing tableau, presenting in one page the proper pronunciation of vowels and of diphthongs, as they are to this day articulated by Gaelic-speaking Irishmen; and, in the other, the correct sound of the same vowels and diphthongs in Latin, as spoken from the days of Tiberius and Caius Graccus, when they harangued the tenant-righters of olden Rome in the Campus Martius, to the time of Quintilian and Suetonius. The modern pronunciation of Irish Gaelic confirms the truth of Roby's views regarding Orthoepy.

And before this chapter is brought to a close, it is well to select a few of the consonants, and to compare their sounds in Latin and in Irish Gaelic.

Take "s" for example :—The letter "s" receives in Irish always the same sound which double "ss" in English represents. There is no exception to this in Irish. Now its correct sound in Latin is precisely that of "ss," English. "S" coming before or after the slender vowels "e" and "i," is articulated like "sh" English; as "ꞅın," *that*, is pronounced *shin*, "ꞅı," *she*, like *shee*; "ꞅe," *shch*; "ꞅıon," *sheeon*, a storm; and so, in every single instance in Irish. This point shall be fully explained in a coming chapter. The sound of the third letter in the "A. B. C." is at present, and has been for the past half century, a subject of literary dispute in England, Scotland, Ireland, and America. In French, in Italian, and in Spanish, its soft sound of "s," or "tsh," or "t," before "e" and "i" is settled. In Germany, on the other hand, no one disputes its hard sound of "k." Those who speak the English language alone have been disputing the sound which "c" and "g" ought, in Latin, to receive before the vowel "e" and "i," for, the sound which it receives before "a," "o," "u," is correct; it has never been, and never will be questioned.

CORRECT LATIN SOUND OF "C."

Be it as it may with the sound of "c" and "g" in the English language, at one time "k," at another, "s," or "tsh," Roby proves plainly against Professor Max-Müller, and others, that in the days of correct Latin speech, the consonant "c" always received the sound of "k." In Irish-Gaelic "c" never has had any other sound before or after "e, i," as well as "a, o, u," than "k." Correctly spoken Latin and good Irish Gaelic are alike therefore in the mode of articulating the vowels, diphthongs, and consonants.

Take a few of Roby's arguments in favour of the hard sound of "c." (p. xlv). (1) "C," he says, is invariably represented in Greek transliteration by "k" (*Kappa*); and "k" is invariably represented by the Latin "c." Again (2) Latin "c" was always represented by Gothic "k;" example (Latin) *Caesar*; (Gothic) *Kaiser*; (Latin) *Carcer*; (Gothic) *Karkara*; (German) *Kerker*.

Third—There are only four instances in which, before the seventh century, "ci" is found for "ti"—that is, in which "c" is made to represent a soft sound. But in the early Latin period, in the golden age, there is found not one. Even these four instances are African, or are found to be misspelt or badly copied.

Summing all up, he repeats in page 50—"There is not one particle of trustworthy evidence before, at least, the fifth or sixth century, for any other pronunciation of "c" than that of the sharp guttural "k."

Thus, by tracing the lines of different routes of history philology, antiquities, inscriptions, comparisons, analogies, we find them converging to one terminus. Thus, the learned Fellow of St. John's College, Cambridge, arrives, after long investigation, at a truth which Irish-Gaelic points out at once. How is this? Because Irish-Gaelic, quite unlike the languages of Europe, owing to the insular position of the country, as the tongue of the Gaels being free from phonetic decay, has, up to the present retained unimpaired that sound of the vowels and of the consonants by which the letters had been known thirteen centuries before the Christian era, when first the Milesians started from Spain for Inisfail,* the isle of destiny.

The coming of a colony of Kelts, known by the name Milesians, from Spain to Ireland, fourteen centuries before the Christian era, is thus made memorable by Moore, in one of his admirable melodies :—

I.

They came from a land beyond the sea,
  And now o'er the western main
Set sail, in their good ships, gallantly,
  From the sunny land of Spain.
Oh, where is the isle we've seen in dreams,
  Our destined home, or grave?
Thus sung they, as by the morning's beams
  They swept the Atlantic wave.

II.

And, lo, where afar o'er ocean shines
  A sparkle of radiant green.
As though in that deep lay emerald mines,
  Whose light through the wave was seen.
"'Tis Inisfail—'tis Inisfail!"
  Rings o'er the echoing sea;
While bending to heaven, the warriors' hail
  That home of the brave and the free.

III.

Then turned they unto the Eastern wave,
  Where now their day-god's eye
A look of such sunny omen gave,
  As lighted up sea and sky;

* "Inis" (Gaelic) island; "fail," destiny; root, "fat," reason cause; "ail," great, powerful, omnipotent; "fail," the great cause, destiny.

Nor frown was seen through sky or sea,
  Nor tear o'er leaf or sod,
When first on their Isle of Destiny,
  Our great forefathers trod.

The vantage ground gained bravely by Roby in 1871, and defended and maintained by Professors Munro and Palmer, against Max Müller and others, has at last been ceded by universal consent, and by the unanimous voice of the educated of England, to the party of progress.

The writer at present holds in his hand a small tract styled *Syllabus of Latin pronunciation*, drawn up a few years since at the request of the head masters of schools in England. In this compendium of the views of the Latin professors, in the English Universities, it is stated that in 1871 the Head-masters of the classic schools, then assembled in conference, declared the system of Latin pronunciation prevalent in England, *unsatisfactory*; and they agreed to ask the Latin professors of Oxford and Cambridge to draw up and issue a joint paper to secure uniformity in any change contemplated. This request was repeated in 1872. Accordingly, in the October term of that year, Professors Palmer and Munro drew up the *Syllabus of Latin pronunciation*. It is published by Deighton, Bell & Co., Cambridge; and by Parker & Co., Oxford. The following is a summary of the views presented.

" The tyranny of accent over quantity is as marked in Italian as in English, and the professors maintain that it is essential to distinguish between *long* and *short* syllables. English appears in its sounds so different from those known in old Latin, that often it is not easy to find in English even single sounds to present as adequate representations of an old Latin sound." What, then, are the correct sounds of the vowels and diphthongs in Latin, and of the consonants?

"We propose, then" say they, "that the letters of the Latin should be sounded as follows:—

A, as *a* Italian, or *a* in *father*.
E, as *ai* in pain.
I, as *i* in machine.
O, as *o* in *more*.
U, as *u* in *rule*, *lure*
Au, as *ow* in power, as *laus*,
Eu, *e* and *u*, sounded quickly.
Ei, *e* sounded with *i* in rapid succession.
C, always as *k*.
G, as *g* in *get*.
S, as *s* in *sin*; *j*, as *y* in *yard*.

The pronunciation of Latin is now fixed and settled for ever in English schools. The change in every particular regarding the sounds of vowels, consonants, and diphthongs is nothing more or less than the pronunciation precisely given in Gaelic to the same vowels, consonants and diphthongs. "A" (Gaelic) as "a" in *father*; "e" (Gaelic) as "e" in *where*, or "ai" in *pain*; "i" (Gaelic) as "i" in *machine*; "u" as "u" in *rule*, &c. (see page 128, supra.)

Thus it has been shewn both by authority and by the reflected light of truth beaming forth, that Irish Gaelic is an excellent medium and a great help by which scholars and linguistic scientists can safely arrive at the correct pronunciation of the language of the educated Romans and speakers of Latin throughout the Roman empire, from the days when Caesar fell at the base of Pompey's statue to the days of Trajan.

HOW IRISHMEN OF THE FIFTH CENTURY PRONOUNCED THE LATIN "C."

There has been from the earliest period in the Irish alphabet both the letter "s" and the the letter "c." Now the early Irish borrowed from the Latins some terms as

Sacerdos, a *priest*, which became in Irish Gaelic "*Sagart*," (g hard). It is plainly evident that if *Sacerdos* had been in the fifth century, when St. Patrick and his companions landed on the coast of Down or Drogheda, pronounced *Saserdos* (*s* for *c*) the native Irish would never have called a priest "Sagart," (g hard), they would have called him "Sasart." Hence, from this fact out of many that a priest has been called by the name "Sagart," it is clear that the "c" in *Sacer*, *Sacerdos*, had had at that early period the sound of "k," and not of "s."

We know that the "c" of *ceart* (*kearth*) *justice*, is "k," and this shows how, amongst the Latins, the term *certus* had been pronounced *kerthus*. "C" of *ceard*, an art, a trade, (a tinker), shows that in old times *cerdo* (Latin) had been pronounced *kerdo*, and not *serdo*. *Ceir (kyeirh) wax*, was *kerh*, and not *ser*; and this fact shows how the Latin word, *cera*, *wax*, had been pronouncod *kera*, and not *sera* In this way the Irish *ciste* (*kisthe*) a *treasure*, a *purse*, a *box*, a *place* to put money, an *exchequer*, and *cios (kyos)* *rent*, *tribute*, point out the correct pronunciation of *cista*, *census*, to be *kista*, *kensus*, &c. *Cead*, leave (*kyead*) Lat. *ced-o ; (kedo)*, *ceud*, a hundred, (*keudh*) ; Lat. *Cent (kent*, and not *sent)* ; *ceann*, or *ceand*, a head (pr. *kyan*) is still retained in *king*, (head-man) ; and in *kent*, a headland, a country.

This chapter fitly closes with a letter written for the purpose of proving that the correct sound of the letter "C" in Celtic, is that of "K," and not "S" :—

"KELTIC, OR CELTIC (SELTIC.)

(To the Editor of the Scotsman, Edinburgh.)

"Tuam, Ireland, July 24th, 1874.

"SIR—It is now a month since I received a letter from a gentleman, living in Moy, county Tyrone, Ireland, asking my opinion on the correct spelling and pronunciation of the much-disputed words, Celt, Celtic, " if they should not be pronounced Kelt, Keltic? An Englishman," he writes, ' has given out that the word *Celtic* should be pronounced as if written *Seltick*, giving 'c' the soft sound. Now, before changing my opinion or altering the pronunciation, I request your judgment.' The foregoing questions, taken from the letter of my correspondent, should, in my opinion, receive a satisfactory reply.

" The English gentleman to whom he alludes is, manifestly, John Stuart Blackie, the learned Professor of Greek in the University of Edinburgh. On the 12th November, last year, the erudite professor wrote a short letter, which was first published in the *Scotsman*, and copied into almost every paper published in England, Scotland, and Ireland, and nigh in every English journal in America and Australia. As his opinion has received such world-wide circulation, it is only natural that those who hold the contrary opinion should feel anxious, that for the sake of what they consider to be true in this point of orthography and orthoepy, their view, too, should receive some fair share of circulation, and the reasons in support of that opinion be at least read and fairly weighed by scholars.

" And first, as to Professor Blackie, the present writer candidly owns, that if the authority alone of any living scholar, without reasons assigned in support of it, were to convince him, by its weight in the literary market, and especially in the department of antiquities and in linguistic studies, and if that authority were rendered weightier still by the attractive force of respect and esteem for a learned and a noble-minded man, and a personal friend—such as Professor Blackie is—he would at once bow to the opinion expressed by the most learned scholar of Greek and Gaelic in Scotland. But men, however distinguished and illustrious, cannot change the essences of things. Their opinions possess weight in proportion to the strength and force of the reasons which support them. It has happened more than once that men acquired great fame for knowledge of very abstruse sciences, and have erred in things of the simplest kind. Amongst theologians and philosophers, a great name, of itself, is not enough to offer as quite convincing in support of an opinion regarding a free question, taught in the school of the queen of sciences, or that of her handmaid—philosophy.

"There are other distinguished scholars, too, who hold the same opinion that the learned professor holds; but neither great learning on other subjects, nor personal esteem, nor early training, nor custom, should be reason sufficient to convince the intelligence of any man on the truth of a particular proposition.

"In the first sentence of the short letter, from the pen of Professor Blackie, he states the question :—

"I received a letter yesterday from a gentleman in the neighbourhood, requesting my opinion on the orthography and orthoepy of the English word which is the rendering of the Greek *Keltos.*'

"In the paragraph which closes the said letter, he gives his opinion, and with it the reason on which that opinion rests, as follows :—

"According to the fixed traditional law of English orthoepy, Greek and Latin proper names, commencing with 'c,' or its equivalent 'k,' when followed by a soft or slender vowel (*e* or *i*), are written a 'c' and pronounced like 's.' It is by virtue of this law that we say, *Cicero, Cæsar*, not *Kikero, Kæsar*. It is therefore a wretched affecnation of recent scholars, and, therefore, contrary to the genius of the English language, when *Kelt* is written and spoken instead of *Celt.*'

"So far I quote the professor, with whom I agree, except in one word. It is true that there is of English orthoepy a traditional law—custom has made it such at present—by which Greek and Latin proper names, commencing with 'k,' or its equivalent 'c,' when followed by a slender vowel, are in English written with a 'c' and pronounced like 's.'

"But I reply, first Keltos is not a Greek term. It is Gaelic. That it is Gaelic shall be shewn presently. Therefore, the traditional law of English orthoepy regarding words derived from Greek or Latin cannot in any way affect the term *Keltos*, which is not Greek but Gaelic; nay, more, there is another traditional law, just the very opposite of that relating to Greek words turned into English, which directs the pronunciation and spelling of terms derived from Irish Gaelic or British.

"2. *Direct* proof in favour of the spelling and pronunciation *Kelt*, *Keltic*.

"For the sake of clearness and conciseness, I shall put it in form of syllogism.

"According to the fixed traditional law of English orthoepy, Irish-Gaelic, British, Cambro-British, or Bas-Breton terms, and amongst them proper names, commencing with 'c,' when followed by a slender vowel (*e* or *i*) are invariably in English pronounced hard, and spelled with 'k.'

"But the terms *Keltos*, *Kelticos*, are Gaelic or British; therefore, the terms Keltos, Kelticos should correctly and according to rule be pronounced Kelt, Keltic, and not Celt, Celtic, (Selt, Seltic.)

"Each of the two premises requires proof, and it shall be given.

"It is a fact that in not one single word of the dialects called Keltic, Irish-Gaelic, Scotch-Gaelic, Cambro-British, or Bas-Breton, has the consonant 'c,' in any position and before any vowel, the sound of 's.' It is a fact that invariably it has the sound of 'k,' and when rendered into English it retains that sound, and no other.

"The law in transmuting Gaelic and British terms into English is, always to give 'c' the hard sound, and if before 'e' or 'i,' the soft or slender vowels, to change 'c' into 'k' for clearness and certainty.

"The proof must consist of some terms taken from each of the four dialects,—British, old Irish, Gaelic, analogy with other terms of similar Keltic descent in use at present in the English tongue. Those words only in which 'c' comes before 'e' or 'i' are selected, for 'c' before 'o, o, u,' is invariably hard.

British and Old Irish	Meaning	Modern English Equivalent.
Ceand	Headland	Kent (county of) not sent or cent.
Cean-tıre	Head of country.	Kantire or C'ntire.
Cıaraıġ	Name of a district, from Cıar, a man's name, one of the three sons of Fergus.	Kerry, not Serry.
Columb-cılle	Name of the Apostle of Iona, from columb, dove, and cılle, gen. sing. of cıll, a church, dove of the church, because he was usually in the church,	Columb-kille, not Columb-sille.

	not dove of the churches.	
Ua Ceallaıġ	One descended of Ceallac	O'Kelly, not O'Selly.
Ua Cearnaıġ	One descended of a soldier	O'Kearney, not O'Searney.
Céıle-Dé	Companion of God	Culdee (*c* hard) Kildea, a family name.
Cıll-dara	Church of the Oak	Kildare, not Sildare.
Cıll-mór	Large church	Killimore.

" There are two thousand eight hundred and ninety names of places in Ireland, according to the calculation of the Irish Registrar-General, commencing with the term 'kill,' from the Irish 'cıll,' a church; 'knock,' a hill (from 'cnoc,' Irish), introduces nigh two thousand names; and 'kluaın,' from 'cluaın,' Irish, *a meadow*, very near two thousand names additional. Many names commence with 'ken,' or 'kin,' from the Irish 'ceann,' gen. 'cınn,' as *Ken*mare, *Kin*sale, *Kin*varra, *Kin*con; Cannafahy (from 'Ceann-na-faıṫċe.') Then there are names of places called Caltra, from 'Cealtraċ," an old burial ground, Cappagh, from 'ceapaċ,' a tillage plot.

Again, from analogy with words found in old Irish, British or Gaelic, but not proper names, we have *quatuor*, Latin, and quarter, English, from the Irish 'ceaṫar,' four; and from 'ceap,' Irish, comes keep; from 'cınne,' a race, kin is formed; from 'cıa,' 'ce,' who, has sprung the Latin *qui*, *quæ*; from 'cıaraṁn,' comes Kirwan; from 'ceannaıd,' is formed Kenny. There are hundreds of names formed in this way from Gaelic or British—Keogh, Keating, Kennedy, Coyne, Kyne—in which the Gaelic 'ce' is changed into 'k,' or its equivalent, 'c' hard or 'qu' in modern Anglicised renderings.

"Therefore, in Anglicised Gaelic words '*c*' always is pronounced like' k.'

"It is certainly true (1) that not one single family name, or (2) name of a place in England, Scotland, or Ireland, commencing with 'c,' that is not rendered into English by the letter 'k', or 'qu,' or 'c' hard. The same is true of every name on the Continent of Europe derived from any of the Keltic dialects.

If the sound of 'k' appears harsh or hard in the term *Kelt*, why is it not harsh in the familiar names Kelly or O'Kelly, Kenny, Keogh, Keaveny, Kevin, Kent, Kern, Kells, Kilkelly? Surely, every Kelt and non-Kelt would not pronounce O'Kelly, O'Selly; Keogh, Seogh; and Kilkelly, Silselly. If not, why wish to pronounce Kelt, Selt, and not Kelt? The second premise remains to be proved that 'Kelt' is Gaelic, and not Greek.

"The word 'Kelt' is Gaelic, andnot Greek. 'To determine,' says Dr Latham, 'the abstract or theoretical propriety of a certain pronunciation, a person must have sufficient knowledge of foreign tongues, and a sufficient knowledge of English analogies. He must also have some test by which he can determine to what language a word equivocal in pronunciation belongs.' What testimony exists to show that the term 'Kelt' is Gallic or Gaelic? The testimony of the greatest warrior and general of his own age or of any other, and one of the best scholars of the time in which he flourished, Julius Cæsar, the conqueror of Gaul—writes, in the first page of his Commentaries, 'De Bello Gallico,' regarding the Kelts, '*Qui ipsorum lingua Celtæ, nostra Galli appellantur*." He says they were called Celtæ in their own language, that is, in the language of the people who then inhabited Gaul from the river Garonne to the Seine, a language identical with he Gaelic spoken in Ireland.

"In Dr. Prichard's Eastern 'Origin of the Celtic Nations,' edited by Dr. Latham, these words were read:— 'The author who first uses the word *Kelt* is Herodotus.' Keltoi was the *Greek* name; the *Latin* name was Galli.

"'From what language,' he asks (p. 66) 'did the name reach the informants of Herodotus?' In his opinion, 'From the neighbouring tribes.'

"'The term may have been the name of some of the *Kelts*, but it was the Iberians of Spain and the Greeks of the South who gave it its general import—just as it was the Romans who got the Hellenes called Greeks. The Greeks may have learned the name from the Phenicians.'

"He asks (p. 67), 'can we speculate on its meaning.' But he fails to find it out.*

"I offer one—The 'Galli' of Western Europe were in Cæsar's time, and long before it (Vide Commentaries De Bello Gallico, Libri I. et VI.) and Zeus, ('Grammatica Celtica, lib. vi., passim) distinguished amongst the nations for their military skill and bravery. They were trained to war. Their name Keltoi means 'trained to war.' 'Caṫ,' means war (pronounced *cah*, and ailté, or oılte, trained; root aıl or óıl, to traın, to educate; Latin, *alere*; and in the Irish adage, 'every child is just as he has been trained,'—gaċ leanḃ 'aılteır,' the term 'aıl,' or 'oıl,' signifies to train, to support, to *bring up*.

"The derivation just given is natural; it accords with history, with facts, and with the well-known character of the people to whom the name had been applied.

---

* Max Müller in his "Lectures on the Science of Languages," vol. I, p. 225, says of the Kelts, "The name is a Keltic word; Caesar states distinctly that it was so, when saying "*Qui ipsorum lingua Celtæ, nostra Galli appellantur.* The Greeks used *Keltoi* and *Keltæ*. The word *Keltos* may have meant in the ancient language of Gaul *elevated*, upright, proud, (warlike, brave, trained to battle?) like the Latin *celsus and excelsus*.

"At one time I thought that the Gaelic term 'ceil,' (pr. keill), to conceal, to hide, was the origin of the name, because the Druids, bards, and learned men were regarded by the neighbouring people, and by some of their own nation, as the depositories of hidden knowledge. But were 'ceil' the correct derivation of the term, the name *Keltoi* could, with propriety, be applied only to the learned amongst the race. The meaning of the term as explained above from 'cat,' and 'ailté,' trained, appears correct.

"It is no argument against this proof, to say that, indeed, the Greeks adopted the word. To adopt does not destroy the original character of a term or of a thing.

"Rich beyond measure as Greek is in its etymological fecundity, *it cannot* supply a root from which possibly the term *Keltos* may have been derived.

"It is certain, then, that the term Kelt is Gaelic. It is certain that there exists a fixed traditional law of English regulating the orthoepy and orthography of words rendered into English from Gaelic, and according to that law, the sound of 'c' is always that of 'k,' and the spelling either 'c' hard or 'k.'

"As there is no instance in which the sound of 'c' (from words of Gaelic origin) is soft, it follows that the correct sound of 'c' in Celt is hard (like 'K' in Kelt). To remove all doubt, however, about the correct pronunciation, the better way is to spell the term with 'k,' Kelt, Keltic, and not Celt, Celtic. It must be admitted, however, that to write Celt, Celtic, is quite in accord with the Gaelic or Irish, which retains the consonant 'c,' and has no letter of the form 'k' in the written language.

"Those are my views regarding the sound and spelling of the terms Kelt, Keltic.

"Those views, as they have been here put before the

public, constitute my reply to my learned correspondent from Moy, co. Tyrone.

"I cannot conclude without remarking that if I were to yield to the rules of friendship, or to the impressions of early training, or the usual pronunciation of the present time, as far as I can hear it, I should be content to write Celt, Celtic, and pronounce the 'c' soft. But friendship, esteem, habit, or usage, are not knowledge. The will of man can be swayed by these influences, but his intellect can never. Knowledge alone is the light and the life of the intellect; that alone which convinces.

"There are others who may wish to see these views of the subject; and with them, too, the reasons just presented may be convincing.

I am, Sir,

"Your obedient servant,

"ULICK J. BOURKE, President."

CHAPTER VII.

Irish-Gaelic Continued. It throws light not alone on the correct sounds of the letters, but on points of Classical interest. The planet Venus; key to the planetary world. Linguistic questions (6); the discovery made by Bentley. The Digamma, why so called; its vocal value. The letter lost before the age of Homer; its phonetic value turned to use by the author of the Iliad. The sign and sound lost to those who arose in centuries after Homer's time. The sound tracked and pursued by Bentley, and at last discovered. That the letter was lost is certain. Truth of the discovery. Latin not borrowed from Greek. Latin and Gaelic, elder sisters to Greek in the Aryan family. What does Irish-Gaelic prove favourable to Bentley's discovery. Latin as a language older in most of its forms than Greek. Irish-Gaelic anterior to Latin; reasons and authority. All the Aryan branches, however, are equal in origin and early parentage. (7) Sameness between some simple forms of Sanskrit and Irish-Gaelic. The verb "asmi," Sanskrit, and Irish "as-me.' I am. The termination of the imperfect tense in Latin explained, *amabam*, equal "ama-ba-m," *i.e.* in Irish, *loving was I.* The value of "f" in the conditional and future tenses—"bı" (vee) *was.* Other verbs compared. (8) Inflections of verbs. Grimm's opinion. Dr. Prichard's views. What Geddes thinks on this point. (9) Inflections of nouns. (10) Termination "*tur*" of the Irish passive verb. (11) "*Te,*" Irish-Gaelic, the analogon of "*tus*" (Latin), past participle, as "brıste," broken, Latin, *fractus*; "dírıgte," *directus*, from *dirigo.*

Just at present there is much excitement in the non-scientific world, about all that has been said and written, and the expeditions that have been sent out at the cost of a quarter-million of pounds sterling by the governments of England, and France and Prussia, and Russia, and by the President of the United States, to the far South, to the North and to the East. And for what purpose? For nothing else save to observe a small sable speck on the surface of the sun on the morning of the ninth of December, 1874. To one who does not know the value of astronomical science, it is quite a puzzle to conceive the good of all this. "What," asks the rich burly farmer, or the money-making merchant, "is the meaning of all this preparation? what the profit from all this outlay? What gains to be derived from these expeditions provided and prepared by presidents, princes, and potentates?" An amateur astronomer gives the answer. To note the transit of the planet Venus, as she first appears to touch the bright face of the day-god, or seems to steal away from his presence. Those who put questions like the foregoing to themselves or others, are not aware that, small as that little black mark on the sun's face is, caused by the presence of the planet Venus moving in her orbit across his disk, it is the safest key by which men of science are enabled to open the portals of heaven and to learn with certain knowledge, the height, and breadth, and depth, the speed, and span, the orbits, and times, and weight, of the heavenly bodies. By the knowledge obtained on this occasion many vexed questions amongst scholars, schooled amidst the stars, are set at rest for ever.

Amongst linguistic scholars there have been vexed questions. Sanskrit as a language and Irish-Gaelic help to elucidate much that had been only dimly seen and imperfectly known.

Amongst those questions,—that relative to the discovery of the *Ionic Vau*, in Greek, has excited a grave controversy amongst linguistic savans. So has the loss of the initial "p".

in some Greek words; the loss of the consonant "n"; slurring over certain guttural or dental consonants;—the presence of "m" in the verb *sum*, or in *eimi*; the inflections of verbs; the dative plural of nouns; passive verbs; the past participle; names of historic places and persons. Questions such as those have been discussed by scholars. What light does Irish-Gaelic throw upon them?

SIXTH.—BENTLEY'S DISCOVERY CONFIRMED.

Two centuries ago Dr. Bentley made a great literary discovery that a letter and its sound, had been during the space of three thousand years lost to the Greek language. That strange discovery took the learned of the period by surprise. That letter and its sound he reproduced.

With great judgment and extraordinary persevering efforts, like an astronomer pursuing the dim flickering rays of some distant planet, whose light had for an instant crossed the field of vision, Bentley pursued the lost sound and its sign, until at length he satisfied himself and the literary world that he had gained a great success.

It appears that long before the age of Homer, the Greeks had made use of a letter, holding in their alphabet at the time the sixth place,—and which the grammarians called, from its shape, "digamma," or double Gamma, although it represented in sound the vocal value of the letter "f" or "v." In strict phonetic propriety its name was *vau*, as it was really so called amongst the Greeks, a name sometimes written "b," *bau*, in which "b" represents either the eastern or the Spanish phonetic equivalent of "v." Representing sound the lost letter was called *vau*; *digamma* as representing sign or character.

Modern writers have retained the name of the symbol *digamma*, and not *vau* the name of the sound, partly because the former was made use of by some grammarians of the early ages; partly because Dr. Bentley called it by that name; and partly to distinguish the newly-discovered labial aspirate, from that retained in Latin. As a written letter, the character has been known by the special name *Æolic Digamma*, for, in the dialect of the Æolians, the letter and its sound had been retained longest, even after both had disappeared from the written and spoken forms of the other dialects of the Hellenic tongue. Greek students are puzzled by the name, whilst they forget that the name is nothing. The whole power of the letter rests in the sound "v" or "f."

First.—It is certain that the *vau* had existed in the Greek language anterior to the period in which Homer flourished.

The reasons are, (1) that in the languages Gaelic and Latin,—older offshoots, as shall be shewn, of the Aryan linguistic tree, the letter "f" is found. Hence, naturally enough, a language like the Greek, flowing from the same primæval source of human speech, must at a very early period have had the same letter that the sister tongues had derived from a common parent. (2) In comparing the Greek alphabet with the Semitic, and collating the letters as numerical symbols, it is seen that "f," in Greek occupied the sixth place. (3) At a period later still, the numerical cypher (six) 6, has been in Greek represented by a unique character not unlike a small sigma but in reality a gamma doubled, and written in a cursive hand. (4) Grammarians of the olden time, and the famous Hellenic historian of Roman events, Dionysius of Halicarnassus, states the fact, that the letter "f" had been lost, and that its sound was equivalent to that of the semi-vowel "v." (5) In the oldest Greek monumental inscriptions *gamma doubled* is found. These reasons tend to point out to scholars of the present day that the Ionic *vau* had been in the early ages of Grecian literary culture one of he Greek letters. (6) Th e greatest grammarians of the present and past century, who have studied the matter, fully admit that such a letter had once been in Greek. William Smith, LL.D., and Theophilus D. Hall, M.A., Fellow of the University college, London, (see Student's Latin Grammar, London, John Murray, Albemarle-st, 1873,)—the latest and perhaps the greatest Latin and Greek Grammarians, have no doubt about this point; and Kühner and Roby and the Grammarians of the Port Royal in the last century expressed the same views.

Second.—From all that has been shewn, it is clear the letter 'f,' representing the sharp aspirate semi-vowel, had been lost at a very early date indeed. That it had been lost at a very early date appears, further from the fact that Homer does not in his writings make use of the letter; nor does any Greek poet or historian who flourshed subsequent to the period in which the father of Grecian poets lived.

Thirdly.—Although the letter had been lost, its vocal value was retained in the time of Homer. It is natural to suppose that the Great Hellenic Epic poet employed in his writings the language just as he had heard it spoken in Ionia, during the days of his childhood and manhood. Now in his grand masterpieces of poetry the presence of the 'f' sound is required to complete, in certain instances, the rhythmical and harmonious flow of the verse. That sound must, therefore, have, to his tuneful ear, played a part in the rhapsodies which he composed and recited in his native home of Ionia. So much *à priori*.

Viewing those grand epic poems as they have been handed down to the literary world of the Christian era, and as they are, the sound of the semivowel 'v' or of the sharp 'f' is required for the perfect rhythm of some verses, and for the purpose of developing with due grace, in the language of Homer spoken or read, that uniform harmony required for perfect poetry.

How is this known ?

Many scholars versed in Greek have, in the past and in the present times, discovered a want of smoothness in the rhythmical flow and the metrical form of some lines, both in the Iliad and Odyssey—for instance in the fourth line of his first book of the Iliad;

"*Heroon, autous de heloria Teuche Kunessin.*"

The concurrence of the two epsilons 'e' in *de*, and 'e' in 'heloria,' did not, as critics thought, please. Certain scholars reasoned thus on the point :

The defect or hiatus in the line, arises either from a want of poetic power on the part of Homer, or from some missing phonetic element, known to Homer and adopted by him, although not expressed by any sign or letter, but not known to his readers of the present time. It was a daring thing to assert that the fault lay in the absence of perfect poetic power, or phonetic accuracy in the versification of the immortal bard of Ionia. It must arise then from some missing vocal value known to Homer and practiced by him, and not known in later times. This latter view was right. Dr. Bentley saw it.

But what was that phonetic property known to Homer and infused into the rhythm of his verses, yet lost to posterity ? This was the difficulty ; Dr. Bentley solved it.

The following passage, from a *dissertation* by the Rev. William Trollope, M.A., Pembroke College, Cambridge—London, Longman & Co.,—is suited to the present purpose :—

" Since then, it appears that such a letter did exist in early Greece, and more especially in those parts in which Homer composed his poems, it can scarcely be doubted

that its effects were still perceptible in the poet's time, and that its application may be fairly applied to the removal of metrical difficulties in his writings. Bentley has satisfactorily established his point to a considerable extent, and he would probably have strengthened his hypothesis into a greater degree of certainty, had he lived to prosecute his plans in spite of the paltry and malicious ridicule to which his ingenious discovery exposed him. *The principles* upon which he had proceeded rested upon the observation, that there were certain words in Homer beginning with a vowel, which were never preceded by a consonant; and others of which the two first syllables were short, which were never preceded by a double consonant. In proof of this position, Davis, who followed up the enquiry, has actually exhibited the result,"
and has shewn where the digamma must have necessarily. formed a constituent part of the word.

The Bentlian theory is now generally admitted by the learned, and the weight of argument is certainly in favour of its truth.

Dawes, however, differs from Bentley; instead of the name Æolic digamma, Dawes affirms that it should be distinguished by the title of *Ionic Vau*; and he assigns to it the power of the English "w."

Mr. Knight (*Prolegomena in Homerum*) has supported the opinion of Dawes; and Bishop Marsh (*Horae Pelasgicæ*) maintains that the digamma was pronounced like the Roman "f."

Such was the state of the question some forty years ago, respecting the discovery of Bentley. All Greek scholars now admit fully that the letter "f"—call it digamma or *Vau*—had been lost; that its power was still employed in the spoken Ionic Greek at the time of Homer; that in the seventeenth century Dr. Bentley discovered this missing sound and its symbol (f.) What, then, does Irish Gaelic prove in favour of the the truth of Bentley's discovery?

It shows that at the earliest Pelasgian period the phonetic power of "f," and the symbol to represent it, had been known in the far-off period of primæval Greek speech; just as geology, by the discovery of a vein strewn with bones in a stratum of the earth's crust, shows how races of animals now extinct had, at one time, roamed through the wild woods and perennial prairies of an antedeluvian world, so comparative philology investigates the lost letter, finds it out, shows its place and power in modern dialects, and in this way points out and confirms the ingenuity and keen research of Bentley.

The special force of Irish Gaelic in subjects of this class is handsomely noticed by Professor Geddes, from whose lecture the annexed quotation is taken:—

"The expression for twenty, or two tens, is now *eikosi* in Greek, but the Sanskrit *vins'ati* points to a form *duin*-s'ati or *two tens*; the Latin is *vi-ginti*, where "v" is for *dvi* (two) all that remains of the *two* of the *two tens*. What is the Gaelic? Fıċead. And now that they have ransacked the old stones of Greece for inscriptions, it appears that the old Greeks wrote *Ficate*, also *Bikati* (and not *eikosi*) which is, therefore, the equation of the Gaelic Fıċead. Compare the Irish Gaelic "ḟíon," wine, with *foinos* (Greek) *wine*. Fıos, *knowledge*, *notice*, with foıda and *Fismen* (we know). Or, again, the word for '*evening*.' The Greek is *hesperos*; with the digamma it is *fesperos*; the Latin, '*vesper*, or *vespera* "v." What is it in Gaelic? FEASGAR (f.) 'He would be a bold man,' adds Geddes, 'that would say this is from either Greek or Latin, for the Lithuanian *vakaras* is on the side of the Gaelic, and hence Fick, in his Indo-Germanic Lexicon gives the type-form of the Aryan word for *evening* as *vaskara*, of which, therefore, the most faithful edition is preserved in the Keltic speech."

In Gaelic the derivation of the term *feasgar* is plain from *feasg*, shade, cover, shades of evening, and "rata," period, time, juncture.

The strong point of which Irish-Gaelic supplies proof in favour of the truth of Dr. Bentley's discovery rests on the fact that Latin and Gaelic are elder sisters to Greek, in the Aryan family of languages, and that the three are quite distinct; yet, that they are traceable on a common geneological stem.

It may be useful, then, in this place, to show that Latin is older than Greek, and that Gaelic is the eldest sister of the family; and that the three are specifically distinct and independent.

First, *Latin, as a language, is older than Greek.* Some years ago the common teaching in classic schools in this country was, that Greek was older than Latin, and that, moreover, Latin was derived from Greek.

Comparative philology, as a science and a study, has dissipated this false teaching.

(1) Of two languages that is the elder, in which the sibilant "s" is found as initial in certain words, the equivalents of which begin with a vowel or "h," in the other, as "sex," "septem," "super," in Latin, are in Greek "hex," "hepta," "huper," &c. Therefore, Latin is, in age, anterior to Greek.

(2) James Stuart, M.A., Professor of the Greek and Latin Languages in the Catholic University of Ireland, and late of Trinity College, Cambridge, writes in his *Memoranda in Greek Grammar*, p. 1., published in 1859 by James Duffy, Dublin: "*The Latin language is older than the Greek*; first, because, when a similarity

exists, it is between the Latin and the Æolic, the oldest Greek dialect; and, secondly, because, while it is the tendency of all languages in their progress to substitute auxiliaries and particles for inflections, this is more the case in Greek than in Latin."

(3) Winning has shown that of two languages, the words of which are identical, those which have a vowel prefix are latest or youngest, in point of time. Hence, the Irish-Gaelic and Latin are, as sister languages, older than the Greek, thus:—"*Neart*," in Irish, means strength, manliness; the old Sabine speech had had the word "Nero," brave, manly, and "Neris," manliness; Greek, "a-ner," a man. This "a" of aner is only euphonic; for, "naras" in Sanscrit signifies men. "Aster" is Greek, for star; Latin, "stella," Irish, "reult;" "*o*phrus," Greek for brow—omitting enitial "o,"—old Irish "braoı," modern, "gruaıd,' "g," guttural, changed to "ph," aspirate labial, as "c" of "cos" becomes "p" in "pous. Hence, Greek is younger than Latin or Irish.

Again, Irish-Gaelic is anterior to the Latin.

(1) "The Kelts seem to have been the *first* of the Aryans to arrive in Europe." *Max Muller,—Lectures on the Science of Language, vol.* i., p. 225.

(2) "In a variety of instances," says Newman, *(Regal Rome, p. 25)* "Latin words retain only secondary meanings where the primary ones are manifest in the Irish-Gaelic (Keltic.) Thus, the word "monile," a neck-lace, is from the Gaelic, "muıneal." The word "muıneal" means neck." Hence Irish-Gaelic was before Latin. See pp. 118, 119—Supra.

(3) Dr. Donaldson, in his *New Cratylus*, says:—The earliest population of both Italy and Greece was Irish or Keltic. After these came the Sclavonian, Low-Iranian or Pelasgic element in each country.

(4) An American writer, in an essay, published during the past year in one of the journals of New York, on the Aryan languages, says that the Indo-European family of languages is divided into eight branches ; 1, Sanscrit or Indian ; 2, Zend or Persian ; 3, Keltic or Irish-Gaelic ; 4, Latin ; 5, Greek ; 6, Gothic or German ; 7, Lithuanian ; 8, Sclavonian. This order is, to the thinking of the present writer, the correct one, and that which is borne out by facts.

The writer's opinion is that the Greek, Latin, and Irish-Gaelic languages are tongues of different and distinct migrations or colonies of settlers from the high table-land or the rich valleys of Armenia,—differing in the time of their coming into Europe—and in the routes by which they came.

Modern scholars are convinced that Greek is much later, in point of time, than Latin or Irish. Comparative philology furnishes abundant reasons to show that Irish-Gaelic is an older language than that in which Homer and Sappho, or Virgil and Horace wove their wreathes of deathless song or story.

Hear Max Müller again :—" The only remark which a comparative philologist has to make is, that the idea of making Gaelic the parent of Latin is more preposterous than deriving English from German, the fact being that there are many forms in Latin more primitive than their corresponding forms in Greek. The idea of Pelasgians, as the common ancestors of Greeks and Romans, is another of those grammatical myths, but it hardly requires, at present, any serious refutation."—*Max Muller, Lectures on the science of languages, vol. I, p.* 224.

William K. Sullivan says in his " Keltic Studies," p. xiv., of Dr. Lottner, that he holds the opinion that no special relationship could be scientifically established between the Hellenic and Italic branches of the Aryan family, a doctrine which must appear heretical to most classical students.

Again, he writes, p. xv., "Dr. Lottner, without at all departing from his opinion regarding the absence of special affinities between Latin and Greek, has slightly modified his views about the position of the Keltic." He has shewn that the European bough from the Asiatic tree of language in Armenia, formed a single people. From this people, the Hellenic (he says) first separated. The remainder split into two divisions, the South-west and the Northern. The South-west division was subdivided into the Italic and Keltic branches; while the Northern division became subdivided into Germans and Slavonians; and the Slavonians in turn were subdivided into Slaves proper and Letts. This opinion, says Dr. Sullivan, harmonizes with the ancient Irish tradition respecting the Keltic.

The following passage from MaxMüller makes the genealogical chart regarding all the European languages plain to every scholar. All mists are cleared away. The strange tracings from other hands, quite unscientific, are connected, and the entire question put before the view in its most simple and in its correct state.

"When Sanskrit had once assumed its right position, when people had once become familiarised with the idea that there must have existed a language more primitive than Greek, Latin and Sanskrit, and forming the common background of these three, as well as of the Teutonic, Keltic, and Slavonic branches of speech, all languages seemed to fall by themselves into their right position. The key to the puzzle was found, and all the rest was merely a work of patience. The same arguments by which Sanskrit and Greek had been proved to hold co-ordinate rank were perceived to apply with equal strength to Latin and Greek; and after Latin had once been shewn to be more *primitive* on many points than Greek, it was easy to see that the Teutonic, the Keltic, and the Slavonic languages also contained each a number of formations, which it was impossible to derive from Sanskrit, Greek, or Latin. It was perceived that all had to be treated as co-ordinate members of one and the same class."

SEVENTH—SAMENESS BETWEEN THE PRIMITIVE SIMPLE FORMS OF SANSCRIT AND IRISH.

Instead of mere classes, we hear now for the first time of well-regulated *families* of languages.

The verb *To Be*, Latin *Est*, Greek *Eisi*, can be made to furnish sufficient proof that Latin never could have passed through the Greek, or what used to be called the "Pelasgic" stage, but that both (Greek and Latin) are modifications of the same original language. In the third person plural (for instance "sunt") Latin is more primitive than Greek. The regular form of the verb would be "as-anti;" this in Sanscrit is changed into "santi." In Greek the initial "s" is dropped, and the Æolic "enti" is reduced to "eisi." The Latin, on the contrary, has kept the radical "s," and it would be perfectly impossible to derive the Latin "sunt" from the Greek "eisi."

"Sunt" means "they are." The word is certainly more primitive than the Greek "eisi." Irish-Gaelic is very clear and strong on this point: "sunt," they are, is not far from "as siad," they are.

The substantive verb in Irish-Gaelic is "as," (spelled at present usually "is," but pronounced in the old way, "as," not "ish.")

Irish—as me, *it is I*,
as tu, *it is thou*,
as se, *it is he*,
as sı, *it is she*,
as sınn, *it is we*,
as sıḃ (*siv*) *it is you*,
as sıad, *it is they*.

The words in the third plural, "as-siad," become "'s sıad;" the "d" and "t" are virtually the same. The "t" in "sunt" is accounted for by the "d," in "sıad," third person plural of the personal pronoun. This termination of "nt" in the plural of the verb is still more clearly pointed out by the third plural of the personal pronoun in Welsh, namely, "hwynt," they.

What are the forms of the verb *To Be* in Sanskrit? Curiously enough, they are identical with those in Irish-Gaelic. "Asmı," I am, composed of "as," "ıs," and the personal pronoun "mı," me, or I. This verb is identical in form and in sound with the Irish-Gaelic verb "as-me," it is I, in which the component parts, "as," "is," and "me," I, are not united.

The other Sanscrit form of the verb *To Be* is "bhavami," from the root bhû.

The imperfect tense of the Irish assertive verb, "as," is "ba," or "buḋ," (pr. buh) was, as "buḋ me," It was I; "buḋ tu," wast thou, etc. The regular verb *To Be*, denoting a continuity of existence, is "bıḋ," pronounced "bee," as "bıḋ me," I be; "bıḋ tu," thou art usually; "bıḋ se," he is usually.

The perfect indicative of this verb is "ḃı me," [vee meh) I was; "ḃı tu," thou wast, "ḃı se," he was.

Let the Irish verb, the Sanscrit, the Greek, and Lithuanian appear side by side, so that, the most simple and primitive of all may appear.

1.—Irish-Gaelic.

	First Person.	Second Person.	Third Person.	
Sing.	As me.	As tu.	As se.	As sı.
Plur.	As sınn Old form as muıd	As sıḃ	As siad	

2.—Sanskrit.

Sing.	Asmi.	Asi.	Asti.
Plur.	Asmus, or smah.	Stha.	Santi.

3.—Greek (old form.)

Sing.	Esmi now) eimi)	Essi (eis.)	Esti.
Plur.	Esmes reduced to esmer	Este.	Enti, (Æolic) reduced to Eisi

4.—Latin old (form.)

Sing.	Esum (now sum.)	Esis (now es.)	Esti (now est.
Plur.	Es-umus, now sumus.	Estis.	Sunt.

5.—Lithuanian.

Sing,	Esmi.	Essi.	Esti.
Plur.	Esme.	Este.	Esti.

In all these forms, the radical, simple Irish-Gaelic particle "as" ("s" hard) is found; the endings are pronouns.

6.—English.

"Am" is for "asm," and "that" for "as me." "A" of "am" is a broken form of "as," "is," and "m" is the Gaelic personal pronoun, nominative case. "Art" is for "as tu" (s changed into r) "ıs," is the third person same as "as," or modern Irish "ıs" [iss,] is.

"I need hardly say," writes Max Müller, that the modern English verb "I am," "thou art," "he is," are only secondary modifications of the same primitive verb." *The Science of Language, vol. i., p.* 198.

Observe.—The ending "bam," of the imperfect tense in Latin (and "va" of Italian verbs, and "ba" of Spanish verbs) appears to be derived from the Keltic "ba," was, connected with the root, and followed by the pronoun "me," (I,) as "amabam," I did love or was loving, is equal to "ama-ba-me," that is, loving was I; root "am" loving; "ba," was; "me," I; "ama-ba-s," (su or tu) loving wast thou, etc.

In Irish Gaelic the conditional tense and the future take "f," and this letter is the aspirate labial representing the sound "ḃi," (vee,) has been; as "ḃuail-finn," I was one to strike; "ḃuailfad," I shall strike.

One Tense of the Sanskrit verb "bhavami," I exist, is quite enough to collate with the Irish-Gaelic verb *to be.*

Imperative—SANSCRIT.

Sin.	bhavani	bhava	bhavatu
Plural	bhavama	bhavata	bhavantu

The foregoing is very like the imperfect tense of the verb *to be* in Irish.

IRISH "ḃ," IS EQUAL TO "bh."

Sing.	ḃidinn	ḃidtha	ḃideaḋ se.
Plural	ḃidmuis	ḃidiḋe	ḃidis.

I was usually in a state of existence; thou wast, &c. All these tenses connected with the two forms of the substantive verb are very striking.

It is quite evident to the reader that in the forms here presented of the verb "as-mi." Sanscrit, and "as-me," Irish, the latter is the simpler and the plainer.

In connexion with this special branch of comparative grammar, by which an inter-comparison of grammatical forms and radical sameness has been made between the Aryan sister languages—Irish-Gaelic, Sanscrit, Greek, Latin, English, and Lettish, there is one other point of classical interest to which it is well to draw the attention of the reader.

EIGHTH.—*The point of interest is, the personal inflections of verbs in Greek, Latin, Irish, and Sanskrit.* Grimm declares in his *Grammatik*, p. 1,052, "that the characteristic terminations of the third person singular and plural, viz., D, and N D, appear to him quite *inexplicable by means of the German pronouns.*"

"It is fortunate," says Dr. Prichard (*Keltic Nations*, p. 265—Latham's edition; London, Quaritch 1857,) "that there is one language in which the personal pronouns, as well as the verbal suffixes, have been preserved in a form much less altered from their original state than in any of the more celebrated of the classical dialects, in which philologists have, before his time, sought the means of elucidating the structure of language. I allude to the Keltic dialects—the Welsh and Irish (which he strangely styles Erse). The terminations of words are but little capable of change in the Keltic idioms, as, indeed, are those idioms themselves, of which the people appear ever to have been remarkably tenacious." That has always been the character of the Keltic race. So says Zeuss.

Dr. Pritchard adds:—"It is certain that the Keltic idioms preserve in a more perfect state than any other languages of Europe and Asia the original pronouns of which abbreviated forms enter, as suffixes, into the inflections of verbs through the numbers and persons."

The reader is refered, for the proof, to his work, *The Eastern Origin of the Keltic Nations*, c. v., sections v. & vi.

Every Irish scholar knows that the simple prepositions enter in Irish into composition with the personal pronouns; as "me," I, me; "tu," thou; "se," he, him; "sı," she, her; "sınn," we, us; "sıḃ," you; "sıad," they, them, compounded with "aıg," at, form the compound pronouns—

Sing.	agam	agat	aıge	aıcı
Plur.	agaınn	agaıḃ	aca.	

"Agam," at me, is compounded of "aıg" at, and the pronoun "me," me; agat, at thee, &c.

By this means, the verb "ta" is, art, are, entering into composition with the personal pronoun, efformates the synthetic verb "táım," I am.

Sing.	táım, I am.	táır, thou art.	tá se, he is.
Plur.	támuıd, we are.	tátoı, ye are.	táıd, they are

"Táım" is for tá and me; "táır," tá and tu; "támuıd," for tá and muıd, us; "táıd," is for tá and sıad. In "táır," thou art, "t" is changed indirectly into "r."

In this way the personal inflections of the verbs in Irish-Gaelic are accounted for; and thus, too, are the inflections "mus," "tis," "ant, "unt," and the like in other languages plainly traceable through the Keltic to the broken forms of the personal pronoun.

What does Professor Geddes say on the subject of the inflections of the verbs in the Greek and Latin languages: "No one," he says, in p. 15 of Lecture, "could fail to be struck with the preservation in certain tenses of the primitive personal endings, e.g., "m," as indicating the first person imperative, as "brıseam," let me break, the exact analogon of "frangam," and in Epic, or oldest Greek, "rhegnumi." So "dh," the third person of the same mood "brıseadh," with "se," let him break; the analogon of Latin "frangito"; Greek," rhegnuto." The most remarkable of these is the ending "muıd" of the first person plural, "brısamuıd," let us break. This "brısamuıd" is, by the way, derived from the root "brıs," (a euphonic) and "muıd," an old personal pronoun employed, to this day, by the peasants of Galway in speaking Irish, as, for instance, they say—"Is muıd-ne a bı ann sın," it is we who were there. But, to return to Geddes. The "muıd" is, according to his notion, the analogon of "ometha," and "oimetha," appearing in the Greek verb; whence, brısamuıd is the correlative of "rhegnuometha."

Other Irish tenses compared with their Latin or Greek equivalents.

The linguistic analogies presented by the Gaelic verb, are very nearly divided between the Greek and the Latin.

The "ınn" of the imperfect tense and "fınn," of the conditional, (Irish) remind us of "n" in the first person of the Greek past tenses "etupton," I did strike; "etupon," I struck; and "erregnun," I was breaking.

An important analogy to the Greek infinitive might be found in the cluster of Irish-Gaelic infinitives in "ınn;" as "feuċaın," to try, to see; "tuıgsın," to understand "cluınntın," and "cloıstın," to hear.

The "muıs" (pr. mush,) a plural, first person of Irish-Gaelic verbs, is the analogon of "mus," Latin; as, "frangamus," "brıscamuıs."

"Another gleam of light from the Gaelic is reflected on the formation of the Greek future. From the verb "brıs" (pr. brish) future "brısfas" I shall break, is formed. "Brısfas" is certainly formed by the addition of the substantive verb "as," "is," or "am," to root 'brıs,' that is, I *am* to break, means, I will break. So says Geddes.

In Irish Gaelic the future relative is *fas*, and not *as* simply. The termination *fas* is from "ḃus," an old future form of the assertive verb "as," *is*, *exists*. This "ḃus" is made up of *as*, *is*, and *ba*, *may be*, or *become*. The future "brısfeas," then in Irish-Gaelic means some one who (fas) is about (brıs) to break.

No one, continues Geddes, will doubt that we have one

form of the future tense in Gaelic expressed by the substantive verb *as*, or *is* or *es*, or its future form "bus." "Could a more perfect analogy be obtained to illustrate the formation of the Greek future by means of the substantive verb *es* ?

Greek Future.—*Tup - es - o*, equal to *tupso*, I shall strike.
to-strike-am-I.
" " *reg - es - o*, I shall break.
to-break-am-I

Thus in Irish Gaelic, "brıs-f-as" equals break-about-to-am-I. In *facso*, an old future of *facio*, the Latin language still retains a remnant of the ancient formation of the future tense. "It is a boulder," says Geddes, "of immense value in the eye of the linguistic geologist.

The Latin "bo" of "amabo" has been shewn to come from "ba," was, or "beıṫ," to become. "Nor is there any doubt," says Max Müller (p. 268, vol. I.) "that in the Latin *bo* of *amabo* we have the old auxiliary *bhu*, to become.

NINTH.—INFLECTIONS OF NOUNS. DATIVE PLURAL.

The remarkable termination of the dative plural, in the great body of Gaelic nouns, holds out a striking proof that the Gaelic plural "ıḃ" is the root of the Latin and Greek analogous case-endings. The "ıḃ" is the correlative of the "bus" the dative plural in Latin, the "byas" of the Sanscrit, and the vanishing "phın" of such forms as "nauphin" and "óchesphın." In Greek it is ready to die as early as the time of Æschylus. In Latin the "bus" shows symptoms of decay, as it is found in full force only in the third or consonant declension; but to this day the "ıbh" survives in the Gaelic.

Dr. Prichard writes (*p.* 344, *Eastern Origin*,) "It is worth while to notice particularly the dative plural which generally terminates in "aibh." This termination is plainly related to the old Latin dative in "ubus" and "abus," which was probably the genuine and original form of the case in Latin. The Sanscrit dative plural ends in "abhyas," or, at least, in "bhyas," after a vowel, as "rajabhyas," Latin "regibus," Irish "ríoġaiḃ," to kings. In these respects there is a remarkable cognation between the Keltic and the Sanscrit."

The ending "bus" of the dative plural of Latin nouns is found in the third declension only; in the fourth and fifth, too, but these are mere developements of the third.

This omission is a falling away, and a sign of weakness in the early days of Latin linguistic developement. The termination "iḃ" (ḃ, aspirated, has the sound of "v" when articulated in the same syllable with "i") or "aibh" is found in Irish not in one declension, but in all. Examples, from the *College Irish Grammar, fifth Edition, pp.* 58, 59, 60:—

FIRST DECLENSION.

To it belong all nouns masculine that end with a consonant, preceded by a broad vowel (a, o, u). The gen. case singular and the nominative plural take "i" before the closing consonant.

Eaċ, *m., a steed.*

	Singular.	Plural.
Nom. Acc.	eaċ, *a steed.*	eiċ, *steeds.*
Gen.	eiċ, *of a steed*	eaċ, *of steeds.*
Dat.	eaċ, *to a steed*	eaċaiḃ, *to steeds.*
Voc.	eiċ, *oh ! steed.*	eaċa, *steeds.*

Eiċ, is pl. of eaċ; eaċraid, cavalry, is a noun of multitude.

In this manner is declined every noun masculine of one syllable or more ending in "c" (unaspirated). And in the same manner are declined all nouns of *one* syllable ending in "ċ" (aspirated). But if more than one syllable, and that "ċ" final is aspirated, then it is changed, in the genitive case, into the soft guttural "ġ"; as,

Marcaċ, *a rider.*

From "marc," an old Keltic term for *horse.*

	Singular	Plural.
Nom. Acc.	marcaċ	marcaıġ
Gen.	marcaıġ	marcaċ
Dat.	marcaċ	marcaıġıḃ
Voc.	ṁarcaıġ	ṁarcaċa

"In all printed books, and in most manuscripts of the four last centuries, final "ċ" becomes "ġ" when attenuation takes place; as, "bealaċ," a way, a road; gen. "bealaıġ." But in very ancient Irish manuscripts, and in all printed Irish books in the Irish or Scotch Gaelic the "ċ" (asp.) is retained."—*O'Donovan.*

Bord, *m.*, *a table* (declined with the article "an")

Articulated Form.

Nom. Acc.	an bord, *the table*	na boırd, *the tables*
Gen.	an ḃoırd, *of the table*	na m-bord, *of the tables*
Dat.	do'n m-bord, *to the table*	do na bordaıḃ *to the tables.*

SECOND DECLENSION.

The second declension comprises (1) all nouns *feminine*, of which the characteristic is *slender*—the vowel "ı;" (2) nouns *feminine* of one syllable or more of which the characteristic is broad. The second declension is distinguished from the first by taking, in the genitive case singular, an additional syllable, "e," called by grammarians—because "e" is a slender vowel—the slender increase.

Examples.

Suıl, *eye* (pr. *soo-il*, in one syllable).

	Singular.	Plural.
Nom. Acc.	suıl	suıle (pr. *sooil-le*
Gen.	suıle	sul
Dat.	suıl	suılıḃ
Voc.	ṡuıl	ṡuıle

All nouns of *this class* ending in a consonant, preceded by the slender vowel "ı," are declined chiefly like the foregoing:

A noun *feminine*, of which the characteristic (or final vowel), is broad, and in this respect, is in the nom. and acc. cases, like to a noun masculine, "cos," *f.*, *a foot.*

	Singular.	Plural.
Nom. Acc.	cos, *kos*	cosa, *kossa*
Gen.	coıse, *koshe*	cos
Dat.	coıs, *kosh*	cosaıḃ

THIRD DECLENSION.

(1) Personal nouns in "óır;" (2) abstract nouns in "aċt;" (3) verbal nouns in "uġaḋ, aḋ, eaḋ, aċt, aıl;" (4) certain primitive nouns of one syllable or more. The genitive singular takes a broad increase (a).

Slánuıġteoır, *a Saviour* (with the article).

	Singular.	Plural.
Nom. Acc.	an Slánuıġteoır, *the Saviour.*	na Slánuıġteoıríḋ, *the Saviours.*
Gen.	an t-Slánuıġteora	na Slánuıġteoır
Dat.	ó 'n t-Slánuıġteoır	ó na Slánuıġteoıríḃ
Voc.	a Ṡlánuıġteoır	a Ṡlánuıġteoıríḋ

FOURTH DECLENSION.

Example—Tıġearna, *Lord.*

	Singular.	Plural
Nom.	tiġearna	tiġearnaiḋ, *the lords*
Acc.		
Gen.		tiġearnaḋ
Dat.		tiġearnaiḋiḃ
Voc.		tiġearnaiḋ

FIFTH DECLENSION.

This declension, like the fourth, comprises nouns that end in a vowel (a, e) with a few in "ain." They are, with a few exceptions, of the feminine gender. This declension is distinguished from the former by a peculiar inflection (n or nn) in the genitive singular.

Example.

Pearsa, *f.*, *a person* (with the article).

	Singular.	Plural
Nom. Acc.	an ṗearsa	na pearsana.
Gen.	na ṗearsan	na b-pearsan
Dat	do 'n b-pearsain	do na pearsanaiḃ
Voc.	a ṗearsa	a ṗearsana

The affected consonant is marked with a (·) dot: "ṁ," or "ḃ" (affected or aspirated) has the sound of "v" or "w," "ṗ," of *ph*, "ċ," of *ch*, "ḋ, ġ," of *y*, "ṡ, ṫ," of *h*" "ḟ" silent.

IRISH DECLENSIONS 500 YEARS AGO.

In the mediæval tract on Latin declension, edited by Whitley, Stokes, from a MS. in Trinity College, Dublin, and written in the Irish language over five hundred years ago, the datives plural of the old form are:

Nominative.	Dative plural.
Ceann, *a head*	ceannaiḃ
Rann, *a stanza*, *a division*	rannaiḃ
Aṫair, *a father*	athraiḃ
Cathir, *a city*	cathrachaiḃ
File, *a poet*	filiḋiḃ

Rannaıre, *a poetaster, a rhymster* rannaırıḃ
Cara, *a friend* caraıtıḃ
Talaṁ, *earth* talmanaıḃ
Dıa, *God* Déıḃ.

Thus, in the past, as in the present, the *dative plural of Irish nouns of all classes* terminated in "ıḃ," or "aıḃ."

TENTH.—THE PASSIVE TERMINATION "TAR."

The termination of the passive verb, as "duntar," is shut, is like the "tur" in Latin of "amatur," "diligitur;" "brıstear," is the analogon of "frangitur."

ELEVENTH.—THE PAST PARTICIPLE IN IRISH AND LATIN.

The past participle "te," "ta," in Irish-Gaelic is the analogon of "tus," "tum" in Latin; the participial adjective "tos" inGreek; as "brıs-te," "fractus," "rhektos."

WHAT WERE THEY ORIGINALLY.

A question naturally presents itself here regarding these grammatical forms of the noun and verb. What were they originally? Are they mere arbitrary marks attached to the vocal or written root, as elements unmeaning in themselves, but employed arbitrarily or conventionally to modify the meaning of words; or are they produced like the flowers and leaves and branches springing from a stem? Or, again, are they the worn forms of primitive independent words, that in ages past had a meaning and a purpose? Is it possible to trace them back to their original source, and find out their purpose and meaning.

FIRST—Are these grammatical forms mere arbitrary marks annexed to the root? Some grammarians, amongst whom is Frederick Schlegel, are advocates of this opinion: "Languages with inflections," says he, "are organic languages, because they include a living principle of developement and increase, and alone possess a fruitful and abundant vegetation. The wonderful mechanism of these languages consists in forming an immense variety of words, and in making the connection of ideas expressed by these words, by the help of an inconsiderable number of syllables, *which, viewed separately, have no signification*, but which determine with precision the sense of the words to which they are attached. By modifying radical letters and by adding derivative syllables to the roots, derivative words of various sorts are formed. . . . . Substantives, adjectives, pronouns, are added, and verbs conjugated by employing terminations and augments, *which, by themselves*, signify nothing."—*Transactions of the Philological Society, vol.* ii., *p.* 29. The advocates of this opinion regard inflections or syllables to be words without meaning when taken apart from any connection with the root; and that they have that special form which they present, because, at a very early date certain clans agreed upon it.

SECONDLY—Are they produced like the flowers and the leaves of plants? Many writers give to this question an affirmative answer, and say, that undoubtedly languages are formed by a process, not of crystaline accretion but of germinal developement. This is the common opinion, or it had been so up to a late period. Farrar, and Frederick Schlegel, too, propound it.

"It is held by many with whom poetical phraseology takes the place of sound and severe reasoning." These are sage words from Max Müller. What numbers are deceived daily by poetical phraseology, how many are taken by the gilding and not by the gold of thought!

"The science of language adopts neither of these views. As to imagining language, that is nouns and verbs, endowed with an inward principle of growth, all we can say is, that such a conception is really inconceivable.

Language may be conceived as a production; but it cannot be conceived as a substance that could produce itself. The science of language has nothing to do with mere theories, whether conceivable or not. It collects facts, and its only object is to account for these facts as far as possible. It takes each termination by itself, establishes its most primitive form by means of comparison, and then treats that primitive syllable as it would treat any other part of language, as something which was originally intended to convey a meaning."

THIRDLY—Scholars skilled in a knowledge of comparative grammar know that grammatical terminations were originally independent words, and had a special purpose and meaning. A knowledge of comparative grammar removes every difficulty on the question of early grammatical forms.

Max Müller forecasts, in a very lucid style, and in a way quite attractive, a view of a possible future language fully developed, in ages to come, in its new concrete forms, and by means of this imaginary tableau, shows his readers how the present literary and living European tongues have been efformated from the Aryan, and how the inflections of the verbs and case-endings of the nouns have sprung from independent words, having a meaning and a purpose. The passage is well worth being reproduced in these pages.

"Let us begin with modern formations, because we have here more day-light for watching the intricate and sometimes wayward movements of languages; or, better, still, let us begin with an imaginary case, or with what may be called the language of the future, in order to see quite clearly how what we should call grammatical forms may arise. Let us suppose that the slaves in America were to rise against their masters, and after gaining some victories, were to sail back in large numbers to some part of Central Africa, beyond the reach of their white enemies or friends ; let us suppose these men availing themselves of the lessons they had learnt in their captivity, and gradually working out a civilization of their own. It is quite possible that, some centuries hence, a new Livingstone might find among the descendants of the American slaves a language, a literature, laws, and manners bearing a striking similitude to those of his own country. What an interesting problem for any future historian and ethnologist ! Yet, there are problems in the past history of the world of equal interest, which have been, and are still, to be solved by the student of language. Now, I believe that a careful examination of the language of the descendants of those escaped slaves would suffice to determine with perfect certainty their past history, even though no documents and no tradition had preserved the story of their captivity and liberation. At first, no doubt, the threads might seem hopelessly entangled. A missionary might surprise the scholars of Europe by an account of a new African language. He might describe it at first as very imperfect—as a language, for instance, so poor that the same word had to be used to express the most heterogeneous ideas. He might point out how the same sound, without any change of accent, meant true, a ceremony, a workman, and was used also as a verb in the sense of literary composition. All these, he might say, are expressed in that strange dialect by the sound *rait*, (right, rite, wright, write). He might likewise observe that this dialect, as poor almost as Chinese, had hardly any grammatical inflections, and that it had no genders, except in a few words, such as man-of-war and railway engine, which were both conceived as feminine beings, and spoken of as *she*. He might then mention an even more extraordinary feature, namely, that although this language had no terminations for the masculine and feminine genders of nouns, it employed a masculine and feminine termination after the affirmative particle, according as it was addressed to a lady or gentleman. Their affirmative particle being the same as the English *yes*, they added a final "r" to it, if addressed to a man, and a final "m," if addressed to a lady; that is to say, instead of simply saying *yes*, these descendants of the escaped American slaves said *yesr* to a man, and *yesm* to a lady.

"Absurd as this may sound, I can assure you that the descriptions which are given of the dialects of savage tribes, as explained for the first time by travellers or missionaries, are even more extraordinary. But let us consider now what the student of language would have to do, if such forms as *yes'r* and *yes'm* were for the first time brought under his notice. He would first have to trace them back, historically, as far as possible, to their more original types, and if he discovered their connection with *yes sir*, and *yes ma'm*, he would point out how such contractions were likely to spring up in a vulgar dialect. After having traced back the *yesr* and *yesm* of the free African negroes to the idiom of their former American masters, the etymologist would next inquire how such phrases as *yes sir* and *yes madam* came to be used on the American continent. Finding nothing analogous in the dialects of the aboriginal inhabitants of America, he would be led by a mere comparison of words, to the languages of Europe, and here again, first to the language of England. Even if no historical documents had been preserved, the documents of language would show that the white master, whose language the ancestors of the free Africans adopted during their servitude, came originally from England; and within certain limits it would even be possible to fix the time when the English language was first transplanted to America. That language must have passed, at least, the age of Chaucer before it migrated to the New World; for, Chaucer has two affirmative particles—*yea* and *yes*; and he distinguishes between the two. He uses *yes* only in answer to negative questions. For instance, in answer to *does he not go?* he would say *yes*. In all other cases Chaucer uses *yea*. To a question, *does he go?* he would say *yea*. He observes the same distinction between *no* and *nay*, the former being used as the negative, the latter after all other questions. This distinction became obsolete soon after Sir Thomas More, and it must have become obsolete before phrases such as *yes sir* and *yes madam*, could have assumed their stereotyped character.

"But there is still more historical information to be gained from the phrases. The word *yes*, is Anglo-Saxon, the same as the German *ja*, and it therefore reveals the fact that the white master of the American slaves who crossed the Atlantic after the time of Chaucer, had crossed the Channel at a still earlier period, after leaving the continental fatherland of the Angles and Saxons. The words *Sir* and *Madam*, tell us still more. They are Norman words, and they could only have been imposed on the Anglo Saxons of Britain by Norman conquerors. They tell us more than this. For these Normans or North-men spoke originally a Teutonic dialect, closely allied to Anglo-Saxon, and in that dialect words such as *Sir* and *Madam* could never have sprung up. We may conclude, therefore that, previous to the Norman conquest, the Teutonic North-men must have made a sufficiently long stay in one of the Roman provinces to forget their own and adopt the language of the Roman Provincials.

"We may now trace back the Norman *Madam* to the French *Madame*, and we recognise in this a corruption of the Latin *Meadomina*, my mistress. *Domina* was changed into *Domna, Donna*, and *Dame*; and the same word *Dame* was also used as a masculine in the sense of *Lord*, as a corruption of *Domino, Domno*, and *Donno*. The temporal lord ruling as ecclesiastical *seigneur* under the bishops, was called a Vidame, as the *Vidame of Chartres*. The French interjection *Dame*! has no connection with a similar exclamation in English, but it simply means, Lord! *Dame-Dieu* in old French is Lord God. A derivation of *Domina* Mistress, was *Dominicella*, which became *demoiselle* and *damsel*. The masculine *dame* for *Domine*, Lord, was afterwards replaced by the Latin *senior*, a translation of the German *elder*. This word *elder* was a title of honour, and we have it still both in *alder*man, and in what is originally the same, the English *earl*, the Norse *jarl*, a comparative analogous to the Anglo-Saxon *ealdor*.

"This title, *senior*, meaning originally older, was but rarely applied to ladies as a title of honour. *Senior*, was changed into *seigneur*, *seigneur* into *sciur*, and *sieur* soon dwindled down to *sir*.

"Thus we see how in two short phrases, as *yesr* and *yesm* long chapters of history might be read. If a general destruction of books, such as took place in China under the Emperor *Thsin-chi-ho-ang-ti* (213, B.C.), should sweep away all historical documents, language, even in its most depraved state, would preserve the secrets of the past, and would tell future generations of the home and migrations of their ancestors from the East to the West-Indies.

It is well worthy of the student's attention to note the words in the last paragraph, that in two short phrases, *yesr* and *yesm*, long chapters of history *might* be read. In point of fact long chapters of history are read in the monuments found in words continuously furnished by the science of comparative philology. Irish supplies a large share.

Whitley Stokes, M.D., edited in 1860 for the Irish Archaeological and Celtic Society a work styled *Irish Glosses*—a mediæval tract of Latin declension M.S., copied in the year 1500, but written many years anterior to that date. In the preface to that work, the learned editor asks the question.

"Some persons may ask why should the Irish Archæological Society expend its funds in publishing a document which merely illustrates the Irish language? Let such persons try to understand that every contribution to a more accurate knowledge of the Irish language is ultimately a contribution to Irish history. Moreover, immediate results of high historical importance may be obtained by comparison of the words and forms of the Irish with those of the other Indo-European languages. Chronicles may lie, and often do; laws may be the work of a despot; romances may represent the manners and morals of their readers or hearers; but the evidence given by words and forms is conclusive evidence of the habitat, the intellectual attainments, the social condition of the Aryan family before the Keltic sisters journeyed to the West; evidence of the period—evidence of the relative connection between the Kelts and other Aryan races after the separation."

Comparative philology is a pillar tower of light on the highway of ancient history. It is like photography: nay, it is a stereoscope of past and forgotten events. Under its view the hidden periods of the past are flung out in the fulness of their reality, and in the light which clothed their forms in the days of their actual existence.

CHAPTER VIII.

Stating the position: what has been proved. Certainty of a Primæval Tongue. Irish-Gaelic of Eastern Origin: European Languages Sisters of the same family. Before the dispersion from the cradle land in Persia and Armenia, the Aryan tongue became divided into Low-Aryan, or the primitive speech; and High-Aryan, or the secondary speech. Proofs. (12) Latin, Gaelic, Sanscrit, Umbrian, present a certain sameness of primitive phonetic power, which points to one primæval type, namely, Low-Aryan. Greek, British, or Welsh, Zend, and Oscan, present certain features of secondary phonetic power which point out to the philosophic enquirer that they must have sprung from some early affected source, namely, High Aryan. Proofs. This is the Author's opinion; it is now, for the first time, put forth. (13) Another new view. That Irish-Gaelic in its plastic power and phonetic fecundity possesses, like the parent Aryan tongue, not only the virtual, but the formal germinal developements of dialectic variety. Proofs. (14) Of all the daughter languages from the Aryan, Irish-Gaelic comes nearest in this respect to the primitive mother tongue. (15) Slurring over consonants. (16) The vowel sound in certain cognate radical words is long in Irish-Gaelic. In sister tongues the lingual-dental letter "n" is inserted to fix the quantity. The Author's view. (17) In facility of forming words to express new ideas; in its capability of producing compounds, Irish-Gaelic ranks in the highest place.

The proofs presented in the preceding chapters, and the learned views and grave opinions of those scholars who at the present day are most distinguished for their knowledge of languages, and for their acquaintance with the science of comparative philology, cannot fail to imbue the mind of the reader with the certainty, that there had been a primæval tongue now known by the name Aryan ; and that all the languages of Europe and those of India and Persia have, like branches from a parent plant, sprouted forth from that venerable tree of pre-historic speech.

"That there was such a period," when the Aryan language flourished, "we can doubt as little as we can doubt the real existence of fern forests previous to the formation of our coal fields." These are the words of one of England's greatest linguistic scholars, F. Max Müller, M.A., Professor of Comparative Philology at Oxford. And he adds : "We can do even more. Suppose we had no remnant of Latin ; suppose the very existence of Rome and of Latin were unknown to us, we might still prove, on the evidence of the six Romance dialects, that there must have been a time when these dialects formed the language of a small settlement ; nay, by collecting the words which all these dialects share in common, we might, to a certain extent, reconstruct the original language, and draw a sketch of the state of civilization as reflected by these common words." Again : "In this manner the whole or nearly the whole grammatical framework of the Aryan or Indo-European languages has been traced back to original independent words. This process is what is called comparative grammar, or a scientific analysis of all the formal elements of a language preceded by a comparison of all the varieties, which one and the same form has assumed in the numerous dialects of the Aryan family. After the grammatical terminations of all these languages have been traced back to their most primitive forms, it is possible to determine their original meaning." Pages 271, 272, 273, *The Science of Language*, vol. I., Longmans, Green & Co., London, 1873.

The science of comparative philology has clearly and firmly established three great facts; (1) that, as Pictet well observes, there had been spoken in Armenia and Persia, above two thousand years before the Christian era, "at a period anterior to every historic development," a primæval language admirable for its richness, its vigour, its harmony, and the perfection of its forms; a language which was likely to foreshadow in its own features, naturally and without effort, not only all the impressions affecting it, its nice shades of form and thought, but also its tendency upwards towards a sphere higher still; a language full of images, clear and seen at a glance; a language bearing in its infant state all the future wealth which was to be developed by a magnificent, practical expansion in the region of poetry the most elevated, as well as of thought the most profound. This is the language, at first one and the same stock, that served as the common medium of inter-communication among the people of this primitive race, as long as they did not extend beyond the limits of their own country. (2) That new forms of that language had been wafted, at the very earliest period, southward across the Ganges, and westward by the Ister, the Rhine, the Rhone, the Tagus, the Severn, and the Shannon. (3) That the Keltic tongue, of which Irish-Gaelic is the living leading dialect, had been borne by the very earliest emigrants to the north of Italy and onward to Iberia or Spain, and to the south or west of Gaul, and to Eire, where the vanguard of emigrants had been forced by the onward march of those myriad migrations that followed.

"The Kelts seem to have been the first of the Aryans to arrive in Europe; but the pressure of subsequent migrations, particularly of Teutonic tribes, has driven them towards the western parts."—*The Science of Languages.*

One must bear in mind, however, that emigrants in the remote past acted rationally and naturally in their march, much in the same way as emigrants act at the present day. The people of a province or of a district do not go all at once *en masse*, as it is said, to a country. When natives of Ireland or of Scotland emigrate now-a-days to America, they do not all go in one year, nor do they all go to the same special spot. So it was in the days when emigrants came from Asia to Europe.

It is equally true that those who have lived in the same district, country, province, in the old home, in the new home love to dwell together. Inhabitants from the west of Ireland cling to each other when they go across the Atlantic and seek for themselves a home in the lands of free America.

As a rule, too, those that are weakest are forced to the west ; it is also true that the latest comers, if few, are forced to seek the farthest-off lands. All this, which is true at the present day, had been equally true in the days of early Keltic migrations to Europe. The circumstances differ ; but the code of principles that have guided mankind in their acts, adventures, and pursuits in life have never changed. Again, the words of Max Müller on this point are apt. He connects what happened four thousand years ago with that which is going on before our eyes at present, and hesitates not to put the emigration of the Aryan from his land of Iran to his new home in Eirin, and the emigration of the Irishman to his new home in America, on a par in the same sentence. "The pressure of subsequent migrations, particularly of Teutonic tribes, has driven the Kelts towards the westernmost parts, *and latterly from Ireland across the Atlantic.*"

The early migration from the cradle-land of the human race took its rise long before Thare, the father of Abraham, brought his son, and Lot his son's son, and Sarai his daughter-in-law, the wife of Abram, his son, out of Ur of the Chaldees, to go to the land of Chanaan. They came only as far as Haran " in Armenia," and dwelt there. Westward was the cry before Abram was desired by God to go out of his country, and from his kindred, and from his father's house to a land which he would be shewn, the land of promise for him and his seed; nay, before Misraim colonised Ægypt, before the cities of Thebes and Memphis were founded. The inspired author of the Pentateuch hints at the time when the earth was of one tongue and of the same speech. And when they removed from the East they found a plane in the land of Sanaar. The tower had not been built. Even then the Keltic migration commenced. The question regarding the confusion of tongues is not one that comes within reach of the science of comparative philology. The field of investigation respecting it remains untouched, for there are other primitive tongues besides the Aryan. A. W. Schlegel and Bopp point to languages of monosyllabic roots not capable of entering into composition, and others capable; then, there is the Semitic speech with roots of two syllables. The path pursued in this work is that pointed out and illumined by the light that flows from the lamp which the science of comparative philology holds before the student's eyes. The Irish-Gaelic language, in connexion with the primitive Aryan speech, is the special subject which, in these pages, engages the writer's attention.

TWELFTH—A TWO-FOLD TONGUE.

Regarding the Aryan speech, he states (1) that before the people who spoke that primæval tongue had commenced to emigrate, a difference of dialect had arisen. That favoured region in which the Aryans dwelt, along the fertile valleys, through which the rising waters of the rivers Euphrates and Tigris, and the ancient Araxes and Cyrus flow, was encompassed on the north, east, south, and west, by ranges of mountains, with Ararat in the centre, standing up like a giant figure keeping watch over the surrounding hills. As soon as the rich lowlands had been peopled, the long ranges of land on the mountain sides offered a home and a healthful abode to those who had been forced from the valleys by the ever-increasing population.

It soon came to pass that those living in the highlands of Armenia, and in the mountain ranges to the south and east, as far as Herat and Hindoo-Koosh, began to speak the language of their fathers with a new tone and accent, brought about by the change of location and accident of climate and new domestic and social relations.

That this dialectical difference arose, scholars distinguished in the field of comparative philology assert. "The mountaineers spoke," says Donaldson, "a harder and and a bolder dialect." The Aryan tongue was split into two dialects, known by the name Low-Aryan and High-Aryan. The Low-Aryan was the older or primitive tongue; the High-Aryan, the younger, or that which had been formed by accent and dialectic mutation from the mother tongue. The fact is proved plainly from the effects to this day publicly stamped on the languages of the Aryan races. Irish-Gáelic, Sanscrit, Latin, the early Sabine speech, or Umbrian, bear the impress of the unaffected, primitive, original language of their Lowland Aryan progenitors; while Welsh, Zend, Greek and Oscan point to the affected, derivative, dialectic character of the language spoken by the Aryan inhabitants of the mountains, who, at a far-off period, had, in all probability, been their common primitive progenitors.

How is this seen? Hear Professor Geddes once more:—

PROOF.—SANSCRIT, LATIN, GAELIC *versus* ZEND, GREEK, WELSH.

How nearly allied the sounds of "s" and "h" are is noticeable in the speech of certain children. Some of them have difficulty in enunciating the initial "s." I happen to know a child just now who says regularly "hault" for salt. "Give me home hault;" "haumon" for salmon," and the like. She is following in such words the example of the early Greeks, Welsh, and Persians. A few instances may suffice—

LATIN.	GAELIC.	WELSH.	GREEK.
sal	salann	halen	hals.
senex	sean-aos	hěn	henos.
somnus	suain	hyn	hypnos.
sedes	suidh	heddu	hedos
salix	saileog	helig	helix.
sol	solus	heul	helios.

Or, than which no better example could be found, the adjective—*like*, "samail."

similis	samail	havail	homoios.
"	so, or su, *easy*		eu
"	do, *difficulty*		dus
sic	so, sin	hyn	ho, hěh

From the *College Irish Grammar, p.* 89, the following table of the numerals is copied. It illustrates the close early relationship between Latin, Irish-Gaelic, and Sanskrit, and between Greek and Welsh:

What a very close affinity exists among the several early branches of the great Aryan family of languages may be well perceived from a list of numerals in the several languages:

Symbol	Latin	Irish-Gaelic	Welsh	Greek
1	unum	aon	un	hen
2	duae } duo }	dá } do }	dau } dwy }	duo
3	{ tres { tria	trí	trí	tres } tria }
4	{ quatuor { *qu*=*c*, or *k*,	ceaṫar	pedwar	pisur petor
5	quinq*ue*	cuig	pump	pempe
6	se*x*	sé	chwech	hex
7	sept*em*	seaċt	saith	hepta
8	oct*o*	oċt	wyth	okto
9	nov*em*	naoi, pr. *nhwee*	naw	ennea
10	dec*em*	deiċ	deg	deka
20	viginti	fiċe	ugain	ficate
100	centum	ceud	cant	hékaton

Pisur, *petor*, Greek for four, *pempe*, for five, are Æolic, for *tessares*, four, *pente*, five ; also *ficate* for the common *eikosi*, twenty.

Teutonic	Sanscrit	Zend
ein	eka	yak
tue	dwau	dú
thri	tri	sih
fiuuar	chatur	chahár
finfe	pancha	panj
sehs	shash	shash
sibun	saptan	haft
ohto	ashta	hasht
niguni	navan	nuh
tehan	dasan	dah
tuentig	vinsati	bist
hunt	satam	sad

"All this (history developed by philology) and even more, may be read in the vast archives of languages. The very name of India has a story to tell ; for India is not a native name. We have it from the Romans, the Romans from the Greeks, the Greeks from the Persians.

And why from the Persians? Because it is only in Persian (Zend) that an initial "s" is changed into "h," which initial "h" was as usual dropped in Greek. It is only in Persia that the country of Sindhu (Sindhu is the Sanscrit name for *river*), or of the *seven* Sindhus could have been called Hindia or India instead of Sindia. Unless the followers of Zoroaster had pronounced every "s" like "h," we should never have heard of the West Indies."—*Science of Language*, *p.* 265, *vol.* I.

The foregoing are only a few examples. It would be out of place to fill those pages with a fuller list.

The reader will perceive that the natives of Hindostan who spoke Sanscrit, a branch of the Aryan speech retained the "s" and its sound; whilst the ancient natives of Persia omitted the "s" or "f," and retained its affected sound, that of "h." The Latins, and before them, the Umbrians and Sabines, and those who dwelt in the north of Italy, retained the "s" and its sound, whilst the Greeks and those who, like the Oscans* dwelt in the south of Italy, rejected it. To this day the Gaels of Ireland and of the Highlands of Scotland, retain the "s" and its sound; the Welsh reject it in words which are, amongst the two peoples, employed to convey the same idea and to express the same thought. Can this uniformity of effect arise from chance, or from a cause? If from a cause, that cause must have existed before the Greeks came to the Peloponessus; before Athens was

---

* "Oscan sides with Greek and Welsh; Umbrian with Latin and Gaelic. The Sabine race were a branch of the Umbrians." —*Regal Rome, by Francis W. Newman, p.* 3. *London: Taylor. Walton, and Maberly*, 1852.

Again, on actually comparing the Latin vocabulary with that of the Greeks, Germans, and Kelts, a far closer similarity to the Kelts shows itself.—*Idem*, *p.* 4.

founded by Cecrops; before the foundation of Argos, or Mycenæ, with its broad ways, was laid.

The earliest population of both Italy and Greece was Irish-Gaelic. The Pelasgian emigrants were Low-Aryan; those in northern Italy were Low-Aryan, and, therefore, from the same stock as the Irish-Gaelic. After the Pelasgic, the next shoal of emigrants were High-Aryan, the progenitors of the Hellenes, or Greeks of Homer's time.

"The only point," says Newman, "left uncertain, is whether the oldest Latin itself, or only some of its affluents, was the Keltic influence. The Sabines used a vocabulary which was akin to the Gaelic.

"Nor, in fact, of all the Indo-European tongues," says he, (p. 19, *Regal Rome*,) "has one so near a likeness to the Latin as the Gaelic has.

"The argument appears to be unassailable, except by admitting a relation so close between the oldest Latin and the Keltic as to imply a recent divergency from a common stock."

Latin and Gaelic and Sanscrit are certainly from the older stock of the Aryan tongue, because they retain in the initial forms of the words of those languages the primitive, radical consonants ("s" or "t" or "f") and their sounds; whilst Greek, and Welsh, and Zend must have sprung from the Aryan tongue spoken in the mountain regions; because all these languages have not the natural or primitive sound, but only the affected and secondary form, and its symbol "h" in the commencement of terms apparently primitive.

From the foregoing statements and proof the following conclusions can fairly be drawn:—

(1) That all the European tongues came from the Aryan is certain, just as the six Romance languages of Europe have sprung from the Latin.

(2) That Irish-Gaelic, Latin and Sanscrit have come direct from Low-Aryan is equally certain.

(3) It is not certain, however, but it is probable in the highest degree, from the reasons just given, that Welsh and Greek and Zend came direct from the High Aryan, or the dialect spoken in the mountains of Armenia and Persia.

The writer says, " probable in the highest degree, but not certain ;" because some scholars in the field of comparative philology are of opinion that Greek and Welsh had had the initial " s " at one time in those words from which, at a later period this letter was omitted. Geddes writes, " There is reason to believe that the use of ' h,' for the initial ' s,' is, at any rate, in Welsh, of later development. In the Greek tongue we can trace a kind of conflict going on, which sometimes resulted in the retention of two forms, one with ' s,' the other with the aspirate ' h,' as *hus* [a boar] in Greek, and also *sus*, like the Latin *sus*. So in Welsh it seems probable that ' s ' had once occupied a similar position where now ' h ' appears. The great river encircling their country on the east, which they now call *Hefren*, would appear to have been pronounced by the ancient Britons with an ' s,' when the Romans took their *Sabrina*, and we our ' Severn."—*Lecture*, p. 13.

But this particular instance would prove nothing against the truth of the main proposition respecting the Welsh language, for the inter-communication between the Irish Gaels and Cambro-Britons was so frequent that the latter may have borrowed some primitive terms from the Gael, or may have adopted for some special reason the Gaelic sound and name. Charles Mackay, LL.D., in his new work, *The Gaelic Etymology—London, Trubner*, 1875, writes :—" Three branches of the Keltic language were spoken by the British people prior to the Roman, Saxon and Danish invasions—the Kymric or Welsh; and the Gaelic spoken, to this day, in the Highlands of Scotland, in the Isle of Man, and Ireland, and formerly *spoken in the greater part of England.* Gaelic was the language of the Britons at an early period." Dr. Prichard in his *Eastern Origin of the Keltic Nations*, 2nd edition, p. 187, tells us that Edward Lhuyd, too, held this opinion; and he tacitly insinuates that it is his own. He remarks: "It was observed by Edward Lhuyd, that 'h' is never the first, or proper initial of any word in the Irish language, but that words beginning with 'f' or with 's' change, according to the laws of permutation peculiar to this dialect, that initial into 'h.' Hence he (Lhuyd) infers that these words in their primitive form began with 'f,' or 's,' or 't'; and that cognate words which begin with 'h' in other languages *have lost their proper initial.* In like manner some Greek words now beginning with an aspirate have lost an originae digamma (f), while others, *hepta* and *hex*, corresponding with *septem* and *sex* in Latin, and with *sapta* and *shash* in Sanscrit, have lost an initial "s.'"

Herodotus, styled, justly, "The Father of History," writes that the ancient inhabitants of Greece, the Pelasgi, spoke a language which appeared foreign to the Hellenic races of later times. He says they spoke a barbarous tongue, "barbaron tén glossan hientes,"—that is, a tongue which the Hellenists did not speak. We know, too, from Homer, that the Helli who dwelt about Dodona, were called *Selli*, or *Helli*; so were the Helli of Thessaly styled *Selli.* This primary sound of "s," instead of its secondary or aspirate "h," employed by the Greeks at a later period, had been retained from the early Pelasgic settlers, the Greeks before Homer's time.

In this way, the use of "s," in its primitive state, can be accounted for as existing in some few, very few, words in Greek and the language of the Cambro-Britons.

"Thus, the Welsh," continues Dr. Prichard, "as well as the Greek language, drops the "s" or the "f" entirely and substitutes the aspirate in words which originally had either "s" or "f" for their initial; while in the Irish the aspirate is still used as a regular inflection of words properly beginning, and retaining, (with aspirate mark, when required,) the "s, or f, or t."—p. 191.

EXAMPLES.

The writer takes up *Spurrell's Welsh Dictionary*, and looking over the columns of words beginning with initial "h," he sees, at a glance, that most of them are affected Gaelic terms; the only difference apparent is that the initial letter has the secondary sound, and not the primary. The following, with their derivative and compound forms, make up at least two hundred words. Primitive terms, for the most part, have been selected for insertion here :—

Welsh	Irish-Gaelic
halen, *salt*	salan
hallt, *salted*	sailte
haliu, *saliva, spittle*	seile
haliwio, *to salivate*	seiluġaḋ
Halog, v., *defile*	saluiġ
halogi, v., *to defile*	saluġaḋ
halogwr, *one who soils or spoils*	salaċóir
hanes, *old stories*	seanaċas
hanesai, *a story-teller*	seanaċaiḋ
hanesel, *full of stories*	seanaċaṁail
hanesgan, *an epic poem*	seanaċais dán
haneswr, *a recorder of stories*	seanasoir
haf, *summer*	saṁ
havail, *like*	saṁail

haid, *a swarm*	scaoṫ
hawddfod, *a state of ease*	sostad
hedd, *peace*	sıṫ
helyg, *willow*	saıleog
hen, *old*	sean *(pr. shan)*
elistir, *flag weed*	selıstır
heul, *sun, light*	sol, *sun;* solus
hil, *seed*	sıol
holht, *cleft*	scoılt
hir, *of long duration*	síor
hin, *that* (pronoun)	sın *(pr. shin)*
hinon, *fair weather*	soınean
hun, *sleep*	suan
hé, hó (per. pronouns)	sé, *he;* so, *this*
hebóg, *a hawk*	seabaċ
helá, *hunting*	sealga
helliwr, *a hunter*	sealgaıre
helva, *herd*	sealḃ
helw, *possession*	seılḃ
hesg, *dry, barren*	seasg
hwth, *thrust*	saıṫ
hwyl, *sail*	seol

Irish Gaelic presents the fullest and clearest impress of its parent prototype—the Aryan language.

In its plastic power and phonetic fecundity, Irish-Gaelic possesses, like its primitive Aryan parent tongue, not only the virtual but the formal germinal developments of dialectic variety.

This proposition will sound strange to the ears of many. They will be inclined to say—such speech is pretty much like what poets and Irish patriotic adventurers spout regarding the "Green Isle." The natives are ever boasting of the antiquity of their family genealogy. Every "O" and "Mac" traces his parentage not only up to Noah, but to Adam. They were before every other people; and they speak a language, as some of their writers say, that

Adam and Eve spoke in Paradise. Hear Professor Blackie :—

" A deal of nonsense was talked about the antiquity of Gaelic. It was said to be the oldest language in the world ; as old as Hebrew, and perhaps older. This was said in all soberness in a Gaelic poem by the famous Allister MacDonald, in praise of the Gaelic tongue.

> Si labhair Adhamh a b-parrthas féin
> S'ba snasmhar Gaelig a m-beul aluin Eabha.

And again—

> Och tí chaill agus tí uireasbha gan í,
> Gloir gach—a labhradh caint acht í.

Which means—

> This tongue Sire Adam spoke, believe
> In Paradise ; and this
> Flowed from the lips of sinless Eve.

" They know, however, that the Gaels were one of the earliest peoples who had come from the East, and that they brought with them their language, which, of course, would be at least 4,000 years old. But what was the use of talking so much about the language ? Was it like wine—was it always the better the longer it was kept ? Or was wine even always the better the longer it was kept ? He doubted that very much. He did not see what good could be done to Gaelic merely to say that it was the oldest language under the sun. Philologists did not know anything about the comparative antiquity of languages as a whole.. Taking Greek, Sanscrit, Latin, or Gaelic, they could not say, as a whole, that the one was older than the other. They could, however, say that one had certain forms which were certainly older, according to well-known principles of philology. They could not say that Sanscrit was the mother of Greek. They could only say that these two languages were two sisters ; and so he said that Latin and Gaelic were two sisters, and also sisters of Greek."—*Speech delivered at a grand Keltic conversazione, Edinburgh, in the Museum of Science and Art*, 1872.

The writer is of the same opinion as Professor Blackie. A deal of nonsense has been spoken and written about the antiquity of Irish-Gaelic. Numbers of our simple people say the wildest things regarding it; that it is older than Hebrew; that is the language spoken in Paradise. All this is dreamy nonsense.

It is no use to talk of its great antiquity, to which, undoubtedly, it can lay just claim. It is at least four thousand years old. Its early rise dates from the period when Abram removed from Haran to Sichem, or Bethel; when the great Pyramid was built. That is antiquity quite sufficient. Workers are wanted; thinkers are wanted; literary aid is required. Few or none are ready to do any practical work, though spouters abound, praising Irish-Gaelic, yet doing nothing either to retain it in life or to strengthen its decaying existence.

Professor Blackie says, further:—"What was the lineage and kinship of the Gaelic language? In 1830 it was regularly admitted to be a real orthodox, full-blooded member of the great Aryan or Indo-European family of languages, in which year Prichard published his book on the subject.

"Originally the Aryan tongue was the language of the leading classes on the high table-land of Persia, who at length divided—one half (at different periods) going east into Hindostan, and the other west into Europe. Gaelic, therefore, as the earliest in her migration westwards, was one of the oldst branches of this ancient family."—*Ibid.*

That Irish-Gaelic, in its plastic power and phonetic fecundity, possesses not only the virtual but the formal germinal developments of dialectic variety, is a proposition that can, as the writer says, be readily proved by means of a little knowledge of the science of comparative philology.

Proof:—The Aryan tongue is declared to have been a potent agent in *the process of developement*; a language admirable for its richness, its vigour, its harmony, and the perfection of its forms. Again, that it had been such as it has been here described is proved by its effects. How are the perfections of a cause known? From the perfections of its effects. Witness the varied perfections of the Greek, Latin, Gaelic, British; of the Zend and Sanscrit. It was from the Aryan tongue, as from a fountain, these perfections were derived. It was potent in its process of development. It produced the High Aryan. It gave to the East the Sanscrit; to the West, all the European tongues. Such was the Aryan.

How is Irish-Gaelic like to it? First, in its varied phonetic power. Second, in its stems of one syllable; third, in its power of combination and of efformating new terms to express factitious ideas. In these striking features Irish-Gaelic appears to present a strong resemblance to its parent prototype.

(1) Greek has only one phonetic law, one conduit of articulate sound, which admits, of course, a variety of notes, yet, still all these notes are only one in their phonetic identity. The same is true of Latin, and of British, or Welsh, of Zend and of Sanscrit, of German, too, and of Lithuanian and the rest of the Indo-European tongues. No doubt, the sounds of consonants are not always the same when terms of cognate meaning are turned from one language to serve in another. Yet, for all that, it is true to say that in each specific speech, the sounds of the consonants and vowels are uniform, and that this unifor-

mity proceeds from a simple principle of phonetic sameness. Does this singleness of sound exist in Irish-Gaelic? By no means, as shall be shewn.

THIRTEENTH—The terms formal and virtual, as understood in the foregoing paragraphs, are best explained by examples:

An example of formal germinal developement is presented in an egg having a double yolk fecundated; in a nut with two kernels; in a uterus with several distinct embryos.

An example of virtual developement is seen in a ray of light, which, single and simple, possesses the power of producing, by passing through a pellucid prism, all the colours of the rainbow.

Each consonant in Gaelic has four formally distinct sounds. Every Gaelic speaker is aware that, in the speech of the Gael, the consonants all, except "l, n, r," receive, in certain instances, and in the same sentence, owing to their position or to their connexion in composition, a secondary or affected sound, as well as a primary or natural sound. For instance, the affected sound of "b" and of "m" is "v" or "w;" of "p," "ph;" of "c," "ch" (guttural); of "s," "h," of "t," "h," and "f," at times "h," otherwise silent, of "d" "dh," "th," naturally, and its affected sounds are guttural; "g," too, has a secondary sound. The terms "sagart," a priest; or "salan," salt, are "sagart," "salan," with "s" having a "ss" sound; or "halan," with "h" sound, that is the aspirate. Both sounds are in the very same sentence, as "Is mait an salan mo ṡalan-sa," it is good salt, my salt. The possessive pronoun "mo,' causes the sound of "s" before which it is placed, to become affected; and thus, the natural sound of "s" is changed into its affected or secondary sound of "h." In this way Irish-Gaelic possesses, at the same time, in the same sentence, *two formal sounds of the consonan's.* Welsh presents only one; Greek, one; Latin, one; German, one. Bear in mind, still further: in Irish-Gaelic, as shall be shewn, *each* consonant receives a slender sound and a broad sound—each of which differs, as much as a flat in music from a sharp. Thus, each consonant spoken has in the same sentence four formal articulate developements. These are easily learned by ear.

To illustrate this point clearly, let an example be taken. For instance, the consonant "b" in the word "bord," a table; and in the term "bean," a woman, "b" before "a, o, u," has a broad sound, as in the word *broad* itself; and a slender sound before "e" or "i"—(see c. x in this vol). The sound of "b" in "bean," is called slender or sharp; that which it receives when sounded in union with "a, o, u," broad or flat. Again, if the possessive pronoun "mo," my, go before the term "bord," the broad sound of "b" becomes affected or aspirate, and receives the sound of "w;" but if it precedes the word "bean," the affected sound of "b" in "bean" is that of "v." Hence there are two natural sounds of "b," flat and sharp; and two affected or aspirate sounds—

(1) "bord," table, (flat, natural.)
(2) "bean," a woman, (sharp, and natural.)
(3) "mo ḃord," my table, "w" or affected flat sound.
(4) "mo ḃean," "v" or affected sharp sound.

To a foreign ear a fourfold formal articulation is presented in the sound of one consonant "b;" to the uneducated Irish, and to Irishmen of learning, speaking Irish, but not schooled to a knowledge of its written or phonetic forms, this varying articulate value of "b" appears single and unchangeable. The peasantry are, as it were, naturally familiar, from infancy, with the modulated sounds of the same letter in altered relations, just as the ear of a singer is attuned to the air of a song. Hence, to learn Irish, it is necessary to hear it spoken, and to be for a time conversing with those who speak it,

Manx Gaelic is phonetic Irish. In Manx, one form of the varying sounds of the consonants was adopted, and the words have been spelled accordingly. In Manx the radical primitive in many terms, those beginning with "b, m, f, t," has been lost.* Thus, it was in times primæ-

NOTE—Example: The verb "to be," in Irish, is, in the interrogative form, "fuil," as, am I, "ḃ-fuil me?" The initial radical "f," is eclipsed by a softer sound "v," expressed in Irish by "ḃ" (aspirated) thus:—

Singular.

ḃ-fuil me,	*am I,*	pr. will me
ḃ-fuil tu,	*art thou,*	will thoo.
ḃ-fuil se,	*is he,*	will sheh.

Plural.

ḃ-fuil sinn,	*are we,*	will shin.
ḃ-fuil siḃ,	*are you,*	will shiv.
ḃ-fuil siad,	*are they,*	will sheeath.

What is the verb "fuilim" in Manx? It is—

	Singular.		Plural.	
"Vel"—as	Vel me,	*am I,*	Vel shiu,	*are we.*
	Vel oo,	*art thou.*	Vel shiu,	*are you.*
	Vel eh,	*is he.*	Vel ad,	*are they.*

Manx: vel oo rea, *art thou ready.*
Irish: ḃ-fuil tu réid, *art thou ready.*
Manx: ta me rea, *I am ready.*
Irish: tá me réid, *I am ready.*

Take the following piece, written in Manx. It relates to the first King of Man, *Manannan-beg-mac-y-Lheirr.* The date assigned to the piece is 1504. Who the author was is unknown, but the honour of being the first Manx poet is awarded to him. It seemingly relates to Magnus the Northman, who about the beginning of the 11th century ravaged Man and Anglesea, and made his son king over the Manx, having first obtained for him to wife, "with good grace," the daughter of Murchath, "chief man of Ireland:"

MANX.

1.

Manannan beg va Mac y Leirr
Shen yn chied er ec row rieau ee;
Agh myr share oddym's cur-my-n-er,
Cha row eh hene agh An-chreestee.

val, the Zend, Greek, Oscan, Welsh, adopted one form of the Aryan mother tongue; Sanscrit, Latin, Umbrian, Irish-Gaelic, retained the other, which had been unaffected by change.

This inherent power is certainly a potent agent for a process of developement. Irish-Gaelic is admirable for

---

2.

Cha nee lesh a Chliwe ren eh ee reayll
Cha nee lesh e Hideyn, ny lesh e Vhow;
Agh tra aikagh eh Lhuingys troailt
Oallagh eh ee, ny geayrt lesh Kay.

3.

Yinnagh eh Doinney ny hassoo er Brooghe
Er-lhieu shen heno dy beagh ayn Keead;
As shen myr dreill Manannan keoie
Yn Ellan shoh'n ayn lesh cosney Bwoid.

The foregoing stanzas are here rendered into modern Irish by the present writer:

I.

Manannan beag ḃı mac an Leır
Sın an ċeud-ḟear aıg a raıḃ 'rıaṁ ı;
Aċt mar ṡe ıs feárr feıdım-se ċur mıan' aır
Nı raıḃ ṡe feın aċt an-ċrıostaıḋ.

II.

Cıḋ nı leıs a cloıḋeaṁ rınn' se ı rıgaıl
Cıḋ nı leıs a ṡoıgıdean,' nı leıs a ḃoga;
Aċt traṫ feıcfeaḋ se luıngıs a' trıalt
Falloċaḋ se ı, a g-cuaırt, leıs ċeo.

III.

Déanfaḋ se duıne 'nn a ṡeasaḋ aır ḃruaċ
Aır leıṫ sın féın do ḃeıṫ aon ċeud
Is sın mar do rıagaıl Manannan cutaċ,
An oılean so, ann aon leıs cosnaḋ buaıḋ.

A literal English version of the Manx and of the Irish just presented above:—

Little Manannan was son of Leirr; he was the first that ever had it (the island); but, as I am able to conceive best regarding him, he himself was a non-christian.

It was not with the sword he ruled over it, neither with arrows or bow, but whenever he would see ships sailing, he would cover it round with a fog.

its richness, its vigour, its harmony, its unaffected roots. Hence, Irish-Gaelic presents the fullest and clearest impress of its parent prototype—the Aryan language.

FOURTEENTH.—SLURRING OVER CONSONANTS.

Owing to the real inherent power possessed, in Irish-Gaelic, by the consonants, of producing phonetic variety, at one time sounded naturally and fully; at another, changed into sounds of secondary value, or not sounded

---

He would set a man standing on a hill apart appear as if he were a hundred; and thus did wild Manannan rule that island along with defending its superiority.

In this passage, the reader cannot fail to perceive that the language spoken in the Isle of Man is Irish-Gaelic, written according to sound.

An Irish song penned by a student from words dictated by a peasant who has had the stanzas by rote, lies on the desk before the writer. It could be printed and published as Manx. A copy of Pittman's pamphlet lies on the table, written in English of course, but spelled on the principle of phonetics, of which he is the great advocate in England. To any person not knowing English, the language, as published in this pamphlet must appear quite foreign from every tongue that ever sprung from its parent Anglo-Saxon. English written phonetically appears a new language. Such is Manx compared to Irish. Just take a few words: "Dı," in Irish has much the same sound that "Dı" has in French, or rather perhaps of "gı" Italian, or of "je," English. The term for God in Irish is "Dıa," pronounced correctly like *Dieu* in French, or commonly and vulgarly *Jeea*; gen. case "Dé," of God. How is it spelled in Manx? Thus, *Jee*, God; as,

Jee-yn-Ayr, God the Father.
Jee-yn-Mac, God the Son.
Jee-yn-Spyrryd Noo, God the Holy Ghost.

The origin, the beauty, the orthographic value, and the philologic worth of the term "Dıa," is lost for ever in Manx. Take another example, which completely destroys the origin of the word. "Dé," of; "dí," for "de ší," of her; "féın," self; "dí féın," of herself. What is it in Manx? *Jee-hene*. Again, "Dıbırt" (Irish), to banish, is written *jeebyrth*. All connexion with the family of terms ("bear," take; "dıṫ," want, away) is utterly broken in *jeebyrth*. So it happens with every word in Irish beginning with "c"; the said "c" is metamorphosed into "k," as "cıall" (pr. *kyail*), sense, is in Manx *keeayll*. "Bala," a wall, *voalley*.

at all, the vocal value of consonants is, at times, likely to be slurred over and lost.

Now, slurring over consonants is a very common process, well known to every classic student. This habit is noticeable, especially in the six Romance languages. French students possessed of any discriminating power, and who have made the language of old Latium, or of Gaul, at any given period, their study, must have observed this gradual falling away of primitive radical sounds of the consonants.

Italian, as a language, Spanish, too, and at an earlier date, French, have come forth from the household of the Latin family. A few words in each are contrasted here, in order that the Keltic trait of phonetic falling away in the power of consonants may be readily perceived :—

Latin.	Italian.	Spanish.	French.	English.
fo*c*us	fuo*c*o	fue*g*o	feu	fire
se*q*ui	se*g*uire	se*g*uir	suivre	follow
pa*t*er	pa*d*re	pa*d*re	pére	father
mater	ma*d*re	madre	mére	mother
frater	frate	frayle friar	frere	brother
soror	sorore	sor.	soeur	sister
obed*i*re	obed*i*re	obe*dec*er	obeir	obey

The words *pere, mere, frere,* and *soeur*, in French, bear no trace of the original "t" in *pater, mater, frater* : or of "r," middle, in *soror*. Can Irish-Gaelic come to the aid of the student in explaining the fact? Yes; the slurring over consonants, and their finally omitting them in spelling, is almost a natural trait of Gaelic speech, although the language of the Gael still adheres to the ancient radical spelling, and still holds fast to, and we trust will continue to hold fast to, the old perfect pronunciation.

The sound of "t," (aspirated) in Irish in the foregoing, is only that of the aspirate "h"—this, in process of time, is readily omitted in sound, and soon, after a time, omitted from the spelling.

The omission of the sound of *ent*, at the end of French verbs is very striking and quite like the slurring which, in Irish takes place in pronouncing "aḋ," or "uġaḋ," final, like "oo" in the present participle, in verbs and in nouns.

FIFTEENTH—THE LOSS OF THE LETTER "P" INITIAL.

This falling off has sprung from a cause cognate to that just explained in the foregoing paragraph. There are a few words in which Irish-Gaelic appears to be in accord with either Greek, or with some primitive speech spoken before the earliest migration from the plains of Persia. These are (1) Irish "aṫaır" *(awhyr)*, father, gen. case "aṫar *(awhur)*, of a father; Latin and Greek *pater*; Hebrew (commencing with "a") *abba;* (2) Irish, "ıasg," *a fish;* Gr. *ichthus*; Latin, *piscis;* (3) Irish "orc," a pig, a prince, diminutive "orcán," urchin, and "orcín," the same; Latin *porcus;* (4) Irish "ıarun," *(eearun)*, iron; Latin *ferrum.* The "f" in Latin is either lost in Irish; or the Latin and Keltic had it not originally; then the Latin in time assumed it; Gaelic did not. Initial "f" and "p" (Latin) are liable to vanish in Irish sometimes n grammatical regimen. So the words "aṫaır," "ıasg," "urcean," are for "pathair" *(pater)*, father; "pıasg" fish; "puırcean" *(porco)*. *Hedo* (Latin) was *fedo* in the Sabine language; so *arena* was *fasena.*

SIXTEENTH—A change takes place in Greek when the sound of "n" or "nt" is followed by a sibilant (s sound). The "n" disappears, and its absence is compensated by making the vowel sound before "n" long. This is a feature well known to classic scholars; for instance, in *titheis*, a participle for *tithent*, from the verb *tithemi*, I put, This classic turn the Irish-Gaelic carries out to the full extent, and beyond even what the classics sanction. The "n" is omitted not only before "s," but before "f," and before the dentals.

Examples.

Mens of *mensis*, month (with s after n) becomes "mís" (Irish) a month.

Cens of census, tax, (s after n) Gaelic "cís," rent (pr. *kees*).

Mens of mensus and mensura becomes "meas" in Gaelic, signifying estimate, esteem, value, respect, regard. Again, before "t" and "d," and "c" or "qu"—

Centum, "t" after "n," a hundred, becomes "ceud."

Vigenti becomes "fícead"; Gr. *eíkosi;* and

Tendo, to stretch, becomes "teud," a cord, a rope.

Dens, a tooth, "deud," the gums.

Quinque, *i.e.*, *cuínce*, five, becomes "cuíc."

In this way the presence of *nt* in Latin and Greek words has been explained by scholars well schooled in the science of comparative philology.

The writer's view of the subject is just the opposite of that taken by his brother philosophers. Why? First, we are certain that Irish is the oldest sister in the Aryan family. Therefore, Irish has not, strictly speaking, formed those words just enumerated above, from Greek or from Latin; nor has it therefore omitted "n" from these words.

The Aryan mother tongue had had "n" in those words, or not; if it had had, then the Irish simply omitted "n," from the Aryan and lengthened the vowel; if it had not had "n," then Irish-Gaelic, in this respect, gives another proof of its wonderful likeness to its parent model. It is the writer's opinion that the letter "n" had not been in the original Aryan mother tongue. And why does he entertain this view? Because he knows that Greek and Zend and Welsh resemble high Aryan more closely than the primitive low Aryan spoken in pre-historic times, in the valleys of Armenia and Persia. He is of opinion that words in those languages possess the secondary rather than the primary forms of the initial consonants. What, then? Nature always endeavours to supply as best she can the deficit caused by a want or defect. To supply, in these instances, for the omission of the initial radical consonants, the words take "n," as "siad," Irish, *personal pronoun*, meaning they or them, and pronounced "sheeath," makes *hwynt* Welsh.. How? The sound of "s" is omitted, or its affected form "h" assumed in its stead; "t" and "w" are the letters which in Welsh express the vocal value of the Irish "d" and "n." Thus, "siad," they, becomes *hwit*, and, to supply for the omission of "s," "n," is inserted before the final consonant, *hwynt*; so "ceud," becomes *cent*, Latin; *ekaton*, Greek; "cuig," five, *quinque*; "teud," is *tendo*; "deud" is *dens, dentis*.

SEVENTEENTH—CAPABILITY OF IRISH-GAELIC OF PRODUCING COMPOUNDS.

The third reason assigned just above for the great family likeness between Irish-Gaelic and its prototype is, that in its plastic power it presents, in a pre-eminent degree, a ready facility for composition and a wonderful adaptability to express fresh or factitious ideas, as they are called, by new combinations of efformatives and preformatives.

What does Zeuss say of its power in this respect? And no scholar living in the present century or in the past knew better than he what the resources of Irish-Gaelic are in this way. He was a thorough master of his native language—the German. Latin and Greek were as familiar to him as his own tongue, for, he wrote in

Latin; and his knowledge of Greek was not inferior to that of his classical acquaintance with the writings of Cicero, and with those of every writer from the days of the poet Livius Andronicus, 238 A.C, to those of M. Annæus Lucanus, and of Suetonius, and the witty Erasmus. German is pre-eminent amongst the Aryan languages for its compositive capabilities. Greek is known to every school-boy who has read the first chapter of the Gospel according to St. John; or the Works of Xenophon or Plato, to be a language enriched by its power of compositive developements. The Greek language is one of the richest and the most prolific that has been spoken by man. Latin has never been surpassed for fullness, for dignity, and for beauty and variety of forms. Nevertheless, Zeuss, a German scholar, fully aware of the richness and the copiousness of those classic tongues, says of Irish-Gaelic, that it does not yield; it is not inferior to the Sanscrit, Greek, or German; and that it is far and away before Latin and Slavic in its ready facility for forming compound terms. His words are:—"*Compositionis facultate lingua Celtica non cedit linguis affinibus, quæ ut Indica, Græca, Germanica, ea maxime excellunt, et longe superat eas quæ ut Latina, Slavica, eadem minus valent.—Grammatica Celtica, p.* 818.

It is a high position for Gaelic to hold, to be considered amongst the first by the ablest scholars in Europe—not merely by a few enthusiasts in a remote town in the west or south of Ireland, but by the deepest read linguistic savants in the world.

A MARVEL.

If Irish-Gaelic is really so excellent a language, and if it hold, in the opinion of the learned, so high a place amongst the languages of Europe, why is it that it has been regarded at home, and at present looked upon, as one of an inferior status ?—why is it so poor, comparatively, in its literary developements, in its published works? The reason is, the language has never received common fair-play. In the third and fourth chapters of this work, it has been shown how Irish has been trampled to the dust, despised, outraged, persecuted, banished, laws enacted and severe penalties enforced to put it out of existence; even its own people have learned to despise it, to banish it, to annihilate it in every way that can be devised. Irish-Gaelic is the Cinderella of the sister languages of Europe.

ROOTS, REAL WORDS.

"After we had explained every thing in the growth of language," says Max Müller, vol. i, p. 405, "there remained, in the end, as the only inexplicable residuum, what we called roots. These roots formed the constituent elements of all languages. This discovery has explained the problem of the origin of language immensely." Hebrew has only 500 roots; Greek, about the same number; Chinese, 450; Gothic, 600; modern German, 250. What, then, are these roots? "In our modern languages, roots can only be discovered by scientific analysis; and even as far back as Sanscrit, we may say that no root was ever used as a noun or as a verb. But originally roots were thus used; and in Chinese we have, fortunately, preserved to us a representation of that primitive radical stage which, like the granite, underlies all other strata of human speech.

The Aryan root, *da*, *to give*, appears in Sanscrit *da-nana*, Latin, *do-num*, gift, as a substantive; in Latin, *do*; Greek, *di-do-mi*, I give, as a verb; but the root *da* can never be used by itself. In Chinese, on the contrary, the root *ta*, as such, is used in the sense of a noun, *greatness*; of a verb, *to be great*; of an adverb, *great* or *much*. Roots, therefore, are not scientific abstractions; but they were used originally as real words."—*Max Muller*, *p.* 407, *vol. i.*

" Take the root "ár," which to this day is employed in Irish-Gaelic to signify *to plough*, *to open the soil.* Max Müller takes this very root (p. 292). From it we have the Latin *ar-are*, the Greek *ar-cun*, the Lithuanian *ar-ti*, the Russian *ora-ti*, the Gothic *ar-jan*, the Anglo-Saxon *er-jan*, the modern English *to ear*. Shakespeare says *(Richard II.)* :

To ear the land that has some hope to grow.

From this root comes the Latin term for plough, *aratrum ;* in Greek *aro-tron ;* in Lithuanian, *arkla-s ;* in Cornish, *aradar ;* in Welsh *arad.*

A more primitive formation of the root *ar* seems to be the Greek *era*, earth; the Sanscrit *ira* or *ida;* the Gaelic *ithir*, fresh earth. It meant originally the ploughed land, afterwards *earth* taken generally. Even the word *earth* must have come originally from *ar*, and must have been taken to mean ploughed or cultivated land, from *ear*, to plough ; or "ár," Irish.

The Greek *aroura*, and the Latin *arvum*, a field, have to be referred to the root *ar*, to plough. . . . I have no doubt that the words *ars*, *artis*, and our own word *art*, meant originally the *art* of all *arts*, first taught to all mortals by the goddess of all wisdom—the *art* of cultivating the crops.

The root *ar* is called a predicate root, because it predicates one and the same conception, whether of the *plough* or the *rudder*, of the *ox* and of the *field.*

There are two kinds of roots—*Roots Predicative* and *Roots Demonstrative.*

In the present enquiry, however, the writer purposes to adhere to the usual *prefixes* and *suffixes* in their relation to the *predicative* root.

As examples of a few affixes, let us take the endings of adjectives in "aṁaıl," "aıl," "eıl," "aċ." These terminations answer to the Latin *alis*, *ilis*, *icus*, *ax*, Gr. *ikos*.

Take "aṁaıl" (pr. *awil* in Irish-Gaelic), a broken form of "saṁaıl," like, resembling. It is in Irish an independent word; as "Rıġ-aṁaıl," *King-like* and contractedly in Scotch-Gaelic "rıghàıl" (kingly); Latin, *regalis*. The *ly* English is a broken form of *like*. In Irish-Gaelic "aṁaıl" is preserved in all its fulness; in Scotch-Gaelic and Manx it is fragmentary, (*ail*,-*al*,) "fear," a man, makes "fearaṁaıl," contractedly "fearaıl," Latin, *virilis*; "sgrıos," destruction, "sgrıos-aṁaıl," destructive (root, "sgrıos," destroy, and "aṁaıl," like) *lethalis*.

The author writes in his *College Irish Grammar* (p. 172 5th Edition)—The second class of derivative terms are adjectives; these end in "aṁaıl, mar, aċ, ıḋ, ta, da, or ḋa."

"These spring from nouns as roots, or from adjectives rarely from verbs, because it was from things of which nouns are only names, and from their qualities expressed by adjectives that mankind first formed notions or ideas and therefore the names of such things and their qualities were the earliest germs of human speech, of the genealogy of which history and philology point out the Keltic as one of the earliest offshoots,—*Easy Lessons, by the present writer, p.* 247. *Dublin: Mullany; also New York: P. M. Haverty, Barclay-street*, 1873.

aınm, *name*	aınmaṁaıl, *nameable.*	nominabilis
aoıbe, *delight*	aoıbaṁaıl, *delightful*	delectabilis
barr, *top, increase*	barraṁaıl, *growing big*	superabilis
saoı, *a gentleman*	saoıaṁaıl	sociabilis
sıans, *pleasure*	sıansaṁaıl	desiderabilis

Adjectives ending in "aċ"—

Irish.	Latin.	Greek.
amplaċ	vorax	harpax
soılseaċ	"	heliakos

All names of individuals, ending in Latin in *ax* or *us*, end in Irish-Gaelic in "aċ." Adjectives ending in "aċ" are derived from the passive participle of verbs by changing the final vowel into "aċ," as "feallta," deceived, betrayed, "fealltaċ," deceptive. Patronymics, surnames, nicknames, end in "aċ," as, "Albanaċ," a Scotchman; "Breatnaċ," a Welshman; "Burcaċ," Bourke; "Seabaċ," a hawk, Hawkins.

FORMATION OF IRISH COMPOUND TERMS.

In purely compound terms, as well as in derivative words, the principal groups embrace nouns, adjectives, verbs.

A noun may have, as its prefix, another noun, or adjective, or a verb; and in the same way, the adjective may have a noun, another adjective, or a verb; and thus the verb also may have as its prefix, a noun, an adjective.

A FEW EXAMPLES OF EACH.

"Breug-faıḋ," a false prophet, from "breug,' a lie spoken or acted, and "fáıḋ," a *fate*-teller; "faıḋ,' is from faṫ, cause, principle.

"Breug-ríġ," a pseudo-king, a pretender; "breug-ṗápa," pseudo-pope.

"Ceart-lár, right-middle, the very centre, from "ceart," right, and "lár," centre.

"Clap-solus," twilight, from "clap," close, gather, and "solus," light.

"Clog-teaċ," a belfry, a round-tower, from "clog," a bell; and "teaċ," house.

"Fear-ıonad," from "fear," a man; and "ıonad," a place, one who holds the place of another—a lieutenant, a vicar.

In the catechism taught to the Catholic children, the question is put, "cıa ḃe an Pápa?"—who is the Pope; and the answer is "cean na h-eaglaıse, agus fear-ıonad

Iosa Criost air an talaṁ,"—the head of the Church and the vicegerent of Jesus Christ on earth. The simple Irish-speakers easily understand the term "fear-ionad," (man-place), but they could never understand the Latin word, *vicegerent*, or *lieu-tenant*.

"Oiġ," pronounced "Oee." means a virgin, one who is "óg," young and pure.

"Oiġ-ḃean," a maiden, a virgin grown to the age of womanhood, a bride.

"Oiġ-fear," a virginal youth, grown to the age of being a man.

"Ór-slat," gold rod, sceptre.

"Teas-grád, ardent love, from "teas," heat, and "grád," love.

"Tír-grád," patriotism, from "tír," country, and "grád," love.

For complete list see *College Irish Grammar* (by the author) pp. 175, 176.

London is derived from "long," ship, "dion," protection.

Liverpool, from "lior," the sea, or waters of the sea; and "pol," a deep pond.

"Lir" is the Keltic name for Neptune, god of the sea. Thomas Moore has composed a plaintive melody—"Silent, oh, Moyle, be the roar of thy waters"—on the sad fate of "Lir's lonely daughters," who, changed into swans by the enchanter's wand, were doomed, as the sad story relates, to wander for ages on the white-crested billows of the lonely sea around the "maol," or headlands of Cantire, in Albion, and the headland along the coast of Antrim, in Eire.

From combinations like those just seen, are derived some proper names, found in Caesar's Commentaries on the Wars in Gaul, as *Dumnorix*, world-king, "doṁain-riġ;"

Bituriges, life-king, "beata-riġ;" *Caturiges*, battle-king, "cata-riġ." Riġ means king; "doṁan," the world; "beata," life; "cata," of battle (gen. case.)

The prefix "bean," a woman; Latin *femina;* changes the gender of the noun, as "tiġearna," a Lord; "bean tiġearna," a lady; "bean-naoṁ," a female saint; "bean-oglaċ," a female attendant. "Leat," half, has the meaning *of one of two*, as "leat-taoḃ," a side, one of the two sides; "leat-suil," one of two eyes; "leat-láṁ, not half-hand, but one of two hands; "leat-ċos," not half-a-foot, but one foot of two feet, &c.

Again, there are compounds in which the second noun is governed in the genitive case by the first; as, "fear-feasa," a man of knowledge, a seer; "feasa" is gen. case of "fios," knowledge; "cu-mara," an otter, literally, dog of the sea; "mara" is gen. case of "muir;" "mac-tíre," a wolf, literally, son of the country; just as in French *chemin-de-fer*, or in English man-of-war.

In this way other nouns of Keltic origin are explained; as *Orgetorix*, means "urra-gaċ-toruis," that is the-stay (*urra*) of-every-journey; "torus," a journey, makes gen. case "toruis" (pr. *torrish)*; to which the Latin sound *torix*, is nearly equivalent. We say in Irish just now—"Is mait an urra tu," you are a good "urra," that is a support, one to fall back on, a bail; *Cinngctorix*, (fear) "cinn-gaċ-toruis," the head-man-of-every-expedition; root, "ceann," head, gen. "cinn"-fear *man* omitted. *Vergobret*, "fear-go-bret," a man for judgment, from "fear," a man, "go," for, "bret," judgment. *Vergilius*, Virgil, is of this class; it is derived from "fear," a man, Latin, *vir*, and "geal," fair, a man of fair hair. *Vortigern*, or *Vertigern*, the name of the king who called in the Saxons, comes from "fear," man, and "tiġear-na," Lord, that is, the man-sovereign. The name "Ailban" given first to Britain, and subsequently to the north of Britain, or Scotland, is derived from "aıll," a mountain steep, a high hill, and "ban," white. The Latin name of the river *Garonne*, or *Garumna*, rising in the Pyrenean mountains, and rushing in a north-westward course into the sea, is derived from "garḃ," (pr. *garuiv*) rough, and "aṁaın," (pr. *awin*) a river, meaning the rough river. Rome derives its name, according to Newman, because it is built on the "ruad," "án," or yellow river, the Tiber; "ruad" means *rufus*, or a dark yellow color, and "án," for "aṁaın", river.

The Prepositive Adjectives, thirty-six in number, usually in composition go before nouns, before other adjectives and verbs, are not noticed here. For a full list, see *College Grammar*, *pp.* 177, 178, 179. *Fifth Edition. Dublin: Mullany.*

The second class of compound terms are those which have prefixed to the stem, or to a noun, adjective, or verb branching from it, certain syllables, which are either primitive terms, or broken forms of primitive terms. These prepositives are well known by the name prefixes, and are thirty in number: An, aıṁ, aın, as aınḟır, aıs, (a foot print), aṫ, co, con, coṁ (together), dı, dıṫ, (want defect) do, so, su, e, ea, eag, ear, eas, fóır, frıṫ, ıol, ıom,' ıon (fit), ın or ı (in), mı, mıs, neaṁ (in Scotch-Gaelic *neo*) oll, rıġ, ro, sar, sıar, ıar, seaċ, suas, uas, uıle.

To treat of each would not be in keeping with the work in hand. A few prefixes—an, do, so, sar, seaċ—are se lected.*

---

* Explanation.—"An" and "aın," are the same prefix; they express completeness, fulness, perfection, and in a few instances over-doing, therefore excess. "An," as a root, is found in the Latin word *annus*, a year, a full circle of the sun's apparent yearly course; in *annulus*, a ring, in "aıne," beauty, embodiment of beauty; "aıṁ," or "aṁ," are the same prefix, and denote rawness, sharpness, sourness; as, "gar," conve-

"An."—This prefix expresses a two-fold view of the term with which it enters into composition; the exact meaning is regulated by usage. It is *intensive*, or increasing the natural force of the word; or *negative*, denying or reversing what is conveyed by the root-word.

Now, in Greek, *a is intensive*, and *a negative*. This coincidence is, to say the very least, singular; and if effects in their sameness are to be ascribed to a common cause, primary or secondary, there must have existed in

---

nience; "amgar," hardship; "am" is found as an adjective; as, "ub ám," (pr. oov av) a raw egg.

"Ais," a side, and "eis," a foot-print, are nouns; "air ais," back again; "tar air ais," come back; "eis" is a foot-print, a track, as, "ann eis," in the track of, after; "eis-eirige," rising again, resurrection; "eis-eirige na marb," the resurrection of the dead; "at, re," again, as, "déan," make; "at-déan," remake; "at," as a root, means next, second, as, "lá," day; "at-lá," next day; "at-bliadain," next year; "co, con, com," mean with, together, like "go," Irish, or "con," Latin; or "sun" Greek; "di, dit," (pr. dyee) means want. We say today, "Tá dit orainn," there is want on us; we are in want. It is opposed to "sit" (pr. shee), happy, having peace and abundance.

"So" means positive worth, readiness in doing anything, derived from the substantive verb "as," is, in being, exists; "do" means difficulty, and is formed from "dí," and "so," as "di-so," "di-ho," "dio," and "dó;" "su," same as "so;" "e, ea, eag," away, deprivation; "fóir," front; "frit," frequent, repeating; "iol," many, varied, is of the same root-family with "uile," all, "oll," all, total; and "ál," prodigious; as "al-neart," of prodigious strength; "iom" is a secondary form of "uime," about; "ion," fit, as a noun, it is of the same origin with "an," as explained above; as "ion-déanta," fit to be done, meaning that there is within it an inherent power, and everything ready for its completion. We say in Irish, "Tá se annam," it is in me, meaning I am able to do that. "Rig," a noun, means king; "ró," rapidity; "sec," turn, side, modern spelling "seac;" "sár," superiority (from "so," good, and "ár," growth) "iar," means back, rear; hence west, "siar," westwards; "oir," front, east; "soir," eastward (see Easy Lessons in Irish); "uas," up; and "suas," upwards; "ios," down; "síos," downwards; "car," end; "eas," same as "as," out of, deprivation; as, onóir," honor; "eas-onóir," dishonor, drudgery; "mi" and "mis" loss; as, "ád," fortune; "mi-ád," misfortune.

the primæval tongue from which both claim direct or indirect descent, a principle which has left its impress in this striking orthographic sameness.

"An," in Irish-Gaelic, is very common, as an intensive prefix. To this day it is, by Irish speakers, with whom the writer daily and hourly converses, made use of before nouns, adjectives, verbs, adverbs; as, "An lá maiṫ ṡe," is it a good day? "seaḋ ıs an lá sc," yes, it is a tip-top day. "An" before "lá," a day, expresses the idea of *excellent* in its kind. Again, "capal," a horse, "an-ċapal," an excellent horse; "cur," a sowing, a crop, "an-ċur," a first-class crop, a very excellent crop.

It is before adjectives, however, that "an," as an intensive prefix, is chiefly employed; as, "fuar," cold, "an-fuar," very cold; "breáġ," splendid, excellent; "an-ḃreaġ" very splendid, very excellent. By placing the participle "go" before the adjective, an adverb is formed; as, "go ȧn-ḃreáġ (pr. *guh han-vryah*), very excellently.

"An," in its negative power, is rarely employed, except in the following, and a few other words: "eolas," knowledge; "an-eolas," ignorance (and all its compounds as "an-eolgaċ." ignorant); "fıos," knowledge; "eágna," wisdom; "an-eagna," folly; "dlıġe," law, "an-dlıġe," want of law; "deıse," comfortableness, suitableness; "an-deıse," affliction.—*See College Irish Grammar, p.* 182.

This particle "an" and "aın," is a radical word, and signifies *beauty, perfection, excellence, surpassing greatness.* It is found in "aıne," beauty, the Irish name for Venus; also in the term "aınfır," *a maiden full grown*, from "aın," beauty, and 'fır," of man, the embodiment, as it were, of human beauty, for woman, as a type, is styled *the fair sex*, in contradistinction to the sons of Adam, who as a class are not so fair. This derivation of "aınḟır," meaning a maiden full grown, is in accordance with truth and its correct acceptation, rather than that usually given by the Most Rev. Dr. O'Brien, Bishop of Cloyne, and others—namely, from "aın," fit, suitable for, and "fır," of man; for "aın," as a prefix, has not that meaning. "Aın" is not an adjective, and, therefore, should not, strictly speaking, be translated by a term which presents the acceptation in which adjectives are usually taken; "aın" is either a full-blown radical noun, or a broken form of "aıne," beauty. Again the fact that the second part of the term is in the genitive case "fır," and not "fear," the nominative, is proof positive that "aın," is a noun, and a radical primitive term, and hence it must be translated—if correctly—by the English equivalent, beauty surpassing excellence, perfection, "aınfır."

That "an" expresses the idea of greatness, even to excess, is proved by the term "an-tıġearna," a tyrant, that is, a lord acting the part of a master to excess.

The original meaning of "an," as a prefix, was intensive; in process of time it assumed the negative by conveying the idea of over-leaping the bounds of propriety; as "dlıġe," law; "an-dlıġe," want-of-law—that is, where the law was all on one side, and in excess, creating, necessarily, a want of all law for the party oppressed.

The next pair of particles which are full of interest to every classical connoisseur are "so" and "do." They are correlative in sense and sound; and in their primitive office, with the Greek particles *eu*, and *dus*.

Their use and application in Irish-Gaelic is, at the present moment, as common as the language itself in all its forms, for the peasant Irishman who still clings to the speech of his Melesian progenitors.

"so," signifies easy, gentle, affable.
"do," „ difficult, harsh, repulsive.

From a list of about eighty examples, the following few are selected :—

Nouns.

SO.	DO.
soċaır, *gain, advantage.*	doċaır, *loss, disadvantage, from* "do," and "car,' *friendly, aid.*
so-ḋuıne, *a good man, from* "so" and "duıne," *a person, in the sense of the French* "*bonhomme.*"	do-ḋuine, *a harsh man.*
soınıon, *fair weather, from* "so" and "sıon,' a blast.	doınıon, *foul weather, a storm.*
sólás, *solace.*	dólas, *sorrow.*
saoı, *a sage, a gentleman, sir.*	daoı, *a dunce, a sot.*

Adjectives.

saor, *free, cheap.*	daor, *slavish, dear.*
soléır, *clear, lucid, from* "so," and "leur,' *light,* as "nı leur dam ṡe, *it is*" *not (in) sight to me.*	doléır, *dark, obscure.*

Verbs.

saoruıġ, *free, cheapen.* &c., &c.	daoruıġ, *condemn, make dear.*

Past participles passive, too, take the prefix "so" or "do," which not only changes the meaning of the radical term, but imparts to the participle the force of adjectives, ending in *able* or *ible,* as

feıcsın, *to see.*	feıcsınte, *seen.*
so-ḟeıcsınte, *seeable, visible.*	do-ḟeıcsınte, *invisible.*

cuımsıġ, *to get about,* (root, "cum or cuım, *the waist,*) *to comprehend*; cuımsıġte, *comprehended, understood.*

so-ċuımsıġte, *easy to be comprehended, or to be got into one's head.*

do-ċuımsıġte, *incomprehensible, hard to be comprehended, &c.*

In this way, nigh every term in the Irish-Gaelic admits, as far as may be required, the use of "so" or do," to affect or qualify its meaning.

Is there anything like this process in Greek? Certainly:—*eu*, good, easy; and *dus*, bad, difficult, are found as prefixes to many derivative and compound terms, as

Greek, dus-arithmos, *difficult to count.*

Irish-Gaelic, so-ıırcaın, *easy to count*; do-aıreaın, *difficult to count.*

Greek, dus-emeria, *bad weather.*

Irish-Gaelic, do-aımsır, *bad weather.*

Greek, eu-meria, *good weather.*

Irish-Gaelic, so-aımsır, *good weather.*

Greek, eu-aggellion, *Latin evangelium, good news.*

Irish-Gaelic, so-sgeul, *good news, gospel.*

Greek, dus-angellion, *bad news.*

Irish-Gaelic, do-sgeul, *bad news.*

Greek, duspistos, *hard to believe.*

Irish-Gaelic, do-ċreıdsın, *hard to believe.*

Greek, eupistos, *easy to believe.*

Irish-Gaelic, so-ċreıdsın, *easy to believe.*

"In surveying," says Geddes, "relics of the oldest form of speech, such as these, we seem as if walking amongst the fragments of a forest primæval, and in their presence the philologist feels as Quintilian did towards Ennius—"*Sicut sacros vetustate lucos adoramus.*"

Above Latin in antiquity, these particles ascend far beyond Cicero, beyond Quintus, Ennius, or Plautus, (200 A.C.) The speech of Varro has lost them in all the periods of its history. Even Greek shows symptoms of weakness, as it has modified one of them, metamorphosing "su" or "so" into "eu." For "eu" is the affected form of "su." That which is natural precedes that which is affected; "so" and "su" are natural "eu" affected.

"So" springs from the substantive verb "as" or "is" and denotes real worth, excellence; "eu" has no part of that verb; it is the shadow of "so." The only tongue," he continues, "that can compete with Gaelic in this respect is the Sanscrit, where they appear in similar form, as *su* and *dus* and *dur*; Ex. Sanscrit *su-manas* gentle-minded—*cumencs* (Gr.) "dur" means *foe=dusmanas*, (Gr.) dusmenes In Irish-Gaelic "mein" means *mind*; "so-ṁeinеаċ," *gentle-minded*; and do-ṁéinеаċ, *bad-minded* (See Irish song, "the Cuilin.")

Geddes says, with the heart and head of a real lover of learning, that the recognition of these linguistic truths, in reference to *eu* and *dus*, Greek, and *su*, and "do," Irish, has given him more personal pleasure than any other single fact in Keltic and Greek analogies.

Linguistic lore, like this, is to the student of comparative philology what a rich vein in a gold-field is to a Californian money-seeker.

To sum up, then: Irish-Gaelic, therefore, as a primitive tongue, is as valuable as Sanscrit, for philological enquiry and research, and supplying, withal, rich veins of linguistic lore, deserves and demands the earnest study of every true student of languages and of antiquity.

CHAPTER IX.

GRIMM'S LAW—EIGHTEENTH REASON.

Resemblance between words of the same meaning in different dialects. Examples. Discoveries. Grimm's discovery of a linguistic law. Praised by some, by others ignored. Pedantry and ignorance. Principles of phonetics. The "law" explained. A paradigm. Examples of the law. Objections. C into p and b. The principle of the law derived from the Aryan mother tongue. Connection between Grimm's Law and aspiration and eclipse in Irish-Gaelic. The law of aspirating and eclipsing has come down the stream of time from the earliest period. Laws of glossology. Law, its origin. The Eternal Law; St. Bernard's notion of it; St. Augustin's; Milton's. Divine Law. Natural Law. Written Law. Law, as understood in the schools of science. Law subjective and objective. Laws of nature are principles put into practice. Grimm's Law. The expression of a principle. Laws within laws. Examples. Dialectic renewal, a law within a law.

Any student possessed of ordinary talent devoting his attention for a few years to the study of the ancient languages of Greece and Rome, and to the tongues spoken at home,—English, German, French, or Gaelic—cannot fail to notice, in comparing the ancient classic speech with the modern European dialects, or with the dialects of German or Keltic, that there exists a striking resemblance—often amounting to sameness—between many primitive words common to Látin, Greek, German, English, Irish, Gaelic, and the Romanic dialects of Europe.

To illustrate what has been just stated, let us take a term of frequent occurrence—*fer*, Latin, which no student, no matter how heedless in the study of languages, can have failed to notice. *Bear* (English) is in Irish "beir," in Gothic, *baira*, in Sanscrit *bhri;* in Old High German, *piru*, in Greek *pher*, in Latin *fer*. The word represents in each language the same idea, and is identical in sound, "b" in English, Irish, Gothic. The Sanscrit radical "b" sound assumes the aspirate force, and in Old High German the word is found to commence with a hard labial "p,"—which in Greek is again aspirated "ph," and this aspirate form is preserved in Latin, and expressed by "f," for, there is no modified form of "p," to represent the aspirate sound, such as "ph," English, or "ph," Greek. Such is the fact as far as regards the *soft* labial letter "b," with its aspirate or affected form "bh;" and its *hard*, cognate equivalent "p," with the aspirate "ph" or "f."

Scholars for the past two hundred years could not have failed to note this interchange of the cognate consonants, "b," "bh," "p," "ph," in words presenting, in different tongues, the same meaning, yet no one publicly propounded the principle up to the time of Jacob Grimm.

Many scholars from the time of Ptolemy, in the second century before the Christian era, to the time of the indomitable Polish Priest, Copernicus, knew that the earth was not really the centre of our astronomical system, yet it was reserved for Copernicus to put forth the light of this scientific truth to the world. The glory of being the father of modern Astronomy was reserved for the humble and laborious Father Copernic.

Before Columbus had set sail from Spain, and ere he had on the morning of the 12th October, 1492, beheld the coveted coast of San Salvador, the earth was an orb. In those days there were clever men, and yet how few except Vergilius had come to the conclusion that the globe on which they dwelt was round. Columbus alone was certain of the earth's rotundity; by his genius, his enterprise, and energy, he showed to an admiring world the truth of the theory of which he had himself been convinced; and he opened up the vast hemisphere beyond the Atlantic to the world at large, and to science.*

Before Kepler had spent nigh twenty years calculating the orbits, the motions and the bulk of the heavenly bodies, those famous astronomical laws which have rendered his name imperishable, had been for ages producing their stupendous results, always in order and harmony. Why were not all those simple, yet sublime laws, discovered by some other philosopher as well as by Kepler? Such a discovery demanded genius, patience, knowledge, a love of learning, labour. It was not by chance these laws in the heavens were read by the author of *The New Astronomy* and of *Harmonics of the World*. Kepler spent seventeen years pursuing those investigations which led to the discovery of his third great law.

Bodies had fallen time after time to the earth. The principle which produced gravitation had lain hid. Newton saw an apple fall, and in the fall beheld with

---

* Vergil, or rather Vergeal, in Irish-Gaelic "Feargeal," was a native of Ireland. His name is derived from "fear," a man, and "geal," fair. He went to France during the time of King Pepin, by whom he was recommended to the Duke of Bavaria. For holding views, then considered strange, regarding the earth and the antipodes, he was reported by St. Boniface, apostle of Germany to Pope Zachary. The Pope summoned the Irish priest to Rome, and on account of his advanced knowledge of science, and for his virtues raised him to the see of Saltzbourg. St. Basil, the two saints Gregory and Athanasius, knew that the earth was round.

the ken of a philosopher's eye the law of gravitation. Hally also came at the same time to a similar conclusion.

The electric fire, with its twofold developement—positive and negative—had permeated earth and air and sky, and all material space; it had flashed from pole to pole, from planet to planet, from star to star, it had contributed to cement and sever earth and sea; it had, like a universal soul, kept all nature in motion, producing its myriad effects long before the Professor of Science at Bologna—Galvani, or his lady—witnessed the sudden tremulous quiverings of a frog suspended from a copper hook on an iron frame. Galvani saw in the spasmodic twitching the action of that fluid which keeps the universe in motion. That was a great discovery, yet it was a little thing. The eye of genius beheld, in the beatings of the headless frog, the pulsations of that vital flow which alone quickens the material world. The genius of Galvani turned the incident to account. The effect today is seen in the almost supernatural results of electrical science.

So too, up to the present century, to the time of Jacob Ludwig Grimm, Professor of German literature, and Librarian of the University of Gottengen, no scholar put the question:—Does this interchange of sound and of letter spring from a principle, or is it a mere accident; is it the effect of a cause continually acting—that is, of a law of language? or, is it the result of mere chance? Again, is this interchange peculiar to the labials, "b," "p," "bh," "ph," "f," "v," "w," or is it common to the other two classes called gutturals, "c," "k," "g," "gh;" and dentals, "t," "d," "th," "dh," "z," "l." From the year 1818, to the year 1838, the learned, hard-working German philologist, author of *Geschichte der Deutschen Sprache*—*the history of the German language*, investigated this philological question, and after twenty years of study discovered the law, and announced it to the world; that the interchange of the consonants and of their sounds as perceived in the Aryan dialects was the direct issue of a principle, established by the Creator in the intelligent nature of man, or the effect of a primitive cause producing its effects in the primæval speech of the great Aryan race, and not the outcome of chance. *

In the language of philologists, the principle from which the facts proceed in order, and by which the phonetic effects of cognate consonants are regulated, is called a law. What physical laws are shall be explained further on in this chapter.

This newly discovered law of language has, like all discoveries of value, been praised by some, by others dispraised.

Regarding those who do not appreciate this linguistic law Max Müller writes :—"I feel convinced that however important the facts may be which have been arranged under the name of Grimm's Law, a true appreciation of the causes which underlie these facts is more important still. Nothing has caused so much confusion as the vague way in which these changes have been spoken of even by scholars who generally think deliberately and speak cautiously. I am not so pedantic as to consider it necessary to protest against the statement that Greek 't' becomes Gothic 'th,' and Gothic 'th' becomes the old High-German 'd,' as long as such a statement is used simply for the sake of brevity. But when phrases are taken literally, and when the changes of Greek *treis* into

* Jacob Ludwig Grimm died a few years ago in September 1863, at the advanced age of 78.

Gothic *trais* and old High-German *drei*, is represented as an historical process, it is high time, indeed, to protest. Why have all accurate scholars so strongly protested against looking upon Sanscrit as the mother of Greek and Latin? Are all the lessons of Greek scholarship to be thrown away? No Greek scholar would now venture to derive *Attic* from *Doric*, or *Doric* from *Attic*; nor would he allow the existence of a uniform Greek language a kind of pre-historic common speech, from which the principal dialects of Greece were derived."—Vol. ii. p. 232. *Science of Language. Longmans, London.*

Again, in p. 225, "None (of the languages) is borrowed from the other. None was *before* or *after* the other. All must be taken as national varieties of one and the same type or ideal."

He puts the question: "Who tells us that Greek 't' ever becomes 'th?' What definite idea do we connect with the phrase so often heard, that a Greek 't' becomes Gothic 'th?' Does a Greek become a Gothic consonant? Even an Italian consonant never becomes a Spanish consonant; an Italian 't,' as in *amato*, never becomes a Spanish 'd,' as in *amado*. They both come from a common source—the Latin; and so the Greek and Gothic and Gaelic come from a common source—the old Aryan language. We trace back all European languages to a common source, from which each may have started, fully equipped in its peculiar consonantal armour."—p. 219, vol. ii.

The Oxford professor has stated in the first paragraph just quoted that nothing has caused so much confusion as the vague way in which these changes, by which Grimm's Law is illustrated, have been spoken of even by scholars who think deliberately and speak cautiously. The present writer has heard men, distinguished for learning, speak of this new law of language, not only vaguely, but describing it as a pedantic piece of chance interchange, and stating that any other possible combination of consonants would suit in explaining the system, just as well as those which Grimm and his followers bring forward, explanatory of the principles of phonetics.

It is quite certain that the men who have spoken thus have expressed their views without any serious reflection, and from a want of knowledge on the special subject. It is a piece of pedantry not uncommon in the present age with men who have studied law or theology well, to suppose, because they are good lawyers or theologians, that, therefore, they are also good scientists, or good linguists. This is a great, and a very common mistake. It is easy for any man, gifted with fair talent, to become a good theologian or a good lawyer. The angelic Doctor has placed the queen of sciences, for the past six centuries, on such a colossal foundation that no one now or in time to come, needs to add to the Divine superstructure. The ground in the region of Catholic theology is clear; the mapping and the outlines have been all well and distinctly defined; all that is required on the part of a student is fair application and close attention to the teaching of theologians. Such, however, is not the case in the region of modern sciences such as geology, philology, hermeneutics, exegetics, chemistry, and sister sciences. Above all, a man may be learned fairly as a theologian, and be utterly at sea, as frequently happens, in the sciences. It is really hard to be obliged to listen to men of fair ability, and of considerable knowledge in theology, or in law, pronounce that the lingual laws by which languages are governed in the interchange of certain consonants and their sounds, are a mere jumble. The man who speaks so, displays his own ignorance, no matter how much the few friends around him may appear to sustain the sense, or sapiency of such oracular utterances.

But to return—What is this law discovered by Grimm? It may be stated fully in this wise:

"There are in the Aryan language three principal points of consonantal contact, the guttural, the dental, and the labial 'k,' 't,' 'p.'"

The consonant "k" represent the guttural, or throat-letter; "t," the dental, or tooth-letter, and "p," the labial, or lip-letter. The consonant "k" is articulated chiefly by the action of the throat, opening the mouth and uttering a volume of voice from the chest; "t," by the action of the tongue pressed against the front teeth, raised slightly, and "p" by pressing the lips hard, and then emitting the breath quickly through the partially re-opened mouth.

These are the three points at which articulate sounds are produced—the throat, the teeth, the lips.

Now, "at each of these three points there are two modes of utterance,—the hard and the soft; each in turn is liable to aspiration, though only in certain languages."

Hence we have the hard checks at the three points,—"k" or "c," "t," "p;" and the soft checks, "g," "d," "b."

The guttural "k," (hard) if uttered with a soft check, is "g," like "g" in "gum;" the dental "t," if uttered with a soft check, become "d," and the hard labial "p" becomes "b," when uttered quietly and softly, as "pen," "ben," "pin," "bin."

"We know," says the Professor of philology at Oxford, "from the physiological analysis of the alphabet, that three or sometimes four varieties exist for each of the three consonantal contacts. We may, for example, pronounce 'p' as a hard letter by cutting the breath sharply with our lips; we may pronounce it as a soft letter, by allowing the refraining pressure to be heard while we form the contact; and we may pronounce it as an aspirate by letting an audible emission of breath follow immediately on the utterance of the hard or soft letter,"—p. 220, vol. ii.

Hence, there are three classes of consonants—the guttural "k" and "g," the labial "p" and "b," the dental "t" and "d."

Now each of these is liable to aspiration; "k" and "g" to become "kh" and "gh," "p" and "b" to become "ph" and "bh," "t" and "d" to become "th" and "dh."

"In Sanscrit," says Max Muller, (p. 216, vol. ii.) "the system is complete; we have the hard checks 'k, t, p;' the soft checks; 'g, d, b;' the hard aspirated checks. 'kh, th, ph;' the soft aspirated checks, "gh, dh, bh,' And," he adds, "the soft aspirated checks are in Sanscrit of far greater frequency and importance than the hard aspirates." This rich variety of consonantal contact is to be found, however, in highly developed languages only. Among the Aryan dialects Sanscrit alone can boast of possessing it entire.—p. 220. Irish-Gaelic can make the same boast.

The learned Oxonian professor of philology says of Keltic—the four aspirates are likewise absent. That assertion may be true of Welsh or Manx; but it is not true of Irish. In Irish-Gaelic the six aspirates are to-day found in almost every sentence—"kh" or ch; ph, th, gh, bh, dh." Irish-Gaelic is, in this respect, as varied as Sanscrit; it possesses in full the rich variety of consonantal sounds, hard, soft, with the hard aspirates and soft aspirates, as "k, kh, g, gh, t, th, d, dh, p, ph, b, bh."

What is Grimm's Law, then? It is this:—"If the same roots or the same words exist in Sanscrit, Greek, Latin, Keltic, Slavonic, Lithuanian, Gothic, English, High-German, then wherever the Hindus and the Greeks pronounce an aspirate, the Goths, Low-German, English, Irish, pronounce the corresponding soft check, and the old High-German the corresponding hard check. In this change the Keltic, Gothic, Slavonic, and Lithuanian are in accord. Hence the following formula :—

I. Greek and Sanscrit, kh, th, ph, hard asp.
II. Irish-Gaelic and Gothic, g, d, b, soft checks.
III. Old High-German, k, t, p, hard checks.

The letters used here are symbols of the sounds, viewed philosophically, and not as the letters which occur in the respective languages. Thus, "kh" represents the "gh" of Sanscrit; the "ch or chi" of Greek; the "h, or gn, or m" of Latin : "th," also is the symbol of the Sanscrit "dh ;' the Greek *theta* "th," and the Latin "d" or "d ;" "ph" stands for "bh," Sanscrit; "ph," Greek; "f," Latin.

IV. Again, if Greek have g, d. b, soft checks
V. Irish-Gaelic and Gothic have k, t, p, hard checks
VI. And old High-German, ch, th, or z, ph, or f, hard aspirates. Lastly—
VII. If Greek have k, t, p, hard,
VII. Then Irish-Gaelic and Gothic have kh, or ch, h, alone or g, th, kh, f, bh.
IX. Old High-German, g, d, b.

Thus in one schema.

	Gutturals.	dentals.	Labials.
Sanscrit, Latin	c, k, kh or ch, g, gh	t, th, d, dh	p, ph, b, m
Irish-G'lic English	ch, kh, g, g, k, k	th, d, t, z	ph, f, b, ph, v, bh, v, w,
Old High German	g, g, k, c, kh, ch	d, t, th, th	b, p, ph, f,

The word which commences with "p" in the original is found in another language to have "ph" or "f" as its initial; and in a third, "b" or "bh." If a term have "c" in one language, its equivalent in another has "ch" or "kh," and in a

third "g;" lastly, the "g, d, b" become again in a fourth dialect "k, t, p," and in this way the cognate consonants go through a cycle of changes:

c, or k hard.	**ch, kh aspirate.**	**g, or gh soft**
t „	**th „**	**d, or dh „**
p „	**ph „**	**b, or bh „**

And over again "g," and "d," and "b" soft become "c, t, p," hard.

The first stage in the process of change which the hard consonants, "k, t, p," undergo is aspiration, by which they become "kh, th, ph." The second stage should naturally be into the soft consonants, "g, d, b;" and then if these changes were the result of phonetic decay, the sounds and their signs should ultimately vanish. "Phonetic corruption always follows one and the same direction. It always goes downward, but it does not rise again. But the raising of the soft to a hard is a movement upwards; *hard to an aspirated letter is a move* in the opposite direction. This phonetic law is compared by Grimm to a three-spoked wheel. Whenever it turns round, it causes that which is a rise in one spoke to appear a fall in the other. If, therefore, we consider the aspiration of the hard "t" as the beginning of a phonetic inflection ("th") which gradually led to the softening of "t" to "d," we should again have, on the other side, to account for the transition of the "d" into "t," by a process of phonetic invigoration. In this way the cognate consonants pass through a cycle of changes without any fear of decay.

EXAMPLES.

Irish-Gaelic.	English.	Sanscrit.	Latin.	Old High-German
beir.	bear,	bhri,	fero,	piru.
tu,	thou,	tuam,	tu,	du.
tri,	thee,	trayas,	tres,	dri.

Observe—As a rule, Irish-Gaelic accords with Sanscrit and Latin, and not with Greek, or Old High German.

In the foregoing formulas, it has companionship with Gothic and English, because in many instances—as in "beır" (Irish), *bear* (English)—they are not unlike.

OBJECTION TO GRIMM'S LAW.

"It is a very remarkable fact," says the learned Edward Lhuyd, "that a considerable number of words, whose initial in the British language is a "p," begin in the Irish with a "k" or with "c."

Keltic.	English.	Irish.
paul, W.	a pole,	cual.
peth,	a thing, a share,	cuıd.
pa,	what,	cá.
pask,	Easter,	cásg.
pencas, Cornish,	whitsuntide,	cıncıs.
peiswin, W.	chaff,	caıtın.
pesuch,	a cough	casaċt.
pen,	a head,	ceann.
puy,	who,	cıa.
puylh,	sense,	cıal.
plant,	children,	clann, or cland.
plyv,	feathers,	cluıṁ.
peduar,	four,	ceaṫar.
pymp,	five,	cuıg.
pair,	cauldron,	coıre or cuır.
pren,	a tree,	cran.
par,	couple,	coraıd.
pridh,	earth,	crıaḋ.
pryv,	worm,	cruṁ.
pob,	every,	caċ.
map, or mab,	son,	mac.

Does this interchange between palatals and labials come against Grimm's Law? By no means. Dr. Prichard gives the answer.

Dr. Prichard says:—"The interchange of cognate letters is a thing familiar to everybody—('b' for instance into 'p,' &c.,)—but the permutation of palatals into labials ('c' to 'p') appears much more improbable. Great as the difference is between such elements of articulation as 'k,' and 'p,' we find them to stand as representatives for each other in two different dialects of the same language. Some dialects of the Greek language afford well known exemplification of this remark. The Ionians and Æolians inserted *kappa* in a variety of words instead of *pi*, used in all the other Grecian dialects. This remark has been made by many of the scoliasts and old grammarians, and more fully by Vossius, who says:— "*Iones in interrogativis et relativis mutant* p *in k (kappa) Ita* kos *dicunt pro* pos; hokos *pro* hopos; ke *pro* pe, kote *pro* pote: *Æoles quoque uti* kappa *pro* pi *testatur Etymologici auctor in* koios; *sic Latini* jecur *pro* hepar, *et scintilla a spinther.*"

Again, *Lupus*, Latin, for *Lukos*
equus „ for *hippos*.
relinquo from the *Æolic leiko*, for *leipo* to leave.

In the most polished language of the old world—Greek—the interchange of "p" into kappa is not uncommon. If this occurs in dialects which are so very near akin, it is no way surprising to find the same special law operating in dialects so wide apart as Irish, Gaelic, and Welsh. The cause of the change came from the Aryan region.

In his ample explanation of these interchanges, Jacob Grimm falls into one great mistake, which, owing to the undeveloped knowledge at the period respecting the Aryan mother tongue, he could not at the time he wrote have avoided. Grimm supposes that all these interchanges of consonants was brought about by time, and that one language deduced them from another, like families inheriting the varied traits of character peculiar to the primary and intermediate parentage from which they sprung. This view of Grimm's is opposed to all that is known at present of the great primæval Aryan mother tongue, and the European daughter languages that have sprung from her bosom.

Hear Max Muller once more:—"Before the Aryan nations separated, some of them, at all events, had elaborated a threefold modification of the consonantal checks." —p. 222.

"Throughout the whole of this process there is no transition of one letter into another, no gradual strengthening, no gradual decay. From the very beginning different branches of the Aryan family fixed the cardinal points of the common phonetic horizon differently. While the Hindus fixed their East on the 'gh,' 'dh,' and 'bh,' the Low Germans and the Gaels fixed it on 'g,' 'd,' 'b;' the High Germans on 'k,' 't,' 'p.' All the rest was only a question of what the French call *s' orienter*. It would follow, if not of necessity, at least according to intelligible principles. To make my meaning more distinct, and to impress Grimm's law once for all upon your memory, I shall use a familiar illustration, and ask you to recall to your mind the arms of the Isle of Man, three legs on one body, one leg kneeling towards England, the other towards Scotland, the third towards Ireland. Let England, Scotland, and Ireland represent the three varieties of consonantal contact; then Sanscrit would bow its first knee to England ('dh') its second to Ireland ('d') its third to Scotland ('t'); Gothic would bow its first knee to Ireland ('d'), its second to Scotland ('t') its third to England ('th'); Old High German would bow its first knee to Scotland ('t'), its second to England ('th'), its third to Ireland ('d'). The three languages would thus exhibit three different aspects of the three points of the phonetic horizon:—we should not have, according to Grimm's simile, one three-spoked wheel; but three concentric wheels fixed each from the beginning in its own position." Max Muller—*The Science of Language*, vol. ii, p 231, 232. London, Longmans, Green, & Co., 1873.

Grimm's Law, and the Rules for Aspiration and Eclipsis in Irish are founded on the same principles.

The thought has, doubtless, arisen in the mind of the learned reader to ask what has all this to do with Irish Gaelic? Grimm's discovery has been, to be sure, a great triumph in the field of comparative philology, but what connexion is there between this splendid success achieved by the votaries of linguistic science, on the one side, and the study of Irish Gaelic on the other? The answer is, much in every respect. It is now admitted beyond cavil;—the fact is certain, for Grimm's discovery is styled a law,—that is, as shall be shown, a directive influence which invariably produces, in the same circumstances, uniformity of results—that this interchange of the consonants proceeds from a principle of harmony and in accordance with a scientific directive agency. The interchange of consonants in Irish caused by aspiration and eclipsis is identical with that which has led to the discovery of Grimm's law, and therefore, is the scientific result proceeding from a principle of harmony and an intelligent directive influence. The effects are identical—the cause must be the same. So the discovery made by Grimm has been practically known, under another form and name, for the past thousand years and longer, in Irish-Gaelic; nay, the modifying phonetic principle, and, perhaps, the practice of it came from the plains of Persia ages before the supposed historic Cadmus had set foot on the Hellenic shore.

The first phonetic modification which the *hard* checks, "c, or k, t, p," undergo in the interchange, according to Grimm's law is, that "k" becomes "kh; "t," "th," and "p," "ph" (that is "f"). What does Irish-Gaelic say? This is just what is produced in Irish-Gaelic by *aspiration*, "k" becomes "kh, "c, ch," "t," "th," "p," "ph." The second modified phonetic effect results in "kh" becoming "g;" "th," "d;" "ph," "b." By the laws of eclipsis in Irish, "p" assumes a new sound, "b;" "c," that of "g;" "t," that of "b;" "f," that of "v," ("ḃ.") The aspirates "ch, th, ph," are a middle element between the *hard* checks, "k, t, p," and the *soft* ones, "g, d, b."

Exceedingly singular, indeed, is the agreement between this system of changes and that which is carried out in the Irish language of the present hour, both in its spoken and written forms.

ASPIRATION.

When two words are to be joined, in order to form a compound, as "sean," old, and "bean," woman—old woman, the compound term in Irish is not "sean-bean," (shan-ban) but it is "sean-ḃean," "ḃ" aspirated, (pro. shan-van). And in this way the first letter of every word, as a rule, forming the second part of a compound term, becomes aspirated.

Why? Because words cannot, according to the spirit of the language, coalesce or harmonize without the introduction of a middle sound. The need on the part of the Gaelic language is supplied by this process called "aspiration." It arises (1) in composition; (2) in the vocative, or nominative case of address; (3) in past tenses, in the conditional tense, in the infinitive mood of verbs; (4) after prepositions.

What is aspiration? It is a change of the natural or primitive sounds of the consonants, ("l, n, r," excepted) into others of homorganic articulation."—*See College Irish Grammar, p. 27, Fifth Edition.* The change in the sound is in Irish-Gaelic noted by a (·) over the affected consonant; in Scotch-Gaelic by the use of "h;" in Welsh, by a change of letter; in Manx, by a change of letter. It is found to exist, in a modified way, in Latin and Greek; the principle, at least, is not wholly overlooked.

PROCESS OF ECLIPSING—What is eclipsis in Irish-Gaelic? It is the suppression of the sound of the initial mute consonant for that of a *cognate* letter which, in the written language, is prefixed to that consonant of which the sound is silenced, as "go d-tigid do rigaṫt," that may come thy kingdom (thy kingdom come); "t" of "tigiḋ" is eclipsed by the sound of "d," and to express that change, "d" is inserted before "t;" "d" tells the change of sound; "t" (though not sounded) points out the radical word "tig," come.

Again—"Ar b-posaḋl," our marriage; "posaḋl" signifies marriage, from "pos," root, "bo," a cow; "bosaḋl," giving cows; or from "bos," the palm of the hand, by which mutual troth is plighted; "p" points to the radical word, "b" to the new sound; "p," for the time, is silenced or eclipsed. Hence the name eclipsis.

Observe—Both in the process of *aspirating* and *eclipsing*, the change of sound, like *shandi* in Sanscrit, can never be into any other than that of a cognate consonant; "p" cannot be affected by any other consonant than by "b" (in eclipsing) or "ph" in aspirating; "c" can never be affected by any other than by "g" soft, or "ch," when undergoing aspiration. In Welsh the eclipsed consonant is omitted. The radical consonant in Kymric sometimes undergoes fully four changes. Gaelic retains the radical letter while it points out the phonetic change. In this respect it is right.

By aspiration in Irish-Gaelic, and in obedience to Grimm's law:

	Hard.		Aspirate.	
I.	c	becomes	ch, or ċ	(aspirated)
	t	,,	th, ṫ	,,
	p	,,	ph, f, or ṗ	,,
	soft.			
	g	becomes	gh, or ġ	,,
	d	,,	dh, or ḋ gh, y,	,,
	b	,,	bh, or ḃ, v, w	,,

BY ECLIPSIS.

	Hard.		Soft.
II.	c	is eclipsed	by g, ar g-cara, *our friend.*
	t	,,	d, ar d-teanga, *our tongue.*
	p	,,	b, ar b-pian, *our pain.*
	Soft.		
	g	,,	by n, ar ngort, *our enclosed field, our garden.*
	d	,,	n, ar n-dan, *our poem.*
	b	,,	m, ar m-bord, *our table.*

The consonant "f," which is equal to "ph," a hard aspirate, loses its sound when under the influence of a process of aspiration:—The new aspirating action destroys its value as a consonant: Ex. "Sean-ḟear," old man, is pronounced "shan-ar. "F" is eclipsed by "v," that is "ḃ" (in Irish); in Scotch-Gaelic, "bh;" "s" aspirated, becomes, in its secondary form, "h;" it is eclipsed by "t," as "teaċ an t-sagairt," house of the priest; here "t" precedes "s," and is sounded, while the phonetic value of "s," for the time, is lost.

In olden times, whenever eclipse took place, the radical consonant was doubled, as "ar ccara," our friend; now "ar g-cara;" "ar tteanga," our tongue, now, "ar ḋ-teanga," our tongue.

In one word, then, the *hard* consonants are eclipsed by their *soft* cognates; the *hard* and *soft* are alike modified by aspiration into a sound aspirate, but invariably of cognate value.

Eclipsis, like aspiration, is a toning down of the hard consonants into thin, soft cognates; and of the soft consonants into others softer still, (as "b" by "m," "g" by "ng," "f" by "v,") to accord with the spirit and requirements of the Gaelic tongue. The principle that directs eclipsis is the same as that which directs aspiration, but proceeds one step further, for variety as well as harmony. It calls upon the soft consonants and not the aspirates.

Grimm's law, therefore, from what has been just seen and stated, is to the European languages, what the laws of aspiration and eclipsing are in Irish-Gaelic. (1) There is an interchange throughout all the languages of Europe in the initial of certain consonants; there is an interchange like it in Gaelic. (2) That interchange is found to arise in certain consonants; the interchange in Irish is confined to the same class and to the same consonants. (3) The change from one letter to another is always between cognate consonants—never otherwise. (4) The first infected alteration is from a hard consonant to its aspirate; next, to its soft cognate. So, in Irish-Gaelic, by aspiration the consonant receives its first bend from the natural form; by eclipsis, the soft cognate is installed in the phonetic chair of the hard primitive.

This phonetic system, which is so full of beauty of perfection and harmony, has been known to flourish in Irish-Gaelic since the days of the Abbot of Boyle—six centuries ago—and under a more archaic form, long before that period. It must have come from the cradle of the Keltic race east of the Caspian. Like the sound of *Vau* or the *Digamma*, in the time of Homer, it must, from the earliest period, have had an influence on the spoken tongue, although, in the early monuments of the written speech, its specific effects have not been stamped with sufficient distinctness. Such is the high origin of these phonetic processes.

It is seen how beautifully they accord with the grand discovery made by Grimm: his law has been much lauded. Aspiration and eclipsis in Irish-Gaelic can no longer be condemned on phonetic principles.

Within the past decade of years Grimm's law has received from scholars that attention to which it is entitled. The lectures of the learned professor of philology at Oxford has helped to render Grimm's name, and his discovery, valued amongst scholars of the present and coming time.

FAVORABLE TESTIMONY.

"The laws of glossology are fixed by the same mind that fixed the laws for the formation of a crystal or the growth of a tree. Grimm's law threw as much light on the science of tongues as Newton's law threw on the physical world. All that we read about phonetic decay and dialectic renewal, is interesting in the highest degree; for in them we trace the working of the Hand that covers the orchards with fruit or melts the icebergs as they float from the polar seas."—*God in Creation, p.* 17, *by Rev. Fr. Rawes, O.S.C.*

It is well that young students not skilled in philosophy or theology should form, at the start, a correct notion of law as understood by men of science.

Let them for a moment ascend in thought to the first fountain of all law, and trace its descent downwards from the great central source of knowledge and wisdom to the mental light that guides the simplest peasant, or the principle that controls the motions of the summer breeze.

(1) The knowledge and wisdom which first planned creation, and the governing action of the Creator is the

great eternal law. *Lex eterna creatrix et gubernatrix est universitatis.*—St. Bernard.

(2) The visible expression of that divine wisdom, as seen in creation—the wonderful order which, like beauty, shines forth in Nature's works—is termed a law by St. Augustine, Bishop of Hippo; and by Paley; and by the author of *Essay on Man.—Order is Heaven's first law.*

(3) We come down from the hights of the mountain of the Creator's intelligence and wisdom, and from that universal order, which, like light, is shed over all his works, to the world on which man dwells; the same Divine mind rules the natural order, pointing out what is to be done, and what to be avoided. This special view of the Divine will made known to man, directing the order of things to be preserved and not to be broken, is called the Divine Law. *Lex divina est ratio vel voluntas Dei naturalem conservari jubens perturbari vetans.—St. Augustin, Lib.* 22, *contra Faust*, c. 27.

(4) And a knowledge of the Divine will implanted in the breasts of mankind, showing them by the light of reason what is right to be done in accord with equity and truth is called the Law of Nature.

(5.) In general that is termed amongst men, a law which is in the first place according to reason; and which, secondly, directs the movements and the operations of things to their proper end. This view of law is given by the learned Gerson: *Lex est recta ratio practica, secundum quam motus et operationes rerum in suos fines regulate ordinantur.*

From the views here presented, it appears that intellectual guidance receives the name of law; secondly, that the repeated action itself in the objects, or the directive principle, whatever it is, residing in the objects and producing uniform results, is known as a "law." Hence the term conveys the idea of mental directive influence, or subjective guidance, as well as objective uniformity of results.

Law, then, conveys the idea of intellectual or subjective direction; and of objective action combined however with order.

(6.) The knowledge of what is right, and what is wrong is called the Natural Law.

It is a gleam of the Divine mind infused into the intelligent nature of man anterior to the time when the "law" was given to Moses. That law received by Moses is known as the Written Law. The Apostle of the Gentiles contrasts the two laws, the Natural and the Mosaic, in his epistle to the Romans—c. 14, 15. *For when the Gentiles who have not the law do by nature those things that are of the law,—these having not the law, are a law to themselves; who show the works of the law written in their breasts,—their consciences bearing witness to them and their thoughts between themselves, accusing, or also defending one another.*

(7) As mankind, in their natural state are, as St. Paul shows, a law to themselves, even without any written code, knowing what is right and what is not, by the light of that knowledge which the Creator has given them, so the non-intelligent creatures of God, and the world of matter in its substance, in its qualities, in its relations, is guided in all its motions by fixed principles. These principles, whatever they are, like the centre of gravity, or like the electrical or magnetic forces, when viewed in relation to uniform action, are termed laws. Fire, therefore, and water, and their effects,—heat and cold, fluids and solids, in the aggregation or elimination of their constituent elements, in their substance, properties, results;—the sun and the moon, the planets, the

earth, tides, the lands and its animals; the sea and its living freight, have all their fixed laws, according to which they always act, and by which they are governed, unless when an inner law—the result of another principle,—or when the intelligent Legislator who first established that law, demands, in some special instance its suspension.

It is worth knowing some of these principles which govern God's creation. A few of the laws from different sciences should not, in this age, be kept hidden from the eye of young students.

There are, first, the three great laws discovered by Kepler, after a life of labbr and study, the most wonderful in their way that ever have been conceived by the intellect of man, and arrived at by the principle of induction.

The first of the three laws he discovered is, that each planet revolves round the sun in an ellipse, and the centre of the sun is in one of the foci. The second, that the radius-vectores of the planets sweep out equal areas in equal times. The third, which is the most astounding of all, and which cost him the largest amount of study and thought, that, if the squares of the times of the revolutions of the planets around the sun be divided by the cubes of their main distances, the quotient will be the same for all the planets; or in the usual form, the squares of the *periodic times* of the planets are as the cubes of their distances.

Newton's law of gravity has been alluded to already. It is this—That the force of the attraction of gravity varies inversely as the square of the distance. This same law is equally true of heat and of light; and of electrical and magnetic attraction. If two sit at a fire, and one is twice as far removed from it as the other, the degree of heat the former receives from the fire is four times less than that which the latter enjoys.

Dalton's law in chemistiy shows that chemical combination is always in multiple proportion. And the writer will here quote from Rev. Father Rawes, who is exceedingly accurate in all the scientific proportions which he introduces into his discourses. There are five distinct chemical compounds of nitrogen with oxygen. The weight of nitrogen is the same in each, but the weight of oxygen is 16, 32, 48, 64, 80, that is, in arithmetical proportion, 1, 2, 4, 5, 6."

Another law, regarding light:—"The signs of the angles of incidence and refraction of light have a constant ratio to one another." And in gases, Boyle's law shows that the volume occupied by any gas is inversely proportional to the pressure to which it is subjected. And this law—the densities of all the elements known in the gaseous state are identical with their combining weights. And again—"the velocity of diffusion of different gasses is inversely proportional to the square roots of their densities." Then there are laws of medical science, of physiology; laws regarding vegetable and animal life, which are quite astounding, yet simple.

All these laws and others of a kindred character, which govern and direct matter, are to the eye of the man of real science glimpses of the mind of God. They are, as has been said, a part of that eternal wisdom which at first planned and directed not only the creation of matter and life, and mind and spirit, and grace and sanctification, but established principles, and infused them for guidance into their subjects at the moment of creation, enabling all, in their respective orders, to attain that special end for which, in the general order, he has destined each creature. "God beholds the ends of the world," says Job, "and looks on all things that are under heaven. He made a weight for the winds and weighed the waters by measure. He gave law for the rain and a way for the sounding storms. He saw it, and declared it, and searched it." Grimm's law, which governs the interchanges of phonetic variety and of dialectic renewal known to philologists is as certain as Newton's laws or Kepler's laws in astronomy; or as Boyle's or Marriotte's law in the science of chemistry. Each is the result of scientific induction. Each law is a glimpse of the mind of the Creator. Grimm's linguistic law is of this class.

LAWS WITHIN LAWS—PHONETIC DECAY, DIALECTIC RENEWAL.

One who has not studied with sufficient care those principles, which according to the teaching of the masters of physical sciences, affect matter and exercise a directing influence over its varied forms—solid, liquid, and gaseous—is sometimes surprised to find effects produced quite different from those which, in the circumstances, he had been led to expect.

The surprise of the student will be increased when after fuller investigation he shall have found that such results spring from the guiding action of another law, which, compared to the former, seems like a law within a law. The same intelligent director of the general law has made these exceptions. He alters and directs the action of nature as He willeth.

1. By the law of gravitation, water flows down an incline. By the inner law of capillary attraction, fluids ascend; that is, they go up, when by the general law one expects them to go down.

2. Fluids expand with heat and contract with cold. But as soon as water arrives at a certain degree of cold-

ness, it ceases to contract and suddenly begins to expand; and on freezing, is found to expand considerably.

3. Cohesion is a law of nature, but in gases one finds expulsion when cohesion ought to take place.

4. In the downward pressure of solids and fluids force is always in proportion to weight, but in the hydraulic paradox, the weight of one gallon of water can be made to act with the pressure of a thousand tons. This is strange.

5. One line continuously approaching another must eventually meet that other, but in the parabola the asymptote continually approaches the curve, and yet science proves plainly that it never will touch the curved line.

6. Every child is aware, just as well as if he were a member of the fire brigade in a large city, that water quenches fire; that there is a destructive war ever being waged between the elements of water and fire, so that, water in sufficient amount destroys fire; in a word, that water and flame cannot exist together in the same place; yet, it is a fact, that oxy-hydrogen light will blaze in the midst of water; further still, water reduced to its original elements of oxygen gas and hydrogen, produces light the most brilliant and heat the most intense, by igniting the gases just in the same ratio of combining elements, that are required in the production of water from the union of oxygen and hydrogen gases.

7. A ray of light viewed as coming from a luminous centre is simple, yet by means of a solar spectrum it is resolved into those elements which produce the primary colours, and each colour or subdivision of a ray of light is itself the product of a number of lines, or of undulations. The length of the waves which causes, for instance, the red ray is such, that it would take thirty

seven thousand of them to make an inch, and that for the same red ray, there are four hundred and fifty-eight billions vibrations of the ether in a second.

For the violet color there are sixty-five thousand waves in an inch, and seven hundred and twenty-seven billions of vibrations in a second.

8. Some laws are as certain as that the sun shines, but quite beyond the comprehension of man's mind:

For instance, the tropical year is being shortened three-fifths of a second in the space of one hundred years.

9. The sidereal year is being lessened in length daily, so that it will be shorter than at present by a second of time in a hundred and sixty-five thousand years. This is wonderful.

10. The plainest action of the eye is a mystery to a man of science. How is the point of a pin seen? By rays of reflected light from the pin entering, as photographers know, the pupil of the eye, in the same way as they enter the double convex lens in a photographic camera, and leaving their impression with the image on the retina at the back of the eye. The retina conveys the sensation, that is the image to the brain—the brain to the mind. Now, if ten millions of eyes were to look at one pin, they should all see the pin's point,—that is ten millions of rays pass from the point of the pin. An equal number pass from every other point. Hence millions on millions of rays of reflected light proceed from an object one inch in length. What myriads come from the endless variety of objects which, at one view, come within the sphere of vision. No mind can conceive the thought which is capable of compassing the specific calculation. And yet all these myriad rays, bearing their respective images, cross each other every moment that one in any illumined space beholds objects.

11. Who can comprehend the wonderful fleetness of light—in round numbers, two hundred thousand miles a second. That is something prodigious. Who can know how the electric fluid runs along the wire and through the wire with the speed of light?

More wonderful, still—how is it that two currents of the electric fluid will rush from opposite batteries with the fleetness of light at the same moment and through the same wire, and not meet, or, at least, not disturb in the least their relative action?

12. The phenomena of the electric fluid are bewildering. Positive electricity is not negative, and negative is certainly not positive; yet, the negative will produce the same results as the positive. Each will cause a magnetic current to pass at an angle of ninety with the line of direction of the electric current. How magnetism produces electricity, and electricity magnetism, is a mystery. How does electricity build up, and yet destroy—combine and lock together, as if in a vice, the elements of matter, even water, and all the while never cease to eliminate and to waste all the component elements, to pass away and yet never be lost? How is that positive and negative electricity, with the magnetic fluid, are three distinct fluids, and yet only one fluid? These are a few of the astounding counter laws which come under the notice of men of science in viewing the works of God.

CHAPTER X.

NINETEENTH—Another Law in Irish-Gaelic: the Law of Vowel Assimilation. The former Law relates to the Consonants, this to the Vowels, and their Phonetic and Orthographic Influence. Rationale of the Law of Vowel Assimilation. The *Atlantis.* The Division of Vowels into Broad and Slender is true, viewed Philosophically. It is true, in fact, in Irish. It has been known and practised two thousand years and longer. The Ancient Rule "Caol le Caol, agus Leaṫan le Leaṫan" is the Law of Vowel Assimilation literally Crystalised. Traces of the Phonetic Vowel changes in the Romance Languages show that there was a time when the law in the early Latin and Greek mother tongues had been fully known. What does French say? What does Italian, Wallachian, Spanish say? What does the English? Conclusions: Objections. The Palatal Power of "e" and "i." These affect the Consonants by their Palatal Influence. The results of the Vowel-Law in Gaelic uniform, unchangeable. Hence the Spelling and the Sounds always sure. All this bespeaks the reality of the Law. The results two-fold, extending along the whole field of Gaelic Pronunciation, and directing the system of Gaelic Spelling. Examples. Beauty of the system in Irish-Gaelic. How to know English words of Keltic and not German Origin. A Discovery.

The new and important subject—Grimm's law and its relation to certain rules and usages in Irish, have been fully discussed and explained. How the principle on which it is founded has been by a process of induction reached, and what is the character of the law itself, have been shown. Its permanent and uniform effects; the identity of these effects with kindred processes of aspiration and eclipsing in Irish-Gaelic, and the nature of physical laws, have been pictured in these pages just past.

There exists to a degree, quite remarkable in Irish-Gaelic, another law which may be called *the law of vowel assimilation*, possessing a vitality that has lasted for two thousand years and longer, and exercising a phonetic influence which completely permeates the spoken language, while it controls and directs the rules of the written Gaelic speech.

The foregoing law, allied to Grimm's, which is the fountain and source of eclipsing and aspirating in Irish, is founded on the principle of consonantal harmony, and affects the consonants only; but this law affects the vowels chiefly, and rests on the principle of vocal pitch, or comparing vowel sounds to notes in the musical octave,—on their relative height in the scale of harmonic sounds.

In the explanation of the subject of classic pronunciation (pp. 122, 130 of this volume) it is shewn that the vowels in Irish are five; that they are pronounced just as they had been pronounced (p. 127) by the Latin races, from the days of Plautus to Suetonius; that the sound of—

a is *aw*, never *e*. *e* as first *e* in where.
i as *i* in pique. *o* as *o* in told.
u as *u* in rule, or *oo* in tool.—See pp. 127, 128.

" Irish or Keltic," remarks Geddes, " is, in its pronunciation, ever *sound* where the Scottish and English are *false.* It can be shown," he says, " to be sound where both are false.—*Lecture*, p. 9.

" The phenomenon presented by most letters in English

of sound and sign, having but a fortuitous connection, is nearly unique. The real sound is quite different in English from that which one is taught to give it. There is nothing like this in any language. At all events, there is nothing in Irish like such irregularities.

"The pure vowel sound of 'a' exists in English in the 'a' in *far*; of 'a' in most words in which that letter occurs. But the "e, i, u," (in English) do not represent perfect vowel sounds, but mixed ones, and we have accordingly to look for the true simple vowel sounds under others; thus 'e' will be found to be best represented by the 'a' in *name*; 'i,' by the 'e' in *theme*; while 'u' is expressed by the 'oo, in *cool*".—*Atlantis, No.* 1, *p.* 16.

"In English, 'e' *long* has evidently lost its original sound, for it is now pronounced *ee* (not *eh*); like 'i' *long* in all ancient and modern languages."—*Dr. O'Donovan.*

And the learned Doctor remarks, "that 'e' still keeps its ancient long sound in a few words, as in *where, there, ere,* in which words it corresponds exactly with 'e' long in Irish."—p. 11.

What diphthongs are, has been shown in p. 127. And in pages 193, 194, the four distinct sounds of consonants in Irish is plainly proven.

RATIONALE OF THE LAW OF VOWEL ASSIMILATION.

The vowel sounds have, by philosophical writers, been viewed in the light of musical notes, and from the analysis made, it appears that "i" and "e" are the highest in vocal value; and that "a, o, u" are the lowest in the vocal scale. This view is confirmed by the following extract, taken from *Atlantis, vol.* 1, *pp.* 60, 65.

"The reason of such a division is quite philosophic, for every vowel sound is produced 'by the passage of the air through the opening of the glottis;' and thus all intonated vowel sounds 'partake somewhat of the character of musical notes, while, at the same time, they constitute the elements of speech.' In the musical octave each successive note, from the highest to the lowest, is sounded with a volume of voice deeper than that of the note preceding; and conversely the preceding is sounded with a higher, that is, a more *slender* (we shall so call it) volume of voice than its succeeding note. The two highest are, therefore, the two which may properly be called *slender*, when compared to those which, lower in the scale, are pronounced deep, or *broad*. In this manner intonated vowel sounds, as far as they partake of this musical character, are some slender, some broad. Let us arrange them, then, in the philosophic order, from the highest to the deepest; thus, i, e, a, o, u."

There are such sounds, therefore, founded on the nature of vowel intonation, as *slender*,—and others compared with them, *broad*. And the vowels that represent a *slender* sound are "i" and "e;" and those that represent a *broad* sound are "a" "o" "u." This is the conclusion at which philosophic analysis of vowel intonation has arrived. This is the clear outcome of linguistic investigation of vowel sounds.

Now, what does Irish-Gaelic say on this nice point of vowel intonation, and of the division of vowel sounds into broad and slender?

1. Why, the distinction between broad and slender vowels has been known by Irish grammarians and Irish writers from the days of Aongus O'Daly Fionn, surnamed the Divine in the sixteenth century, and of Donogh Mór O'Daly, Abbot of Boyle, in the thirteenth century, and long before these two celebrated Irish poets flourished.

2. It is a fact that even before the Christian faith had been preached and practised in Ireland poetry was

fashionable, and Keltic bards were a public institution amongst all the princes and sovereigns of Ireland. It is well known, as Zeuss attests, that these princes of poetry fashioned their bardic effusions according to settled laws, which on no account could be violated.

What were these laws ?—*Assonance*, or as it is called by the Irish bards "Comarda," was, at all events, the fourth indispensible requisite. Assonance was of two kinds, "slán," or perfect, and "briste,' or broken. For perfect assonance it was necessary that vowels of the same class, broad (a, o, u) should chime with broad; or slender (e, i) should chime with a slender vowel in the final syllable. Therefore, the division of vowels—now proved to be philosophically correct—dates from the earliest times, even before the Christian period.

It is true that in the written Irish prose previous to the twelfth century, the division of the vowels into broad and slender, is not so striking and perceptible as in the writings of periods subsequent to that time. Nevertheless, the songs and bardic compositions of the very earliest period clearly point to this division of the vowels into broad and slender. Dr. John O'Donovan says:— "The principle upon which this division is founded is observable in the oldest fragments of Irish composition remaining to us."—*Irish Grammar, pp.* 3, 4. One can be morally certain, therefore, that from the most remote historic periods, the division of the vowels into broad and slender has been known.

The ancient rule in Irish: "Caol le Caol agus Leathan le Leathan," is the law of vowel assimilation literally crystalised.

3. The historic truth regarding this point, like the round towers, or the stamped tiles with which the palaces of Palmyra were built, has been engrained into the con-

stitution of the language. This fecund elementary truth has given birth to the grammatical dictum, "caol le caol, agus leaṫan le leaṫan," that is a slender vowel with a slender, and a broad vowel with a broad. The following observation is from the *College Irish Grammar, p.* 16 :—"This division of the vowels into *broad* and *slender* should not be lightly noticed by the student; for the spelling of all the words in the language depends much, nearly entirely, on the position which the slender and broad vowels hold with regard to the consonants. There is an old Gaelic rule which directs that a consonant, or consonants, should in every written word, lie between either two *slender*, or two *broad* vowels; and consequently, that a broad vowel, such as 'a,' 'o,' 'u,' could not correctly go before, while a slender vowel, either 'e' or 'i' comes immediately after a consonant, but if a broad vowel precede, so should a broad one follow; if a slender vowel precede, so should a slender vowel follow."

Dr. John O'Donovan says:—"The influence of the vowels over the consonants which exists to some extent in every language, has given rise to a general rule or canon of orthography which distinguishes the Irish from all the European languages."—*Irish Grammar p.* 3.

In page 9 of *Celtic Studies, from the German of Dr. Hermann Ebel, by William K. Sullivan, Ph., D., M.R.I.A. Williams and Norgate, London*, 1863, read the following words:

"The Irish rule of 'broad to broad, and slender to slender,' may be looked upon as progressive assimilation, the Irish broad vowels being 'a, o, u,' and the slender 'e, i.' Wherever this rule is followed, a consonant or consonants should, in every written word, lie between either two broad or two slender vowels; or, in other words, if the vowel of a syllable be broad, the vowel of the next succeeding syllable should be broad; if the vowel be slender, the following one must likewise be slender."

4. In the Finnish-Tartarian language—say the Russian, the vowels are divided into hard and soft—"a, o, u," are hard vowels. Now, if the root syllable in these dialects be hard (a, o, u,) the vowel of the suffixes must be hard. This principle is very remarkable in Russian. A distinct character is framed to note the hard or soft sound.

5. Is there any trace to be found in the Romance languages, or in English, to point out that, in former times, a division of the vowels like that which exists and flourishes at present in Irish-Gaelic, had existed? To this question an answer in the affirmitive must needs be given.

Every body who is any way acquainted with the French language is aware that the consonant "c," before the vowel "e" and "i," is invariably pronounced like "s;" and before "a, o, u," the same consonant is articulated (hard) like English "k." What else is that but a remnant of the slender-vowel action of "e" and "i?" The influence which these slender vowels have exercised on "c," as a consonant, has, in process of time, resulted in the pronunciation which, at the present time, the consonant "c," before "e" and "i," receives, in contradistinction to that which it receives before "a, o, u." It has happened, owing to vocal modifications, and owing to changes and times and dialectic renewal, that this difference is not so fully or so strongly marked in other consonants as it is in "c." "L" is an exception. The action of the slender vocal force of "e, i," on the liquid consonant "l" is such that in some words the "l" sound is nigh lost.

Let us take the Italian language next. What says Italian? what says Wallachian? That with regard to the articulated changes in the consonant "c" before "e," it cannot be denied that this letter coming before the slender vowels "e," "i," has an articulate value which it has not before "a," "o" "u," and hence, that the action of the slender vowels has told on this consonant in Italian. And thus these vowels, "e," "i," have, in the other mutes, to a less perceptible and to a less distinguishable degree, however, shown the influence that they have exercised on the consonants, with which in sound they unite.

Next, what says Spanish? Before "e," "i," "c" has the sound not of the Italian and Wallachian "tsh," but of "th" sharp; before "a, o, u," it has the common articulate value of "k." Hence, in the language of Castile and Arragon is to be seen the same phonetic feature that presents itself in Italian, Wallachian, and French.

Does this affection or change of sound before the vowels "e, i" exist in English too? Yes, it is found in English.

This division of vowels into broad and slender, "leatan le leatan, agus caol le caol," has never, though resting on the first principles of melody and euphony, been philosophically treated, nay, even noticed by English philologists, yet its use is not foreign to the Saxon tongue; for "c" and "g" before the broad vowels "a, o, u," are pronounced, "c" like "k," and "g" like "g" hard;

	a	o	u
as, c,	*cat*;	*cow*;	*cud*;
" g,	*garden*;	*gone*;	*gun*;

while before the vowels "e, i" called slender, the same consonants are pronounced soft—

e	i	
cent;	*cider*;	*ginGER*.

From the statements and the proofs just presented, the following conclusions are certain :—

(1) The vowels can, naturally and in strict propriety, owing to their character as musical sounds, be divided into two classes, broad (a, o, u,) and slender (e, i). (2) In Irish-Gaelic this division into hard and slender has been known and put into practice by the bards and grammarians, from the earliest period of Ireland's history. (3) In other languages this division is not unknown; nay, it holds an important place, at this very hour, in Russian, in which a special character is employed to point out the presence of the broad or slender vowel sound. (4) As the broken pillars of Pompeii tell of the architectural columns that stood perfect two thousand years ago, so the shattered remnants of the slender sounds of "e" and "i," scattered among the six Romance languages, point to the perfect use of the slender or sharp vowel sounds of "e" and "i," in days of early Roman pronunciation. It cannot, however, be inferred that "c," before "i" in Latin, had at any period the sound of "s" or "ts." For it is certain, as has been shown in chapter VI. of this work, that the sound of "c," even before "e" or "i," had, in Latin, always been the same as that of "k." (See c. vi., pp. 127, 128, 129).

OBJECTION.

How, then, has "c" in the Romance languages, daughters of Latin, the soft and hard sound ?

The answer is: "c" in Latin was always hard before "e" and "i," as well as before "a, o, u." Every consonant partakes of the nature of the vowel in union with which it is sounded. Now, the vowels "e" and "i" are the highest in the scale. They are slender; they are palatal. They give a pitch upwards to the articulate vocal value of the consonants—to "c," to "d, l, m, n," to "s." Hence consonants sounded with "e, i," must have a higher palatal potency than when sounded in union with "a, o, u."

The remnant of this high palatal power of the slender vowels, "e, i," is perceptible at this hour in the sounds which some consonants (notably "c, l,") receive in the Romance dialects, and in English.

In Irish-Gaelic the original sound of "c" before "e, i" is preserved in all its integrity and fulness. Its sound is the sound of "k," but "k," as in *Kyrie*.

Note,—The high palatal sound consonants receive from the presence of the slender vowel sounds, is well represented by "y" in English.

Hence, as a rule, an Irish consonant followed by "e," is represented in English by the same consonant, with "y" annexed.

"The sound of a slender consonant in Irish-Gaelic becomes, to an English student, distinct and perceptible by blending the sound of 'y' with the common consonantal articulation."—*College Grammar, p.* 20.

The consonant "s" in Irish, is a strong instance of the effect produced by the slender vowels: Before or after "a, o, u," its sound is "s" (like "ss" English); before or after "e, i," it is "sh," without an exception, as, "se" (sheh) he; "sion," (sheeon) a storm.

The "y" sound with the vowels "e, i," is plainly perceived in the second column of the following terms when contrasted with those of the first:—

bo, (pr. *bow*) cow; beo, (*byow*) alive.
cό, (*koh,*) as; ceo, (*kyeo*) or (*keogh*) fog.
do, (*dhoh,*) to; deo, (*dyoh*) life, ever.
cá, *kaw*, what; cia, (*kyah*) what.

"C" and "d" and "b," before "e" or "i," are palatalised, like "t" in *tune*; or like "ky" in *kyrie*

in kind, "a," in card; so the Irish word, "ciun," calm, is pronounced *kyooin.*

It is evident, therefore, when this vocal value of the slender vowels has been through ages retained in the Irish language; and when to this day the phonetic and the orthographic influence of the slender sounds permeates every syllable of Gaelic speech, and when, as has been shown, the sounds of the vowels is identical with the phonetic values of the same vocables in the Latin tongue, that a law like that now known in Irish as *vowel assimilation* must have existed at one time in Latin. The shadowy outline of the full figure of that law is to this day seen in the Romance descendants of the parent Latin tongue.

To sum up, then, it is certain that at an early period in the Latin as well as in the Irish language, a radical difference existed between the influence exercised by the two classes of vowels—the *broad* and the *slender*. This radical difference is found not to have floated down the stream of time, presenting, all through its varied course, the impress of a distinct phonetic feature, in any language so well as in Irish-Gaelic. In Latin it is lost except in its broken transmitted forms. In Ireland it is perfect still. This is important.

THE VOWEL LAW—ITS RESULTS UNCHANGEABLE: SOUND AND SPELLING ALWAYS SURE.

The effects of this principle of vowel assimilation in Irish permeates the whole of the language spoken and written.

One cannot breathe without air, nor see without reflected light, so one cannot speak Irish-Gaelic, or write it without a knowledge of this principle. Like rhythm in poetry, or melody in song, it is entwined with, and it gives life to the living breathing language of the Gael. For all this, the Irish speaking natives of Ireland do not advert to the presence of the principle; just much in the same way as we do not advert to the presence of the air by which we are surrounded.

All the phonetic and orthographic properties of Irish-Gaelic take their rise from this principle of vowel assimilation, just as branches sprout from a stem, and the leaves and flowers spring forth and bloom. Some of these properties are (1) fullness of articulate sound; (2) correctness of pronunciation, (3) an unchangeable spelling, quite in keeping with the settled pronunciation of the language. This principle may be regarded as a law of Gaelic speech: for its effects bear the impress of order, of harmony, of continued and lasting uniformity; of a directive influence on the language even in points the most minute.

What is the leading effect of this rule? It is simply that vowels of a certain class, for instance "e, i," affect the consonants (in union with which they enter, in producing Gaelic sounds, either of syllables and words,) to that degree, that not only the consonants are stamped with the vowel value which they derive from the connection, but the syllable coming directly next in order receives, so to speak, a starting note from the closing vowel of the preceding syllable. The effects produced are two-fold—first, on the consonant; secondly, in directing the character of the next vowel in the coming syllable.

EXAMPLES.

"Slanuıġteoır," a saviour, from "slan," safe, and "slanuıġ," to save; the slender vowel "i" precedes "g," and, therefore, a slender vowel "e" is the first in the annexed syllable, "ṫeoır," and not "toır." Again, "fuasgaltoır" ends in "toır," and not "ṫeoır," for in the primitive root, "fuasgal (with "a" before "l") closes with a broad vowel ("a"). In verbs this law is strikingly remarkable, as "cuir," put, "cuir-tear," (and not "cuir-tar,") is put; "buail," strike, "buail-tear," is struck.

Irish-Gaelic, therefore, adheres fully to the law of *vowel assimilation*, which, generally speaking, has been lost throughout Europe.

"Thus we see that the classification of vowels made by Irish grammarians accords exactly with that which the investigations of philosophy point out as correct. There are in Gaelic, therefore, two classes of vowels clearly and philosophically distinguishable. Do they differ in their influence and in their effects?

"Vowels and consonants constitute the one grand, universal family of letters. Consonants derive their name from the fact that they *are sounded along with*, or by the aid of the vowels. When articulated, they partake, of the sound of that vowel by the aid of which they are enunciated. Irish vowel sounds are, as we have seen, of a twofold character, *broad* or *slender*; each consonant must, accordingly, partake of a twofold articulation, *broad* or *slender*, according to the broad or slender intonation of the vowel by the aid of which it is sounded. This twofold articulation can, in some measure, be applied with truth to consonants in any language; but, with the exception of the Keltic dialects, and particularly Irish, we know of none in which this phonetic distinction in the articulation of consonants has retained its radically distinctive philosophic character.

"The influence of a twofold sound of the vowels thus acting on the consonants, and causing them to participate in it, is so fused into our national language that it has stamped its pronunciation and orthography with a complexion and individuality quite different from everything English. To Irish-speaking natives this individuality appears quite easy and natural, and, like accent, with which it is essentially blended, is naturally acquired and practised by them without knowing or adverting to the existence of the principle from which it springs; yet, to those who do not speak the language, it appears at once strange and difficult.

"As the language is spoken and written, the effects of the influence exercised by the twofold division of vowel sounds extend to both departments—the written and spoken Gaelic. These effects may well, therefore, be called *articulate*, or phonetic, and *orthographic*.

"The *articulate* regards the sound of each consonant when it is intonated with a broad or slender vowel. The *orthographic* regards the laws of spelling."—*Easy Lessons, or Self-Instruction in Irish, Part III., pp.* 200, 201; *Dublin, Mullany, publisher.*

It appears to arise from a principle of euphony, according to Latham:

"The Irish-Gaelic, above most other languages, illustrates a euphonic principle that modifies the vowels of a word. The vowels 'a, o, u,' are full, whilst 'i, e' are sharp. Now, if to a syllable containing a small vowel, as, 'buail,' there be added a syllable containing a broad one, as 'am,' a change takes place. Either the first syllable is accommodated to the second, or the second to the first, so that the vowels respectively contained in them are either both full or both small. Hence arises, in respect to the word quoted, either the form 'bualam,' or else the form 'buailim."—*Latham on the English Language, 3rd ed.*, § 228, *p.* 158. And from a principle of harmony, according to Professor W. K. Sullivan.

GRAND RESULTS: CERTAINTY OF SOUND; SURETY OF SPELLING.

Two grand results spring immediately and directly from this principle:

First—A perfect system of phonetics, and a correct common standard of pronunciation. The vowel sounds of "e, i" are high, and lend to the consonants a palatal character. The tongue, in pronouncing the consonant with "e," must touch the palate. The sound once uttered does not rest with the consonant. It does not stop there, but passes on to the first part of the next syllable. The action of this sound may well be compared to a man going up a hill. He attains the height he sought. He cannot, in descending, come down all at once. He holds for a time to the high position he has attained. So it is with the vowel sounds. When the articulate value of "e" or "i" has been heard in any syllable, that pitch or palatal power it has attained is kept up; and hence the next syllable coming directly after it must, in part, re-echo the vowel pitch. In this way each syllable ending with "i" must have "e" or "i" first in the succeeding syllable. Such is the law of phonetics in Irish. It is the precursor of the law of spelling; and spelling is moulded on its rules.

Second—A correct system of spelling. Let a student only learn the roots of words; the prefixes and suffixes; and then, by the application of the rule, "Caol le caol, agus leatan le leatan," he can spell any word in the Irish language. Let us take, for example, in Irish:

THE LORD'S PRAYER—AN PADAIR.

Ar n-atair a tá air neam go naomtar d' ainm, go d-tigid do rigeact, go n-déantar do toil air an talam mar gnidtear air neam. Tabair dúinn ann n-iúd ar n-arán laetamail, agus mait duinn ar b-fiaca mar maiteamuid-ne da 'r b-fiacainaib féin, na léig sinn a g-catugad, act saor sinn ó olc. Amén.*

*Terms, or Words Explained.—"Padair," a prayer, derived from the Latin *pater*, father; it means the *our father*, and

The Iliad. By his Grace the Most Rev. Dr. MacHale, Archbishop of Tuam.

Bruṫ Acuil, seinn, óiġ neaṁḋa, 'gus buan-ḟearg,
Acuil Mic Péil, an gaisgiḋeaċ, teinteaċ garg;
Do scap tríḋ sluaġ na n-Greug, trom leun a's ár,

---

hence a prayer; "aṫair," father; after "ar," *our*, one of the plural possessive pronouns, "n" is prefixed to *avoid* any want of smoothness of sound; "aṫair" either lost initial "p," or came as it stands without "p," from the primitive Aryan speech; "a," who; "tá," is, art, are; "air," on; "air," preposition, is distinguished from "ar," our, by taking the vowel "i" before "r:" "air," pronounced *arh;* "ar," is pronounced *ur;* "ár," destruction, is *awr;* "a" in "ár" is accented in "ar," *our*, it is not; "neaṁ," pr. *nyav*, heaven; "flaiṫeas" means the principality (of God), indirectly heaven; "go," that; "naoṁ," a saint; "naoṁṫar," may be blessed, may be sanctified; "d" for "do," thy, formed from "tu," thou, as *thy* is from *thou*, *tuus* (Latin) from *tu*; "ton" and "tá" (French) from *tu*; "tig," come; "tigiḋ" (*thigee*), may come; "rig" (pr. *ree*), a king; "rigeaċt," kingdom; the correct spelling is "rig" (root of word *a king)*, and not "riog," and its suffix is "aċt," a state. By vowel assimilation "aċt" becomes "eaċt," because the vowel in "rig" is slender. "Déan," do, act, make; "déantar" (and not "déan-tear") may be done; "a" in "déan" is broad and final; hence the suffix is broad, "tar" and not "tear"; on the other hand the passive ending after "gniḋ," to do, is "tear," because "i" in "gníḋ" is the closing consonant. "Talaṁ," earth; Latin *tellus*, *terra*; "taḃair," give; "duinn," to us, composed of "do," to; "sinn," us; "diu," to-day, spelled also "uiḋ," as in French *huy*; "arán," bread, takes "n," like "aṫair," above, after "ar," our; "lá," a day; "lae," of a day; "lae-ṫ-aṁail," day-like, daily; "ṫ" is inserted between "lae" and "aṁail," like, for euphony; "maiṫ" (pr. *may-eeh)* forgive; "fiaċa," debts, after "ar," our, "f" is eclipsed by a medial aspirate "ḃ," that is by "v;" "mar," as; "maiṫeamuid," we forgive; "muid" is the plural ending to "maiṫ," forgive, "ea" is inserted for fulness of sound "ne" is suffixed to "muid," to make the term emphatic. We say, "sinn," we, "sinn-ne," we-ourselves; so also "ne," an old form like *nos*, Latin, is suffixed to verbs to express emphasis and contradistinction; "na," not; "léig," lead; "sinn," us; "a," into; "caṫ," (pr. *cawh)*, a fight; "caṫuig," to fight in battle; "caṫugaḋ," temptation, a fight with the adversary of our souls; "c" is eclipsed by "g," a softer sound; "c" is retained in the spelling, but not sounded; "saor," v., free; "sinn," us; "ó," from; "olc," evil.

'S d' ḟág móran laoċra treun,' ro luaṫ air lár:
Raiḃ a n-aḃlaiġ fuilteaċ' sracta air an ḃ-feur
Aig madraiḃ seanga, 's fangaiḃ gortaċ' geur.
Bud 'n-dán réir ṫola Ioiḃ, go d-tiocfaḋ an t-eug
O ċuaiḋ ċum imris Acuil a's flaiṫ na n-Greug.
'Ċeolraiḋ an ḃinnis, craoḃ-sgaoil, de na Deá
Cia 'n neaċ do ṫionsgnuiġ gleo ó 'r ṡíolruiġ an cráḋ?
Do sgaoil mac lonraċ Ioiḃ a ġaeṫe teo,
'Gus ṡeoil go riġeaċt an ḃáis na sluaiġte beo;
Mar ġeall air ḋímeas díbliġ ṫug an riġ
D'a ṡagart naoṁta,—dearc an leun gan sciṫ,
Aig teaċt go tiuġ a's go tóban air a lorg,
Mar díoltas ccart air Ċeanfart uailleaċ, borb.
Ċum longa na n-Greug, do ṫriall an sagart sáiṁ,
Le taḃartas trom 'gus seoide ann gaċ laiṁ;
Mar ḃi fleasg craoḃ, 'ḃi fillte air a ċeann,
'Gus bacul óir, gnáṫ-ḃrata Ṗeuba teann,
Do ġuiḋ an sluaġ go léir aċt fós go buan,
Ġuiḋ dís claim Aitríḋ taosaiġ árd' na luan.
Go raiḃ an troiġ faoi sgrios na n-Deaṫa, bán.
A gaisgiḋṫe Greug,' a's go raiḃ ḃur seolta lán,
Le gaoṫ a ḃéarfas siḃ air ais ċum ċuain
Ḃur d-tír a's ḃur muintir sealḃuġaḋ móran suain
Aċt déanaiḋ truaiġ air ṡeanóir crom faoi leun
'Gus taḃraiḋ air ais dó arís a leanḃ féin,
Glacaiḋ mo ḋuais, a's sgaoiliḋ cuid mo ċroiḋe,
'Gus taḃraiḋ móḋ do Ḋia na n-gaeṫe buiḋe!
Aig freagairt impiḋe, ġáir na Grug' go mór,
'Gus ṫug dó coṁairle eisteaċt le n-a ġlór.
Do ġuin an coṁairle ceart an-ċlant' an riġ
'Gus d' ḟoillsiġ freagraḋ geur garḃ-ṁéin a ċroiḋe.
Leig leat, a ṡeanóir, na déan moill, na sgiṫ,
Measg lung na n-Greug, aċt fill air ais sa t-sliġe,
Air cagla gád naċ d-taróċaiḋ ort aon sgiaṫ,

No do ċaıl caoṁ, no bacul fós do Ḋıa.
Nı leıgfad uaım an óıġ go d-tıg an traṫ,
A críonfas aoıs, a sgéım, a cruṫ, 's a bláṫ;
Aċt béıḋ sı gabṫa leıs an t-seol go buan,
'S a gleusaḋ leaba ann a ngeıbfead suan,
O'n m-baıle 'g-cıan: teıṫ uaınn: na brostuıġ an Ceann.
Do ġeıt an fear le eagla an rıġ 'ḃi teann,
'Gus d' eulııġ leıs go sostaċ, trom, faoı ḟearg,
Le ȧıs na d-tonta glóraċ, géımneaċ garg;
Aıg meaḃruġaḋ cuıtuıġaḋ 's aıg agaırt coımırc De.
Mıc mna na n-deas-dlaoıġ' sgeıṫeas dealraıḋ an lae.
A rıġ na gaeṫe geal. a's na bóġa bán,
A ḃ-fuıl na ínse le do ṡolus lán *

THE ILIAD—NOTES.—"Bruṫ," anger, brooding anger; "fearg' passing anger; "seınn," sing; "óıġ," (pr. *o-ee)* virgin; "neaṁda," heavenly; "'gus" "agus," *and*; "buan-ḟearg" lasting anger; "f" in "fearg" is aspirated, on account of the compound word: A change to an aspirate form is in composition required in Gaelic. "Mıc," gen. case of "mac," son; "gaısgıdeaċ (pr *gawishgeeach)*, a hero, a chivalrous fellow; "teınteaċ" fiery, from "teıne," fire; "garg," rough; "do" is sign of the perfect tense; "a," who, is omitted before "do," for "a do scap," who did scatter; "tríd," through; "sluaġ" (pr. *slooa)*, as in *Ballinasloe*, that is the town (baıle) of the hosts (na sluaġ) "trom-leun," heavy woe; "a's" and, "ár" destruction; "ḟág," left; "f" aspirated in perfect tense active; "mórán," many; "laoċra," heroes; "treun," brave; the name "Traynor," is derived from "treun," brave, and "fear," a man; "ro luaṫ," too soon; "aır lár," on the centre, stretched, lying—an adverbial phrase, meaning *laid out*, stretched, lying low; "raıḃ," was; "a n-aḃlaıg," plu. of "aḃlaċ," a carcase; "fuılteaċ," from "fuıl," blood; "sracṫa," torn, mangled; "feur," grass; "aıg," at, by; "madraıḃ," dogs; "seanga," thin, wasted; "fangaıḃ," vultures; "gortaċ," hungry; "geur," sharp, biting; "buḋ," it was; "n-dán," in destiny; "réır," according to; "tola," gen. case of "toıl," will; "Joıḃ," gen. case of "Job," Jove; "go," that, "tıocfaḋ," would come; "eug," death, takes "t" for sound between "n" of the art; and "e," the vowel, as "an t-eug;" the death; "an t-aṫaır," the father; this occurs only in the nom. and in the accusative cases singular; "ó," from, referring to time, *since*; "ċuaıḋ," went; "ċum," to, towards; "ımrıs," gen. case of "ımreas," contention; "rıs" in

Translation by John Stuart Blackie, F.R.S.E.—Vol. II. Edinburgh: Edmonston and Douglas, 1866.

The baneful wrath, O goddess, sing, of Peleus' son, the source
Of sorrow dire, and countless woes to all the Grecian force;
That wrath which many a stout heroic soul from joyful day
To gloomy Hades hurled, and left their mangled limbs a prey
To dogs and vultures; thus the will of mightiest Jove was done;
Since first contention keen arose, and sundering strife begun
Between Atrides, king of men, and Peleus' godlike son.
Which of the gods between them twain the rancorous feud inspired?
Latona's son; for he against the king, with anger fired,
Shot through the camp a sore disease; the people drooped and died;
For that Atrides to his priest the righteous suit denied.
When to the swift sea-ploughing ships came Chryses with a prayer,
And for his daughter's freedom brought the precious ransom rare.
He on a golden sacred staff, with outstretched arm, displayed
The wreath of the far-darting god, and thus to all he prayed,
But chiefly to the kingly pair, whose word the host obeyed:
Ye sons of Atreus, and ye Greeks with burnished greaves, give ear;
You may the gods with conquest crown, and grant with mastering spear
To sack old Troy, and sail with joy to friends and country dear:
But me—my daughter dear restore, and let rich ransome follow,

---

"ımrıs," in the gen. is pronounced *rish*; "s" after "ı" has the sound of *sh*, in every instance; "ımreas" is same as "ımréıdeas;" "réıd" means ready; "reıdeas," evenness, smoothness, quietness; "ım-reıdeas," non-quietness, hence contention; "flaıt," a prince; "flaıtaṁaıl," princely; "ceol," music; "ceolraıḋ," songster; "bınn," harmonious; "bınneas n' craoḃ," a branch; "sgaol," loose; "craoḃ-sgaol," reveal, show out as a branch pulled of a tree, what is hidden beneath the surface; "tıonsgnuıġ," commenced; "síol" seed; "síolruıġ," was generated; "tos," and "taos," and "tús," commencement, beginning; "tosaċ" and "tusaċ," a beginner, a leader; "taosaċ," a leader, &c.

Fearing the dread, far-darting god, the son of Jove, Apollo.
Whereto the Achæan host replied with loud-consenting cheer,
And bade him grant the old man's prayer, and his wreathed staff revere;
But ill was Agamemnon pleased, and forth his anger brake;
Away he sent the priest, and thus with fell reproof he spake:
Old man, if near the hollow ships I find thee here again,
Or lingering now with laggard foot if thou shalt dare remain,
Thy hand shall show the sacred wreath, and bear the staff in vain.
The maid I'll not restore; no, not till hoary age shall come
To her at Argos, in my house, far from her father's home:
There shall she tend the loom, and share my royal bed; but thou,
Begone! fret me no more! thy speed shall be thy safety now!
He spake! the old man feared; no word of sharp reply gave he,
But silent went to the billowy beach of the vast and voiceful sea.
There from the ships apart he stood, and poured the pleading prayer
To the son of Jove whom Leto bore of the lovely-flowing hair:
Hear me, O god of the silver bow, who rightly claim'st for thine
Tenedos' isle, and Chryse's walls, and Cilla's towers divine!

An English gentleman, a man of considerable learning, heard this system at one time explained by the present writer, and he cried out suddenly—"How beautiful!" He was right. The system of vowel assimilation in Irish is really beautiful.

What is beauty? It is harmony of parts producing a uniform single developement. It is the expression to the eye, or to the perceptive faculty, of truth, of wisdom, and outward grace. In physical things, it is fulness of developement produced by symmetry and harmony.

In all that is said of the beautiful there are two leading ideas, without which, a conception of beauty cannot be formed; these are oneness, combined with multiplicity and truth, to which, according to some, ought to be added extrinsic grace, or the reflex of light.

We say, "the beauty of creation,"—that is, the grace and external show of that order and harmony which shines forth in all that the eye beholds, the astronomer's glass reaches, or the microscope presents. We say, "the beauties of nature—a beautiful poem; a thing of beauty is a joy for ever," to express the delight of the mind at the variety and singleness with fulness of development, that are presented in the objects, and which, on that account, are called beautiful.

Beauty must be natural, must be founded in truth; like the color of gold, it must be the gleam of real worth, or like nature's budding rose that opens its petals to the morn. Nothing artificial, nothing made up, nothing however pleasing to the eye, yet deceitful or deceptive, can be justly styled beautiful. Imitations, no matter how well painted, passing for what they are not in reality, can never be pronounced beautiful. Again—show, and richness, and power, without harmony of parts and oneness of combination, cannot constitute beauty.

The English language is very rich in wealth of words, in strength and in power; yet, its system of orthography or of phonetics cannot, by any means, be pronounced "a thing of beauty."

Not so in Irish Gaelic. All the rules for orthography, all the minor principles of phonetics, are the developements of the one great law of vowel assimilation.

The principle which produces this law is like the principle of polarity. The slender vowels "e, i" always tend to one pole; "a, o, u," to the other.

If a student learns this Gaelic law as it has been explained in this chapter, and makes it his aim to put it into practice both by writing the language, and speaking it to some one who knows it, each day for one month, there is no doubt, but even at the end of that short period, he will be able to speak Irish-Gaelic fairly. English scholars, whose natural accent and tone from childhood are opposed almost naturally to the guttural sounds of Irish-Gaelic, have learned in two months to speak many sentences and to write the speech of the sons of the sister isle of Britain.

Learners and those not practised in the language commonly err in reading and spelling by giving to Irish letters the sounds which, in the English speech they are accustomed to bestow on the same letters, and combinations of letters. This is, of course, a great mistake. Apply English sounds and English accent to French, and what a phonetic jumble the language of Fenelon or the rhyme of Racine becomes.

FROM ONE PRINCIPLE BOTH LAWS PROCEED PERHAPS.

This chapter is brought to a close by putting before the notice of the learned reader and every philologist who may peruse these pages, a view respecting the *law of vowel assimilation* such as it exists in full in Irish Gaelic, and in fragmentary form in the Romance *dialects*, on the one hand; and Grimm's law, or that which in Irish regulates the processes of *aspiration* and *eclipse*, on the other. They appear to be distinct laws; and no doubt they are in their results. But every physicist knows that though all the colors formed from light are distinct—green is not orange, nor orange green; yet, all blend so harmoniously, that a person cannot well perceive where, in the diversity of the rainbow tints, the one comes to a close, and the other takes its rise. It is so in the aggregate of virtues, they form the circle of perfection; if one is omitted, the rest are imperfect, or, like the stones that compose an arch, they affect yet support each other. Thus it appears to the writer that a common phonetic principle, like the magnetic fluid, acting on the vowels, produces the law of vowel assimilation; and on the consonants, is the origin of aspirating and eclipsing.

Thus the Welsh term *tref*, a habitation, (in Irish "treiḃ" a tribe, a class of people) is *threv*—"th" when "a" precedes; *marw* (dead), Irish "marḃ," becomes, when compounded with "di" (want, defect) *di-varu*, immortal ("m" into "v.") So in Irish "marḃ," dead; "dı-ṁarḃ," immortal; "m" is aspirated by the influence of "i," in "di:" and "f" in "dıḃfeırge," wrath, eclipsed. The harmonic action of the vowel sounds leads to aspiration and eclipsis.

This view, just now presented, has occurred to the writer for the first time while penning this page. He suggests it but does not hold it as an opinion. No doubt, like colors, or some notes in distinct octaves, the two laws have at least a remote and an indirect relationship. Regarding the law of vowel assimilation, however, his opinions are settled. He has devoted attention to it from time to time, since he was eighteen years old. He has read all the views of all those who have written on the subject. Some writers—they are few—have declared the division of the vowels into broad and slender, is the in vention of bards or rhymers. This was the opinion of Dr. John O'Brien, Bishop of Cloyne; of Colonel Vallancey, of Halliday, of P. MacEllegott—but these writers never gave the subject the slightest thought, at least they, in their writings, give no reason for their strange opinions.

The science of comparative philology had not been known when they lived. Some of them were very inaccurate in thought, and very illogical in reasoning. Few scholars now-a-days care to notice Colonel Vallancey, and poor Halliday died when only a young man. Had he lived he would doubtless have become a distinguished Keltic scholar.

There is at present a work being published on the languages of western Europe, by a distinguished Scotch Gaelic Scholar, Charles Mackey, LL.D. When it will have been published, then, many words, now commonly deemed of German or Gothic origin, will be seen to derive their parentage, as Matthew Arnold has shewn, from a primitive Keltic ancestry.

GENERAL RULE TO GUIDE ONE IN DISTINGUISHING WHETHER A WORD IS OF GAELIC OR GOTHIC PARENTAGE.

There is one general characteristic worth noticing, that, as a rule, Keltic primitives side with Latin and Sanscrit, while English shows, in the initial letter of words that are regularly changed, a decided relationship with the Gothic, or low German.

Every word in English, therefore, which has not, generally speaking, the same initial letter as that which distinguishes its German cognate equivalent conveying the same idea, has come to us from Keltic parentage. For, the Latin race is more than half Keltic. The Greeks, too, received much of their *vivida vis animi* from the primæval Pelasgic plantation who founded Thebes, built Argos, laid out the broad-ways, and erected the magnificient mansions of Mycenæ, left monuments of their knowledge of architecture on the Acropopolis, at Athens.

The term *day*, for instance, which is a very simple common word, shows that it has sprung from a Keltic stock. The High German is *tac*; Low German, *tag*; Old Gaelic, *dia*; as "dıa-luaın," Monday; "dıa-maırt," Tuesday, &c.; and in the word "n-de," for "lá-an-dé" yesterday,—day-of-day; ".dıu," to-day; and spelled "ann-dıu,". and contractedly "n-dıu:" Latin *die*, and *ho-die*, to-day.

Now, to which of the two languages is the term "day," judging from sound and sign, more a-kin? Certainly to

Gaelic. All the late students of comparative philology admit that Irish or Keltic is the oldest of the Indo-European tongues; that the Keltic branch of the Aryan tree was the first off-shoot to Europe, and that the speech of the Gael had taken a "fixed set" before any of the other branches had attained their natural developement. It is the oldest language, therefore; and the term *day* must have been retained in English from the British or Irish.

A RICH VEIN DISCOVERED IN THE MINES OF PHILOLOGY.

Reverting once more to the law of *vowel assimilation*, as it exists in Irish-Gaelic, and as it is known in the languages of Europe, the writer must observe that if a distinguished German scholar, after twenty years study, like Jacob Grimm, should discover such a law, tracing it, now in French, again in Italian, and Spanish; finding it half-revealed in Latin monumental analogies, and inscriptions prior to the Punic period; collating terms of cognate sound in Latin and Æolic, comparing Oscan with the Greek of Dorians or Ionians; and perhaps higher still, seeing what relation had existed between Old Keltic pronunciation, as far as it can be known, and the Phenician speech of the primeval period. Such a discovery, which he might conveniently call *Aryan vowel assimilation*, would be hailed with delight by every intelligent philologist in Europe.

The language of Ireland lays before the savants of Europe the beautiful discovery in the science of comparative philology, which, as a law of her life, lay hidden for ages past. For this she seeks no reward.

CHAPTER XI.

Twentieth—Subjects arising out of the foregoing. 1. Had the Irish Gaels before the Christian Era any knowledge of letters? 2. Had they a knowledge of the Art of Writing? 3. What alphabet did they use? A literary fight waged for centuries on this battleground. The combatants on either side, in the past and in the present. The two classes in opposition. Those on one side wrote without any knowledge of the subject, or from prejudice, or pay; the other, native born, with knowledge, matured study, and great research; without pay or hope of reward. The views and reasons of each side stated. The science of Comparative Philology rises high above all party views, and looks at the question *a priori*. It proves that the early Pagan Irish were a highly literary people. How far late historic research is in accord with the teaching of Comparative Philology. Gist of all the Manuscript History presented by O'Curry in accord with the proofs from Philology. The early emigrants from the Aryan region literary. The Kelts as the first emigrants had, therefore, before others, a knowledge of letters and of the arts. They had, therefore, an alphabet. They did not borrow letters from any nation, Greece or Phenicia. Two kinds of Alphabets, a public or common form of writing, and a secret writing—the Ogham Advanced knowledge of the Pagan Irish in Arts. The Book of Kells. The Round Towers. The Number of letters in the Irish Alphabet The letters—called Irish character—are Roman of the seventh century. Why not use modern Roman with diacritical dots now instead of the old dotted character. Wisdom of this course. The aspirate "h" and the (·) dot. Which is the better to mark the phonetic mutation. Summary.

There are in Irish-Gælic subjects of interest connected closely with that which has been put before the reader's view in the chapter just closed, regarding the phonetic law of vowel *assimilation* in Irish, and the all-pervading influence, which, in the spoken and written language it exercises on every syllable spelled or spoken.

These subjects are best shewn by putting the following questions:

1. Had the Irish-Gael, before the Christian Era, and consequently before the Gospel was preached in Eiré, possessed any knowledge of letters, and to what extent?

Coming directly next in order is another subject wound up with the foregoing, but nevertheless special, and on that account demanding a special answer to a particular proposition.

2. Had the Irish-Gael who flourished in the first century of the Christian Era, or immediately before that time any knowledge of the art of writing?

3. What alphabet or form of written letters did they use? Were they Semitic, that is, Hebrew, Chaldaic or ancient Phenician, or were they of Aryan origin, coming down from the great ancestral home in Persia, before the first migration of Aryans had found a new home in the Isle of the West?

Questions like the foregoing, at times in the same interrogatory form, have been put, but never satisfactorily answered. The discussion regarding the early literature of the Irish, and their knowledge of the use of letters at the very earliest historic period has been going on since the days of Henry II. to the present hour.

The literary fight has been waged since the times when the native Irish were first pronounced half savages by Giraldus de Barry, well known as Cambrensis to all who desired to raise English power and English civilization by the process of despising the Gael in their own country and exhibiting them in the light of advanced barbarians. Cambrensis had hosts of followers. He had the press and the power of the dominant race at his back. So much did his teaching prevail, that foreign writers like Bollandus believed the early Irish were devoid of learning, and had in the Pagan period no acquaintance with letters until the arrival of St. Patrick in Ireland. It is only a few years ago since James Anthony Froude stood up in New York before the American public, to show from history, that not only Pagan Ireland, but Christian Ireland had, previous to the coming of the English amongst them, been half savages, strangers to refinement; and, like the Hottentots to whom Pinkerton likened them, had been far removed from the softening influences of civilization and literary culture. The very rev. historian, Giraldus Cambrensis, and Rev. Father Bollandus, S.J., with Pinkerton and Froude, are the leading men of the past and present who directed the literary campaigning against the civilization and literary character not only of the Pagan Irish, but of the Christian Irish who had lived before the landing of the English on the southern shores of Ireland.

On the other hand, the cause of Ireland's civilization and literary character has been very ably handled by learned and clever Irishmen, lay as well as cleric. Strange to say, many of these defenders are themselves the descendants of the very men who, as invaders, came with Henry II.; *v.g.* Rev. Dr. Thomas Burke, the erudite author of the *Hibernia Dominicana*; Very Rev. Dr. John Lynch, Archdeacon of Tuam, author (1662, A.D.) of the celebrated *Cambrensis Eversus.* According to the testimony of the Very Rev. Mathew Kelly, D.D., Professor of *Belles-lettres* in St. Patrick's College, Maynooth, translator and editor for the Celtic Society of *Cambrensis Eversus*, the author, John Lynch, was one of the most eminent men who rose with such promise about the close of Elizabeth's reign. He was born in Galway, and descended from a family who claim descent from Hugh De Lacy, one of the most successful of the first race of Anglo-Norman invaders.

The Very Rev. Dr. Geoffrey Keating the Herodotus of Ireland, the foremost and ablest in the sixteenth century, or, indeed, at any other period, in defending the truth of Ireland's history, was of Norman descent. The illustrious Irish scholar and erudite historian traces his lineage to the distinguished family of that name, "whose various branches held high rank and large possessions in the counties of Wexford, Kildare, Carlow, Waterford, Tipperary, and Cork." According to the traditions of the family legalised by the books of Heraldry in Ireland—the founder of the house, whose original name is unknown, for surnames were at that time being introduced (12th century), was one of the pioneers of the Norman invaders, who lighted the beacon fire that lit the way of Fitz-stephens." The story is worth relating, for it tells how it happened that as the founder of the Keating family, lay by his watchfire, a wild boar chanced to prowl quite near, and was on the point of attacking him, when the sparkling and crackling of the fire frightened the animal, and caused him to flee.

The first of the Keating family, thus providentially saved, adopted as his armorial "sign," a wild boar rampant, rushing through a brake, with the motto *fortis et fidelis*. The surname which he assumed is from the Irish compound term, "ceud-teinne, meaning first fire, or *cetein*, hence Keating.

This origin of the name appears very pretty; but the

narration cannot create conviction in any mind desirous of real historic data. Halis Keting was the founder of the family; and twelve years after the landing of Fitz-stephens, the name of Halis Keting is found as subscribing witness to a grant to Dunbrody Abbey, by Henry of Montmorencie. About the year 1570, Geoffrey Keating was born at Tubrid, not far from Shanbally, in Tipperary. Amongst other able supporters of the cause of historic truth, are to be ranked Sir James Ware, and his faithful expounder, Harris; also Archbishop Ussher; Roderick O'Flaherty, author of the *Ogygia, seu rerum Hibernicarum Chronologia ex Pervetustis Monumentis fideliter in se collatis, Londini,* A.D., 1685.—The truth of Irish history was defended by Brother Michael O'Clery, the erudite and noble leader of the last literary hope of Ireland before the fatal war of 1641; by John Colgan, by Dr. Petrie, Dr. O'Donovan, O'Curry, by the late lamented Very Rev. Dr. Mathew Kelly, Maynooth, by Dr. Todd of Trinity College, the Hon. D'Arcy McGee, by most of the able scholars connected with the Royal Irish Academy, the Archæological and Keltic Societies; lastly, amongst the living, by the Very Rev. Thomas Burke, who ably and victoriously vindicated the cause of historic truth and of Ireland's title to the honorable distinction bestowed on her by the Venerable Bede, "the island of saints and scholars;" by the Most Rev Dr. Moran, Lord Bishop of Ossory, by Sir William Wilde, and Lady Wilde (Speranza), by the most laborious and voluminous writer in modern times—Rev. John O'Hanlon, of St. Michael and John's, Dublin, who has, for the past thirty years, labored with wonderful research, to compile from all possible authentic sources the lives, not of a few, but of all the saints of Ireland; by Sister Mary Frances Cusack, religieuse of the Order of Poor Clares, Kenmare—a lady who commands the most facile pen of all the distinguished writers of the present time, and certainly the most gifted authoress of this century; by Alexander Sullivan, M.P. for Louth, and author of the Story of Ireland; by Martin Haverty, Esq.; and, though last named, not the least distinguished for learning and for the impartial historic testimony he has given during an eventful life—John Mitchell.

And touching this controversy concerning Ireland's claim to a literary name in the fifth century, and in her pre-christian days, it must be stated at the very outset, regarding those who have been engaged in it, that all who gave their views in a spirit of hostility to the Irish race, have been either absolutely ignorant of the special subjects concerning which they wrote; or if not ignorant, filled with prejudice, as in the instances of Giraldus de Barry and that of James Anthony Froude; or from the one-sided view which they took, or were obliged to take, they distorted facts, and presented past events in the historic light in which it was their wish or their office that posterity should view the deeds of past periods along the high-ways of Irish history. A man may be learned in one subject or in a thousand subjects, and yet be very ignorant of others, concerning which he has had no information, and cares to have none. Clever men may be very learned in history and in science and in Catholic theology, if you will, as the Flemish Father Bollandus had most certainly been, and, nevertheless, they might be, as they actually were, very ignorant of the private laws and history of either Japan, or of Ireland.

Now the Irish people had been in the past as unknown to those writers, as the Japanese in the past and in the present have been to many Europeans.

On the other hand, those who have vindicated the character and cause of Ireland, who say that she was a hive of learning from the year A.D., 432 to 800, a period when, as Aengus states, there were countless hosts of illuminated books in Erin; that previous to St. Patrick's coming to preach the faith to the Irish, she possessed a history and a literature of her own; that a literary order—the Bardic—had been in the reign of Conor MacNessa, and long before that period, a standing national institution amongst the Irish Gaels, as it had been, hundreds of years previous to that time, amongst the tribes and people of Keltic descent; that they had an alphabet; that they had the Brehon Laws written; that there were books written "and in the possession of the Druids before the arrival" of our national apostle,—were all native-born writers, and they display, in reality, the greatest amount of research and knowledge in antiquities and in history.

TWO CLASSES OF WRITERS IN OPPOSITION.

These two classes of writers are opposed one to the other. The one side maintains and gives strong proofs to show that the pre-Christian Gaels possessed a literature, and practised a mode of writing and of keeping records; and that they had an alphabet quite different from, and independent of, both the Greek and the Roman form and character. The others who do not adopt these views, reject the arguments, repudiate the authority of the writers cited as that of mere rhymers and storytellers, no way worthy of credit.

The three subjects, the very early Christian and pre-Christian civilization,—literary fame—and the alphabet letters are so blended one with the other, that it is not well to separate them.

COMPARATIVE PHILOLOGY.

The arguments drawn from the science of comparative

philology rise above all these debated points of history, and throw, on the question of Ireland's early civilization, a new light which, up to the present time, has never beamed on the pages of Eire's ancient story. Critics cannot cavil with certain philological facts, the deductions from which are quite clear, and strong enough to convince any candid lover of truth.

And first, let the question be put before the reader from the pages of the latest and best work written on the early records of ancient Eire—*O'Curry's Manuscript Materials of Irish History.* To give extracts from all the works at hand on this interesting subject would fill a volume. Three or four quotations must suffice.

"Amongst the large quantities of MS. records which have come down to our times, will be found examples of the literature of very different periods of our history. Some possess a degree of antiquity, very remarkable, indeed, when compared with similar records of other countries of modern Europe. Those manuscripts, which we now possess, belonging to the earliest periods, are, themselves, we have just reason to believe, either in great part or in the whole but transcripts of still more ancient works."

"At what period in Irish history *written* records began to be kept it is, perhaps, impossible at present to determine with precision. However, the national traditions *assign a very remote antiquity and a high degree of cultivation to the civilization* of our Pagan ancestors."

1. Without granting to such traditions a greater degree of credibility than they are strictly entitled to, it must, I think, be admitted that the immense quantity of historical legendary and genealogical matter relating to the pagan age of ancient Erin, and which we can trace to the very oldest written documents, of which we enter-

tain any account, could only have been transmitted to our times by *some form of written record.*

What was the probable state of learning in Erin about the period of the introduction of Christianity by St. Patrick?

2. There is abundant evidence in the manuscripts relating to this period (the authority and credibility of which are readily proved), *to show that St. Patrick found on his coming to Erin a regularly defined system of law and policy*, and a fixed classification of the people according to various grades and ranks, under the sway of a single monarch, presiding over certain subordinate provincial kings."

3. "We find mention likewise of books in the possession of the Druids before the arrival of St. Patrick, and it is repeatedly stated (in the Tripartite Life of the Saint), that he placed alphabets, *primers* or *lessons*, in the Latin language in the hands of those whom he wished to take into his ministry."

4. "We have also several remarkable examples of the literary eminence which was rapidly attained by many of his disciples, amongst whom may be particularly mentioned Benen, or Benignus; Mochoe, and Fiacc of Slebhte, or Sletty. This last is the author of a biographical poem in the Gaelic language, a most ancient copy of which still exists, and which bears internal evidence of a high degree of perfection in the language of the time in which it was composed. And it is unquestionably in all respects a genuine and native production, quite untinctured with the Latin, or any other foreign contemporary style or idiom.

There are, besides, many valuable poems, and other compositions referable to this period which possess much of the same excellence; and among these are even a few *still extant* attributed to Dubthach Ua Lugair, chief poet of the monarch Laeghaire, who was uncle on the mother's side, and preceptor of the Fiacc just mentioned."—From the body of *Lecture I, pp.* 4, 5.

The following paragraphs are from the Appendix, No. II., to *O'Curry's Manuscript Materials, pp.* 463, 472.

OF WRITING IN ERINN BEFORE ST. PATRICK'S TIME.

"It is, perhaps, impossible now to arrive at any certain conclusion as to the *nature of the writing* in which the records were kept, and history, poetry, and literature preserved amongst the Gaels of Erinn, *in the ages which preceded the coming of St Patrick.*"

In the absence of any known remains of the writing of the pre-Christian period, it may, indeed, be reasonably asked, what reason there is *to think or believe that the Gaels were at all acquainted with any form of written characters? Do we find* any names still preserved in the Gaelic language and ancient writings for *a book, parchment,* writing pen, ink, page, line, stave, in use in, or having reference to, these early ages.

"These," says O'Curry, "are important questions, and I must confess," he adds, "that I have not paid so much attention to their consideration as to enable me to give anything like a full or satisfactory answer to them. At the same time I must observe that I believe the subject to be one which it is now too late to attempt to clear up, so scanty are the remnants, and so widely dispersed are those of our ancient books, or rather of those copies, a few only of which have come down to us. Enough, however, to my mind, remains to show (at least, I myself feel perfectly satisfied) *that the pre-Christian Gaels possessed and practised a system of writing and keeping records quite different from, and independent of, both the Greek and the Roman form and characters, which gained currency in the country after the introduction of Christianity in the first part of the fifth century*, if, indeed, they were not known here even a considerable time before that era."

"It is not," says O'Curry "my business here to offer any opinion as to the characters in which the 'Saltair of Tara,' and the 'Cin Droma Sneacta,' were originally written; though I dare say, it may have been the modified Roman character of the time."—p. 464.

And at the close of his learned remarks in p. 472, he writes:—

"My own opinion is, that these books—'Saltair of Teamhair' and the book of 'Drom Sneacta,' probably, were not written (in Ogham) *but in the popular Roman characters* of the time, modified, perhaps, as at present (?); and that these characters were first brought in (to Eire) by the Druids and Poets, who, from time to time, had travelled in pursuit of their studies to the continent, or had attended the many *distant foreign expeditions which took place from this country even previously to the period of the Incarnation.*

A LITERATURE IN IRELAND IN PAGAN TIMES, CERTAIN.

1. It is, at all events, quite certain that the Irish Druids and Poets had written books before the coming of St. Patrick, in 432, since we find the statement in the ancient Tripartite Life of the Saint, as well as in the annotations of Tireachan, preserved in the *Book of Armagh*, and which were taken by him from the lips and books of his tutor St. Machta, who was the pupil and disciple of St. Patrick himself.

2. The "Saltair of Tara," to which reference had been made in the foregoing quotation, was composed, or compiled, by Cormac MacArt, son of Conn, in the third century.

"Cormac, the prudent and good,"
Was a sage, a file (or poet), a prince;
He was a righteous judge;
Was a good friend and companion.
Cormac gained fifty battles;
He compiled the *Saltair of Tara*,
In that saltair is contained
The best summary of history.

3. "It is certain," says O'Curry, "such a compilation existed." Cormac MacArt died in the year 266, A.D.

4. The manuscript "Cin Droma Sneacta" is said by Dr. Keating to have been compiled before St. Patrick's mission to Erin.

"It was compiled by Ernin, son of Duach, son of Brian, king of Connaught, an *Ollamh*, and a prophet, and a professor in history, and a professor in wisdom; it was he that collected the genealogies and histories of the men of Erin in one book, that is the "Cin Droma Sneacta." Duach, twenty-fourth son, the youngest, of Brian, King of Connaught, was alive the time of St. Patrick. He is progenitor of the O'Flaherties, the O'Connors, the O'Maddens, O'Murphys, and O'Ruarks —*See Iar Connaught, edited by Hardiman.*

5. The "Seancus Mor," or the compilation of the Brehon Laws now translated, and edited, were compiled in the year A.D. 439, under the direction of a committee of nine—three Kings, three Bishops, and three Filés. The four most illustrious of these nine were St. Patrick, apostle of Eire; Laeghaire, the chief monarch of Eire; and Ros, the chief File of Eire, at that time, and Benignus. *See Ancient Laws of Ireland, preface to vol.* 1, *Seanchus Mor*, 1865; *published by order of the Government, and printed by Alexander Thom, Dublin.*

O'Curry enters fully into the well-known subject of

Ogham writing. In eight pages he makes the matter very plain and certain from a historic point of view. Indeed there is no doubt at all that the pre-Christian Gaels of Ireland wrote in Ogham. Proofs to this effect are scattered broadcast in every page of our ancient M.SS. The records of the Royal Irish Academy abound in well authenticated facts.

Dr. Graves has written very learnedly on the subject of ancient writing in Ireland—Ogham. So has William Williams, Esq., of Dungarvan—one of the most erudite and accurate antiquaries in Ireland.

Dr. Graves writes: "Whether the ancient Irish, before the Christian era, possessed a primitive alphabet differing essentially from that in use in other parts of Europe, is a question which has been debated by scholars with great earnestness. Those who maintain the affirmative, appeal to the concurrent authority of the most ancient manuscript histories, according to which an alphabet called Ogham was invented by the Scythian progenitors of the Gael race, and was introduced into Ireland by the Tuatha de Danann, about thirteen centuries before the birth of Christ. They also refer to the oldest romances, which contain frequent allusions to the Ogham, either for the purpose of conveying intelligence, or in sepulchral inscriptions on pillar stones erected in honor of distinguished persons. Finally, they point to existing monuments of this very kind, presenting inscriptions in the Ogham character, and argue, from their rudeness and other circumstances, that they must be ascribed to a pagan period.

"Those, on the other hand, who dissent from this hypothesis, allege that (1) the legendary accounts of the invention of the Ogham bear all the marks of fiction; and they contend that the nature of this alphabet, in which the vowels and consonants are separated, furnishes internal evidence of its having been contrived by persons possessing some grammatical knowledge and acquainted with alphabets of the ordinary kind. They impugn the authority of romantic tales by questioning the antiquity of those compositions. Lastly, they assert that a considerable number of the existing Ogham monuments are proved by the emblems and inscriptions which they bear, to belong to Christian times."

The truth lies in both—Ogham was written first in Pagan, and afterwards in Christian times.

HARRIS'S VIEWS.

"Now, it is absurd to think," says Harris, *(Antiquities of Ireland, vol.* ii. *p.* 25.) if *Benignus* and *Fiech* had before been unacquainted with the Irish characters, that they could be so soon such masters of the language as to write elegantly and poetically in it. But the truth of the matter seems to be this. The *Irish*, before their conversion, were utterly unacquainted with the *Latin letters*, without the knowledge of which, St. Patrick considered that his new converts were utterly incapable of reading the Scriptures, reciting the offices of the Church, and reading other good books. . . . . This, therefore, was the cause which induced that indefatigable preacher of the Gospel to dictate the Latin alphabet to his new converts, to enable them to instruct others. On the other hand, his new converts, being well skilled in their native letters, became, with all the ease in the world, proficient in the Latin elements—so much so that we are told St. Fiech was so great a proficient, that he became master of the psalter, some say in one day, others, in fifteen days; of which great progress Hugh Ward, making mention, expressly interprets the alphabet taught by St. Patrick to be the Latin elements. Thus much I thought absolutely necessary to observe upon the unguarded expression of *Bollandus*, because, should his notion prevail, there would be an end put at once to all the antiquities and to the history of Ireland, antecedent to the introduction of Christianity amongst us."

Again, he writes in same chapter, iii., vol. ii.: "Upon the strictest enquiry I could never find any alphabet, no, not the *Runic* itself, in the structure or order, like the *Ogham* or "*Beth-luis-nuin*" elements. It follows, therefore, that as there was no prototype to copy them from, they must be original. What I mean by original language here, is not the first language spoken, but I mean such as were introduced into the world upon the confusion of the first language."

WHAT HAVERTY SAYS.

Haverty, as a living authority, whose history of Ireland is a solid work full of matter, at once well selected and truthful, says:—"There are indisputable authorities to prove that the Latin mode of writing was known in Ireland some time before St. Patrick's arrival, as there were unquestionably christians in the country before that time."

We hold on the authority of Cuan O'Lochain, who held a distinguished position in this country in the beginning of the eleventh century, that the Psalter of Tara did exist and was compiled by Cormac MacArt in the third century, and consequently that the Pagan Irish possessed a knowledge of alphabetic writing at least in that age.—*See Petrie's History of Tara Hill.*

In page 38 of his history of Ireland, Mr. Haverty writes:—"Let it be borne in mind that these views are the gist of the testimony without end supplied by all the ancient Irish annals."

Cormac, it is said, at the close of his life adored the true God, and attempted to put down Druidism and idol worship. It is, at all events, certain that he endeavoured to promote education. He established three colleges, one for war, another for history, and the third for jurisprudence. He collected and re-modelled the laws, and published the code, which remained in force until the English invasion, and for many centuries after that time, outside the English pale. He assembled the bards and chroniclers at Tara, and directed them to collect the annals of Ireland and to continue the records of the country from year to year, making them synchronize with the history of other countries. Cormac himself, it is said, had been the inventor of this kind of chronology. These annals formed what is called the "Psalter of Tara."

In his old age he wrote a book called "Teagasg na Rig," or the instruction of kings, which is still in existence.

The "Psalter of Tara," however, has been lost.

Again: "We have ample reason to believe that Ireland, in her *days of paganism*, had reached not merely a point relatively advanced in the social scale, but that Christianity found her in a state of intellectual and moral preparation superior to that of most other countries."

IRISH AUTHORS OF THE PAGAN PERIOD.

"The names of several persons who had distinguished themselves as poets or legislators in the time of paganism are still preserved, as well as some of the compositions attributed to them.

Among those were Ollam Fodla, by whom the Feis (or Parliament) of Tara was instituted:

2. Cimbaeth and other kings of his period.

3. Moran, the chief judge of Ferach—the fair and just, at the close of the first century.

4. Cormac Mac Art, who has left us a book of "*Royal* precepts," and caused the Psalter of Tara to be compiled, —third century.

A few of the pre-Christian bards or poets are:

1. Amergin, brother of Heber and Heremon, to whom three poems, still extant, are ascribed.

2. Congal, the son and poet of King Eochy Feileach (before the coming of Christ).

3. Adhna, chief poet of Ireland.

4. Forchern and Ferchertne, the author of the *first Irish grammar*, Uraıcaċt-na-n-Eıgeas, or "the rudimentary lesson of the learned; "ur" means fresh or noble, or "uraı" surety, support, foundational principle; "caċt," a lesson; "eıgeas," those who aspire to "eágna," wisdom; or as it were "eagna-aos," wisdom-race, wisdom-class, all who love learning.

"Men like these could not have been produced in an entirely uncivilized state of society."

"The noble language of ancient Ireland had already in their time attained a high degree of perfection, being most copious in primitive roots and expressive compounds."—p. 59.

In *Ogygia*, part III. p. 214, 245, Roderick O'Flaherty devotes thirty-one pages to the discussion of this subject, chiefly, however, in support of the Ogham writing.

CONCLUSIONS.

From all that has been proved and known historically, the following propositions may be regarded as true.

1. It is certain that the golden age of Irish literature, ecclesiastical, civil, and scientific—as far as science had been then known,—medical, astronomical, legal, was within the period from 432 A.D. to 800.

2. It is certain from the Tripartite Life of St. Patrick that he gave the Roman alphabet, or primers in the Latin language, to all the ecclesiastics of Ireland.

3. It is certain that the Druids before St. Patrick's coming to Ireland wrote books and studied manuscripts.

4. It is certain that in the pre-christian period the Druids and the learned Gaels made use of a secret writing called "Ogham," of which there were many kinds, something like the modern shorthand, and that even in the Christian period this kind of writing was not and is not to this day wholly forgotten.

5. It is not certain whether the books known in Ireland a century or longer anterior to the coming of St. Patrick were written in Roman letter, or not. O'Curry (*Manuscript Materials of Irish History, p.* 472) gives it as his own opinion that some books at least were not written in the Ogham of the time, but in the Roman character, a knowledge of which they had learned on the continent of Europe.

His words are:—"So far, then, for our accounts of the possession of an independent alphabet and mode of writing from the most ancient times by the pre-christian Gael, or Scots of Erin (and the Britons appear to have had a similar mode of writing, at least until they lost it, as well as their native literature itself, under the Saxon rule); but whether the books of Erin were written in this Alphabet (the "Ogham"), whether, for instance, the "Cuilmenn," the "Saltair of Teamhair," and the book of "Drom Sneacta" were written in it, is quite a different question. My own opinion is that they were not written in Ogham, but that they were written in the popular Roman characters of the time." p. 472.

6. The only historic point which, in the writer's opinion, is doubtful, is whether or not the books compiled by the Druids were written in Aryan letters resembling those used by the Latins or Greek, or Phœnicians; or in their own secret characters. The writer's views are, that books were written in the characters peculiar to each. The Druids wrote in Ogham, those works intended

for the druidicial order, or for private use; the public records like the "Seancuȝ Mor" were written in a common, well-known, and not secret letter, be it Roman or Aryan.

THE MATERIAL MADE USE OF IN WRITING.

Without entering into detail, the opinion of learned writers on this subject may be fully taken :—It is certain that, besides stone, tablets of wood were employed by the pre-Christian Gaels of Ireland. The very name (feada) in Irish, to this day, for tablets and writing material prove this truth.—*See Ogygia, part III, p.* 233. *See Harris's Ware, vol. II, c. III. O'Curry's Manuscript Materials, with appendix II*, p. 470.

WHAT LIGHT DOES THE SCIENCE OF COMPARATIVE PHILOLOGY THROW ON THE QUESTION.

The following passage will serve as a prelude to the answer. It is taken from O'Curry's posthumous work, edited by the President of the Queen's College, Cork :—

"While on the one hand no one can deny that the discovery of the use of metals marked an era in human culture, and that, previous to that discovery, the tools and weapons were made everywhere of stone, bone, and horn; on the other, *there is no real evidence that the art of making bronze, or even copper*, preceded that of making iron. According to the results of linguistic paleontology, ascertained by M. Adolphe Pictet, the Aryans, at the period of their dispersion, were not only acquainted with the four metals—gold, silver, copper, and iron—but knew how to make bronze—a fact which M. Pictet thinks implies a knowledge of tin. . . . . . If we admit M. Pictet's conclusions—and whatever difference may exist as to certain steps in theanalysis, there is no doubt that they are, in the main, correct—*all the branches of the Aryan race carried with them, as they migrated from the original home of the race, a knowledge of the principal metals.* The Romans, Kelts, Greeks, Germans, and Slaves, all alike knew iron; and consequently the use of the terms "stone age," "bronze age," or "iron age," are, except in a very limited sense, incorrect as regards those branches, though they might be strictly true, if applied to the parent Aryans." By a parity of reason the writer states:

If we admit Mr. Pictet's conclusions all the branches of the Aryan race carried with them, as they migrated from the original home, a knowledge of the arts and sciences, and a knowledge of letters. The Romans, Kelts, Greeks, Germans, and Slaves, all alike, had in early times a knowledge of letters, consequently the early inhabitants of Eire, who were the first colony that had left the cradle of the family in Persia, had, from the start, a knowledge of learning and of letters. The Keltic names for writing "sgrıoḃ," Latin *scribo*; and *graf*, to inscribe; and names for tablets, tend to show this fully. No one nation borrowed in the primæval period a knowledge of learning or of rudimentary letters from another. Hence the early Irish did not borrow from the Phenicians, nor the primæval Greeks from the Phœnicians.

This truth can be illustrated by that which, at the present day, takes place throughout most of the nations of Europe.

England has a literature of her own, and a form of letters such as are daily seen in newspapers and printed periodicals. The young and the uneducated who have not been trained in the school of historic knowledge call those characters *English letters.* France has a literature of her own, and makes use of the same letters. Frenchmen call them *French letters.* In like manner, the Italians and Spaniards have the same right as the French or English to call the letters in which their published periodicals and papers are printed, Italian or Spanish. What are the facts? Did the English borrow them from the French?—did the French borrow them from the Italian, or *vice versa*? No; all alike have obtained these letters from the Roman. The Roman mould and letter-press was, as it were, the common matrix for all the printing type of Europe. And thus, too, it happened in the early migrations from the Aryan table-land all along the east of the Caspian and the boundary line of the River Oxus. When the Keltic colony left—and they did not all leave in one body—they brought with them a knowledge of the arts, sciences, and of literature, as known to the Aryans at the time; when the Oscan and Umbrian races left, they acted in like manner; when the Pelasgi migrated westwards, and settled down in the fertile vales of Thessaly, or entered the Peloponnesus, they were not inferior in the knowledge of their arts and of literature to their Aryan relatives whom they had left behind. Hence the Kelts cannot be said to have borrowed from the Greeks or from the Phœnicians that knowledge of letters which, according to the testimony of Irish annals, the early settlers possessed.

The story of Cadmus, coming with his sixteen letters from Phœnicia, and his brother Fenius Fearsa, arriving about the same time in Ireland, does not, as the early Greeks knew well, indicate the act of an individual, but of a people and of a historic event connected with that people. It is certain that the early Greeks—even the Pelasgi—had a knowledge of letters, and far a better knowledge, too, than the Hellenes had at a subsequent period. The common opinion at present regarding Cadmus is, that there was no such individual; but that as the Greeks had had a knowledge of letters, the early introduction of the alphabet into Europe should be ascribed to some representative new-comer. Cadmus suits admirably for that purpose. The historic fact is there. The individual is nothing.—*See Introduction to the Study of Greek Classic Poets, by Henry Nelson Coleridge. London: John Murray, Albemarle-street,* 1846.

In page 88, Mr. Coleridge writes: "But the title of Cadmus to the invention, or rather introduction of letters, was not undisputed by the Greeks themselves: Æschylus boldly ascribes it to his mythic Titan; and Euripides gives the invention to that hero who is reckoned amongst the contemporaries of the Trojan War.

Another tradition attributes the *phi* and the *chi* (X) only to Palamedes."

"The reader," says Coleridge, "will attach what faith he pleases to the lives and adventures of Cadmus and Prometheus and Palamedes; but of one thing there can be no doubt, that the Greek alphabet is essentially of Oriental origin."

What Mr Coleridge says of the introduction of letters into Greece, and of the character of the Greek alphabet, the same can, with truth, be said of the early Keltic. The reader will attach what faith he pleases to the story recorded in our Irish annals regarding Fenius Fearsa. Whether such an individual as Fenius lived or no, matters not; of one thing or of two things there can be no doubt, that the earliest races which came to Ireland had a knowledge of letters, and that the Irish alphabet is essentially of Oriental origin. So much *a priori*—namely, that the primeval colonists had a knowledge of letters and the arts, and that the alphabet had been borrowed or copied from the one parent alphabet used by the mother nation.

And the arguments *a posteriori*, prove the same. First,

the number of letters in Irish and in early Greek, is the same; secondly, the sounds and vowels are alike; thirdly, a primitive sameness is easily seen in many of the root words.

This opinion is quite in accordance with late investigations, and with the practical views of historians who treat of the origin of the great races of Europe. Dr. Leonhard Schmitz, in his history of Greece, from the earliest times (*London, Longman, Brown, Green and Longman*, 1852) says, p. 15," the idea that the early inhabitants of Greece were half savages, without laws, without a knowledge of letters, without fixed habitations, or any notion of agriculture, is merely an application of a speculative theory entertained by some, that man, at first, was little better than the brute creation, and that only by degrees he emerged from the savage state into any degree of civilization." Now, comparative philology, as a science, shows that this opinion of some writers hitherto has been founded on a gross error. The early inhabitants of Ireland, therefore, as well as the early inhabitants of Italy and of Greece, were more advanced in civilization than those who, in the same countries, succeeded the early colonists. Wars, and incursions of strange tribes, destroyed, oftentimes, peace and quiet and learned leisure and the fostering care which the cultivation of letters and of the arts demand. The Cyclopian and magnificent buildings of Argos, of Mycenæ, of Thebes, of the Acropolis in Athens; the pyramids of Ægypt, the tombs of Tuscany, prove, beyond doubt, that the early settlers in Greece, in Ægypt, and in Etruria, had a higher knowledge of arts and of letters than the races who succeeded them. So, in Ireland, those who erected the pillar-towers were better masons and better science scholars than those who lived at a later period.

Pagan Ireland had a literature and letters. The truth of that proposition appears from all that has been written in the present chapter. The fulness of the proof proceeds from various sources.

1. From the amount of authentic historic testimony handed down to the present period from the earliest Christian times, the lives, for instance, of St. Patrick and of his immediate successors and companions; the lives of the myriad holy men and women, the story of whose actions is still preserved; (2) from the publication of the Brehon Laws now presented to the reading public by order of the Government of England,—a digest of laws made under the eye of the holy Apostle of Ireland and his companion St. Benignus, from a larger pile composed in Pagan times; (3) from the abundant materials in Ogham character, still extant on stone, which the Irish antiquarian can read, just as truthfully as the astronomer reads from the signs on the surface of the moon—that there is no atmosphere surrounding that satellite, nor water; therefore, nor vegetable nor animal life, no sound on leaf or tree, all is silent as the tomb, and lifeless as a buried city.

4. The tales and poems regarding Pagan times are, to a certain extent, a proof that there was once a people in Ireland who professed a knowledge of some, at least, of the arts. In every tale resting on tradition, as Professor Blackie well observes, there must be some foundation of truth. An epic based on a pure fiction does not last.

So much *a posteriori*, gleaned from the written page of history, and from the broken footprints of Pagan power, and pre-christian civilization in ancient Ireland.

Owing to the science of comparative philology, the old Keltic representations of a Milesian colony and of earlier migrations are touched with a pencil of freshening chromatic power, and the traits latent for ages appear developed. This science acts like an acid solution on a photographic plate, developing the latent impression and exhibiting the picture in all its fulness of outline. It is like light too; it brings out the dark colors into view, and shows forth those that lay hidden. Before the morning rises the various tints of the most beautiful flowers lie unnoticed—under the beams of the rising sun, their brightness and beauty become developed. Comparative philology is to the early history of Ireland what light is to color, to beauty, and truth.

The first inhabitants—the very oldest of the Keltic family—must, as descendants of the great Aryan race, have had a knowledge of literature, such as it had been known in the East, and with it a knowledge of letters. The science of comparative philology plainly proves that statement.

The next question that arises is,—What is the number of letters in Irish?

Here, again, another proof of the eastern origin of the Gaelic race, and with it a proof of their knowledge of literature and of letters, presents itself.

It is a question which must be treated fully.

There are only seventeen letters in Irish or Gaelic. There had been only seventeen letters in Greek at the earliest period. From this fact, resting, of course, like one of the stones of an arch, for support and strength, and unity, on its connection with others, it appears that the Greek language and the Irish came from one Eastern motherland. To the writer the fact appears to form a strong link in the chain that connects Ireland and Greece in the earliest pre-Christian period with the Armenian and Aryan motherland, from Ararat to the Hindco Koosh mountains.

The writer fancies he hears some learned scholar cry out—as certainly many of those who attend the modern universities cannot fail to cry out when they will have read the foregoing,—What, this man knows nothing of history!—just listen to what he has stated, quite against all that we have ever read in Grecian history, that there had been seventeen letters in Greek at the earliest period. Seventeen letters! Every historian who has written on early Greece says *sixteen* How does it appear now that all writers have up to the present been wrong. Had all the early historians of Greece gone astray? The answer to questions like these, which must naturally arise in the mind of the learned reader, is at hand. A chapter has been already devoted to the subject of the *lost letter* in early Greek. It has been shown on the most convincing proofs that the very earliest colonists of Greece had had the letter "f," *Æolic Vau*; that they lost it even before Homer had written his immortal Epic; that the loss had been perceived in times past; that it was reserved to the genius of modern Greek scholarship, in the person of Bentley, an English schoolman, to discover it that it has been found, and is known under the strange name of *digamma* so called from its shape; that, therefore, as a letter, it is, or it should be, rightly installed amongst the number of early Grecian letters.

All the ancient and modern Grecian historians and all grammarians, completely ignorant of the loss in the past, or the gain in the present, of the letter "f," make no allusion to it. They state that sixteen letters was the total number known to the early Hellenes. If to this number sixteen, the lost is added, seventeen is the result; just the number which, in the present and in the past has ever been known and made use of in Gaelic.

Stranger still is the coincidence, that not only is the number of letters which the oldest Greeks had had, and that which is to this day employed by Irishmen in Gaelic, equal, but the letters are identical—twelve consonants and five vowels.

The consonants in Greek are:* b, g, d, k, l, m, n, p, r, s, t.
The consonants in Gaelic are: b, c, d, f, g, l, m, n, p, r, s, t.

Regarding the Greek letters, the learned Lancelot writes in his *Port Royal Greek Grammar*, that these sixteen letters had been introduced into Greece by Cadmus, that they are sufficient to express the different sounds of the Greek language. "The other eight," he says, "were invented afterwards more for convenience than necessity." 250 years after the arrival of the Phœnecian adventurer Cadmus, during the siege of Troy, Palamedes invented four aspirate consonants; and 650 years after the Trojan war, Simonides invented the remaining four, the long vowels *Eta*, *Omega*, and the double consonants *xi*, (x) and *psi*.

The account furnished by Pliny the Elder and Tacitus' regarding the introduction of letters, differs very little from the narration of the event supplied by Lancelot. All agree that sixteen letters were at an early period introduced by Cadmus; they do not, however, agree on the invention of the eight additional letters.

According to Aristotle *phee* and *chee* (x) were invented by Epicharmus, the Sicilian, the double letters and *Omega* by Simonides, the Younger, a little before the Persian war. Hence the full Greek alphabet of twenty-four letters was not known, and, of course, not made use of until after the time of Thales and Pythagoras, and a century

*Kappa in Greek, is the same as c, in Gælic; g, is found in each; f, is the only letter in Gælic which is not found in the Greek column.

before the birth of the Father of Moral Philosophy in Greece—Socrates.

In any case, it is certain that the number of letters in the first ages when Greece was colonized, had been the same as that known and made use of in Ireland—seventeen and that the letters were identical.

HISTORY AND COMPARATIVE PHILOLOGY.

Viewing this particular subject regarding the introduction of letters into Greece, it is, in a historic point of view, filled with difficulties. In the light of comparative philology it is plain. One class of writers assert that Cadmus, a native of Phœnicia, came into Greece at an early period and brought with him sixteen letters; that they were called *phoinika*, because derived from Phœnicia, that eight other lettters, three double, and three aspirate, and two long vowels, were added at different periods up to the middle of the fifth century, before the Christian era. The other class of writers say there was no such individual as Cadmus; he was only a representative of the rise of letters and literature in Greece. The exact date of his coming is not known. It is not certain whether it was 1045, B.C., as Newton states, or 1493, B.C., the common system, or 1550, as M. Schoell states. The letters were called *phoinika*, because they were written on leaves or tablets, of the phoinix, or palm-tree; that Herodotus was the first who stated those letters had been brought from Phœnicia into Greece. Herodotus's words were repeated by others. Pliny the Elder, and Tacitus adopted the statement of Herodotus. Repetition is not proof. The father of Grecian history thought that letters had been brought from Phœnicia by Cadmus because, in the Temple of Apollo, at Thebes, he saw letters which the priests of the Far-Darter called *phoinika*, or

Cadmeian. That incident on which Herodotus founded his knowledge regarding the introduction of letters proves nothing, for the priests of Apollo might have called the letters *phoinika* because they were in some measure like the Phœnician, or styled them Cadmeiar, from the name of some person who first inscribed them or ordered them to be inscribed on the walls of the temple of the god of day. Euripides and Æschylus scout the idea that there was any such personage as Cadmus. The authority of Herodotus is, therefore, not worth much on this particular point.

On the other hand, viewing this special subject by the light shed on it from the scientific lamp of comparative philology, everything fits rightly and naturally in its own place. The Greeks, as a people descended from the Aryan family, had had from the start a knowledge of letters; they had the identical number of letters, too, which another sister branch of the same Aryan family possessed—namely, seventeen letters—twelve consonants and five vowels. All this is very easy and natural, and before this light all the difficulties connected with the historic views of Herodotus vanish like vapour before the meridian sun.

In the comparison which has just been made here between the two ancient sister Aryan languages, Irish Gaelic and Greek, a proof in favour of the greater antiquity of Gaelic is preserved. How?

Greek, it seems, had, at one time, the letter "f." That is certain. Gaelic could never have borrowed that letter from Greek. Hence, Gaelic as a daughter of the Aryan mother tongue, must have had possession of that letter long before Greek had lost it, that is from the earliest period, and, therefore, it must be inferred, had it from a source independent of all Grecian influence.

There are striking coincidences between the written languages of the two peoples—the Grecian and the Gael—one dwelling in the South of Europe, the other seated, as it were for centuries past, in the Islands of the North Western Sea, yet both races have manifestly sprung from Aryan progenitors. Each people emigrated at a primeval period from the East, but at different times, and in different migrating shoals.

According to the theory of Frederick Wolfe (1759). in the prologomena on Homer and his writings, there was no knowledge of letters of any kind at the period the great poet is supposed to have flourished; that there was no such person as Cadmus; no knowledge of letters up to the time of the Persian war; that Homer never wrote the grand poems attributed to him. All one-sided views generally fall into excess. Wolfe's opinion is of that class. He does not reason strictly like a scholar who is conversant, not only with books, but with mankind. "A principle may be perfectly true, whilst its growth runs wild in unpruned license and tyrannous excess." It does not follow, though one admits there was no such personage as Cadmus, that, therefore, there was no knowledge of learning amongst the early Greeks. Professor Blackie states rightly, that Wolfe treats with levity the tradition of the Greek people in reference to Cadmus—the mythic position of whose name seems to be sufficient to prove a knowledge of letters in Greece, some centuries before the age of Homer. Professor Blackie admits that Cadmus is a mythic personage, yet, though mythic, the exponent of a knowledge of letters in the early dawn of Grecian literature.

In any hypothesis then, either of history or of comparative philology, that can be made, it is certain, as opposed to the Wolfian theory, that a knowledge of letters existed, and that it existed at the very earliest age, say 500 years before the time of Homer.

ANOTHER IMPORTANT QUESTION.

How do the seventeen letters in Gaelic supply, as Lancelot said regarding the Greek sixteen, every articulate form of utterance? How is it that Hindostani makes use of the extraordinary number of 48 consonants; Sanscrit, 37; Turkish, 32; Persian, 31; Arabic, 28; the Kafir (Zulu) 26; Hebrew, 23; English, 20? Again, Latin has 17; Finnish has 11; and some Austrian languages have only 8. It is worthy of remark that those languages in which the largest supply of consonants abounds are a composition of dialects, as they borrow a great fund of words from other primitive tongues; for instance, Hindostani uses Sanscrit, Persian, Arabic, and Turkish words. Turkish, on its part, admits Persian and Arabic: English, German, Keltic, Latin, Greek, French. But, how is it that Irish-Gaelic can supply every form of articulate sound with its 12 consonants and five vowels? This is the answer :—

1. The division of vowels into *broad* and *slender* has been already explained, and ought now to be well known.

2. The action of aspiration and of eclipsing has been explained to the reader. By the use of the slender and broad vowels, and the process of aspirating and eclipsing, there is no form of palatal, guttural, labial, or nasal sound, slender or broad, that cannot be readily articulated by an Irish speaker.

1. Take the labials,

m.
b.
p.
f. } Labial letters in their natural state.

These letters, by aspiration, become:

ṁ.—v or w in sound	Labials affected.
ḃ.—v or w "	
ṗ.—ph or f "	
ḟ.—h "	

Now, each of the consonant letters in its simple natural state, has a twofold sound—broad or slender, according as it is articulated along with "i" or "e," (slender vowels) or "a, o, u," (broad vowels).

Each affected consonant, also, has a twofold sound. Hence, the four labials, "m, b, p, f," produce, in their natural and affected forms, sixteen different sounds.

The gutturals, "c, g," (ċ, ġ, aspirated) produce eight; the dentals, "d, t," and the sibilant "s,"—twelve; that is thirty-six distinct articulations of the consonant sounds.

In this way, every variety of articulate sound is produced from the twelve consonants and the five vowels, just as from the seven notes of the musical scale is is produced every tone required for purposes of melody and harmony: or, as from the three primary colors, red, yellow and blue, is produced by combination every variety of hue and cromatic grace that can charm the eye.

From this process, in Gaelic, not only are the hard checks, "k, p, t," and their aspirates, "kh, ph, th," produced, but the medials and the medial aspirates; and the soft and their soft aspirates are formed. Irish-Gaelic, in its consonantal forms, is, with its 12 consonants, richer than Sanscrit, with its 37. Sanscrit has no "f," or its equivalent "ph." Irish has; Sanscrit has no soft sibilant; Irish has (s before e or i.)

"Greek," says Müller, "has no 'y,' no "w,' no 'f,' no soft sibilant. Latin has no soft sibilant, no 'th,' 'ph,' 'ch.' English is deficient in guttural breathing like th German *ach, ich.* Arabic has no 'p.'"

Again, the Mohawks, never, as infants or grown-up

people, articulate with their lips; they never say "pa," "ma," "ba." Chinese never pronounce "r." No Chinese can pronounce Europe—but *Eulopa*; and they must call America, *Ya-ma-li-ka.*

Irish-Gaelic, in its simplicity and perfection, is something worthy the admiration of scholars.

CAUSE OF THIS—TESTIMONY OF CONSTANTINE NIGRA.

This variety of articulate sounds arising from twelve consonants is mainly owing to the division of the vowels into slender and broad. As slender and broad they influence diversely the consonants in their affected as well as natural state. How wide and wonderful the effect of this system had ever been, has just been shewn.

In 1869 the Italian Ambassador at Paris, Constantine Nigra, published his work "Glossae Hibernicæ Veteres codicis Taurinensis," with a copy of which he honored the present writer. In page 8, he writes, regarding the action of the slender and broad vowels in Irish.

"Nulla alia lingua tam delicate sensit, quam hibernica, hanc mutuam sonorum inter sese actionem, nulla alia ad leges harmoniæ et ponderationis toni tam arcte subegit flexiones et eleménta radicalia, quæ apud cætera arianæ originis idiomata majore tenacitate servantur."

No other language directs so sensitively as the Irish this mutual action of the sounds in their respective relations; no other language has so closely moulded to the laws of harmony and to depth or power of melody, the inflections and radical elements which in the other dialects of Aryan origin are kept up with a kind of unflinching tenacity, in their natural bent.

Two other points connected with this interesting subject (1) *the early Irish alphabct;* (2) *and Irish writing*—remain to be discussed, and correct opinions regarding them to be presented to the reader.

1. What is the origin of that *letter* or *character*, which, at present is usually called old Irish character—not alone by those who have no acquaintance with Irish literature, but even by many who have some reputation for Irish scholarship.

Has the shape of the letter had its origin from any source, purely Irish or Keltic. Is it Roman? If so, why call the letter *old Irish character*?

There had certainly been two forms of Keltic writing amongst the Pagan Irish (1) Ogham, and (2) Roman. There may have been, as has been said above, a third, which one may be allowed to call Aryan (bearing a resemblance to early Greek or Phœnician, since the Kelts, like the Helenes, came from the east, and the Greek letters were not unlike the Phœnician, though the latter were not of Aryan origin). Regarding this last class of letter, it is not certain that it had ever been in use amongst the pre-Christian Irish. The question, then, is one confined to the Ogham and Roman alphabets. The old manuscript and printed character used in Irish is not Ogham. Therefore, *a priori*, it is Roman; and, as a historic fact, proved by numberless manuscripts, it is Roman. Therefore, it is a misnomer to call these letters in printed Irish books and manuscripts *old Irish character*, whereas, in real truth, they are old Roman characters. The Irish people of the fifth century and of the sixth received these letters from the hands of St. Patrick.

If the Irish people in the past had borrowed the old semi-uncial letter of the fifth and sixth century—as the early manuscripts, written in Latin and in Irish abundantly testify—how can it be out of place for Irishmen of the present day to borrow again from Rome the round, full, pleasing, and therefore beautiful letter of the present period, which all the Romance dialects have borrowed, and which many of the Gothic and German races have made their own? *

Is there any portion of the so-called Irish character to which Ireland can lay claim.

There is the (˙) dot, or diacritical mark alone which points out to the eye the phonetic fact, that a change has taken place in the sound of the radical consonant. That portion of the character, and that alone, is Irish. The present writer then suggests, and he has himself adopted the plan, to make use, like most of the peoples of Europe, of modern Roman character, retaining, the while, the dot over the letter to note to the eye the change of the sound which the affected consonant represents. Thus the new letter is Roman, while it is Irish. Hence he has styled it Romano-Keltic.

He has matrices of this form moulded in London, and two founts of Romano-Keltic struck off. It is in type

* From a review—*Ancient Irish Art*—written in 1869 by Lady Wilde (Speranza) on Professer Westwood's Work:—"And here it may be noticed, in passing, that the so-called Irish alphabet is simply the Latin alphabet, modified by the first missionaries to suit the Irish sounds, as Ulphilas, the apostle of the Goths, invented an alphabet of mingled Greek and Latin characters, in order to enable him to make his translation of the Gospels into Gothic; and, as the Greek missionaries invented the Russian alphabet, which is a modified form of the Greek, for a like purpose. That the Irish should retain the old form of the Latin letters, while most of the other nations of Europe have discarded it, is to be regretted, as nothing would facilitate the study of Irish so much at the present day, when one has so little leisure to spell out with much painful endeavour the barbarous symbols of a by-gone age, as the adoption of the modern Roman alphabet. The first Irish book that was ever printed appeared in 1571, and is now in the Bodleian Library. It is a catechism of Irish Grammar, and the Irish alphabet has suffered no modification or improvement since. In the Keltic journal, an admirable periodical recently started at Manchester to perpetuate the study of Irish, the Irish letters are printed in modern Roman characters—an innovation welcomed by all students.

of that mould the Irish Gaelic in these pages has been printed.

2. The second point regards the mark that should note to the eye the affected sound of the vowel and consonant. The change is pointed to in Scotch-Gaelic by the use of "h" immediately after the consonant and before the vowel. In Manx, the modified sound is noted by a change of letter. In Welsh, too, the radical letter is changed, not once but frequently—in some instances, three times. In Irish the radical letter is retained to show the origin of the word. The (·) dot or point placed over the consonant sufficiently indicates a phonetic mutation, and the use of an eclipsing letter before a radical consonant adjusts in written form for the eye, the softening of sound conveyed to the ear, when eclipsis occurs.

The question is, then, which of these systems is the best?—which is most fully supported by reason and authority?—which is most in accord with the laws and rules, at once, of phonology, orthography, and orthoepy?

These two subjects have been fully discussed by the present writer in the annexed letter, published within the past year:—

To the Editor of the Highlander.

St. Jarlath's College, Tuam,
Feast of St. Elizabeth, Queen of Hungary,
November 19th, 1873.

Et hanc veniam petimusque damusque vicissim.—Hor de Art Poet.

Dear Sir,—In the issue of the *Highlander* of the 15th of November just past, a letter from the pen of an Irishman, Thomas O Neill Russell, on the subject of the Gaelic language of Scotland and Ireland, has been published. In it my name is introduced, not for any personal reason, but as representing a certain reaction in favour of the renascent language of the Gael.

The gentleman who wrote the letter is entitled, like every freeman, to hold his opinions, and to express them publicly in the columns of any journal favourable to his views, or otherwise inclined to encourage freedom of discussion. Whilst this right is freely conceded to him, to others the same concession should not be denied. Hanc veniam petimusque damusque vicissim:

Taken on its literary merits, the letter before me is not deserving of any notice; yet, as it professes to deal with points of phonetic and orthographic interest in connection with the written language of the Gael of Albion and of Eire, it is only fair to our cousins in the Highlands, and to "Clan na Gael" at home and abroad, especially in America and Australia, to show the reasons why Irishmen for the past thousand years have made, and still do make, and will continue to make use of the (·) dot, and not of the aspirate "h," to express the modified or altered sounds of the radical consonants, "b, m, p, f, c, g, d, t, s." It is fair to show also why the proprietor of the *Tuam News* has for the Gaelic department of that journal adopted the Romano-Keltic style of type,—Roman of the present day to be up to and in harmony with the style of letterpress made use of throughout Europe, yet Keltic in the diacritical mark which tells the eye of the change in the sound of the radical consonant. It will be said that a (·) dot is a small point to establish a thesis on. No doubt it is, but the use or the non-use of it in the written Gaelic, like the white flag of the Bourbon Dynasty with the Count de Chambord, represents a principle. It is one of the most striking points of difference between the written Gaelic of Scotland and of Ireland.

My object in penning this letter is to present to the lovers of Gaelic all over the world what I believe to be the correct view on the subject at issue. On this account I address myself to you, Mr Editor, and, through you, to all the readers of your journal, rather than to Mr R., with whom, as a single member of the great Gaelic Family, and with his opinions I have no right to interfere.

SHAPE OF LETTER.

And first, as to the shape of the Romano-Keltic letter employed by the proprietor of the *Tuam News*.

From my letter written to you early in July last, and subsequently published in the *Highlander*, I take the following abstract :—

The oldest Irish writings are in Roman letters. Any one who wishes to see Irish and Latin manuscripts, at present in the Bodleian Library, Oxford ; or in the British Museum, or those preserved in Irish and Latin, which the Belgian Government sent some twenty or thirty years ago over from Brussels to Trinity College, Dublin, in order that copies of them should be made by the learned and ever to be lamented Dr. O'Donovan, and Eugene O'Curry, Professor of Archæology in the Catholic University, will, after he shall have seen and read those manuscripts, as I have, not hesitate to admit the proposition as true. It is equally correct to state that most Irish books are printed in type fashioned according to the shape of the manuscript Irish letter, *i.e.* in Roman, dotted, of course, to mark the affected or aspirate sound. And it is only stating a fact to assert that Irish and early Scotch Gaelic manuscripts are written in a hand resembling that made use of by the Anglo-Saxons. Ireland received from Rome, through the hands of St. Patrick, alphabets of the character made use of at the time in Rome; England received the same faith and the same Roman letter through St. Augustine. The manuscript books which he brought from Rome are to be seen to this day at Trinity College, Cambridge. And Germany received, through the teaching of missionaries from Ireland, the same form of letter, and the same faith that they themselves had first received from Rome.

On this special point the author of the letter in the issue of the *Highlander* just to hand and myself are, it seems, quite in accord. For he remarks: "It is evident that the Irish type is going out of favor, for almost all the new publications are printed in Latin (Roman) letters. The Rev. Canon Bourke, in the *Tuam News*, is using modern type in the Gaelic department of that paper." It is clear, from those remarks about the *Tuam News*, Mr. R. is of opinion that the use of modern Roman letter is an improvement on that employed in the past. For he states: "Just as these (German) letters have interfered with the spread of the German language, so has the use of the Irish type (in the past) interfered with the advancement of ours" (Irish language). Again: "The angular, awkward characters in which most of our Irish books are printed do not deserve to have one word said in their favour. They have not even the merit of antiquity; for it is a well-known fact that the older our manuscripts are, the more closely do they approach the present Latin type in the form of the letters in which they are written."

So far, the writer of the letter on the Gaelic language and the writer of the present letter hold the same views. Here we part.

THE (·) DOT, OR "H," TO NOTE THE ASPIRATE SOUND.

In the next sentence he tells very plainly what are his opinions on the use of the (·) dot in expressing modal changes of the natural sounds of consonants. What does he say? Hear it:—"Father Bourke has stuck to the pernicious system of using the (˙) dot for aspiration and mutation instead of the 'h.'"

That is a strange expression. It does not become an Irishman to speak so of the written speech of motherland. Such an expression by no means becomes any man of pretensions to scholarly attainments; and, above all, the proposition grates on the trained ear, as one unheard of in any school of ancient or modern philosophy—to take for truth, without any assigned reason, the utterances of any individual.

The use of the (˙) dot is characteristic of the Gaelic of Ireland; the use of "h," of the Gaelic of Scotland. Mr. Russell addresses the Gaels of Scotland and says: "You in Scotland deserve great praise for using the letter 'h' instead of the (˙) dot for expressing modified or altered sounds of consonants." Thus, without rhyme or reason, he turns his back on Ireland, flings to the winds a system of phonetic notation adopted by her and her sons for a thousand years.

What is the state of facts in regard to the spoken speech of the Gael? Every Gaelic speaker in Scotland, Ireland, America, knows that in the spoken language the sound of the consonants after "mo," my, "do," thy, "a," his; or, in composition, or again the nominative case of address, suffers modification of sound. "M" for instance, in the term "mac," son, is not the same as that in "mo ṁac" ("mo wack") my son, and "a ṁic" ("a vick"), O son. "B" of "bean," a woman, is not the same in sound as the identical but affected "b" in "sean-ḃean" ("shan-van"), old woman. Those who do not speak Gaelic are supposed to have learned this much at least from the *Easy Lessons in Irish.*

It is a fact then that in the *spoken* language this modal change in sound takes place. The vocal value of "p" becomes that of "f;" the sounds of "m" and "b" are changed into that of "w," or of "v;" "c" (k) has its phonetic value altered into "ch" guttural, like "ch" German, or "gh" in lough: "g" into "gh;" "d" into "y;" "s" and "t" into "h." Such are the facts in the spoken speech. In the written how are these modifications of sounds to be expressed, still preserving intact the leading consonants of the radical vocable?

There are at present only three ways employed to express in written forms this phonetic mutation.—(1) by change of letter; (2) by the annexation of "h" to the consonant which represents the affected sound; (3) by means of the diacritical (˙) dot. The Welsh, the Manks, and in some measure the Greeks, adopt the first; the Highland-Gael, the second; the Irish-Gael, the third.

If success is a test of sound principle, the Welsh people are, in this matter, right. All honour to them, at all events, for the nobility of soul and the unflinching energy which they have displayed in cherishing the tongue of the Cambro-Briton.

With regard to changes in Welsh, the initial radical consonant is changed three times. The letter "c," for instance, of "car," a friend, becomes "g," in *ei* gar, his friend, and "ch" in *ei* char, her friend, and "ngh" in *fy* nghar, my friend. Success is oftentimes the result of energy rather than of soundness of principle. And even with the literary success of the Welsh, learned men are of opinion that the system of changing the radical initial consonants to point out mutations of sound, is calculated to ruin the orthography and the original purity of any language. The original Keltic purity of the Welsh has already in many instances disappeared.

The question then at issue on the present occasion is reduced to this—which of the two, the Irish-Gaelic system or the Highland-Gaelic system, the use of the diacritical (·) dot, or the use of the "h" is correct in expressing mutations of sound; which of the two systems is the readier, the more practical; which is best calculated to meet the ends in view—namely, to express phonetic changes combined with varying sameness of written form, which of the two systems is the more firmly supported by reason and authority ?

Each people are naturally inclined to regard that system as the best which has been adopted by the nation, and to which, from childhood's days, they are habituated. But that is not a fair way to come to a just conclusion on the subject. Let the question be judged on its merits.

WHAT IS "H ?"

What is "h ?" (1) "H" represents a secondary sound ; (2) "h" is an aspirate mark. All admit it is an aspirate mark. "Other nations," writes a professor of the Catholic University, Dublin, "besides the Greeks, distinguish the spiritus asper by a peculiar letter, for example, "h"—*Atlantis, vol. 1, p.* 62. "The letter "h" is no articulate sound, but only a breathing."—*The English Language, Latham*, (3 *Ed., p.* 144.)

(2) Others say it is a letter. Well, it is *not* a radical letter. It stands for the secondary sound of a consonant which has lost its primary power. This is Dr Prichard's opinion; and it is the opinion of the celebrated Welsh antiquarian, Edward Lhuyd. Prichard says "h never stands as the initial of a word in Irish. . . . It is merely a secondary form of some other initial."—*Eastern Origin of the Keltic Nations, p.* 165. And Lhuyd remarks that "h" is never the primitive initial of any word in

Gaelic. It is the aspirated form of "f," of "s," or "t." He infers that cognate words beginning with "h" in other languages have lost their proper initials—that thus *hex* (six) in Greek, must at an early period have been written *sex*, as in Latin. This truth has gone far to prove that Latin, compared with Greek, is an older branch of the Indo-European stock. Numbers of words in Irish commencing with "s,' are, in Welsh, spelled with initial "h." It is plain, then, to every student of philology that "h" is not only a sign of aspiration, but that it is moreover the written form of a spent radical consonant, which, as a letter, has lost its primitive power.

Let this view of "h" be treated, first, *as representing a secondary sound.*

ARGUMENTS AGAINST THE USE OF "H."

The argument then is, there is no law of language to show that a single modified new articulate sound is expressed by the combination of any two consonants, such as that of "h" with any other consonant would be. Now "h," as representing a secondary sound, is a consonant; its union, therefore, with another consonant cannot, according to existing phonetic laws, become the exponent of a sound distinct at once from "h," and from that consonant with which it is allied. Now, this is what takes place in Scotch-Gaelic. The letter "h" is united in the written speech with the letters "b, p, f, m," and the throat letters "c, g," and the dentals, "d, t, s." The digraphs "ph, th, ng, gn, cc," &c., and the like, do not come against the thesis as explained. But it will be said—this mode of arguing or of reasoning is not fair. We who favour the opposite opinion say that "h" is *not* a letter; it is a symbol of aspiration, and nothing more.

SECOND ARGUMENT—Very well. Be it so: "h," as an *aspirate* mark, is (1) clumsy, (2) unsightly, (3) like a crutch in the hands of a hale man, it causes the consonant to which it is joined to look misshapen; (4) it bewilders a learner with the countless times it appears before the eye even in single sentences; (5) it makes Gaelic appear to many what Professor Wilson's brother used to say of it: "Gaelic is a language which few persons can read, and nobody can spell;" (6) it is not easy for a tyro to attempt—not knowing the radical structure of the language—to spell a word of four syllables, having a "h" in each syllable. "In the spelling of those aspirate sounds," says Latham—*English Language, p.* 156—"by means of English, we are hampered by the circumstances that "th" and "ph" were already in English used in a different sense from that of "th," which is equation for "h," and "ph," for "f," only in Gaelic.

THIRD—An *a pari* argument: Taking "h" as the symbol of aspiration, it must be said that the Greeks employed it for a long period, and at length gave it up and adopted an inverted comma (ʽ). I quote the words of his Grace the Most Rev. Dr. Dixon, the lamented Archbishop of Armagh, and Primate of all Ireland: "The Greek spirits and accents were not earlier, in the opinion of most writers, than the seventh century. If the very ancient Greeks were particular in using the "h" to mark the spiritus asper, it fell into disuse as early even as the first century."

---

* His Grace the Most Rev. Dr. Dixon, must have meant the seventh century *before* the Christian era. The letter "h" was, it seems, made use of as an aspirate, as at present, from the time of its introduction into Greece up to the period (5th century B.C.) when Aristophanes flourished. "H," says Henry Wilson Coleridge, in his *Introduction to the Study of the Greek Classic Poets*, p. 86 (Edition, 1846. London: John Murray), "did not at first express the long vowel sound of 'e,' but simply the strong-breathing which power it exclusively carried with it into the Latin, and has ever preserved in English and in some other modern languages."

Why did the Greeks give up the use of the "h," after having made use of it from the time of its invention or introduction into Greece to the time of Aristophanes? Doubtless, amongst other reasons, because it was not a convenient sign to express the aspirate change.

FOURTH ARGUMENT.—The phonetic process in Irish called by the name "aspiration," should rather be, save in a few instances, styled softening or mellowing. This is Professor Blackie's opinion: "This aspiration or breathing," says the Professor, "is the simplest thing for the human organs to do. It is not harsh at all, but soft, and was one of the commonest sounds in Greek, as well as in Gaelic. His fault with Gaelic was, that it was *softened* too much."—*Speech at Edinburgh*, 1873. As a rule, aspiration in Irish was, as a fact, though the name announces the contrary, a softening process. Now, I ask is it in accord with correct judgment to adopt a character (h) essentially an *aspirate*, to express an effect contrary to the nature of an aspirate? Again, in some instances (say f) the aspirate mark completely annihilates the radical letter. Does the presence of an aspirate (with f) fitly express complete loss of phonetic value? I do not say that it is wrong to adopt "h," but I say that there should be a suitableness between the sign and the thing signified.

It will be said, all these objections come against the use of the dot (·) just as well as against the use of "h?" I answer—No; "h" is regarded in most of the languages of Europe as an aspirate; the dot (·) is not; it is made to represent simply all the modified sounds of the radical consonants when affected by a vowel, or semi-vowel in the same Gaelic sentence.

ARGUMENTS IN FAVOUR OF THE USE OF THE (·) DOT.—1. The rejection of "h." 2. Its plastic power of preserving at once the radical consonant unchanged in its written form, while it points out the model change of sound. 3. It is conformable in a great measure to the aspirate notation in Greek, and resembles the dagesh (·) dot in Hebrew. 4. For Irishmen it has the sanction of a series of ages, and no Irishman ought to fling to the winds a system so venerable, if not so good, without first finding a better. For all this, the Gaels of Scotland can, and probably will, retain the use of "h." *De gustibus non est disputandum.*

AUTHORITIES.

"The addition of 'h' to the primitive consonants seems," says Dr. Prichard, "only to render it obtrusive, or in other instances to obliterate it.—*Prichard's E. Origin of the Keltic Nations, p.* 16.

And O'Mahony, a great Irish-American Gaelic scholar editor, too, of an Irish journal, says :—"The use of the adventitious 'h' after silent or aspirated consonants has been considered objectionable. It has been repeatedly found that the insertion of this parasite character in positions where it is not employed in modern European languages, and where in Irish the change of sound is merely expressed by the dot (·) placed over the consonant so affected, does but prevent one who can read only English from any attempt at the pronunciation of those words in which it is found; or if such persons should make any attempt to pronounce them, the result is as unlike the real Irish sounds as it is possible to conceive."—*Keating's History of Ireland by O'Mahony—Translation, Preface; p.* 14. *New York, Haverty,* 1857.

Having thus given the reasons and the authorities for each system, I leave the reader to draw the legitimate conclusions from the views just presented.

To assert that the language of the Gael has no modern standard, is to enunciate a proposition which in part, is true, and untrue in part. It is true in this sense, that Irish scholars and persons beginning the study of Gaelic have no standard dictionary. They have two—O'Reilly's, published by Duffy, Dublin; and one by Right Rev. Dr. John O'Brien, Bishop of Cloyne, of which in one hundred and five years there have been only two editions. Neither of those two dictionaries is a standard work. The Gaels of Scotland are, in that respect, in advance of their cousins in Ireland.

The proposition is, however, not true, if it is intended to convey the notion that scholars who cultivate Gaelic as it is spoken and written have not standard sources of correct spelling, of correct orthoepy. The principles on which the sounds of the letters in Gaelic rest are unchangeable. In respect to phonetic uniformity in pronouncing the same letters and syllables, Gaelic is a model language when contrasted with the ever-varying sounds of the same combinations of letters in English. Any one who knows and who has learned Gaelic thoroughly can never make a mistake in spelling correctly. But, of course, a person who has not studied the language cannot acquire in a short time this ready habit of spelling correctly.

HOW SCOTCH-GAELIC AND IRISH DIFFER.

It is, nevertheless, true that Highland Gaelic and Irish-Gaelic differ in the terminations and suffixes to primitive words. Take, for instance, the term which, in the two countries, is one and unchanged—Grád, love, (Irish-Gaelic), gradh, (Scotch-Gaelic); gráduiġ, v., love thou (Irish); gradhaich (Scotch). The primitive term is the same in each dialect; the derivative words differ. You of Albion annex "aich;" we of Eire, annex "uiġ."

My own opinion is that you are correct in retaining "c," (aspirated) or "ch," in the verb because it is found in the Irish derivative, "gradaċ," loving, and in the future and conditional tense of Irish deriv. verbs. Ex: "gráḋóċaid me," I will love. You are not correct in retaining "a" before "i," an "aic" (suffix); "u" before "i" is more in conformity with the principles of phonetics; with the present pronunciation of the vowel "u," which in Gaelic serves only as it does in Spanish to give a free, full, open sound to the annexed vowels. The termination "aċt" as in "beannaċt," a blessing; "mallaċt," a curse, is to be preferred to the ending "achd," with "d" and "c," usual in Scotch-Gaelic, as *beannachd*, *mallachd*. It is a principle of phonetics that letters of the same class in sound harmonize; those which are not of the same phonetic class cannot be allied in sound, and therefore should not be allied in the written language. Hence, Latham (*the English Language, third edition, page* 152) says, "the combination *aȝt*, to be pronounced, must become either *akt* (that is *act*) or *agd*." It is for the Gaels of Scotland to say why they retain the termination "aċd."

A GAELIC COMMITTEE.

It is not difficult to imagine how a professor could be found, who, with the aid of two or three intelligent Keltic scholars, aided by the learned Professor of Greek in the University of Edinburgh, and by two or more learned Gaelic scholars from the south and east of Ireland, might, in a short time, show how much is correct and how much is not correct in each dialect. The time, however, for such a union has not yet come. Judging from the past, no professor in Trinity College, Dublin, or in the National Catholic College, Maynooth, will ever advance the cause of the language of the Gael at home or abroad. Lovers of the speech of the Gael must depend on themselves.

There were scholars in the days before the uncial letter had been adopted, and long before the miniscule or small round character of the middle ages had been thought of.

The art of printing afforded wonderful facilities for the reproduction of books; but the art of printing has not of itself made scholars. In the opening of the twelfth century multitudes in the French capital thronged around William of Champeaux as he lectured from his chair in the cloister of Notre Dame; and five thousand young students flocked from every country in Europe to Paris to hear the brilliant lecturer, and to be charmed and instructed by the marvellous eloquence of William's successor, Peter Abelard. As these five thousand sat on benches or on mats, as was the custom, and took notes of the lectures, or transcribed manuscripts, for there were no printed books at that period, that scholar would have been, indeed, fortunate who had a copy free from contractions or occult symbols. One thing is print; manuscript writing another.

And yet men of the greatest learning flourished in that age. From the school of Abelard alone, as Guizot remarks, came forth one Pope (Celestine II.) nineteen cardinals, more than fifty archbishops and bishops, French, English, and German, "and a much larger number of those men with whom popes, bishops, and cardinals had had often to contend."

Few universities of the present day can boast of twenty thousand students. It was not so in the days of William of Champeaux, of St. Bernard, of Abelard, of Albertus Magnus, and of the Angel of the schools, St. Thomas Aquinas, and our own countryman, Scotus. There were giants in those days.—I am your faithful servant,

U. J. CANON BOURKE, President.

What has been stated in this chapter from the pages

of authentic history, and the proof from comparative philology, show clearly that (1) Ireland had a literature, not only in early Christian, but in pre-Christian times; (2) she had an alphabet—the Ogham, as a matter of certainty—the Roman, too, almost certain—and, it is very probable, a third—the Aryan—brought by the early emigrants who came fifteen hundred years before the Christian era to the Isle of Destiny; (3) the shape of the so-called old Irish character is that of the Roman letter; (4) modern Roman, with the dot (·) to denote the modified sound, suits every useful orthographic and phonetic purpose; (5) the diacritical dot is to be preferred to the use of the aspirate "h."

"With Christianity came to Ireland," says Lady Wilde, "the knowledge of letters. At least no older inscription has been found than that on the pillar stone of Lugnadon—St. Patrick's nephew—which may still be seen beside the ruin of St. Patrick's oratory, in one of the beautiful islands of Lough Corrib; and the oldest manuscript existing in Ireland is the Book of Armagh—a copy of St. Jerome's Latin version of the Gospels, written in the old *Roman letters*, and very valuable for the beauty of the writing and the various drawings it contains. Learning was at once consecrated to the service of God in those early days, and to multiply copies of the Gospels was the praiseworthy and devout task of the first great teachers and missionaries."—From a review, March 11, 1869, on *Fac-similes of the Miniatures and Ornaments of Anglo-Saxon and Irish manuscripts*, executed by J. O. Westwood, M.A. London, Quaritch, 1868.

CHAPTER XII.

What Archæology proves. How Comparative Philology supports its sister science. Both prove that Pagan Ireland had advanced wonderfully in the arts of writing; of illuminating; of blending colors; of dyeing. The knowledge possessed by the Ancients of the Art of Building has never been surpassed, nay, equalled. Knowledge of the Arts and Sciences amongst the Aryan races. Instances from ancient history. The Irish-Gael as an Aryan race possessed therefore the earliest knowledge of those arts and sciences known to their progenitors, and handed down for ages in the same families. (1) The Book of Kells a proof of the Art of Writing, Illuminating, Painting: The Proof has a retrospective power, by tracing effects to causes. It is not in one century a people could of old have become advanced in knowledge. 2. The Round Towers are a permanent living proof of the skill which the Pagan Irish possessed of the Art of Building. The several views presented for the past seven centuries regarding the Round Towers:—Danish, Pagan, Christian. Reasons for each view. Which is the most probable. 3. Jurisprudence; the Just Administration of the Law, known and put into practice by the ancient Irish. The Brehon Laws, now published in Irish and English by order of the British Government, show this fact. The Social and Civil Habits—the love of dress, the love of the beautiful, domestic arrangements—evince an advanced state of civilization in Ireland in the pre-Christian period.

Archæology presents proofs of primeval progress in the Arts and Sciences even in Ireland.

What does the science of comparative philology teach regarding the arts of writing manuscripts and of illuminating, of coloring or dyeing, and of painting, of building, of social life and government in the pre-Christian period in Ireland? We shall see. Books have been preserved in stone for upwards of three thousand five hundred years, and presented within the past three decades of years to the literary world to be perused by scholars skilled in archaic knowledge, and by this means to tell the tale of life and manners that had been known long periods before the Trojan War.

Sir Henry Creswick Rawlinson, K.C.B., who, from 1833 to 1840 held offices of position and trust in the kingdom of the Shah, has brought to Europe a brick or stone of about twenty inches long and ten wide, containing an entire treatise on mathematics. The writing was perfectly illegible without the aid of glasses.

"The Rock inscriptions of Persia show what can be achieved by the science of comparative philology," says Muller, p. 3, vol ii., Lecture, *Materials for the Science of Language.* "I do not wonder," he adds, "that the discoveries due to the genius and the persevering industry of Grotofend, Burnouf, Lassen, and Rawlinson should seem incredible to those who only glance at them from a distance. Their incredulity will hereafter prove the greatest compliment to those eminent scholars. What we at present call the Cuneiform inscriptions of Cyrus, Darius, Xerxes, Artaxerxes I., Darius II., Artaxerxes Mnemon, &c., what were they originally? A mere conglomerate of wedges, engraved or impressed on the solitary monument of Cyrus in the Murghab, on the ruins of Persepolis, on the rocks of Behistún, near the frontiers of Media, and the precipice of Van in Armenia."

In 1802, Grotofend proved they were letters; that they

followed each other, as in Greek, from left to right. Tychsen observed there was a sign to separate the words. Still it was unknown in what language these inscriptions were composed. It was unknown to what period they belonged. All these difficulties were removed one after the other. The proper names of Darius, Hystaspes, and of their god, Ormusd, were traced. With an imperfect alphabet, other words were deciphered, which clearly shows that the language of these inscriptions was ancient Persian. With the help of the Zend, the language of Persia previous to Darius, with the aid of modern Persian and Sanscrit, "outpost after outpost," says Müller, "was driven in, a practical breach effected, till at last the fortress had to surrender and submit to the terms dictated by the science of language."

"The inscriptions of Babylon and Nineveh, the hieroglyphics of Egypt, the records in the caves of India, on the monuments of Lycia, on the tombs of Etruria, on the broken tablets of Umbria and Samnium, want to have their spell broken or their riddle read by the student of language."—p. 6, vol. ii.

The testimony, then, of the Oxford Professor of comparative philology has been here presented to the reader to confirm the statement made regarding the discovery of Rawlinson.

The stone or brick containing an entire treatise on mathematics—one of a pile of such material brought from Persepolis—tells a great deal regarding the knowledge of the arts and sciences which the descendants of the Aryans in Persia possessed. The material of which the brick was composed, the manner in which it was moulded and prepared to stand the brunt of thousands of years, show the consummate art of the makers. The skill which enabled the artificer to engrave or impress letters so small that a microscope was required to see their outlines in detail was wonderful; and, lastly, the science that enabled one to compose a treatise, no matter how scant, on mathematics, proves a proficiency in philosophy and mathematical knowledge such as has seldom been realised since the foundations of Persepolis had been first laid.

It is related of Cicero that he had, in his day, seen the entire of the Iliad of Homer, which is a poem as large in the number of letters as the New Testament, written on one sheet of parchment, of material so fine, and the letters, too, so small, that the whole was rolled up in a nutshell. Of course, the writing was imperceptible to the ordinary eye. In modern times the Lord's Prayer has been frequently written on a paper the size of a silver sixpence. The declaration of American independence has been written within the compass of a quarter of a dollar. Had the Iliad seen by Cicero been photographed? During the siege of Paris, the London *Times* was transferred on a piece of paper four inches square, and sent, under a dove's wing, into the beleaguered city, where the Parisians quickly enlarged the copy and read the news. If so, photography is no modern invention.

Apropos to the wonders of art in olden times, going as far back as the period when the primitive Aryan race flourished, the following passages from a lecture on the Lost Arts, delivered in March, 1873, at New York, by that well-known American scholar and statesman, Wendell Philips, will be found interesting :—

THE ANCIENTS OUR MASTERS.

Take poetry, painting, sculpture, architecture, the drama, and almost everything in works of any form that relates to beauty. With regard to that whole sweep, the modern world gilds it with its admiration of the beautiful. Take the very phrases that we use. The artist says he wishes to go to Rome. "For what?" "To study the masters." Well, all the masters have been in their graves several hundred years. We are all pupils.

You tell the poet, "Sir, that line of yours would remind one of Homer," and he is crazy.

Stand in front of a painting, in the hearing of the artist, and compare its coloring to that of Titian or Raphael, and he remembers you forever. I remember once standing in front of a bit of marble, carved by Powers, a Vermonter, who had a matchless, instinctive love of art, and perception of beauty.

I said to an Italian, standing with me: "Well, now, that seems to me to be perfection." The answer was: "To be perfection," shrugging his shoulders. "Why, sir, that reminds you of Phydias;" as if to remind you of that Greek was a greater compliment than to be perfection.

ALL MEN BORROWERS.

Well, now the very choice of phrases betrays a confession of inferiority, and you see it again creeps out in the amount we borrow. Take the whole range of imaginative literature, and we are all wholesale borrowers. In every matter that relates to invention—to use, or beauty, or form—we are borrowers.

IN THE ARTS.

You may glance around the furniture of the palaces of Europe, and you may gather all these utensils of art or use, and when you have fixed the shapes and forms in your mind, I will take you into the Museum of Naples, which gathers all remains of the domestic life of the Romans, and you shall not find a single one of these modern forms of art, or beauty, or use, that was not anticipated there. We have hardly added one single line or sweep of beauty to the antique.

SHAKESPEARE A BORROWER.

Take the stories of Shakespeare, who had, perhaps, written his forty odd plays. Some are historical. The rest, two-thirds of them, he did not stop to invent, but he found them. These he clutched, ready-made to his hand, from the Italian novelists, who had taken them before from the East. Cinderella and her slipper is older than all history, like half a dozen other baby legends. The annals of the world do not go back far enough to tell us from where they first came.

All the boys' plays, like everything that amuses the child, in the open air, are Asiatic. Rawlinson will show you that they came somewhere from the banks of the Ganges or the suburbs of Damascus. Bulwer borrowed the incidents of his Roman stories from legends of a thousand years before. Indeed, Dunloch, who has grounded the history of the novels of all Europe into one essay, says that in the nations of modern Europe, there have been 250 or 300 distinct stories.

He says, at least, 200 of these may be traced, before Christianity, to the other side of the Black Sea.

TEACHINGS FROM GLASS.

I had heard that nothing had been observed in ancient times which could be called by the name of glass; that there had been merely attempts to imitate it. I thought they had proved the proposition; they certainly had elaborated it.

In Pompeii, a dozen miles south of Naples, which was covered with ashes by Vesuvius 1800 years ago, they broke into a room full of glass; there was ground glass, window glass, and cut glass, and colored glass of every variety. It was undoubtedly a glass-maker's factory. So the lie and the refutation came face to face.

CHEMISTRY.

The chemistry of the most ancient period had reached a point which we have never even approached, and which we in vain struggle to reach to-day. Indeed, the whole management of the effect of light on glass is still a matter of profound study. The first two stories which I have to offer you are simply stories from history.

The first is from the letters of the Catholic priests who broke into China; the latter were published in France just 200 years ago. They were shown a glass, transparent and colorless, which was filled with a liquor made by the Chinese, that was shown to the observers, and appeared to be colorless like water. This liquor was poured into the glass, and then, looking through it, it seemed to be filled with fishes.

They turned this out and repeated the experiment, and again it was filled with fish. The Chinese confessed that they did not make them; that they were the plunder of some foreign conquest. This is not a singular thing in Chinese history, for in some of their scientific discoveries we have found evidence that they did not make them, but stole them.

The second story, of half a dozen, certainly five, relates to the age of Tiberius, the time of St. Paul, and tells of a Roman who had been banished and who returned to Rome, bringing a wonderful cup. This cup he dashed upon the marble pavement, and it was crushed and broken by the fall. It was dented some, and with a hammer he easily brought it into shape again. It was brilliant, transparent, but not brittle.

These are a few records. When you go to Rome they will show you a bit of glass like the solid rim of this tumbler—a transparent glass, a solid thing, which they lift up so as to show that there is nothing concealed, but in the centre of the glass is a drop of colored glass, perhaps as large as a pea, mottled like a duck, finely mottled with the shifting colored lines of the neck, and which even a miniature pencil could not do more perfectly.

It is manifest that this drop of liquid glass must have been poured, because there is no joint. This must have been done by a greater heat than the annealing process, because that process shows breaks.

GEMS.

The imitation of gems. They deceived not only the lay people, but the connoisseurs were also cheated. Some of these imitations, in later years, have been discovered.

He referred to the celebrated vase of the Geneva Cathedral, a vase which was considered a solid emerald. The Roman Catholic legend of it was, that it was one of the treasures that the Queen of Sheba gave to Solomon, and that it was the identical cup out of which the Saviour ate the Last Supper.

It was venerable in his day; it was death at that time for anybody to touch it but a Catholic priest. And when Napoleon besieged Genoa—I mean the Great Napoleon—it was offered by the Jews to loan the Senate 3,000,000 dollars on that single article as security.

Napoleon took it and carried it to France, and gave it to the Institute. In a fool's night, somewhat reluctantly, the scholars said: "It is not a stone; we hardly know what it is."

In the Roman theatre, the Colosseum, which could seat 100,000 people—the Emperor's box, raised to the highest tier—bore about the same proportion to the space as this stand does to this hall, and to look down to the centre of a six acre lot, was to look a considerable distance.

Pliny says that Nero, the tyrant, had a ring with a gem in it which he looked through and watched the sword play of the gladiator's—men who killed each other to amuse the people—more clearly than with the naked eye. So Nero had an opera-glass.

So Mauritius, the Sicilian, stood on the promontory of his island, and could sweep over the entire sea to the coast of Africa with his *nauscopite*, which is a word derived from two Greek words, meaning "to see a ship." Evidently Mauritius, who was a pirate, had a marine telescope. You may visit Dr. Abbott's museum, where you will see the ring of Cheops. Boonson puts him at 2,300 years before Christ.

The signet of the ring is about the size of the quarter of a dollar, and the engraving is invisible without the aid of glasses. No man was ever shown into the cabinets of gems in Italy without being furnished with a microscope to look at them.

If you go to Parma they will show you a gem once worn on the finger of Michael Angelo, of which the engraving is 2,000 years old, on which there are the figures of seven women. You must have the aid of a glass in order to distinguish the forms at all.

I have a friend who has a ring, perhaps three-quarters of an inch in diameter, and on it is the naked figure of Hercules. By the aid of glasses you can distinguish the interlacing muscles, and count every separate hair on the eyebrows.

Layard says he would be unable to read the engravings on Nineveh without strong spectacles, they are so extremely small.

Now, if we are unable to read them without the aid of glasses, you may suppose the man who engraved all this had pretty strong spectacles. So the microscope, instead of dating from our time, finds its brothers in the Books of Moses—and these are infant brothers.

THE OLD DYES.

So if you take color. Color is, we say, an ornament. We dye our dresses and ornament our furniture. It is an ornament to gratify the eye; but the Egyptians impressed it into a new service. For them it was a method of recording history.

Some parts of their history were written; but when they wanted to elaborate history they painted it. Their colors are immortal, else we could not know of it. We find upon the stucco of their walls their kings holding court, their armies marching out, their craftsmen in the shipyard with the ships floating in the dock, and, in fact, we trace all their rites and customs painted in undying colors.

The French who went to Egypt with Napoleon said that all the colors were perfect except the greenish white, which is the hardest for us. They had no difficulty with the Tyrian purple. The buried city of Pompeii was a city of stucco outside, and it is stained with Tyrian purple—the royal color of antiquity.

But you never can rely on the name of a colour after a thousand years. So the Tyrian purple is almost a red—about the color of these curtains. This is a city of all red. It had been buried 1700 years, and if you take a shovel now and clear away the ashes this color flames up upon you, a great deal richer than anything we can produce.

You can go down into the narrow vault which Nero built him as a retreat from the heat, and you will find the walls painted all over with fanciful designs in arabesque, which have been buried beneath the earth 1,500 years; but when the peasants light it up with torches the colors flash out before you as fresh as they were in the days of St. Paul.

Your fellow-citizen, Mr. Page, spent twelve years in Venice studying Titian's method of mixing colors, and he thinks he has got it. Yet come down from Titian, whose colors are wonderfully and perfectly fresh, to Sir Joshua Reynolds, and although his colors are not yet a hundred years old, they are fading; the color on his lips is dying out, and the cheeks are loosing their tints. He did not know how to mix well.

ANCIENT MASTER-ARTISANS.

Taking the metals, the Bible in its first chapters, showed that man first conquered metals there in Asia, and the wonder is that on that spot to-day he can work more wonders with these metals than we can.

One of the surprises that the European artists received when the English plundered the Summer Palace of the King of China, was the curiously wrought metal vessels of every kind, far exceeding all the boasted skill of the workmen of Europe.

EGYPT'S MECHANICAL MARVELS.

Taking their employment of the mechanical forces, and their movement of large masses from the earth, we know that they had the five, seven, or eight mechanical powers, but we can not account for the multiplication and increase necessary to perform the wonders they accomplished.

In Boston, lately, we have moved the Pelham Hotel, weighing 50,000 tons, 14 feet, and are very proud of it; and since then we moved a whole block of houses 22 feet, and I have no doubt we will write a book about it; but there is a book telling how Dominico Fontana, of the sixteenth century, set up the Egyptian obelisk at Rome, on end, in the Papacy of Sixtus V. Wonderful! Yet the Egyptians quarried that stone and carried it 150 miles, and never said a word about it.

ABIDING PROOFS OF LITERARY KNOWLEDGE IN IRELAND.

Is there any abiding record that a knowledge of writing on stone, or on brick, or on vellum, with elegance, and perfection, and beauty of outline, had been known and practised in Ireland in the first century of the Christian period in Ireland? There is. The present writer has himself, seen a work written in the early part of the sixth century—just one hundred years after the coming of St. Patrick to preach the Gospel to the Irish people—one hundred years after the period when the apostle distributed the Roman alphabets to the Ecclesiastics of Ireland.

The work which, it was his good fortune to have seen and examined, is that written by St. Columba himself, and preserved to this day in Trinity College, Dublin. It is now thirteen centuries since the skilled, saintly hand of St. Columba traced those wondrous lines, and yet the letters are as perfect to-day, and the coloring as brilliant, and the ornamentations as lustrous, and the figures as vivid as on the day in which the wonderful book came from the pen of the Doctor of the Irish and Picts, as Mathew of Westminster calls St. Columba—*Doctor Scotorum et Pictorum.* Like the ruins of the early Irish churches, or Westminster Abbey, or the church at Durham, this glorious manuscript copy of the Gospels is a living proof of the artistic knowledge possessed by the old monks, through whose genius, skill and energy, such magnificent works had been perfected. The Book of Kells is in a special manner a convincing proof that, not only the art of writing had been known in Ireland during the first hundred years after the Irish had received the light of Christian faith, but that a knowledge of writing and illuminating must have been practised, as Professor Westwood of Oxford, in his splendid work on the art of illuminating, shows (*Palaiographia Sacra Pictoria.*) The proof can be legitimately urged further still with a retrospective bearing to show that the Irish must, before the coming of St. Patrick, have practised the art of writing and illuminating to a wonderful extent. For, it is not credible that in one hundred years from the time that St. Patrick spread a knowledge of the Christian faith, and with it a knowledge of the art of writing, the people of Ireland would have made such strides in the art of copying books, and of illuminating them in a style to which there is nothing at present, and at the time there existed nothing in Europe so beautiful.

Her Majesty, Queen Victoria, came to see the manuscript Book of Kells, and expressed her wonder at such a magnificent work of human skill. She gives it the highest praise in her book. All amateurs and critics are filled with admiration and wonder at its artistic elegance and beauty. The Book of Kells is more decorated than any other existing copy of the Gospels, and it is pronounced by all to be the most beautiful manuscript in existence of so early a date, and the most magnificent specimen of penmanship and illumination in the western world. The work is written in the Latin uncial letters common at the time.

From an essay by the present writer on the art of illuminating. Dublin, 1868: Mullany.

The style of illuminating which prevailed amongst the literary labourers of those Christian ages in this island, and in Scotland and England, was not borrowed from the East nor from any other country. It was original and peculiar to Ireland. "Long, however," says Wyatt, "before Byzantine art had time to deviate much from its ancient traditions, and even while it maintained an easy supremacy over the Western empire, . . . a formidable competitor for the leadership in the art of illumination had sprung up in the extreme West, in the island homes of the Keltic races. It is not necessary now to prove what historians have freely admitted, that Ireland was certainly Christianized for a long time previous to the date of the mission of St. Augustine to England." And again: "Before proceeding to examine the precise form assumed by this *original* art, it may be well to remind the student that the general character of the decoration of all writings, *previous to the origination of the Keltic style in Ireland*, had been limited to the use of different colored golden and silver inks, on stained purple and white vellum grounds; to the occasional enlargement of, and slight flourishing about, initial letters; to the introduction of pictures, generally square or oblong, enclosed in plain or slightly bordered frames; and occasionally to the scattering about throughout the volume of a few lines and scrolls" (p. 18).

Lady Wilde's views on J. O. Westwood's wonderful work, are worthy of a place here:—

"The earliest manuscripts of Greece and Rome show nothing like this distinctive Keltic art; nor the Italian museums, nor the wall-paintings of Herculaneum or Pompeii—beautiful as are the representations of the human figure found there; nor does Byzantine art afford any similar types. From whence, then, did the Irish, the acknowledged founders of Keltic art in Europe, derive ideas of ornamentation? *This is one of the historical mysteries which, like the origin of the Round Towers, still awaits solution. One must travel a long way, even to the far East, before finding the decorations* of the ancient Hindoo temples anything approaching to the typical idea that runs through all Irish ornamentation. It is, however, an incontrovertible fact, and one proved to demonstration by Mr. Westwood's learning, labour, and researches, that at a time the pictorial art was almost extinct in Italy and Greece, and, indeed, scarcely existed in other parts of Europe—namely, from the fifth to the end of the eighth century—a style of art had been originated, cultivated, and brought into a most marvellous state of perfection in Ireland absolutely distinct from that of any other of the civilized world; and which, being carried abroad by Irish and Saxon missionaries, was adopted and imitated in the schools of Charlemagne, and in all the other great schools and monasteries founded by them upon the Continent.

CONTINENTAL SCHOOLS ADOPT THE KELTIC ART.

"It is no idle boast to say that the Irish were the teachers of Europe from the seventh to the ninth century in art and religion. Mr. Westwood has visited all the great libraries of England and the Continent, and found abundant evidence that Irish art, or Hibernio-Saxon art, was diffused over Europe during that period. The Greek and Latin manuscripts are not illuminated, but are adorned with intercalated pictures; Irish art differs from them in many respects—amongst others, in having the figures and rich ornamentations printed on the leaves and borders of the book itself. He has given *fac similes* from

Irish manuscripts now existing, in the libraries of Oxford, Cambridge, Durham, Lichfield, Salisbury, Lambeth, the British Museum, and other places; and, passing to the Continent, has laid under contribution the great libraries of Paris, Rouen, Boulogne, St. Gall, Milan, Rome, Munich, Darmstadt, Stockholm, Copenhagan, and even St. Petersburgh, and thus proved the excellence to which Irish artists, or Saxon artists educated in Irish schools, attained more than a thousand years ago.—*Review, March* 1869.

And thus it appears the style of the illuminating art as practised throughout Europe, as well as that which the Anglo-Saxons prized, was that of which the missionaries, St. Columba and St. Columbanus, had acquired a knowledge in Ireland, and had brought with them to the countries which they civilized or enlightened. "The art of illuminating had attained a perfection in Ireland almost marvellous; and this, in after ages," says Westwood, "was adopted and imitated by the continental schools visited by the Irish missionaries.'

Students in ecclesiastical colleges should not only know the fact, but should be familiar with it; and young boarders who receive their education in convent schools should have no misgivings on the subject, that the preservation of the literary labours of the learned in ancient Rome and Greece, as well as of all monuments of religious learning, has rested mainly on the guardian care, the industry, zeal, and the laudable custom of copying manuscripts, for which the monks who studied in Ireland, Iona, and Lindisfarne, in conventual seats of learning established by missionaries from Ireland had been so eminently distinguished.

ART IN PAGAN IRELAND.

The following argument appears suasory in favor of

the existence in Ireland of the art, not only of writing, but also of illuminating manuscripts before the coming of St. Patrick to Ireland. St. Columba was born A.D., 520, St. Patrick began his mission in 432, A.D. History tells us that no people become perfect in literary arts in a few years, say a century or two. The growth must be natural. In the year 540, St. Columba was, it is known, a splendid adept at illuminating and copying books. His love for manuscripts and for translations led to a pitched battle, and ultimately to his exile from Ireland. The Book of Kells, which is the wonder of the world to this day, is his work. How did the saint acquire such a knowledge of the art of writing, or illuminating, and to such perfection, that his work to this hour is the marvel of all European antiquaries. Digby Wyatt observes that in delicacy of handling, and minute but faultless execution, the whole of paleiography offers nothing comparable to the ancient Irish manuscripts, especially the Book of Kells, the most marvellous of them all. He attempted to copy the ornaments, but broke down in dispair. In one space about a quarter of an inch superficial, he counted with the aid of a magnifying glass no less than one hundred and fifty-eight interlacements of a slender ribbon pattern, formed of white lines edged by black ones upon a black ground. "No wonder" says Wyatt, "that tradition should allege that these unerring lines should have been traced by angels." Now Columba must have had masters to teach him. These must have learned from others. Who were they? Were they Roman? No. Were they Irish? Yes. Natives? Yes. The Irish had received a knowledge of letters from Rome, if you will, *but they did not* receive a knowledge of the art of illuminating: and this for two reasons; (1) the shortness of the period between 432 and 540; (2) the fact that the

Romans themselves did not begin to practice the art of illuminating till about that period, or a century earlier, and when they did begin, they had nothing so beautiful or grand as the illuminating school in Ireland, even at the earliest period, produced—(See Lady Wilde's words quoted above.) The art as practised in Ireland was, *toto cœlo* different from the Roman. The earliest manuscripts of Greece and Rome, says Lady Wilde, " show nothing like this distinctive Keltic art. . . . Hence, she asks, " From whence did the Irish, the acknowledged founders of Keltic art in Europe, derive their ideas of ornamentation? . . One must travel a far way, even to the far East, before finding in the decorations of the ancient *Hindoo Temples, anything approaching to the typical idea that runs through all Irish ornamentation.*"

The famous Rev. Gerald de Barry (Cambrensis), who did not regard the Irish of any period to be *much* above the level of barbarians, was obliged to admit the beauty, finish, and perfection displayed in the penmanship, in the painting, in the pictured letters of the Book of Kells. His words are :

Si autem ad perspicacius intuentium oculorum aciem invitaveris, et longe penitus ad artis arcana transpenetraveris tam delicatas et subtiles, tam acutas et arctas, tam nodosas et vinculatim colligatas, tamque recentibus adhuc coloribus illustratas, notare poteris intricaturas, ut vere hæc omnia angelica potius quam humana diligentia jam asseveraveris, esse composita.

It is seemingly Lady Wilde's opinion that this Keltic style of ornamentation is of Eastern origin. This view harmonizes with all that has been stated and proved in the foregoing chapters respecting the Eastern origin of the Kelts of Ireland. It is certain the early Irish in the first age of their conversion to the Catholic faith, practised the art. Westwood's Work *(Fac Similes of the Mi-*

niatures and Ornaments of the Anglo-Saxon and Irish Manuscripts) of which a copy is to be had at the Royal Irish Academy, Dublin, and the Book of Kells, are standing proofs of this truth. It is certain that the style of art has not been borrowed from any country on earth. The style is essentially Irish. Professor Westwood says that art, cultivated in Ireland and by Irishmen, and known as Keltic, *was absolutely* distinct from that of all other parts of the civilized world; that it had attained, in Ireland, a perfection almost marvellous, and that it was in after ages adopted and imitated by the continental schools, visited by Irish missionaries.

Whence did the native race derive that knowledge? Either they invented it, or, as Lady Wilde seems to divine, they had it from the East. The science of comparative philology bears out Lady Wilde's views. These views appear to the writer the best and the truest.

In any case, the art was known even before the arrival of St. Patrick. For no people on earth could, in one century, have become such perfect limnists as the Book of Kells and Westwood's work prove them to have been.

On the other hand, if the Irish Pagan Kelts had invented the art, and brought it to such perfection, without any traditional knowledge from the early mother land, they must have been the most extraordinary inventive race on the face of the earth. This is the strongest possible proof of a high state of Pagan civilization.

All writers admit that the Keltic race were most tenacious of old rights, old customs, and traditionary knowledge of all kinds.

To this very hour the Irish race will, despite all innovation of the nineteenth century, cling to many of the old customs; and rightly, if the customs are good. If it is so now, it was much more the habit of the Keltic race, in the early ages. Zeuss and Constantius Nigra bear ample testimony to this special trait of character: *Morum priscorum semper tenacissimi fuerunt Celtici populi*—(*Grammatica Celtica Lipsiæ*, p. 915.)

Lady Wilde says: "The Irish adhered with wonderful fidelity to their peculiar art ideas for at least eight hundred years (say twice eight hundred). While the Saxons coquetted with Frankish art, the Irish continued their exclusive devotion to the ancient and national Keltic type. *They gave ideas to the world, but received none in exchange.*"

The nature of the Pagan polity, and the Druidical laws in connection with the religious system, fostered this traditional conservatism, as at present it is fostered amongst the Brahmins of Hindostan. Hence it is in no way surprising if the first dawn of the light of the Keltic "illuminatory art" had come from the East; and if a knowledge of it had been preserved, and even improved amongst the Druid teachers and their scholars. The youth of these countries have been taught to regard the Pagan Druids as educated savages, whereas they had the same opportunities for acquiring knowledge, and had really possessed as much, perhaps, as the Pagans of the Peloponesus.

ART OF MIXING COLORS KNOWN IN PAGAN IRELAND.

All that has been stated and proved in the foregoing paragraph receives additional strength and confirmation from the historic proofs that remain to show the extraordinary knowledge which the Pagan Irish possessed of the art of mixing colors. This art of producing and combining colors was as well known by our Pagan forefathers, as it had been by the Tyrians.

W. K. Sullivan writes:—"The intimate acquaintance of the ancient Gaels of Erin with the cardinal colors in their higest degree of purity, and with a great variety of other shades and tints, can be clearly established by existing evidence of a very certain character. The Book of Kells, which is an ancient copy of the four Gospels, preserved in the library of Trinity College, Dublin, contains, in its pictorial representations as well as in its illuminations of the written text, a display of beautiful coloring sufficient of itself to prove the taste and knowledge of the beautiful in colors, possessed by our remote ancestors."

"When Ireland fell under the Norman sway, in the twelfth century," says Lady Wilde, "Norman ideas naturally became triumphant; but everything that is most beautiful in antique art belongs to the pre-Norman period. All those evidences of high cultivation and artistic skill were in existence long before Normans had set foot on our shores."

"Wherever, amongst the early manuscripts in foreign libraries, one is found surpassing all the rest in the singular beauty and firmness of the writings, there at once an Irish hand is recognised as the worker, or an Irish intellect as the teacher. . . . The border of the pages in Irish manuscripts seems powdered with crushed jewels." *Lady Wilde. Review, March*, 1867. The figures in the Book of Kells are, no doubt, ecclesiastical and scriptural, but this circumstance does not in the least invalidate our claim to originality in the production and combination of the colors used in the vestments there pourtrayed. On the contrary, the fact of finding them in illuminations such as these, still preserving all their brilliancy in a book written, perhaps, about A.D. 560, only bears the strongest evidence of the truthfulness of the use of brilliant dyes in the coloring of costume. The purity and brilliancy of the green, the blue, the crimson, the scarlet, the yellow, and the purple of the book, like its penmanship, stand unrivalled, and can only be recognised by an actual examination of this very beautiful manuscript."—*Manners and Customs of the Ancient Irish, vol. iii., p.* 12.

COLORING AND BRILLIANCY OF DYES.

The coloring, and the brilliancy, and variety of the dyes is evidence of the knowledge the early Irish possessed in that department. The form of the figures, the symmetry of the written letters, the minute delineation, the skill in the execution, the harmony of detail, present a picture of human workmanship that cannot be surpassed. The process of combining colors was a public art.

The dresses of men and women, from the prince to the peasant, from the queen to the quaint housewife, were regulated in color:

> " . . . . . . Blue to women,
> Crimson to kings of every host,
> Green and black to noble laymen,
> White to clerics."—*Book of Ballymote.*

Amongst the princes and princesses, there was then, as there is now, a rivalry in the superiority and excellence of the coloring of the dresses worn.

Not only was the specific color named which each class should adopt, but the number of colors also helped to distinguish the different grades of Irish society in the Pagan period.

" One colour in the clothes of servants.
Two colors in the clothes of rent paying farmers.
Three colors in the clothes of officers.
Five colors in the clothes of chiefs.
Six colors in the clothes of Ollams and poets.
Seven colors in the clothes of kings and queens."—*Manners and Customs of the Ancient Irish, p.* 89, *by O'Curry. Edited by W. K. Sullivan, President of the Queen's College, Cork.*

These extracts show what strict attention the ancient Irish in Pagan times paid to the art of diversifying and improving colors. Hence at the time of St. Columba, it is in no way surprising that natives of ancient Eire were then superior to any other people in their knowledge of combining colors, of ornamenting, of writing and painting.

A striking instance of the style of dress, and of the color of the cloak worn by kings and queens, is given in the Irish Epic of the early part of the first century.—*The Taim bo Cuailgne.*

Queen Medb is described as: "A beautiful pale, long-faced woman, with long, flowing, yellow hair, a crimson cloak, fastened with a brooch of gold over her breast; a straight ridged '*sleagh*,' or light spear blazing red in her right hand."—*Lecture xxiii, vol. ii., O'Corry, supra.*

All this is evidence of the knowledge and practice of the art of coloring in the days of Paganism in Ireland. It is no wonder that a people so conversant with the art of combining colors should, in the early years of their conversion, become so soon such adepts in dyeing, in mixing colors, in illuminating, and in penmanship.

The thoughts of Lady Wilde on this subject of the art of illuminating in Ireland appear so truthful, so natural, so beautiful, that the writer prefers to present them than to express his own:

"It was about the end of the sixth century that the fame of Irish learning and the skill of Irish artists began to extend to England, and from thence to the Continent; and Irish scribes were employed to make copies of the Gospels and teach the splendid art of illumination in the English monasteries. From that period till the end of the ninth century the Irish were a power in Europe from their learning and piety—eminent in Greek as well as in Latin, and the great teachers of scholastic theology to the Christian world. The Gospels of Lindisfarne, executed by monks of Iona in the seventh century, and now "the glory of the British Museum," form a most important element in the early history of Keltic art, as this book seems to have been the principal model for succeeding artists.

"In the splendid Folio copy of the Gospels at Copenhagan of the tenth century, supposed to have been brought to Denmark by the King Canute, the figure of St Mathew seated, while another saint draws back a curtain, is copied from the Gospels of Lindisfarne, while the border is in the tenth century style The Gospels of St. Chad, now in Lichfield Library, are in the Irish style of the eighth century, and are very noticeable as having marginal notes in Latin, Anglo-Saxon, and ancient British, the latter being the oldest specimen of the ancient British language now in existence. The illuminations also are copied from the Lindisfarne book. St. Chad, it is known, was educated in Ireland, in the School of St. Finian. There are Irish Gospels at Durham of the eighth century. The Gospels of Mac-Regal are at Oxford, and the Gospels of Mac-Duran, the smallest and most beautiful known, are in the Archbishop's Palace at Lambeth. As Saxon art progressed and became influenced by Roman models, the Irish scribes were chiefly employed wherever harmony of colour and extreme delicacy of touch were particularly requisite, as in the borders and initial letters. Thus, the Psalter of St. Augustin, said to be from Rome, and which resembles in style the manuscript Virgil, of the fifth century, in the Vatican, is framed in pure Keltic art. On the Continent, also, the borders of the great manuscripts were generally confined to Irish hands. A Latin copy of the Gospels at Treves, evidently produced by one of the establishments founded by the Irish upon the Rhine, is remarkable for a combination of Keltic, Teutonic, and Franco-Byzantine art. The borders are Irish while the figures are Byzantine. These illuminated borders have the glitter and radiance of a setting of jewels, and are thus admirably suited to fulfil the true object of all ornamentation, which Mr Ruskin defines as being 'beautiful in its place, and perfect in its adaptation to the purpose for which it was employed.'

"In the sixth century St Gall, born in Ireland, accompanied St. Columbanus to the Continent, and founded the monastery in Switzerland that bears his name. Here many interesting manuscripts and fragments are still preserved, remarkable for the old Irish marginal notes to the Latin text. These are considered by philologists of such importance that thirteen quarto plates and *facsimiles* from them are given by Dr. Ferdinand Keller in the Zurich Society's Transactions. An interesting relic of an Irish saint is also preserved in the Cathedral of Wurtzburg—a copy of the Gospels of Killian, martyred in 689, and which was found stained with his blood on opening his tomb about five years after.

"Thus, the Irish can be tracked, as it were, across Europe by their illuminated footsteps. They were emphatically the witnesses of God, the light-bearers through the dark ages, and above all, the faithful guardians and preservers of God's Sacred Word. A hundred years before Alfred came to Ireland to be educated, and went back to civilize his native country by the knowledge he had acquired here, the Christian schools of Germany, under the direction of Irishmen, had been founded by Charlemagne. Through France, along the Rhine, through Switzerland, Italy, and Spain the Irish missionaries taught and worked, founding schools and monasteries, and illuminating by their learning the darkest pages of European history. One of the great treasures of the Imperial Library of Paris is a beautiful Irish copy of the Latin Gospels. The College of St. Isidore, at Rome, possesses many Irish manuscripts—one of them a Psalter, folio size, written throughout in letters a quarter of an inch long, and which is considered to be the finest of the later works of the Irish school. The celebrated Golden Gospels of Stockholm are of Hiberno-Saxon art of the ninth century. This book has a singular history. It was stolen from England, and disappeared for ages, but finally was discovered at Mantua, in the seventeenth century, and purchased for the Royal Library at Stockholm. St. Petersburg also possesses a highly illuminated copy of the Gospels, which was taken from France at the time of the great Revolution, and found its way to the far north. It is a perfect and beautiful specimen of the Irish style of the eighth century, and the initial letters can only be compared to those of the Book of Kells. All those Irish manuscript Gospels are, without exception, copies of St. Jerome's Latin version.

Towards the close of the tenth century the Frankish style of ornamentation, a blending of the Classical and the Byzantine, had almost entirely superseded the beautiful and delicate Keltic art both in England and the Continent, and about the fifteenth century it disappeared even from our own Ireland, the country of its origin. The gorgeous missals and illuminated Gospels, instinct with life, genius, holy reverence, and patient love, were destined to be replaced soon after by the dull mechanism of print; while Protestantism used all its new-found strength to destroy that innate tendency of our nature which seeks to manifest religious fervour, faith, and zeal by costly offerings and sacrifices. The golden-bordered holy books, the sculptured crosses, the jewelled shrines, were crushed under the heel of Cromwell's troopers; the majestic and beautiful abbeys were desecrated and cast down to ruin, while beside them rose the mean and ugly structures of the Reformed faith, as if the annihilation of all beauty were then considered to be the most acceptable homage which man could offer to the God who created all beauty, and fitted the human soul to enjoy and manifest the spiritual, mystic and eternal, loveliness of form, and colour, and symmetry.

Since that mournful period when the conquering iconoclasts cast down the temples and crushed the spirit of our people there has been no revival of art in Ireland. It is not wonderful, therefore, that we cling with so much of fond, though sad, admiration to the beautiful memorials of the past, and welcome with warm appreciation the efforts of able, learned, and distinguished men to illustrate and preserve them.

SECOND—THE ROUND TOWERS.

The pillar-towers of Ireland are a standing proof of the perfect knowledge in the art of building possessed by the people who at first planned and erected those defiant "conquerors of time." Like the Book of Kells, they are, even at the present hour, abiding proofs of the consummate art which left to posterity such enduring monuments. In architecture as well as in the art of dyeing and painting, the ancients had regard to durability; and in this aim they have certainly surpassed all modern schools of science and art. Nothing, at the present day can be executed with pencil or chisel that would like the paintings and pyramids of the ancient world, stand the test of time.

The subject relating to the Round Towers is one that would fill a fair-sized volume; it presents dimensions and outlines far too wide for the writer to compress, and yet elucidate; to trace clearly and fully in one half chapter before the critical eye of the learned student. There is no subject just now in the literary field before men of learning and thought in Ireland, and before men of no learning, and the mere unthinking, yet reading public, so full of knotty and apparently contradictory views as that relating to the ancient towers of Ireland. The subject is worthy the attention of scholars. Men of no learning have, like children looking at the moon, been time after time viewing those towers without any profitable result. Within the past fifty years, however, much has been done by means of the sciences of paleology and comparative philology, and by discoveries made in cities built by the ancients who flourished nigh four thousand years ago. In the seventeenth century the theories of astronomers regarding lightning were the theories of children. One experiment made (June, 1752) by Dr. Franklin with his electrical kite, on the plains of Philadelphia, opened the doors of the material heavens, and all the light that flashes in the spheres, that brightens the Arctic regions at mid-night, that speeds from pole to pole, that darts from the stars. that silently permeates space, was read in an instant by the eye of the philosopher.

By the key of science, a world hidden for ages is opened up in an instant, or a new order of things starts into being. The discovery made by Professor Oersted of Copenhagan in 1819, of the action of current electricity on a magnet, has revolutionised the world and brought the ends of the earth to the bounds of a village home.

Telegraphy is as much a matter of every-day life now as the mail coach had been fifty years ago in the metropolis. Oersted's accidental discovery has led to this moral and social amelioration, not in one kingdom, but throughout the habitable globe.

Pretty much in this way a large amount of knowledge, which lay entirely hidden some years ago, has been gleaned respecting the early history of nations. Fresh and truthful views regarding the Round Towers can, therefore, be presented now-a-days to the learned reader.

It is well to begin, then, to view the subject of the pillar towers as they rise before the view, covered with the mist of ages, like enchanted castles seen at a distance bedecked with a halo under the gilding light of early dawn.

Fiction must be eliminated from facts.

Truth, hidden and unperceived, must be developed.

What is certain must be clearly pointed out, and separated from that which is uncertain.

The most probable opinion can then be found regarding (1) the time in which the towers were built. Next, the object which the ancients had in view, or the purpose which they wished to effect in erecting them, can be ascertained. The two questions are quite distinct. If one arrive at a correct view regarding the time, he will readily perceive the object for which the towers were erected.

WHAT IS CERTAN: WHAT IS NOT.

1. It is certain that to-day the pillar-towers of Ireland "lift their heads sublime," as they have done for the past thousand years, presenting, even still, perennial proofs of primeval proficiency in the practice of the art of architecture. Well does Denis Florence MacCarthy sing of those "grey old pillar temples" :—

The pillar-towers of Ireland, how wondrously they stand,
By the lakes and rushing rivers, through the valleys of our land;
In mystic file through the isle, they lift their heads sublime,
These grey old pillar-temples—these conquerors of time.

2. The period at which they were erected is not certain. To this point the reader's attention is respectfully invited.

3. The object for which they were planned and perfected is a matter entirely hidden from all historic search. It may become known if one could first form a very probable opinion of the time in which the towers were first erected.

According to the anthority of Marcus Keane, M.R.I.A., author of *The Towers and Temples of Ancient Ireland. Dublin : Hodges and Smith*, 1867, there have been one hundred and twenty Round Towers in ancient Ireland. The remains of sixty-six can be traced. However, on the testimony of W. J. O'Neill Daunt, in the catechism of the history of Ireland, there are only fifty-two Round Towers actually existing in Ireland. In page 3, (thirty-fifth edition, 1872, Dublin, Duffy) he asks the question : "Are there any remarkable remains of early Irish buildings?" And he replies, "Yes, there are fifty-two Rround Towers in Ireland of a very high antiquity. Their origin and their purpose are unknown."

The present writer is inclined to believe that there are sixty-six, or the rema ins of that many, as declared by Mr. Marcus Keane, M.R.I.A., because his work is the latest published (early in 1868); and because he has made, for years past, the number of the towers and sketches of them the particular object of his study. The work which he has given the public has been projected and completed in the leisure hours of three years (before the time of publication) and neither labor nor expense has been spared in visiting and closely inspecting the numerous sites and specimens of early architecture, described or illustrated by him. He has travelled, he declares, more than five thousand miles through Ireland, and chiefly on post-cars. As archæologist and tourist, he confesses he that furnishes a trustworthy topographical and pictorial guide to the most remarkable ruins of Ireland. The present writer has read Mr. Marcus Keane's book throughout; and the only point in it deserving of praise is the correctness and fulness of the drawings, and the additional testimony furnished by him as an eye-witness to the number and reality of those conquerors of time.

Having given credit to Mr. Marcus Keane for all that appears to the writer good and useful in the work, he may be allowed to tell those who have not read the book what it is.

Mr. Keane proposes to show that the Round Towers were built by the Cuthites, as he calls the immediate descendants of Ham, or Cham, and the progenitors, according to him, of the Scythian race.—(p. 207.)

NOTE—The Scythians have sprung from Magog, second son of Japhet. Keane and Bryant state that they are descendants of Cham.

Why it is that he makes such a statement nobody but himself can tell.

It is a fact that the Kelts of Ireland—the earliest as well as the latest migration—were the descendants of Gomor, the eldest son of Japhet. The Kimmerii, the Kelts, the Galli, Galatians, the Iberians in the Caucasus and in Spain, those of the Kimmerian Bosphorus and the Crimea, the Irish, Welsh, British, are all of the race of Japhet's eldest son. This view is entirely opposed to all those who say that the Kelts of Ireland are descendants of the Phœnicians.—(*See Biblical Geography, by Dr. Rosenmuller; and Dr. Pye Smith's Biblical Cyclopedia*).

Mr. Keane contradicts, without shewing any reason, the truths which the light of the science of comparative philology has disclosed to the modern literary world.

Hermeneutics, Exegetics, Paleography, and Ethnology are regarded as sciences by learned men; and of course the truths investigated by their aid have been deemed sure and certain. These sciences Mr. Keane does not know. He makes it evident that he never heard of such safe conduits to historic truth.

The book is written without plan. It treats of everything relating to Ireland, Christian and pre-Christian as something mythical, as seen by one dwelling in the land of dreams. The work may well be compared to a stuffed image on which one sees suspended—as on the Hindu Idol Kali—all kinds of grotesque ornamentation. The Hindu idol has four arms and a necklace of skulls. The figure is represented trampling upon an intelligent creature. Such is the book before us. It has no vital force, for it is devoid of plan. It has four arms, for it takes up Paganism and Christianity, and makes use of each, right and left, as it seems to suit the drift of the writer; for, there is no purpose apparent in the work. Very likely the compiler had meant well; but if he had studied the exact sciences in any way, or if he had looked over the pages of the Logic tract, and had consulted a little common sense, he would not, as he has done, make the Irish saints either myths or demons; he would not have stated that all the ruins of Catholic churches and monasteries, even those at our door—for instance, the Abey-knock-moy, and Kilbannon—had been Pagan shrines and temples re-built in modern times. If he had known the Irish language he would not have made the absurd and outrageous mistake of saying that *fidh* is the plural of *budh* (p. 296); that the name of the idol Astoreth or Venus, was derived from the Irish word *a'tore*. *Astore*, in Irish, is a miss-spelling for "a stóir"—oh, treasure! or, oh, store! If he had consulted, for one hour, the Rev John O'Hanlon, M.R.I.A., he would have been convinced that Irish saints—Patrick and Jarlath, Colman and Brendan (see p. 293 and passim) were not Pagan personations, mythical or demoniac, but that they were real men who lived and prayed, and taught and worked, and that their works remain. The inspired narrative of Moses is made to suit the Cuthite theory. Like the Hindu figure, the work tramples to the earth every intelligent thought. The sane opinions of every learned writer—scholars like O'Donovan and Sir William Wilde, and Dr. W. K. Sullivan, Dr Petrie—of all who have penned a line on Irish, are valued as naught or simply ignored. Perhaps the writer had not known them. There is one good, however, regarding the book to be yet noticed; it is, that the writer of it asks no man to embrace his opinions or to uphold his views.

Speaking in general, it must be said, that the most exact and settled sciences, if allowed to be treated without care or order, would soon be reduced to a chaotic state. How much more so do those sciences, like paleography and antiquities, suffer under untrained hands. The most beautiful and the most elegantly arranged garden will soon lose its beauty and fruit, if the fences surrounding it are broken down and every creature allowed to enter and pull up the rarest and most precious plants.

Verily, if the youngest tyro in St. Jarlath's College should have written such a work as the *Towers and Temples of Ancient Ireland*, he would certainly obtain no position of honor in his class, until he should enlarge his knowledge, improve his style, and form some notion of correct thought and logical judgment.

WHAT ARE THE ROUND TOWERS?

For the benefit of many who, in America and in Australia, will read these pages, it is well to tell what the Towers are. Perhaps no better description of them could be given than that furnished by Dr. Petrie himself in the following outline :—

"These Towers are rotund, cylindrical structures, usually tapering upwards, and varying in height from fifty to perhaps one hundred and fifty feet; and in external circumference, at the base, from forty, sixty feet, or somewhat more. They have usually a circular, projecting base, consisting of one, two, or three steps, or plinths, and are furnished at the top with a conical roof of stone, which frequently, as there is every reason to believe, terminated with a cross formed of a single stone. The wall, towards the base, is never less than three feet in thickness, but is usually more, and occasionally five feet, being always in accordance with the general proportions of the building. In the interior, they are divided into stories, varying in number from four to eight feet, as the height of the tower permitted, and usually about twelve feet in height. These stories are marked either by projecting belts of stone, sets off, or ledges, or holes in the wall to secure joists, on which rested the floors, which were almost always of wood. In the uppermost of these stories the wall is perforated by two, four, five, six, or eight apertures, but most usually four, which sometimes face the cardinal points, and sometimes not. The lowest story, or rather its place, is sometimes composed of solid masonry, and when not so, it never has any aperture to light it. In the second story the wall is usually perforated by the entrance doorway, which is generally from eight to thirty feet from the ground, and only large enough to admit a single person at a time. The intermediate stories are each lighted by a single aperture, placed variously, and usually very small size, though in several instances, that directly over the doorway is of a size little less than that of the doorway, and would appear to be intended as a second entrance. In their masonic construction they present a considerable variety, but the generality of them are built in that kind of careful masonry called spauled rubble, in which small stones, shaped by the hammer in default of suitable stones at hand, are placed in every interstice of the larger stones, so that very little mortar appears to be intermixed in the body of the wall; and thus the outside of spauled masonry, especially, present an almost uninterupted surface of stone, supplementary splinters being carefully inserted in the joints of the undried wall. Such also is the style of masonry in the most ancient churches; but it should be added, that in the interior of the walls of both, grouting is abundantly used. In some instances, however, the towers present a surface of ashlar masonry (but rarely laid in courses perfectly regular), both externally and internally, though more usually on the exterior only; and in a few instances, the lower portions of the towers exhibit less of regularity than the upper parts.

"In their architectural features an equal diversity of style is observable, and of these the doorway is the most remarkable. When the tower is of rubble masonry, the doorways seldom present any decorations, and are either quadrangular and covered with a lintel of a single stone of great size, or semicircular-headed either by the construction of a regular arch, or the cutting of a single stone, There are, however, two instances of very ri chly decorated doorways in towers of this description, namely, those of Kildare and Timahoe. In the more regularly constructed towers the doorways are always arched semicircularly, and are usually ornamented with archieves or bands on their external faces. The upper apertures but rarely present any decorations, and are most usually of a quadrangular form. They are, however, sometimes semicircular headed, and still oftener present the triangular or straight-sided arch. I should further add, that in the construction of these apertures, very frequent examples occur of that kind of masonry, consisting of long and short stones alternately, now generally considered by antiquaries as a characteristic of Saxon architecture in England."—*Page* 355.

As to the doorways of Irish Round Towers of the sixty-six towers which remain, only forty-six have got doorways; the others are reduced to their foundations, or else have lost their original entrances.

"Of these forty-six doorways thirty-four are round-headed: The remaining twelve doorways are square-headed. Round-headed doorways generally exhibit a better style of workmanship and materials than are found in the quadrangular specimens."—*Towers and Temples of Ancient Ireland, Keane, p,p.* 392, 322.

WHEN BUILT?

At what period were the Round Towers first built?

For the past three centuries, as is known, and perhaps for many a century previous to that period, the question was asked, and has never been solved. It is not likely that it can be fully and clearly answered on the present occasion. All the present writer undertakes to do, is to put before the reader all those opinions worth knowing, entertained by learned men in the present and in the past, and the reasons on which these respective opinions rest, and then to give that view which, to his own thinking, is the best authenticated and supported. There are three commonly received opinions amongst Irish antiquaries regarding the Round Towers:—First, that they are the work of Danish hands; second, of early Christian times; third, of Pagan origin.

To which the writer adds a fourth, his own; that the Round Towers were first built in the early Pagan period by those of the Aryan race who had settled in this island of destiny; but that after the Gospel had been preached in Ireland, St. Patrick turned the Round Towers, as he did the Pagan fountains, to the service of Christian rites, and hallowed them by Christian practices and religious associations. This fourth opinion is that which seems to his Grace the Most Rev. Dr. MacHale, the most convincing and the best supported by reason and authority.

The first theory is, that the Towers had been built by the Danes while they enjoyed a footing in this island. This view was first published by the Very Rev. John Lynch, Archdeacon of Tuam, one of the most zealous advocates of the ancient glory of Ireland, author of *Cambrensis Eversus*, and cotemporary with Rothe, Ussher, Fleming, Colgan, Keating, MacFirbis, Ward, Wadding, Ware, Stephen White, O'Flaherty.

In publishing this opinion he wished simply to contradict the expression of Giraldus, that the Round Towers—those, for instance, buried in the waters of Lough Neagh, were built (*more patriæ*) in the Irish fashion. This idea of the Towers, said to be sunk beneath the billows of Lough Neagh, has been wedded to song by our national poet, Moore:

On Lough Neagh's banks, as the fisherman strays,
When the clear, cold eve's declining,
He sees the round towers of other days
In the waves beneath him shining.

The learned Father Lynch had no reason in support of his opinion, except the hearsay tradition of the peasantry, who attribute everything of an extraordinary character in the building line to the Danes. This view put forward by the Archdeacon in the spirit of contradiction, and as mere hearsay, was subsequently maintained as a certainty by Peter Walsh, in his work, the *Prospect of Ireland.*

Molyneux adopted the same opinion, not because he had any solid reason in support of this view, but because the Round Towers being a reality, they must have been built by some skilled people. To him it appeared an axiom that the early inhabitants of Ireland had been barbarians. He did not think to doubt it. On this hypothesis they could not, he argued, have built the Round Towers. Hence, as these edifices are a reality, the Danes —for no others are named—must have been the architects. This mode of reasoning was, of course, false—grossly false. His opinion, and that of Ledwich (1739-1823) in regard to the ancient Irish, that they had been savages, is opposed to the truth of authentic history; opposed to the teaching of the science of comparative philology; opposed to Catholic truth; opposed to the testimony furnished by the yet abiding architectural monuments in the East from which our race emigrated. Historians, like Livy amongst the ancients, and a vast number of writers of history in the early part of the present century, start with the notion that the earliest settlers in the countries of Europe and Asia had been rude and ignorant, and only a slight degree raised in the scale of civilization above the ape and the gorilla. This strange view is founded on the theory that man, physically and intellectually, is continuously progressing. Molyneux, then, was, in his time, convinced that the pagan Irish had been savages ; and, as he knew that the English settlers had not built the Round Towers, therefore he argued the Danes must have built them.

Ledwich carried this erroneous opinion farther still. He was convinced that it was an absurdity to suppose tha the early inhabitants of Ireland—not alone the pagan but the Christian natives—had been civilized. Hence, they could not, as he thought, have built the Round Towers. The early Christian Irish were, to his thinking, not much superior to the pagan ; therefore the Christian Irish did not build them. The Danes alone, of all those known to have been in Ireland, were enlightened and civilized ; and hence, they alone, as he supposed, must have erected those mystic and majestic piles.

Well, indeed, and with masterly literary courage, does Doctor Petrie express his own opinion regarding this ignorant, insolent writer, and of what that writer, in his bias and vain flippancy, has left on record. The following are Dr. Petrie's words :—"Nothing but its artfulness can exceed the mendacity of Ledwich's writing."—*Inquiry into the Origin of the Round Towers*, p. 10, *second edition*.

Dr. Petrie is open and candid in all he writes. He gives his views clearly and fairly, and the reasons, too, on which they rest. One has a pleasure in reading the words of such a writer ; but, with men like Ledwich—and there are many of his class, who write to deceive others—it is hard for honest thinkers like Dr. Petrie or Sir William Wilde—men of his own creed—to have patience.

The opinion of the Venerable Archdeacon of Tuam, John Lynch, and the views of Peter Walsh, of Molyneux and of Ledwich are not supported by authentic facts.

This first theory is, then, at present rejected by all. The reasons are:

1. The Danes have never been fully established in Ireland.

2. Their strongest and firmest settlement had been made in Waterford, Wexford, Limerick. One should naturally, then, expect to find in those counties many Pillar Towers; and conversely few or no Pillar Towers in the counties in which the Danes had made no permanent settlement. But such is not the case. Pillar towers raise their heads, to this hour, in counties where the Danes never had obtained a settled footing. And in the counties of Limerick, Waterford and Wexford, the fewest, and those most wasted by the hand of time, are found to exist. The Round Tower built in ashlar at Ardmore, in Waterford, with its circular arch, and Irish style manifested in the moulding, in the working of the arch, in the mason work to be seen under the sill and all round, is, perhaps, the best, and is found yet in a fair state of preservation; so are those which raise their heads to the clouds at Cluaincaoin and Dysart, county Limerick; while the few at Lismore and Dungarvan, at Killmallock, St. Mungret's, at Ardladhran, Ferns, and Wexford, are fast crumbling to decay.

3. If those northmen from Denmark and Scandinavia had built these Towers in Ireland, why did they not erect Round Towers in England, where they once held regal power? Why did they not build those pillar piles, signs of sovereign sway, in Normandy, in Belgium? Nay, why had they not built them in their own land, in Jutland, or Denmark, or Scandinavia? It is as clear as can be, that had the Northmen built the Irish Round Towers they would, at some period and in some other place, have erected similar edifices to commemorate their supreme skill and

their sovereign sway. But no monument of the kind is to be found any where in England, Normandy, Belgium, or Denmark. It is manifest, therefore, that the Danes never built those perennial piles of architectural art. In addition to all that has been here proven, it must be said that the supporters of this first view cannot show that the Danes had, at the time, any adequate idea of that advanced architectural skill of which the erection of the Towers is a proof.

CHAPTER XIII.

Round Towers—second theory. The first theory is that the Danes built the Towers ; the second, that these conquerors of time are the work of Irish Christian hands, and had been built at different periods between the fifth century and the thirteenth. That is Dr. Petrie's opinion. It is held by many scholars at present in Ireland, especially by ecclesiastics. Dr Petrie's Proofs; Positive Proofs ; Negative Proofs. The writer's duty. His views. Refutation of Petrie. An anecdote—the Archbishop and the peasant boy on the subject of the tides. Illogical Scholarship. Literary bores. Silence is not of itself an argument against the truth of an alleged fact. Third theory—that the Round Towers are of pagan origin. Those who support this view. Fourth theory—The Round Towers were built in the early pagan period by the children of the Aryan race who had landed in Ireland ; that after the Gospel had been preached by St. Patrick, the Round Towers were turned to the service of Christian rites, and hallowed by Christian practices. They are pagan in origin ; in use Christian. The great reason Dr. Petrie did not admit the pagan origin of the Towers is, (1) because he could not be certain that the Irish race, before the Christian era, had been skilled in science and arts. Philology proves to a certainty that Kelts were Aryan; their language shows it ; therefore, they were learned. Hence, the Irish language has been useful in elucidating and settling this vexed subject of the Pillar-towers. This argument is strengthened by (2) the character and style of the architecture of the towers. The style is Cyclopian, like that found in Etruria, Mycenæ, Thebes, Persepolis. (3) Corroborative Proofs :—Shape of Doors, Arches. Slanting or tapering superstructures like the Pyramidal piles along the Nile, or those found in Eastern climes, are of the earliest architectural types.

SECOND THEORY.

The second theory regarding the Round Towers :—

These rotund, cylindrical structures, which vary in height from fifty to one hundred and fifty feet, is that they are the work of early Irish Christian hands; that they had been built by Irish Catholics at different periods between the fifth century and the thirteenth, and that the object intended by their use was to serve as appendages to ecclesiastical establishments, as belfries, as monastic castles, as homes of safety in the hour of danger or of surprise, as towers of defence for ministers of religion, as safes for vessels and vestments used at the holy altar. This opinion, which appears so natural, was put forward by Dr. Petrie—himself a Protestant—and has been ably defended by him in a large volume of 450 pp. imper. octavo, entitled *The Ecclesiastical Architecture of Ireland anterior to the Anglo-Norman Invasion, comprising an Essay on the Origin and Uses of the Round Towers of Ireland. Dublin, Hodges and Smith*, 1845. The opinion is, at present, held commonly by nearly all the ecclesiastics in Ireland who have read Petrie's work; it is the view of a great many scholars who have in a passing way paid any attention to the subject. The learned Very Rev. Dr. Mathew Kelly, Professor of Belles Lettres, Maynooth, defended this opinion. He was a great admirer of Dr Petrie. That learned and gentle ecclesiastic and savant has (*Dublin Review, July*, 1845) declared, and deservedly, of Dr. Petrie's book, "that it is a work for which a savant in France would be entitled to a place amongst the nobility." Irishmen cannot hope for honours so great; for, if so, Petrie ought, certainly, to have been raised to a baronetcy.

If respect for the opinion of one under whom the present writer had been a pupil for three years—Very Rev. Dr. Kelly; if early impressions alone were the lights that led to conviction; if a desire to see the name of the early Irish Christian Church hold a distinguished place, as she certainly deserves, not alone for the piety and sanctity of her sons, but for their great learning and wonderful knowledge in past times, he who pens these lines would naturally hold the opinion propounded so ably by Dr. Petrie, and approved and supported by the most erudite antiquarian of the period—Professor Kelly of Maynooth. Impressions received in the days of youth exercise their influence; and so they certainly have done on the mind of the present writer. Dr. Petrie's work came, through the kindness of Mr. Hardiman, who lived at Errew monastery in the year 1845, into the hands of the present writer, then in his sixteenth year. Petrie's views became his views. But time and fuller knowledge have changed the conviction then arrived at regarding the origin of the Pillar Towers of his native land.

DR. PETRIE'S PROOFS.

In order to convince students of Irish history and Irish antiquities, "that the Round Towers are of Christian and ecclesiastical origin, and were erected at various periods between the fifth and thirteenth centuries," the learned Dr. Petrie has been obliged to disprove, according to his knowledge and ability, the arguments brought forward by those who maintain that the Towers had been planned by Irish heads, and erected by Irish hands, at a period of pagan power in Ireland.

The proofs put forward to support the position which he ably upholds and defends are derived from two sources—the one, positive; the other negative.

The positive proofs are :—(1) That the Towers are never found unconnected with ancient ecclesiastical foundations.

(2) That the uses to which the Round Towers are known by a uniform and concurrent tradition of the country to

have been applied—a tradition corroborated by written testimony and authentic evidence—accord precisely with the Christian and ecclesiastical character of those ancient buildings.

(3) That on several, Christian emblems are observable.

(4) That they are of the same style of architecture as that found in well-known Irish ecclesiastical buildings of the early Christian period; or, as Dr. Petrie states, that the architectural style of the Towers exhibits no feature or peculiarity not equally found in the original churches with which they are locally connected when such remain.

The negative proofs are :—(a) That the arguments adduced by General Vallancey, Mr. Beauford, Miss Beaufort, and Dr. O'Conor, are not valid.

(b) That these furnished by Dr. Lanigan, Mr. D'Alton, Thomas Moore, Mr. Windele, can be reduced to the same category with those put forward by Vallancey, and hence are to be refuted by the same process of reasoning as Vallancey's have been.

(c) That supposing the Towers had been built in pagan times, no one can tell either the precise period or the special purpose for which they were erected.

(d) That no mention is made by any writer in any of the early Irish authentic records that the Towers had been built in pagan times.

THE WRITER'S DUTY: HIS VIEWS AND PROOFS.

The present writer must necessarily show how far (1) Dr. Petrie's reasoning is logically conclusive; (2) how much it really proves; (3) how far the positive proofs of the learned author of the *Inquiry into the Origin and Uses of the Round Towers* tend to convince right-minded men and scholars that his theory respecting their Christian origin is correct, and sufficiently supported by facts and valid proofs. (4) In presenting his own opinion he must put clearly before the reader the reasons that convince himself that the Round Towers were built in the early pagan period by those of the Aryan race who had settled in this island; that after the Gospel had been preached in Ireland, St. Patrick turned those majestic pagan piles, as he did the pagan fountains, to the service of Christian rites, and hallowed them by Christian practices and religious associations.

(1) The fact that most of these splendid edifices stand close by or within the precincts of those ruins which all confess to be the remains of Christian or ecclesiastical buildings is, Dr. Petrie states, proof sufficient to show that these Round Towers had been, in some way, made use of by the growing Christian Church of Ireland. Of that fact there is no doubt. The Round Towers were made use of by the early Christians of Ireland for the service of religion and the safe-keeping of vestments, altar plate, and as citadels of safety and defence for priests and religious in troublous times. They had been belfries for a time, and perhaps became turrets to light pilgrims to the sacred shrines. This is one of the strongest, perhaps the very strongest argument put forward by Dr. Petrie in support of his theory. Grant the whole argument. In good truth, what does it prove? Simply that the Round Towers had been for a time in the service of the Church, and honored by being made use of during a few centuries that followed the period of St. Patrick's preaching the faith in Ireland. It does not prove that the early Irish Christians built those Towers.

(2) The argument is developed in this way, that the pillar towers were known by the names "clogteaċ," (clog, bell; teaċ, a house), a belfry; and "cloċ-teaċ" (cloċ, stone, and

teač, house) stone pillar; "gail," a foreign (pillar-stone) erected by "gail," fair looking men, the Gauls (gall is from "ga," a ray, light, brightness; "al," nurtured, not unlike Greek *kalcs*, fair, *ga'a*, milk; "geal," white, Irish); "clogad," from "clog," a bell, and "ed" dress, covering, because the tower has a conical or bell-shaped top; "tig-aifrin," mass-house; "aifrin" is the Irish name for Mass; root, "aifir," to offer, to celebrate, to sacrifice. All these arguments prove simply nothing more than that the native Irish called "these grey old pillar temples," and correctly, too, by those special names, for such, during a period, undoubtedly they were. Nevertheless, the fact that these Towers were known in days of old by these titles, does not prove that the Christians erected those graceful, tapering piles of past time.

3. The argument is pressed still more strongly that the style of at least five Round Towers and that of the ecclesiastical buildings adjoining them, is identical not only in the general features, but in detail. The quadrangular doors of the Towers have not, for instance, the architrave, such as some of the churches have, but it is found on the arched door of the Tower of Roscrea.

4. Christian emblems are carved on those "grey old pillar temples," as at Donaghmore an image of our Saviour crucified is carved in *relievo*; therefore, *all* the pillar temples are of Christian origin.

The foregoing argument, when tested by the light of strict logical reasoning, fades into thin air. It is like the following:—Five men in a parish have a certain cast of countenance, therefore all men in that parish have the same.

In fact, Dr. Petrie's deduction is plainly illogical. The writer has every desire to quote the learned antiquary accurately, and with all due respect for his varied learning. The reasoning is as if he had argued thus:—Five men in this district have not only a certain cast of countenance, but they are hairy; therefore they are descendants of Esau who was a hairy man; nay, *all* the people of this district who are of the same class in society and relatives of those five, must be, like them, descendants of that hirsute progenitor. The argument is vicious in two ways; first, by drawing a *certain* conclusion from premises which are merely *accidental*—as if a person should conclude that a man was always drunk because he had been drunk once; or, that because one man in a college, like Judas amongst the Twelve Apostles, turned out bad, therefore all were bad, and the system in the college bad. Secondly, by imparting to the subject of the conclusion a wider extension than it had had in the premises—applying to the whole body what is true of one only. One sheep in a flock is black, therefore they are all black; one child in a family is vicious or faulty, therefore they are all so—a very illogical, but for all that, a very common argument, indeed. It appears that Dr. Petrie makes use of it—"five towers resemble the surrounding ecclesiastical buildings in the style of architecture, therefore all Round Towers are, in style, like the ecclesiastical edifices around; therefore, the architect who erected the ecclesiastical buildings erected the Towers. Five men in a parish are good or bad, therefore they are all good or they are all bad. Such a mode of argumentation could not for an instant be tolerated. This is Dr. Petrie's argument. It is calculated to deceive. It has deceived even some first-class scholars, as the late Very Rev. Matthew Kelly. It has deceived some clever architects and engineers with whom the present writer has had, within the past month, an opportunity of discussing this vexed subject. The argument of "*ex uno disce omnes*" is not good, except in those instances in which essential qualities are compared. If one man has a soul, all men have souls; this argument is good, because the soul is an essential portion of man's being. If one man has a heart, all men must have a heart, for it is essential to life. But if one man, or five men, have red beard or whiskers, it does not follow that all men have red beard or whiskers. The mere color and the growth of hair, or resemblance in form, is an accident, and from a mere accident in individuals, no conclusion regarding the general body or class can be drawn.

Five towers, or even a larger number, could, in their architectural form be, in style, like the local ecclesiastical edifices, and for all that, not have been built by those hands that erected the churches. What is easier than to suppose a possible and a probable case, namely, that skilled architects imitated, in church-building, the ancient and solid style presented in the Towers. An electro-plated gold watch or an artificial diamond is quite like a pure gold watch, or a natural diamond, yet it is no proof against the worth and the original perfection of pure gold, or the value or history of the Koh-i-noor, which it resembles.

Again, the argument that on several Round Towers Christian emblems are observable, is of no value. The Towers once converted to Christian usages, during the time of St. Patrick, or after that period, could have undergone modifications, and in this way, Christian emblèms could have been inserted to show the new service to which these pyramidal piles had been consecrated. The argument from Christian emblems proves nothing. It is like the following:—The stations of the cross are found, or had been till last year, found in the Colliseum, therefore the Colliseum has been always Christian, and had never been a place of pagan festive rites and brutalizing exhibitions, nor the theatre in which Christian martyrs had been thrown to wild beasts. The presence of Christian emblems cannot change the origin of a pagan edifice.

Next come the negative proofs furnished by Dr. Petrie. And first—

(*a*) That the arguments adduced by Vallancey, Mr. Beaufort, Miss Beaufort, and Dr. O'Conor, are not valid.

It may be useful to remark that the refutation of false or useless arguments which have been offered in sustainment of a view, does not prove that in every instance the opinion is erroneous, or the thesis false; above all, it does not prove that another view offered in its stead is correct. The theory may be right, like the theory of the tides, although, in the views of a peasant, or of an uneducated boy, its explanation is quite meaningless.

In the present instance, it does not follow as a logical sequence, because Dr Petrie proves the arguments brought forward by General Vallancey, Dr O'Conor and others, in favour of the pagan theory respecting the Round Towers to be meaningless and devoid of rational value, that, therefore, the theory itself of their pagan origin is untrue in fact. The learned Doctor simply proves this much, and no more—that their arguments are, as arguments, of no avail in proving the particular proposition. Other arguments, strong and convincing, unknown to Vallancey or to Dr. O'Conor, may exist, and in fact do.

Dr. Petrie shows that Dr. O'Conor's proof from "turagan," a fire-tower; ("tur," tower, and "agan," blaze, torch) is simply a misprint, or an error in transcription for "truaġan," a pitiable person, a hermit; root, "truaġ," pity, wretchedness; and, again, that "fiḋneaṁaḋ" does not mean "celestial index," but sacred trees; root, "fiḋ," wood, and not "fiaḋ," witness, testimony, and "neaṁ," heaven, "neaṁaḋ," or rather "neaṁḋa,' heavenly. He shows that General Vallancey's conclusion, drawing an argument, *a pari*, regarding Ireland's towers and those in Persia and on the banks of the Volga, is a "*non sequitur.*"

"Suppose," says Petrie, "the Persians did worship fire in Round Towers; suppose that Lord Valencia saw in India towers like those in Ireland, and that towers not unlike them are found on the banks of the Volga, and in Bulgaria, does it follow that the towers in Ireland were fire-temples." By no means. The Indians themselves do not know what the Round Towers in Persia were, much less does Lord Valencia know what they were. The towers in Bulgaria are Mahometan minarets. The towers of the Guebres resemble Norman Keeps or large windmills, and are not like the tapering towers of Ireland.

Dr. Petrie has asked—"Does it follow as a logical sequence, because the early Persian race had towers which, probably, were fire-temples, that, therefore, towers in Ireland, which are not unlike those in Persia, were fire-temples? The only answer to that question is—By no means. No logical sequence can result from a mere accidental resemblance. Mere resemblance does not prove identity of origin, of kind, or sameness of purpose, or of end.

Dr. Petrie, and those who adopt his views, must, in turn, be asked, does it follow, because the arguments of Dr. O'Conor and of General Vallancey have been refuted, that, therefore, the thesis proposed by them is without convincing proof? The trisection of a given arch is true in fact; in theory, without proof. Again, does it follow, logically, that Dr. Petrie is right, if Dr. O'Conor and Vallency are not? By no means.

In the summer of 1868, his Grace visited the Western

Highland of Connemara, not for pleasure, but for the purpose of discharging those duties which, as Bishop of the extensive diocese committed to his spiritual care, he was bound to fulfil—preaching, teaching, administering the Sacrament of Confirmation to the growing youth—boys and girls of that extensive district; directing the faithful clergy, cheering them by his presence, exhorting them by his counsel, and consoling them by the example which he has set them of all manner of virtue.

As the Archbishop was journeying from a small town called Ballinakil to Cleggan, a village on the sea shore, just opposite the island of Bofin, an island blessed by the footprints of St. Colman, he entered into friendly converse, in the Irish language, with a young boy—a growing youth of the age of twelve. The tide was ebbing at the time; the sun had just turned the meridian; the wild waste of waters stretching over the bosom of the Atlantic seemed slightly ruffled by a pleasant western breeze beginning to blow inland, and looked like a vast cyclopian mirror damped by the breathing of ethereal beings looking into its glassy surface; or like a mighty monster instinctively moving off from the presence of the sacred ministers and intelligent agents of the God who made all things. His Grace asked the young lad why it was that the sea came in and went out; and then no sooner, said he, is it out than in; and thus, the sea never ceases, but is continuously agitating its waters. Why is this? Tell me for what purpose is all this motion and commotion? By these apparently simple questions his Grace wished to learn what was the naive, uneducated boy's notion of the theory of the tides.

"Ah," said the youth, "don't you know? Sure all this tumbling and tossing of the sea is to give the people sea-weed. If the tide," said he, naively, "did not com in and go out, what should we do without sea-weed." ("Muna d-tiocfaḋ tuile na fairrge asteaċ agus amaċ cad ḋo dḋéanfaḋ an ḟamain"—if the tide of the sea should not come in and go out what would the sea-weed do) an idiomatic form for saying what would become of the sea-weed—there would be none.

Suppose that the theory regarding the tides had no stronger argument to support it than that put forward by the ingenuous youth who conversed on this occasion with the Archbishop, astronomers would feel sorely puzzled in accounting for the tides. The theory regarding the cause of the tidal wave, and of the ebbing and flowing of the waters of the sea is true, although the reason suggested in its support by the unsophisticated youth was of no value.

So, too, the pagan theory regarding the Round Towers may be true, although Dr. O'Conor's reasons are worthless, and General Vallancey's arguments futile. Foolish reasons in support of a theory tend to injure the cause of truth; and literary quacks are the plague of society and of scholars.*

---

* Note—A letter from one of this class has come to the writer's hands within the past year. A certain gentleman from the south of Ireland declared triumphantly that he has made a great discovery regarding the Round Towers. He communicates his thoughts to his Grace the Archbishop of Tuam. The Archbishop did the present writer the honor of asking his opinion on its views and on the merit of the document. Well, what did the sapient writer of that letter say? "I have found out," said he, "all about the Round Towers. The pillar temples are called in Gaelic, 'cuilceaċ,' but 'cuilceaċ' and 'guilceaċ' are the same, and 'guilceaċ' means a reed; therefore 'cuilceaċ,' or a round tower means a *reed*; and these Round Towers were so called because they were built after the organised form of a reed." Such is the substance of a long and labored letter. What follows; simply nothing. It is all a *nil sequitur*.

(*b*) Dr. Petrie does not deal so badly with the arguments and the matured opinions of Dr. Lanigan, Moore, D'Alton, and Windele, as he does with the opinions of General Vallancey, Miss Beaufort, Dr. O'Conor.

Writing of Dr. Lanigan, he says, (p. 32) :—" I have next to notice the arguments in support of the eastern origin of the Towers, of a writer who was greatly superior in solid learning, honesty, and general acuteness, to any of those whose reasoning I have hitherto combatted, namely, Dr. Lanigan, the able author of the *Ecclesiastical History of Ireland.*"

And again he remarks regarding Dr. Lanigan :—" In his labored and ingenious effort to establish a theory on insufficient data, there appears a consciousness of the weakness of the proofs on which it rests."

Dr. Lanigan says that he sees no reason to deny that the Round Towers existed before Christianity, and that their style proves them very ancient.

Literary men of name like his Grace the Archbishop, must bear with the wild notions of foolish writers of this class.

The pillar pile was called "cuılceaċ," which, according to Dr. O'Brien, is by metathesis of "]," a corrupt form of "cloċteaċ." The present writer is of opinion that the term is from (1) "cul," (Latin, *collis)* the nape, or back, or rear, and "teaċ," a house, because each of the Round Towers, except at Clonmacnoise, is built not within the body of the church or monastery, but is found a little apart from the rest of the building. (2) "cul" has, in Gaelic, the meaning of "protection." We say even to-day, of a defender in a fray, "cul-báre," a champion of defence or of victory; "bár," top; "cul," means to defend, to guard, to protect, to cultivate; Latin, *col* in *colo*, to till, to worship; *cultus*, worship, attention, cultivation. The "i" in "cuılceaċ," is inserted, according to the phonetic requirements of the language expressed in the rule, "slender with slender." Because "e" in the second syllable is slender, "i," another slender vowel, must close the preceding syllable.

Dr. Petrie says, in reply, that he sees every reason to deny that they did exist; for, says he, not the slightest evidence has ever been adduced to prove that the Irish were acquainted with the art of building with lime cement before they received the Christian faith; and the architecture of the Towers and that of the ancient churches erected before the twelfth century, is the same in every respect.

Regarding the opinions of our national poet, Thomas Moore, he says, (p. 67) :—"I find little but a repetition embodied in more graceful language and a more logical form of the evidences which I have already examined." And Mr. Windele, of Cork, he styles the "ingenious Mr. Windele." And noticing the reasoning of Mr. Moore, he says: "I find nothing requiring an answer. . . . I pass on,"—p.p. 67, 70, In this way Dr. Petrie handily, though not logically, sets aside all the views of Dr. Lanigan, Windele, D'Alton, Moore.

REPLY :—Not to be able to tell precisely what year this event or that other happened, is no proof that it did not happen at all; if so, many a person could fairly doubt that he had ever been born.

Every person knows the number of literary contests that have taken place on the subject of chronology.

Even the exact time of the birth of the Saviour of men, OUR LORD JESUS CHRIST, has been disputed.

Again, not to be able to tell why, or for what purpose the building was erected, is no proof against the fact that there was a head that planned, and an architect who fashioned it, and men who carried out the work in detail.

Why were the Pyramids built? Who can correctly and truly tell?

Why do Highlanders wear kelts? They cannot well tell. They say it was the primitive dress of the Gaels; but it was not; and even if it had been, why did they adopt that form of dress? To pass the rushing torrent safely? There are torrents in Switzerland.

Why are there a thousand and one strange things done every other day? In examining the time when the Round Towers had been first erected, it is not necessary to know why or for what purpose they were planned or built.

(c) "No mention is made by any writer in any early Irish record extant that the Towers had been built in pagan times?"

The reply to this is, that it is not in every respect true. Although no direct allusion has been made, yet indirect reference has been given that there were Round Towers even in the early part of the first century in Ireland. Allusion has been made to those, for instance, supposed to be under the waters at Lough Neagh. The tradition, vague as it was, showed that the notion of a pagan origin regarding them has been very ancient, and had its rise in pagan times.—See infra, p. 386.

But suppose, secondly, that it is true that no mention at all has been made of their existence, still that proves nothing either for Dr. Petrie's cause or against the pagan origin; it hits right against his own theory, for there is no record to show that the Towers were of Christian origin.

Physicians of the present day know well that before William Harvey's time, two centuries and a half ago, no one knew anything about the circulation of the blood. Did it follow that Harvey was wrong, because for the space of twice a thousand years—from the days of the father of medicine, Hippocrates, to those of Harvey—the doctrine regarding the circulation of blood had been utterly unknown. Michael Servetus hinted at it, but that was all. The same is true of the action of Columbus, of

Copernicus, of the discovery of the electric fluid, even of Bentley and the lost F. Silence respecting the lost letter was no proof that it had never been known. Silence regarding men and events, nay, towns and cities, is no proof that they did not at one time exist. The same mode of reasoning can be applied to things, the knowledge of which has been lost, and to things newly discovered. Silence in the past, to the time of Vallancey, concerning the pagan origin of the Round Towers, proves nothing.

These modern sciences were not known two hundred years ago. The ancient Irish scholars, from the eighth century to the eleventh, had enough to do to keep themselves safe from the incursions of Danes; and in the twelfth century to attend to religion and to the transcription of ancient manuscripts. In later times, up to the opening of the present century, the wonder is, how a native Irish scholar could have lived at all. The awakening sciences of comparative philology, paleology, hermeneutics, are causing men to turn their attention to those ancient departments of knowledge, and to promote enquiry.

If the argument avail at all, however, it comes quite against the views of Dr. Petrie. Suppose for a moment that the Round Towers are, as he thinks, the work of Christian hands, how account for the fact, that no mention is made in any ancient record, in the life of any Irish saint (the writer has read hundreds of them,) in any work relating to antiquities, that the Round Towers had been built, at any particular time or place, by any special man or community of men? In fact, no mention of Round Towers is introduced at all in annal, history, record, life, or chance-writing relating to Ireland; much less, is it stated that a tower was built at such a time and at such a place, or for such an object. How account for this omission, if the Towers had been the work of Christian hands, especially as the name of every saint is recorded, of every king and chieftain, and of the works done by them? Was it not as easy to record the story of the origin of the Towers as it is to tell the history of the churches which the saints founded?

The leading proposition laid down by Dr. Petrie in his able work, and which he endeavours, by means of the different proofs furnished, to sustain, has not yet in these pages received a direct refutation. The following is the proposition:—"That the Round Towers were erected at various periods between the fifth and thirteenth centuries."

The writer is of opinion that that proposition is untrue. The reasons are (1) because he has shown that Dr. Petrie's proofs in support of the thesis have no convincing force; and (2) because in reality, it was simply an impossibility that such works of architectural art could have been built by the Christian population of Ireland, from the years A.D. 432 to 1172, when Henry II. landed on the coast of Wexford. Dr. Petrie himself tacitly admits, and the writer is convinced, that towers of such architectural excellence could not have been erected from the days of St. Patrick to the time of St. Engus, the Culdee. This appears true (*a*) both on account of the evidently imperfect buildings erected during the first century and a-half after the conversion of the Irish to Christianity; and (*b*) because the best stone buildings of the period, still extant in Aran, in the Isles of Bofin and Shark, and High Island, on the coast of Connemara, are in no way to be compared in size, form, in the nature of the stone, in inherent structure with the Pillar Towers; and (*c*) because the Irish Christians in *their first essay* at architecture, (*and on the supposition that before that period they had not known the art of building,*) could never have erected, in a short period, magnificent structures requiring so much skill, and could never have furnished such superb specimens of sculpture, grand and perfect to a rare degree, that they challenge comparison with the best specimens of ecclesiastical edifices of the present period, and excite the surprise and wonder of foreigners who visit our shores.

It was impossible for Irishmen to build the Towers from the first moment an Ostman set foot on the Irish soil, or as long as Danish galleys cruised along the Irish coast. Irishmen were for over two hundred years in daily dread of the fierce "Lochnanaig," (lake-men) from Denmark. To erect buildings during that troublous time was plainly impossible, much more so to erect such splendid superstructures as the Pillar Towers are, and so many of them. That they were not built between the time when Brian fought and defeated the Dane at Clontarf (A.D. 1014) and the landing of Henry II. (A.D. 1172,) is a certainty of history. Therefore, to the thinking of the present writer it was quite impossible that Irish Christians could have, in the circumstances, erected such a number of magnificent buildings from the time of St. Patrick to the time of Henry II. Of course, Catholics of the period performed greater works than the building of such monuments; but in the circumstances of those times, from A.D. 432 to A.D. 800, and again from that period to the final overthrow of Danish power in Ireland, it was impossible that Irish Christians could, in Ireland, have built such elegant structures. Moreover, it is certain from the words of Giraldus, that on his arrival with King John, son of Henry, Towers had been in Ireland, not only at that period, but before the Danes had set foot on Irish soil, that is anterior to the ninth century. Giraldus describes the Towers as: "*Turres ecclesiasticas, quæ more patriæ arctæ sunt et altæ, nec non et rotundæ*"—"Towers for church purposes, which in the fashion of the country (that is, of towers like those in Ireland) are narrow and high, as well as round." They were standing, then, in his time, nay, they were in use for church purposes, therefore they had been manifestly erected long before, say anterior to the coming of the Ostmen to the Irish coast; for, after that period, Irishmen had quite enough to do to live and fight.

Besides the testimony of Giraldus, other historic items are to be found in Irish annals which indirectly corroborate the force of these remarks, that Round Towers had been in Ireland before the ninth century.

A Strong Positive Proof.—That there were ecclesiastical stone buildings erected during the seventh century and the eight, no one doubts. But when the primitive architecture of Ireland is classed with English-Norman of the twelfth, it is quite another thing. In all the Anglo-Norman specimens of architecture there is found one feature common and uniform, namely, the jambs of door-ways and windows are parallel; in all the specimens of early Irish architecture the doorways and windows are wider "at bottom than at top." This constitutes, if no other were found, an essential difference between the two styles—the early Irish and the Anglo-Norman.

In their sculptured ornaments, too, the Irish Towers and early buildings are quite unlike the Anglo-Norman; and Irish architecture appears like the art of Illuminating, quite unique—completely insular and Keltic. The present writer has examined some ten or twelve Round Towers. He has found that the Tower, no matter how nigh to the ecclesiastical buildings, is, nevertheless, completely apart and separate from the adjacent houses. This is true of all, except the Round Tower of Clonmacnoise. Secondly, he has seen that the stones, in their composition, are not, as a rule, of the same sort and of the same stratification as the stones of the ecclesiastical buildings; they are immensely larger, more massive, better prepared for the purpose of building, not laid in the same order, knitted together like huge boulders, but with a scientific sureness combining strength and cyclopic massiveness. Thirdly—The stones of the Round Towers, as at Kilbannon, Tuam, must have been brought a great way, for there are not in the neighbourhood any stones like them. It appears to the writer that the stones of all the Round Towers had been all taken from some two or three quarries, just as in Egypt, the stones which went to the erection of the Pyramids had been all dug from the same quarries in the Lybian mountains, west of the Nile. Fourth—The cement or grouting of stone used in the erection of the Round Towers does not appear, if one wish to analyze it, the same as the mortar found in the circumjacent edifices.

ENDURING CHARACTER OF THE ROUND TOWERS.

The shape of the Tower—its tapering and rotund form—renders it firm and at the same time not liable to be injured by storm. The strongest gale acting against it can never effect its firmness, for the wind has no level surface to act against; the force of the strongest storm impinges only on one line of surface, and, like a ball hitting a convex body at a sharp angle, passes off in a tangent line.

The style of stone made use of in the erection of the Pillar Towers is found suited to the Irish climate, and is, in the opinion of scientists, admirably calculated to withstand the action of the weather.

Taking into note the sloping shape, securing stability, the summit pointed, the rotund form which is of all the very best in resisting the action of external force, especially that of storms, the sort of stone, too, made use of in construction—the Pillar Towers have been admirably calculated to endure, as they have done for ages. Their only foes in the past have been lightning and the unchecked growth of the ivy tree.

Lastly—It is necessary for the advocates of the second opinion to prove, first, that the early Christian Irish had known how to erect edifices of such striking architectural excellence as the Round Towers; and secondly, to show by positive proofs, that they did, *de facto*, build them. It cannot be shewn by direct proofs that from A.D. 432 to 900 A.D. the Towers were erected, or that men of the period possessed knowledge required to raise such pillar piles.

THE ROUND TOWERS OF PAGAN ORIGIN.

THIRD OPINION.—It is now time to come to the third opinion that the Round Towers are of pagan origin.

The advocates of this opinion are General Vallancey, Mr. Beauford, Dr. O'Conor, Miss Beaufort, Moore, D'Alton, Windele, O'Brien, Keane, and others, amongst whom may be classed Giraldus.*

All those agree that the Round Towers had been built in the pagan period, but all do not agree on the time in which they were built, nor on the special object for which they were erected.

The learned reader will observe that the leading ques-

* Note—" Earum antiquitatem ethnicam indicat Giraldus, Saeculo XII, ubi, inquit, extitisse eas antequam Lacus Neach erumperet in Ultonia. Piscatores Turres istas quæ more patriæ arctæ sunt et altæ nec non et rotundæ sub undis manifeste, sereni tempore conspiciunt. Giraldi Topogr. Dist.—(2, c. 9, p. 720.)

tion at issue regards the time of their erection, not the object for which they were erected.

FOURTH THEORY.

The FOURTH OPINION does not, as regards the time of the erection of the Pillar Towers, differ from the third. It states that the Round Towers were first built in the early pagan period by those of the Aryan race who had settled in this island of destiny, but that after the Gospel had been preached in Ireland, St. Patrick turned the Round Towers, as he did the pagan fountains, to the service of Christian rites, and hallowed them by Christian practices and religious associations.

Denis Florence M'Carthy seems to give expression to this view in his famous ballad, "The Pillar Towers of Ireland," for he writes:

5TH STANZA.

" Two favorites hath Time—the Pyramids of Nile,
And the old majestic temples of our own dear isle;
As the breeze o'er the seas, where the halcyon has his nest,
Thus time o'er Egypt's tombs and the Temples of the West!

6.

The names of their founders have vanished in the gloom,
Like the dry branch in the fire, or the body in the tomb;
But to-day, in the ray, their shadows still they cast—
Those temples of forgotten gods—these relics of the past!

. . . .

8.

How many different rites have these grey old Temples known?
To the mind what dreams are written in these chronicles of
stone!
What terror and what error, what gleams of love and truth
Have flashed from these walls since the world was in its
youth!

9.

Here blazed the sacred fire, and when the sun was gone,
As a star from afar, to the traveller it shone;

And the warm blood of the victim have these grey old Temples drunk,
And the death-song of the Druid, and the matin of the Monk.

10.

Here was placed the holy chalice that held the sacred wine,
And the gold cross from the altar, and the relics from the shrine,
And the mitre, shining brighter with its diamonds, than the East,
And the crozier of the Pontiff, and the vestments of the Priest.

11.

Where blazed the sacred fire, hung out the vesper bell—
Where the fugitive found shelter, became the hermit's cell;
And hope hung out its symbol to the innocent and good,
For the cross o'er the moss of the pointed summit stood."

AUTHORITIES.

Dr. Lanigan's views on the subject of the antiquity of the Pillar Towers are expressed in the following passage: " It can scarcely be doubted that the original models, according to which they were constructed, belong to the times of paganism, and that the singular style of architecture which we observe in them was brought from the East.'—*Eccl. Hist. vol. iv, p.* 408.

Very Rev. Dr. Charles O'Conor is of opinion that the Round Towers have come to us from pagan times. And Dr. Petrie says of the Very Rev. Doctor, "that he is a writer whose opinions on every matter connected with the ancient history and literary antiquities of Ireland are justly considered of great weight, and that they deserve, certainly, the most respectful attention." Now, Dr. O'Conor is of opinion that the Pillar Towers are "from time immemorial"—"*ab immemorabili condítas memorari.*" —*Index vol.* 1, *p.* 207.

Thomas Moore, the national poet and the Irish Historian, says: "To be able to invest, even with plausibility, so inconsistent a notion as that, in times when the churches (6th century or 7th) were framed rudely of wood, there could be found either the ambition or the skill to supply them with adjuncts of such elaborate workmanship is, in itself, no ordinary feat of " ingenuity."

Mr. Windele and Mr. D'Alton press their views more forcibly still. The opinions expressed in those pages just now will suffice to give the learned reader an idea of what others think on the subject as well as Dr. Petrie and those who embrace his views regarding the Pillar Towers of Ireland.

DIRECT PROOF IN FAVOUR OF THE FOURTH OPINION.

The convincing force of what is to be stated is derived from sources of philologic truth not known some fifty years ago. Amongst modern sciences, Comparative Philology has, owing to German scholars, made wonderful strides in the onward march of scientific progress. *

Comparative philology, as a science, has not yet seen a complete century roll by. It is only in its infancy, and yet it has effected much. It has shewn, at least, that the early Irish races were of Aryan origin.

* Note—" Une science toute humaine, cultivée d'abord par les philosophes, un peu au hasard, mais dont l'importance ne leur a jamais échappé, c' est la science du langage. . . . . *Il y a moins d' un siècle, la science en était la,* quand la découverte du Sanscrit permit à la linguistique de trouver sa voie, sa méthode, de s' affirmer comme science indépendente. ;Depuis elle a amassé des faits, constitué les lois, classé leur langues, determiné des racines. Elle avance toujours dans son analyse quasi-chimique des mots ; elle a son vocabulaire, ses parties distinctes, sa phonétique, sa morphologie, &c., &c. Quant à son indepence elle s' en montre singulièrement jalouse. Elle ne veut rien avoir de commune avec la metaphysique ; . . . . Voilá donc, cette fois, une science purement humaine détachée du tronc commun. *La psychologie anglaise contemporaine par. —Th. Ribot*, page 3 ; Paris, 1870.

The language spoken and written to this day by the Gaels of Ireland, and of the Highlands of Scotland, clearly proves the great fact that the Irish people are from the East. The scholarship of such professors and teachers as Max Müller and Pritchard, in England; Professors Blackie and Geddes, of Scotland; of such German linguists as Zeuss, Bopp, and Ebel; of Swiss savants, like Pictet, Geneva; and Italian literateurs, like Chevalier Nigra, ambassador at the French Court, and learned antiquarian, make it certain. Our home scholars—those amongst them who are distinguished for antiquarian research, or for their proficiency in the science of language—admit the same truth. Pre-eminent amongst those are W. K. Sullivan, formerly professor in the Catholic University, and at present Rector of the Queen's College, Cork; Sir William Wilde, Dr. Stokes, the late Dr. O'Donovan, and Mr. O'Curry.

The great objection hitherto against the opinion that the Round Towers are of Pagan origin is, that our Pagan progenitors had not, they say, as far as can be known, knowledge or skill and practical power to erect such superstructures. Hitherto, says Petrie, page 2, we have had little on the subject but speculation, growing out of a mistaken and unphilosophical zeal in support of the claims of our country to an early civilization; and even the truth having been advocated only hypothetically, has failed to be established, from the absence of that evidence which facts alone could supply. This objection fades away under the increased knowledge which the light derived from the science of compartive philology sheds on the early history of the Irish race. The early Irish were Aryan, therefore they were a race possessed of skill and power to erect those Towers.

The argument can be put in this way—(1) All the

Aryan nations were skilled in the sciences and arts, especially those of architecture, sculpture, dyeing, and painting. But the early natives of Ireland were, as their language proves, Aryan. Therefore the inhabitants of ancient Ireland were skilled in the sciences and arts, and they possessed a knowledge of architecture, sculpture, dyeing, and painting. Does this argument prove that the pagan Irish built the Towers? Not at all. It only proves that they had knowledge and power sufficient to erect those perennial piles which are a source of wonder to succeeding generations.

The language of Ireland, then, has come to the rescue to settle this vexed question of the early origin of the Pillar Towers of Ireland.

(2) The argument receives additional force from the similarity of style that exists between the architecture of Round Towers and that displayed in the Cyclopian buildings in the East, in Persopolis, Ecbatana, and in Babylon, as far as can be known; in Thebes and in the pyramids along the Nile. Dr. Petrie's strongest argument is that the style of churches built near the Towers and that of the pillar piles are alike in some instances. But, as a rule, the style of the Towers is rather Cyclopian.

The following form will present the new argument in favour of the fourth view in a clear light:—Sameness of architectural features point to identity of origin. But the Round Towers of Ireland present, in the slanting door-way, in the style of arch, in the material used, in the cement, in the shape and size of stones, and in the manner in which they are laid, architectural features which are nowhere to be found, except in the Cyclopian edifices of the earliest historic period. Therefore the Round Towers had been built by men-skilled, at the very earliest period, in the Cyclopian style of architecture.

(3) Abundant proofs of a corroborative kind are furnished in the postumous works of O'Curry—*The Manners and Customs of the Ancient Irish*—that our pagan ancestry seventeen centuries before the coming of Christ, possessed wonderful skill in the art of building as well as in that of dyeing and of painting. Who erected the "Dun," and the "Caiseal"? Who built the palace of Emania? Who erected the palace at Cruachan, where "Madb" Queen of Connaught lived? Who raised the splendid architectural piles at Tara? Was it not the pagan Irish?

If the reader is convinced that those buildings at Cruachan, Emania, and at Tara were splendid specimens of architectural skill, as they are described to have been, and as the ruins to some extent demonstrate, then he must admit that the pagan Irish had been well skilled in the art of architecture. It would enlarge this work too much to enter into further details regarding those early pagan buildings in Ireland than merely to notice the sites in which such buildings had been at one time erected. "The truth is," says Thomas Moore in his history of Ireland, "no one can account for the advanced civilization of the ancients who erected the Towers." Moore declares no one can account for such advanced civilization. Moore wrote before comparative philology had been, as a science, known in Ireland. Moreover, the poet of all circles knew nothing of the ancient records written in the Gaelic language.

The following anecdote regarding the historian and poet, Thomas Moore, has been told by O'Curry, and is found in his *Manuscript Materials of Irish history, p.* 154. *Lecture vii.*:

"The first volume of Moore's history was published in the year 1835, and in the year 1839, during one of his last visits to the land of his birth, he, in company with his old and attached friend, Dr. Petrie, favored me with quite an unexpected visit at the Royal Irish Academy, then in Grafton-street. I happened to have before me on my desk the Books of Ballymote and Lecain, the 'Leabar Breac,' the Annals of the Four Masters, and many other ancient books for historical research and reference. I had never before seen Moore, and after a brief introduction, and an explanation of the nature of my occupation by Dr. Petrie, and seeing the formidable array of so many dark and time-worn volumes by which I was surrounded, he looked a little disconcerted, but after a while plucked up courage to open the Book of Ballymote, and to ask what it was. Dr. Petrie and myself then entered into a short explanation of the history and character of the books then present, as well as of ancient Gaelic documents in general. Moore listened with great attention, alternately scanning the books and myself; and then asked me in a serious tone if I understood them, and how I had learned to do so. Having satisfied him upon these points, he turned to Dr. Petrie, and said: 'Petrie, these huge tomes could not have been written by fools or for any foolish purpose. I never knew anything about them before, and I had no right to have undertaken the history of Ireland.

The first sentence in a new book—*Lectures on the Early History of Institutions*, by Sir Henry Sumner Maine, just published, May, 1875, (London, Murray)—is: "The sources of information concerning the early history of institutions, which have been opened to us during the last few years, are numerous and valuable."

Amongst the sources to which Sir Henry refers are: "The three volumes of the Irish Brehon Laws, lately published by order of the Government, and the works of O'Curry, *MS. Materials of Irish History;*" and *Manners and Customs of the Ancient Irish.*" In these what does O'Curry write about stone edifices in the Pagan period in ancient Ireland ?

So much for the *Rath*, the *Dun*, and the *Lis*, all of which were generally built of earth. The *Caiseal* and the *Cathair* are to be distinguished from these especially, because they were generally, if not invariably, built of stone.

The *Caiseal* was nothing more than a *stone Rath* or enclosure within which the dwelling-house, and, in after-times, churches stood. The *Cathair*, in like manner, was nothing more than a *stone Dun* (with loftier and stronger walls), with this exception, that the *Cathair* was not necessarily surrounded with water, as far as I know.

Our experience of existing monuments enables us to decide that the *Caiseal* and *Cathair* were both of stone, and that the words are cognate with the British *Caer*, the Latin *Castrum*, and the English *Castle*. These terms afterwards came to give names to the towns and cities which in time sprang up at, or around, the various forts so designated, or in which those fortified residences were situated, which naturally became the centres of increasing population. Thus, we have *Rath-Gaela*, (now the town of Rathkeale, in the county of Limerick) ; *Rath-Naoi* (now the town of Rathnew, in the county of Wicklow) ; *Dun-Dubh-linne* (now City of Dublin) ; *Dun-Dealka* (now the town of Dundalk, in the county of Louth) ; *Dun-Chealtchair*, which was afterwards called *Dun-da-Leath-Ghlas* (now the town of Downpatrick, in the county of Down) ; *Lis-Mor* (now the town of Lismore, in the county of Waterford) ; *Lis-Tuathail* (now the town of Listowel, in the county of Kerry) ; *Cathair-Dun-Iascaigh* (now the town of Cahir, in the county of Tipperary) ; *Cathair-Chinn-Lis* (now the town of Caherconlish, in the county of Limerick), &c., &c.

(1) In any attempt to treat of the early or primitive buildings or habitations of Erinn, we must, of course, give the first place to Tara, which, according to all our old accounts, had been first founded by the *Firbolgs*, the third in the series of the early colonists of the island. In the ancient account of the battle of the first or southern *Magh Tuireadh* we are told that the *Firbolgs*, who had been dispersed into three parties on their approach to the Irish coast by a storm, had, on their landing, repaired by one consent to *Rath-na-Righ* (*i.e.* the Rath or palace of the Kings of Tara.)

The "*great House of the Thousands of Soldiers*" was the particular palace of the monarch; it stood within the *Rath-na-Righ*, or "*Rath* of the Kings," and was called, also, *Tigh-Temrach*, or the House of Tara. Of its extent or magnificence in the time of King *Cormac Mac Airt*, in the middle of the third century, we may form some notion from the ancient poem preserved in the *Book of Leinster*, and ascribed to *Cormac File*, or the poet.

As regards the arrangement of the palace of Tara by Cormac, it was larger than any house. The *Rath* was nine hundred feet in Cormac's time. His own house was seven hundred feet; [and there were] seven bronze candelabras in the middle of it. (There were) nine mounds around the house. There were three times fifty compartments (*imdadh*) in the house, and three times fifty men in each compartment; and three times fifty continuations of compartments (*airel*), and fifty men in each of these continuations.

It may be noted here, that the (1) *Rath*, (2) *Dun*, (3) *Lis*, or *Caiseal*, which formed the fortification of ancient residences, often contained within them more than one house; and thus the whole ancient city of *Tara* was composed of seven *Duns*, or enclosures, each containing within it a certain number of houses. We learn this fact from an ancient poem of thirty-seven stanzas, of which there is an old paper copy in the library of Trinity College, Dublin.

Ailenn was one of the ancient palaces of the kings of Leinster. Its remains are standing on a hill a short distance to the north of Old Kilcullen, in the county of Kildare.

AILEACH BUILT SEVENTEEN HUNDRED YEARS BEFORE THE CHRISTIAN ERA—A ROUND TOWER IN IT.

The next great building in point of antiquity and historical reminiscence, is the great *Rath* or rather *Cathair of Aileach*, (in the county of Derry), so well described by Dr. Petrie in the Ordnance Memoir of the parish of Templemore. This great Cathair is said to have been originally built by the *Daghda*, the celebrated king of the *Tuatha de Danaan*, who planned and fought the battle of the second or northern *Magh Tuireadh* against the *Fomorians*. The fort was erected around the grave of his son, *Aedh* (or Hugh), who had been killed through jealousy by *Corrgenn*, a Connacht chieftain.

The history of the death of *Aedh*, and the building of *Aileach* (or "the stone building"), is given at length in a poem reserved in the *Book of Lecan*, which poem has been printed with an English translation, by Dr. Petrie, in the above memoir.

It appears clearly from this very ancient poem that not only was the outer *Rath*, or protective circle of *Aileach*, built of stone by the regular masons, *Imcheall* and *Garbhan*, but that the palace *and other houses within the enclosure were built also of stone* (nay, even of chipped and cut stone). All these buildings, probably, were *circular*, as the house or prison of the Hostages certainly must have been when, as the poem says, it was "closed at the top with one stone." Were these Round Towers?

The material of this house, we are told, was red yew, carved and emblazoned with gold and bronze, and so thickly set with shining gems, that day and night were equally bright within it. I may observe that *Ailcach* is one of the few spots in Erinn marked in its proper place by the geographer, Ptolemy of Alexandria, who flourished in the second century, or nearly two hundred years before the time of Frigrind.

DESCRIPTION OF CRUACHAIN.

There were seven companies in it; seven compartments from the fire to the wall, all round the house. Every compartment had a front of bronze. The whole were composed of beautifully carved red yew; three strips of bronze were in the front of each compartment; seven strips of bronze from the foundation of the house to the ridge. The house from this out was built of pine, (gius). A covering of oak shingles was what was upon it on the outside. Sixteen windows was the number that were in it, for the purpose of looking out of it, and for admitting light into it. A shutter of bronze to each window; a bar of bronze to each shutter; four times seven ungas of bronze was what each bar contained. Ailill and Medbh's compartment was made altogether of bronze; and it was situated in the middle of the house, with a front of silver and gold around it. There was a silver wand at one side of it, which rose to the ridge of the house, and reached all round it from the one door to the other.

The arms of the guests were hung up above the arms of all other persons in that house; and they sat themselves down and were bade welcome.

Such is the description of one of the four "royal houses" which, in the heroic age of our history, that of Ailill and Medbh (the century preceding the Christian era), are said to have stood within the ancient *Rath* of *Cruachan.*

EMANIA.

The description of the *Craebh-Ruadh*, or house of the "Royal Branch," at Emania, the capital city of ancient Ulster (as described in the ancient historic tale of Tochmarc Eimire, or "The Courtship of the Lady" Emer, by Cuchulainn), agrees very nearly with this description of the house at Cruachan; and we know that there were three great houses at least within the circle of the great *Rath* of *Emania*, raised by Queen *Macha*, more than three hundred years before the Christian era.

The best Irish authority in matters relating to ancient Ireland is the author of *Chronicum Scotorum*, copies of which work are in the Royal Irish Academy, and in Trinity College.

The "Trinity College Manuscript," says O'Curry, (Lectures, page 120), is written on paper of foolcap size, like that upon which the annals of *Tigcranac*, in the same volume are written. It is in the bold and most accurate hand of *Dubhaltach* (translated Duvald, Duald or Dudley) MacFirbis, the last of a long line of historians and chroniclers of *Mic Firbisigh* in the barony of *Tir-Fhiachradh*, or Tireragh, in the County of Sligo." (See his life—O'Curry, page 123).

His next great work is the "Book of Pedigrees." The autograph of this great compilation is now in the possession of the Earl of Roden, and a fac-simile of it was made by O'Curry, in the year 1836, for the Royal Irish Academy.

The time and place in which the book was compiled is plainly told by *MacFirbis* himself in the preface:

"The place, time, author, and cause of writing this book are—the place, the College of St. Nicholas, in Galway; the time, the time of the religious war between the Catholics of Ireland, and the heretics of Ireland, Scotland, and England, particularly in the year 1653; the person or author, Dubhaltach, the son of Giolla Isa Mor MacFirbisiġ, historian, &c., &c.; the cause of writing the book is, to increase the glory of God, and for the information of people in general."

MacFirbis, in his *Book of Genealogies*, just described, after giving a long list, say twenty or more names of famous builders in stone—such as Casruba, stone-builder of Ailinn, the Palace of the Kings of Leinster already named; *Troigh Leathan* or *Broad-foot*, the rath-builder of *Tara*; *Bolc*, the son of *Blar*, the rath-builder of Cruachain, the Palace of the Kings of Connacht, *Bainchre*, or fair-face, the builder of Emania, writes:—

"We could find a countless number of the ancient edifices of Erinn to name besides these above, and the builders who erected them, and the Kings and noble chiefs for whom they were built, but that they would be too tedious to mention. Look at the *Book of Conquests* Leaḃar na n-Gaḃala, if you wish to discover them; and we have even besides that, evidence of their having been built like the edifices of other kingdoms of the times in which they were built;—and why should they not? For there came no colony into Erinn but from the Eastern World; and it would be strange if they should not have the sense to form their residences and dwellings after the manner of the countries from which they originally went forth, and through which they travelled. . . . And if those colonists of ancient Erinn erected buildings in the country similar to those of the countries through which they came, as it is likely they did, what is the reason the fact is doubted.

Compare, then, the buildings erected hundreds and thousands of years ago with these, and it is no wonder, except for the superiority of the ancient building over the modern, that not a stone nor an elevation of the ground should mark their situation; yet, such is not the case; for, so great is the stability of the old buildings, that there are immense royal *raths* or palaces and forts (Liosa) throughout Erinn, in which there are numerous *hewn* and polished stones. . . . .

The only cause of doubt is because lime-cast walls are not seen standing in the place, in which they were erected a thousand and a-half, or two thousand, or three thousand and more years since: it is no wonder they should not be; for shorter than that is the time in which the ground grows over buildings, when they are once ruined, or when they fall down of themselves with age. In proof of this, I have myself seen, within the last sixteen years, many lofty lime-cast castles built of limestone; and at this day (having fallen) there remains of them but a mound of earth; and hardly could a person ignorant of their former existence know that there had been buildings there at all.

I leave this, however, to the learned to discuss, and I shall return to prove the fidelity of our national history, to which the ignorant do an injustice.—*From O'Curry's Lectures on the Manuscript Materials of Ancient Irish History*, delivered in the Catholic University of Ireland, pp. 222, 223; translation from *MacFirbis's Book of Genealogies*, the Irish original of which is given in appendix to the same work.

Every one knows how soon buildings perish. The present writer has seen whole villages in a flourishing state—now, there is not, where they stood, even the trace of a habitation. In this town, Tuam, there were two old castles some fifty years ago; the convent of the Sisters of Mercy is now built where the castle of the Burkes of Tuam stood. Such is time! The pillar towers and the old buildings yet remain!!

MODERN DISCOVERIES CONFIRM THE SAME VIEWS.

Just as this sheet is going to press (April, 1875), a work has been issued by Murray, London, which throws more light on the antiquities of the Aryan races than any that has been published for the past hundred years. The work is styled *Troy and its Remains*—a narrative of researches and discoveries made on the site Ilium and on the Trojan plain, by Dr. Henry Schliemann, edited by Philip Smith, B.A. The work is not commonly known, and the narrative concerning Troy must be to scholars agreeable reading. In this place it is well to give the reader some idea of what has been effected for science.

DR. SCHLIEMAN'S DISCOVERIES AT TROY.

In April 1870, Dr. Schliemann commenced his excavations at the mound of Hissarlik, in the Troad—the spot attested as the site of the Homeric Ilium by a tradition extending without a break from the earliest age of historical Greece. He continued, down to June 17, 1873, his explorations, which were then, for the time, brought to a close. In 1874, Dr. Schliemann published the interesting volume containing an account of the discoveries made at Troy; and out of 100,000 objects which had been brought to light, he selected 4,000, representations which he has published with letter-press descriptions in an Atlas containing 217 (two hundred and seventeen) photographic plates. In the English version just published, thirty-two lithographic plates are presented to the reader, together with three hundred of the best illustrations selected out of the four thousand printed by Dr. Schliemann, and these are arranged in a convenient form throughout the body of the work. There have been brought to light thousands of objects in Terra-cotta, made in the shape of wheels or whorls, or of a top-like form. Short descriptions of the style of workmanship, of the material and form of these are given. Such is the new work published during the present week, descriptive of the pre-historic practice and life of the Aryan family.

What does this learned, and latest, and richest contribution to the stores of paleology and historic certainty say of the early Aryan races ? It confirms the Mosaic narrative. Moses assigns the "Isles of the Gentiles" to the sons of Javan. His descendants are called "Yavanas"—(*j* sounds like *y*)—that is *Juvenes* the "younger race" in the old Aryan traditions amongst those who had migrated Westward.

The fact that their names occur on Egyptian monuments, to which Egyptologists ascribe a date not later than the fifteenth century before the Christian era, confirms the very ancient settlement made by Ionians, in North-Western Asia Minor, and along its sea-board. It seems that the name Ionians (another form of *Yavanas*, or descendants of Yavan, *i.e.*, Javan) had been in ancient times the oriental name for the entire Hellenic race. As the mounds of Nimrod and Kouyunic, of Koursabad and Hillah, have revealed the palaces of Assyrian and Babylonian Kings, so the mound of Hissarlik appears to have been the chief city of the primeval "Ionian" Empire. The details of the discoveries made, tend to corroborate this view. The objects discovered in *terra-cotta* are known to have been the most sacred emblems of the Aryan race, and the fact that these have been found in one form or another, at all depths, attests the *common* Aryan descent of all the dwellers on the hill before the historic Ilium. Thus there were peoples, and races, and cities even before Troy had been founded. No trace of Egyptian, or Assyrian, or Cuthite influence has been met with, and the general character of all the remains brought to light has been defined by Professor Conze, of Vienna, as the earliest Aryan, or Indo-European.

Why use such strange words as those employed in the preceding paragraph—"The common Aryan descent of all the dwellers on the hill before the historic Ilium ?" Because some writers speak and write of its earliest inhabitants as non-Aryan; others say that they were not Kelts. If not, they were from the same stock—sons of Javan, brother of Gomer, the progenitor of the Keltic Race. Are we sure the place excavated is the site of ancient Troy ? Yes. Had there been another city anterior to the building of Ilium ? Yes. Has Dr. Schliemann found the Homeric Ilium ? Yes. By means of these excavations, carried on for three years, four strata of remains have been discovered, representing four successive cities, different in the stages and forms of their civilization; cities which arose and have perished on that hill rising above the Trojan plain.

The first, or lowest, discovers traces of a town of primeval civilization. The Iliad speaks of a city which preceded the Ilium of Priam. In this first stratum are recognised vestiges of the earliest Aryan Settlement to which legend points, as built on the Troad.

(2) The second stratum exhibits remains suggestive of civil life which had some affinity to the first, but of a later and a maturer type. This second stratum, according to Dr. Schliemann, is the Homeric Troy.

(3) Above this, in the third stratum are the relics of a third city, which, in the shape and designs of its

"*terra-cottas*," its instruments and ornaments, shows a close resemblance to the second. The Trojans, although of the same race with the Greeks, were superior to them in knowledge and in the art of domestic and civilized life. To borrow an image from the great Epic, the arms of Glaucus were of gold, while those of Diomedes were of brass. The one is emblematic of Troy at the time : the other, of Greece.

The third city was one erected by the Greeks on the ruins of ancient Troy, not, indeed, immediately after the Ten Year War, but after many a long struggle, and after petty feuds for generations.

(4) And, now, what about the fourth ? It comes uppermost, quite unexpectedly, to favor the views put forward in this chapter by the present writer, that civilization had only retrograded from the days of Noah's children up to the coming of Christ; that the early ages had been the brightest in the light of practical knowledge of the arts and sciences; and that the ages coming of late—those approaching the period appointed for a Redeemer to come—constituted the darkest period of paganism.

In the fourth town the only buildings of which traces remain were wooden; the implements found are of flint. All the ancient forms of civilized life had gone. Truly may it be said, in contemplating the remnant of the fourth city, rising over the second ruins of buried Troy: "*Fuit Ilium et ingens gloria Teucrum.*"

The fourth city built on the plain of Troy was founded by the Thracians, who, leaving their settlements in Europe, had migrated across the Hellespont and took up their abode in the Troad. This is proved by the fact that flint instruments, exactly the same as those found in cities of Thrace, have been found in the fourth stratum.

1. In the first or lowest stratum is found one of the earliest Aryan settlements.

2. In the second, a later Aryan settlement, founded by the Phrygians, who called their town Ilium or Troy.

3. In the third stratum, a city built by Greeks, who had conquered the Trojans.

4. In the fourth, a town built by Thracians, who had overcome the Greeks or Phrygians.

The excavations offer to the learned world of the present day a proof the most convincing, that in Pagan times the more primeval the period, the greater was the knowledge of the Pagan progenitors; the less ancient and the nearer the approach to the dawn of the day of Christ's coming, the darker, and the deeper waxed the ignorance of the Pagan peoples.

Before the volume just quoted and summarized, "Troy and its Remains," had appeared, the following allusions to the grand developements of the arts, as shewn in the works of the ancients who had built Babylon, and Nineveh, and Thebes of the hundred gates, formed from history a proof of the knowledge possessed by the ancients in the art of building and decorating, of painting and scientific engineering.

SACRED HISTORY SUPPORTS THE FOURTH OPINION REGARDING THE ROUND TOWERS.

The foregoing arguments receive additional force from all that is handed down to us in the pages of sacred history.

From the records written by Moses, and preserved by the Jewish kings, legislators, and faithfully transmitted by the Scribes, it is manifest that in the days of Noah and of his sons and their immediate descendants, men of the time possessed, in an eminent degree, a knowledge of the arts and sciences.

This statement is true of all who had lived immediately after the deluge, and especially of all those who had been, like Noah, trained by the same elders or teachers under whom Noah had learned. Apart from supernatural illumination, or any direct communication with God, in a special way, as when he was ordered to build the ark, and to fashion it of a certain size and form, Noah's knowledge was very vast. His knowledge of hydraulics and pneumatics, of ship-building, of mechanics, of carpentry, and engineering, must have been naturally acquired. Moses, we know, apart from his being a leader of the people of God, was skilled in all the learning of the Egyptians; and St. Paul had been, at the feet of Gamaliel, trained in all the branches of science and knowledge taught in that eventful period.

The Patriarchal mode of living, and the transmission of lands and learning to the descendants, tended to keep up the succession of advanced knowledge in the Aryan as well as in the Semitic national families.

The sons and grandsons of Noah who saw him build the ark, and all his direct and immediate descendants, must have acquired knowledge from a teacher so learned.

SEM'S SONS.

And hence Sem, the eldest son, with Sem's sons, (1) Elam, (2) Ashur, (3) Arphaxad, (4) Lud, (5) Aram, and (6) Sem, and their descendants for at least seven generations down to Nachor, the grandfather, and Thare, the immediate father of Abraham, must have had the amplest opportunities for acquiring knowledge. And then their age was so remarkable; there was plenty of time for long and mature training, and acquiring from tradition or the mouth of the living elders the great knowledge handed down from the time of Adam.

What is true of Noah's eldest son is equally true of Japheth, the youngest, and his children. These were (1) Gomer, (2) Magog, (3) Madai, (4) Javan, (5) Tubal, (6) Meshech, (7) Tiras, and (8) Japhet. From Gomer have sprung all the Keltic nations. From Javan, the fourth son, have been descended all the inhabitants dwelling in aftertimes along the coast of Asia Minor; the early Greeks, the Ionians.

CHAM'S SONS.

The descendants of Cush (sprung from the seed of Cham or Ham) had, of course, similar opportunities of acquiring knowledge and of putting it into practice. And hence the son of Cush—Belus, or Nimrod (*see Rollins's Ancient History, Book iii, vol. i., p.* 296) had skill and power to build such wonders in the art of architecture, as Babylon and Nineveh. The children of Mesraim or Mizraim, Cham's second son, founded Thebes, in Upper Egypt. The inspired writings of the Hebrew Law-giver record those ancient, yet historic facts.

The researches made by savants within the past seventy years confirm the same truthful records.

A three-fold cord is not easily broken.

The proofs furnished in the foregoing pages of the knowledge possessed by the ancients, are taken from the (1) very excavations made at Ilium, from the walls seen at Persepolis, and works of cyclopean character still to be seen in the East; from the mounds of Nineveh and Babylon; the rock temples of India; from the palaces by the banks of the Nile, at Thebes; at Memphis; from the Pyramids. Again in Europe, from the most ancient cities of Morea and of Magna Grecia, Umbria, Etruria.

(2) From the light pointing to ancient truth, furnished by comparative philology.

(3) From pagan history, and from analogy.

(4) From the inspired pages of the books written by Moses and the prophets. All these proofs, so diverse in their order, and divergent in their sources, tend to establish the same objective historic reality, and to show that the early progenitors of mankind had not been ignorant and feeble in mind, or weak in body, or unskilled in the laws that govern human society, or unacquainted with the arts, or untrained in the teachings of science ; on the contrary, they show that the men who built Babylon had more skill in engineering than those who have re-built Broadway in New York, and the marble palaces of Chicago and those belonging to the prince merchants of that rising city of the new world. For an instant, compare the boasted buildings of modern skill, say those of New York or Chicago, with the edifices in Babylon of old—what a contrast.

Babylon stood in a large plain through which the river Euphrates flowed. The walls of the city—eighty-seven feet thick and three hundred and fifty high—formed a square, each side of which was fifteen miles in length. Along each of these sides were twenty-five gates, that is, in all one hundred, made entirely of solid brass, and fronting and terminating twenty-five streets, which, in length fifteen miles, ran in parallel order right through the whole city. Thus it was not one Broadway that was in those days to be found in Babylon, but fifty of them—twenty-five running due-north and south, and twenty-five due-east and west. These streets ran parallel to the sides of the outer square boundary, dividing the whole city into twenty-six times twenty-six, or six hundred and seventy-six blocks ; each block or small square was at least a half mile in length, and in circuit two miles and a quarter—dimensions large enough to constitute, in modern times, a fair-sized town.

The houses in these squares raised to the height of four or five stories, were, for the sake of cleanliness and sufficient ventilation, and for the purpose conducive to health, a point so much looked to at the present time, not joined in a row, but separate or apart, like the country residences or mansions of the wealthy adjoining great cities. Each house was ornamented on the side fronting the street; each mansion had its own separate parterres, gardens, yards, outhouses, and every accommodation which the laws of hygiene suggest or the promptings of a refined and luxurious taste dictate.

For an account of the quays and bridges, the lakes and fountains, and the means employed to bring water to each house, and to irrigate the plain; for a description of the hanging gardens, built to gratify Amytis, daughter of Astyages, King of the Medes, and raised in tiers, one above the other, in form of terraces elevated on pillars and arches to the height of 350 feet; each garden, a square of which the side was four hundred feet, and containing all kinds of trees, plants, flowers, animals. For a description, too, of the temple of Belus, the wealth of which is calculated by Diodorus to have been equal in value to twenty-two millions of pounds sterling—the learned reader is referred to Quintus Curtius, to Diodorus, and Josephus. A very excellent account is furnished by Rollin in Book iii. *History of the Assyrians.*

Take a view of Nineveh or the City of Ninus, son of Nimrod or Belus, and husband of Semiramis, which was built on the eastern bank of the Tigris, and had been nineteen miles long by eleven wide. When the prophet Jonas sent by God, went to preach to the people of that vast city, sacred writ tells us that "it was an exceedingly great city of three days' journey." Modern excavations show that its buildings had been as grand as those of Babylon. History says that its walls were 100 feet high, and so thick that three chariots could go abreast with ease upon the summit. Fifteen hundred Towers, two hundred feet high, adorned and fortified them.

The pillars of Persepolis, still standing; the remains of Ecbatana; the grand palaces of Karnac and Luxor, with the ruins of Memnonium, near Thebes; the inscriptions found on the Pyramids along the Nile; the Tablets of Umbria and Samnium; the excavations going on just at present, and which for the past five years have been made in the Plain of Troy, and the Mound of Hissarlik, prove beyond all doubt that the people of the very earliest periods had, in knowledge of the arts and sciences, been far and away superior to those who succeeded them, and to those who came immediately before the time when the Sun of Christianity arose, spreading its light on the face of a benighted world.

PALEOLOGY—ANOTHER SOURCE OF KNOWLEDGE.

Now-a-days men are found who do not credit the inspired record of the Jewish Lawgiver and historian, Moses. It is fortunate, as if to confound the incredulity of such people, that within the past four score and ten years a light quite unforeseen has beamed on the early history of mankind. In the year 1797, some engineers in the French army made excavations for the purpose of building a fort near the Egyptian city, Rosetta, in the Delta, through which the Nile discharges, by many openings, its waters into the Mediterranean. Some feet below the surface the men employed found a slab of basalt stone, three feet long, by two and a-half wide, covered with strange writing and hieroglyphical characters. The French were soon after beaten at Alexandria by the English, and this slab was given up to the British commander, and conveyed by him to London. It contained a memorial written in three forms of speech—in hieroglyphics, in Koptic or Egyptian, and in Greek. A key to the interpretation of the hieroglyphic symbols was discovered by Thomas Young (1773–1829), already famous as the advocate of the undulatory theory of light, as opposed to that of emission propounded by Newton. To him, and to J. F. Champollion (1790-1831) and son, M. Champollion, is due the glory of deciphering the monumental records of ancient Egypt. Max Müller, in his Lectures, second volume, points out how this work was pushed on until every sentence and syllable of the hidden characters became plainly revealed. This was a wonderful success.

These records tell that, not in Babylon alone, nor on the banks of the Tigris, had wonders been done in the art of building; but at Thebes of a hundred gates *(Iliad v. 381, L. 1.)* in Upper Egypt; in the Palaces to the East and West and North of that famous pagan city; in the pyramids and obelisks—wonders in the art of painting and sculpture; of dyeing, colouring, and of writing, which exist to this day—had the splendid abilities of Egyptian Kings and men of science been attested before the world.

What was Thebes? The grandest city, either now or then, in the world; from each of its hundred gates, historians say, that it could send forth, at once, two hundred chariots, and ten thousand fighting men.

In the vicinity of Thebes, the ancient capital of Egypt, stand the wonderful ruins of the ancient palaces Karnac and Luxor, and the Memnonium. Karnac surpasses in grandeur every structure in ancient Thebes, or in the world. The approach to Karnac is by a long avenue of Sphinxes, the longest of its kind in Egypt, leading to a succession of portals with colossal statues in front. These are remarkable, even by the variety of the materials in which they are cut. Stone, like marble, and variegated limestone, rose-coloured and black marble of Syene, have all been used in their structure. There are two obelisks, one ninety-one feet high, adorned with sculptures, perfect even to this day in their execution. The principal hall of the palace to be seen at this hour by travellers, is 318 feet long and 160 broad, with a roof supported by 136 columns, seventy feet high and 36 feet thick. Now this immense hall leads into a court where there are four obelisks and twelve colossal figures. Two other courts, of the same kind, lead to the apartments of the Kings. Adjacent to the Palace are many other extensive buildings of the same style. (See description in *Rollin's Ancient History*; also *History of Egyptian Antiquities*, by Cassell, London.)

The entrance to the Palace of the Luxor, about two miles from Karnac, is of the same character. The effect of these ruins on the mind of the traveller looking on even now is that of awe and sublimity. He seems like one who treads, not as Moore describes "The Banquet Hall deserted," but like one conducted through the halls of giant palaces, where demi-gods had revelled in luxury; and where men of science and art had displayed, with princely profusion, the resources of mighty minds and primeval power.

The writer will not describe the Pyramids—those stupendous monuments of human labour and engineering skill. They are sufficiently well known to most scholars of the present time. At Lower Egypt, between Memphis and Heliopolis there are three pyramids, pronounced to be the wonder of the world. There are in all one hundred and eighty pyramidal structures, it is said, strewn along the banks of the Nile, from Heliopolis up as far as Æthiopia. Some are built entirely of stone. The names of the Kings who erected them, and the dates in which they flourished have been wrought in symbolic characters on the stones or bricks. The stones employed in the erection of the Pyramids were taken from one quarry in the Lybian chain of mountains, which, west of the River Nile, raise their heads to the skies.

The huge pillars of granite, one hundred and twenty feet long, ten in breadth, and eight in depth, were hewn, then squared, chiseled, and carried some hundreds of miles on rafts—at times even against the current, and raised to heights varying from one hundred to four hundred and fifty feet. One of the Pyramids at Memphis is four hundred and fifty feet in height—containing thirty-three millions of cubic feet of mason work—and covers thirteen acres of surface.

Thus Egypt stands in her Pyramids a perennial landmark in the domain of the world's history, connecting the period of the deluge with the present. Take away the records written by the pen of Moses, there still remain the Pyramids, raising their heads above all passing mists, and proclaiming the story of the knowledge, and the skill, and the practical power of the immediate posterity of Noah and his children.

Scholars of the present day are enabled, through their knowledge of hieroglyphical science, to understand, to read, and to translate the history of the past greatness of Egyptian power.

Within the Pyramids, still greater proofs of early knowledge and civilization have been found; statues, paintings, figures sculptured in stone; hundreds of thousands of glass images; glass coloured in the process of manufacture; earthen jars; mummies in millions; woven textile; linen fabrics of the finest and most wonderful kind; measures; squares; all pointing out with a voice to the ears of men of science, louder and clearer than if the Pharoes' and Josephs' had again arisen from the tombs, to tell the living generations of the glories of the Egyptians, and their perfect mastery of the arts and sciences.

TO SUM UP.

The ruins of Nineveb, of Ecbatana, and to some extent, those of Babylon, are a proof, to-day, of the knowledge of the art of buildiug possessd by the descendants of Sem. The Pyramids and the palaces at Thebes, and the superstructures at Memphis, show that the descendants of Cham were not inferior in knowledge to those who sprung from the race of Sem. And certainly the cave temples of Persia, the excavations in the Troad, of works erected by the Aryan race, point the proof that Japhet's sons and grandsons had not been inferior to their cousins in the art of building. Now, it is from the eldest son of Japhet the Keltic race have sprung. It is certain that all the immediate descendants of Japhet were skilled in the art of building and in the mechanical arts, and in science, too. The Ionians and all the Greeks were the descendants of Javan, the fourth son; the Kelts, or Gaels, (British, Irish) are the descendants of Gomer, Japhet's eldest son.

Amongst the earliest migrations westward from the Aryan table land, the Kelts, according to Max Müller, and every scholar versed in comparative philology, were the very first. Hence, they brought with them that knowledge which their forefathers had possessed. Their language proves this fact ; their foot-prints through Europe confirm this statement ; and lastly, the cyclopean character, both in size of stone, sloping shape of turret, of pillar, of window and doorway, point out to a kindred origin, if not in race, at least in architectural training, which, it seems, had been at the very earliest period common to the descendants of Japhet (Gomer and Javan) as, well as to the descendants of Sem and of Cham.

WHAT MOTIVE URGED THE ANCIENTS TO BUILD?

One other question remains to be put and answered. Why did the ancients of the primeval period erect such magnificent monuments of intelligent skill and of human power as those, the remains of which are to be found to this very hour by the traveller as he pursues his investigation on the banks of the Euphrates, of the Tigris, or the Nile—in Syria, in the Peloponesus, Etruria or Eire?

The Hebrew Law-giver gives the reason. Before the the dispersion, he tells us that the descendants of the sons of Noah said: "Come, let us make a city and a tower, the top whereof may reach to Heaven; and let us make our name famous before we be scattered abroad over all the Earth." These words of the inspired leader of God's people tells the world now that the first fathers and founders of the kingdoms of earth had been influenced by those human motives, which, to this hour, sway the breasts of the children of men—namely, a desire to avoid death or destruction by a second deluge, and to render their name and fame imperishable amongst men. Motives, such as these, influenced the builders of the tower, around which the city of Babylon at a subsequent period was built. The descendants of these famous builders inherited the skill of their fathers; and although dispersed to the East and to the West, to the North and to the South, they brought with them the same desire for glory, the same love to render themselves and their own names imperishable.

KINDRED MOTIVES URGED THEIR DESCENDANTS.

There is not the shadow of a doubt but that all those who emigrated from the cradle home either to Syria, or to

Palestine, and to Armenia, or to the East as far as the Hindus, and beyond it, or turning southward to Egypt, along by the Nile, or to Europe, Greece, Etruria, Eire, had been influenced by the same desire to render their names imperishable and themselves, as far as could be, immortal. These motives would have been sufficiently strong to urge, in after years, the leaders of the different migratory bands of pre-historic peoples—to settle down, as they did, and erect Pillar Towers—monuments like to those, but not quite so massive, that they had seen built in the cradle-land of their race.

A portion of the descendants of Gomer, in successive emigrations, came across through Europe and founded a colony in Ireland. This fact rests for its certainty on the teaching of comparative philology. The best philologists in Europe proclaim that the Kelts were the first who had emigrated from Asia. MacFirbis, in his Book of Genealogies, says: "There came no colony into Eirinn but from the eastern world." They were thoroughly acquainted with the science of architecture and with the art of building. Their breasts were actuated with the same motives—a desire to be famous, and to avoid the dangers of a second flood—that actuated their progenitors.

(1) These reasons alone are quite sufficient to show why the early Keltic settlers in Eire built the Round Towers.

(2) No doubt, in after times these pillar piles served as prison fortresses; for instance, that at *Ailcach*, in the county of Derry, built, according to the testimony of our ancient records (see p. 387 supra), seventeen hundred years before the birth of Christ.

The house of the hostages, or prison, erected at *Aileach* by order of *Daghda*, king of the *Tuatha de Dannan*, was "circular, and closed at the top with one stone." So it is described in the Book of Lecan. A fortress of that description presents all the features of the Round Tower. It was of stone, and it was circular, it was tapering, it was closed at the top with one stone. Such is the shape and character of those Round Towers that still survive in all their ancient completeness of form; for instance, that at Turlough, county Mayo, at Devenish, and at Antrim.

The Round Towers then may have served for the warlike Kings of ancient Ireland as prisons or fortresses, and for the safe keeping of hostages.

There is a pillar tower at Kilbennan, near Tuam. Before the young Bishop Benignus, or Bennin, had come to the territory of Conmaicne, or Tuam, in the Barony of Dunmore, the place now called Kilbannon had been known by the name *Dun-Lugaidh*, *i.e.*, Louis's Fortress. When St. Benignus, in company with St Patrick, had come from *Donach* Patrick to *Dun-Lugaidh*, it is said that the saint dug a fountain, in the waters of which he baptized nine lepers, who became instantly healed of their leprosy. Niatha, the chieftain of that district, and all his followers and clients, and all the people of the entire country of Conmaicne—St. Jarlath's cousins, himself and his father and relatives—were baptized in that fountain. That well, or fountain, is to be seen to this day at Kilbennan. Its waters gush forth from the foot of the Round Tower which to this hour is to be seen. Two things remain to this day to confirm the truth of the historical event—first, the "Dun" or pillar tower of Lughaidh; second, the fountain gushing forth at its foot. At the time, say, A.D. 440, the *Dun* existed, it was the fortified home of the chieftain Niatha.

St. Patrick and St. Benignus came from Headford to the present Kilbennin—the territory of *Conmaicne*—as the barony of Dunmore, Tuam, had then (440 A.D.) been called.

"Et ibi descendit Patricius de curru; et venerunt ad illum novem leprosi viri Gentiles, antea nunquam credentes, et clamaverunt: Si verus est Deus tuus, sanet nos de lepra ista." Surrexerunt S. Patricius et Sanctus Benignus, et elevaverunt cespitem de terra; et ebulivit fons lucidissimus de terra, in quo baptizati sunt; et in eadem hora sanati sunt de lepra, et dederunt gloriam Domino Et de hoc miraculo iste fons semper nominatur "fons leprosorum." In quo fonte multi infirmi semper sanantur. In quo etiam baptizavit S. Benignus Echenum filium Briani.

Postea venit Dominus illius regionis Niatha filius Dubhani ad Sanctos usque ad illum locum cum filiis quinque suis. . . . . et vovit illam villam Sanctis quia ibi vidit miraculum. In illo loco baptizatus est Niatha cum filiis suis, a Sancto Benigno; et omnes etiam, habitores illius regionis baptizati sunt. . . . . . In *illo loco* fundata est a Sancto Benigno civitas nempe in Dun-Lughaidh, seu in Duno Lugadii filii Niathæ. . . Et specialiter Lugadius, filius Niathæ contulit ipsis *suam arcem* cum predio adjacente, et ibi Ecclesiam extruxerunt quæ olim ex Lugadii nomine *Dun-Lugaidh*, i.e., Dunum Lugadii dicebatur, hodie vero Kill-Beinein, i.e., Cella Benigni appellatur—*Triadis Thaumaturgæ, &c. Lovanii*, 1647. Folio. By Rev. John Colgan.

In the second volume of his magnificent work, Colgan gives a short life of St. Benignus in the third Appendix to the seventh life of St. Patrick. It is from that Appendix the foregoing excerpt has been taken.

Ware, in Vol. II., says of Colgan: He was a native of the County Donegal; a Franciscan Friar in the Irish Convent of St. Anthony of Padua, Louvain. He was Professor of Theology. He was well qualified to collect and write the Lives of the Irish Saints. He died at Louvain, 1658. His learning and his honor, it must be said, held a high place in the esteem of men of letters.

A Round Tower stands to this very hour on the spot where, at Kilbennin, St. Benignus baptized the nine lepers, the Prince and people. The presence of the "fountain," or *blessed well* of St. Benin, as it is called, points out the identity of the present Round Tower with the *Dun* of Prince *Louis*, or at least with the fortress in the *Dun*. This single instance, coupled with the statement made in the book of Lecan, that a circular fortress or prison, with a single stone-covering at the top, had been erected at the Palace of *Ailcach*, in Derry, points plainly enough to the probable truth, that Round Towers had been made use of by the petty princes of Eire as fortresses for the secure keeping of hostages.

The story of Deirdre, who in early youth had been confined in a tower of this description, is favourably suited to show, in a much stronger light, the probability just pointed out, that the towers had been used as fortresses to secure hostages, or as keeps to confine those to whom, in the opinion of the Princes, it was not safe to grant freedom.

The foregoing view, regarding the use of the Round Towers, is quite in accord with the opinion of Sir William Wilde, to which reference has been made in a memoir just published in the *Dublin University Magazine for April*, 1875. He states that they were "places of refuge." A tower intended to keep hostages safe is certainly a fitting place of refuge against hostile attacks from without.

"As regards the Round Towers, for example, one would suppose that everything that could be advanced on every possible view of their origin and uses had been said over and over again. But Sir William, on apparently conclusive evidence, showed that they were intended chiefly as places of refuge."—*Memoir of Sir William Wilde.*

The strange and phantastic theories put forward by Henry O'Brien and Marcus Keane, rest upon chimerical views, or at least on accidental features of similarity found to exist between Hibernian and Persian Pillar Towers. The false and hideous doctrines of Budhism, foul in their features of phallic worship, have been, with much ingenuity, but with no logical reasoning, forced by those writers into the question of the Round Towers, while the simple objects pointed out in the foregoing views have been wholly ignored. The sloping character of these perennial piles had been modelled on a common architectural principle, carried out in Babylon, Thebes, Memphis, and Mycenæ, by which *stability* and *durability* were at the same time secured—stability in the extended base and pointed top; durability in the solid masses of stone, the shape of the structure, the tapering circular form, having always the centre of gravity within the surface on which the tower rests, while on the outside the least possible amount of pressure acted on the building. These are some of the purposes for which the Round Towers had been intended in pagan times. The other uses to which, in Christian times, too, they have been turned, have been told by Denis Florence MacCarthy in his poem already quoted.

WHEN WERE THEY BUILT?

To answer this question is not within the scope of the present work; yet, as so much has been written here, it would seem, that if omitted, the point had been passed over intentionally.

The Pagan period may be divided into two, the remote and the late pagan period. It is certain, from all that has been just stated in these pages, that the Round Towers had been the work of men skilled in the art of building; and we have seen that mankind possessed greater knowledge some two thousand years before the Christian era than they possessed at a later period. The Round Towers must, therefore, have been built at that time, when men were best skilled in science and in the arts of building. The records in stone in Egypt, in Syria, and Persia tell us that this was the earliest period after the deluge, when men were cyclopean, if not in stature, at least in power of mind. Comparative philology proves the truth; and it is quite in accord with all that civil and sacred history testifies.

The science of comparative philology treats this question apart from history, just as geology investigates the truths of the physical world, or astronomy those which treat of the relative movements, size and splendour, times and spaces, of the heavenly bodies. Comparative philology, apart from history, shows that all the migrations to ancient Eire were of Keltic origin. This view is confirmed by the words of Sir William Wilde.

Now all these peoples—those who came with Parthalon, the Fomorians, Nemidians Tuatha de Dannans, Firbolgs,* Milesians—the patriotic navigator along our coasts, the mid-Europe primitive Shepherd and Cultivator; the Northern Warrior, and the Iberian Ruler, were, according to my (Sir William's) view, all derived from one Keltic stock. They spoke the same language, and their descendants do so still. When they acquired a knowledge of letters, they transmitted their history

* Fir, means "men;" "bolg," of bags, Fomorians, "fog," booty, "mara," of the sea. To this day "sea-bathers" are called in Irish "Foghmaires," in Clare and Galway. Thuatha, a tribe, a country, a class of people living in a rural district, *de*, of Dannan—bold people, or Dannans.

through the Irish language. No doubt they fused; but somehow a quicker fusion of races has not been the general characteristic of the people of this country. Unlike the Anglo-Norman in later times, the Milesian was a long way from home; the rough sea of the Bay of Biscay rolled between him and his previous *habitat*; and if he became an *absentee* he was not likely to find much of his possessions on his return. . . . . We find but "one language" among the Irish people until the arrival of the Anglo-Normans, at the end of the twelfth century.

"The linguistic or philological evidence on this subject is clearly decisive. The name of each migrating colony is Gaelic. The residue of the early races, already described, spoke ONE language, called Gaelic; so did the Scotch, the Welsh, and probably in early times the Britons and the Bretons. It was not only the popular conversational tongue used in the ordinary intercourse of life, but it was also employed in genealogies, annals, and other records in a special character, not quite peculiar to this country, but then common in Europe."

The foregoing passage is taken from page 9 of the *Address to the Anthropological Section of the British Association*, Belfast, August 19th, 1874, by Sir William Wilde, M.D.,M.R.I.A.

The conclusion which Sir William, as a scientist, draws from the fact that all the ancient migrations to Eire spoke the same language, is, that no matter by what name they were styled in ancient Irish annals, still they were all of the same generic Keltic stock, marching onward from the Aryan motherland in Persia. Therefore, Parthalon and his companions were Kelts; the Fomorians were Kelts; the Nemedians, Kelts; the Tuatha de Dannans, Kelts; the Firbolgs and the Milesians, Kelts. They were not therefore Cuthites, or descendants of Ham, as Mr. Marcus Keane asserts, nor Phœnecians, and consequently descendants of Ham, through Canaan. "They were descended direct from Japhet," says Sir William Wilde. "Cuthites were not known here then."

OPINIONS REFUTED.

The folly of the Cuthite theory becomes patent to one skilled in the science of comparative philology. The Phœnecian theory, too, regarding Ireland's first settlers melts away before the blaze of modern science, just as the Ptolomaic system of astronomy melted away in presence of the light that arose in the sixteenth century, from the genius of Father Copernic, and the discoveries of Galileo.

But the reader will ask which of these migrating races built the Round Towers? Was it the Fomorians, as Vallencey stated; or was it the *Tuatha de Dannans*, as Henry O'Brien asserts, and as Sir William Wilde intimates; nay, as some scraps from our ancient Irish annals say, the Book of Lecan, already quoted, seems to confirm. Such is the common view of those who supported the third opinion. Was it the Firbolgs, or the Nemedians? Or was it some unknown Keltic race.

This investigation has been treated quite apart, and entirely—in the outline or plot—away from the walk of written records.

The ancient annals of Ireland may be correct, or may not: in them the names of various migrations to Ireland in ancient times are given. But every intelligent reader should ask—first, are all these correct—is the number of colonies named accurate? Had there not been other colonists or migratory bands of men, just as there are now various migrations to the land of the West beyond the Atlantic waves? No Irish historian possessed of any judgment could say that there were not other settlers in ancient Ireland besides those named; nor could he assert, for certain, that those named had been settlers in the precise way in which their achievments and name are recorded. No doubt our ancient records are in substance correct, but much has been omitted, and much has been left to the fancy of historians. The father of history, Herodotus, drew upon his imagination for facts; his sons in Ireland have not, at times, been unmindful of such teaching.

The only fair answer, therefore, that can be supplied from the pages of *Comparative Philology* and *Paleontology* is, that those who built the Round Towers had been Aryans, therefore clever to plan and courageous to execute; that they were of the Keltic stock; and that they were amongst the very first settlers in this isle of destiny. Comparative philology knows nothing about such names as Fomorians, or Firbolgs, or any of the six migrations named. The terms "Fomorian," sea-robber; "Firbolg," bagmen, are accidental. Paleontology deals with races, not parties of a race styled by a technical name. They came, not only at different periods, but they came by different routes; and though originally of one stock, they presented a change at an early period in their *physique* and in their character.

HOW DID THEY COME?

For the present the question is waived—*how* did they come? By what route? Was it by the shores of the south of Europe—or northwards, by the Caucasian passes, through Sarmatia, Dacia, and Germania? Ethnologists and philologists agree that the Aryan highway to Western Europe, and to Ireland, was not confined to one passage, but that the fiery Kelts hastened westward, through Greece, Pannonia, Italy, Helvetia, Spain, as well as through Rhætia, Gallia, Belgia, and Britannia.

Irishmen at home an abroad cling, and justly, too, with wonderful pertinacious force to the story of their early ancient history. This feeling is natural, it is right; it is founded on the knowledge which they possess until they obtain clearer and larger views. Zeuss tells us, that they were so hundreds of years before the Christian era. The reading Irish public, not trained in the sciences of language and of hermeneutics, do not advert to the fact, that the substantial portion of a narration may be true, and yet the colouring false; they do not see into the necessity of examination of other witnesses besides those favourable to their own views, or of cross-examining their own historic witnesses.

In the subject matter before the reader, *history* and *comparative grammar* and *paleontology* pronounce with one accord that the first colonists who came to Ireland migrated from the East; that they were *Aryan* in origin, and *Keltic* in race; but of Parthalon, or the Lady Kaiser, or the Fomorians, the latter do not say one word.

Many Irishmen will not be pleased at this fact. For their sake, then, and to meet the views of ignorant writers on the subject of Ireland's antiquities, the following paragraphs are annexed :—

Sir William Wilde's opinions on the subject of the early Irish races are more deserving of attention than those of any living scholar. He has studied Irish history, not from the pages of the ancient annals alone. His life has been one of deep research in ethnology, philology, paleology. Books have not been the only tablets on which he has read the history of mankind, and especially of the Irish race. His *Catalogue of the antiquities of stone, earthen and vegetable materials, in the Museum of the Royal Irish Academy*, in two volumes, is a work for which Irishmen can never sufficiently thank him. Like Cuvier, he reads the history of a family, or of a race, in a single fossil bone, or in a cinerary urn.*

* With respect to the authenticity of the early chronicles and legends that relate the history of these immigrations—so much sneered at by one set of inquirers and so faithfully believed in by another—let me make two observations, one chronological and the other topographical. Our Irish Annals were first committed to writing by Christian scribes in either Gaelic or Latin, and were not only intermixed with classic story, but with scriptural incidents, particularly those relating to the dispersion of mankind after the deluge. Of a portion of their chronology there can, however, be little doubt; for in recording cosmical phenomena, such as eclipses of the sun or moon, the approach of comets and the like, they scarcely differ by a year from that great astronomical and chronological work, '*L'Art de verifier les dates*,' computed by the French philosophers hundreds of years after those Annals were last written or transcribed. This synchronism, to say the least of it, is remarkably confirmative of those very early Irish Annals. It is just possible that long before the age of alphabetic writing some means by tallies, runes, or other devices may have been invented for fixing the ages of these cosmical phenomena.

Now, the other incident is of equal authenticity in confirmation of the historical statement of our early records. Long, long before the Christian era it is there said that a battle took place on a certain plain in Mayo; and an incident connected with the fight is thus told:—A king or chief was surprised in early morning, while performing his ablutions at a deep well, by three warriors of the enemy, who came upon him unawares. By the prowess of one of his attendants he was saved, who killed his three assailants, and then died upon the spot. Hundreds of years passed by, the locality around had been cultivated and grazed upon again and again; still the valley, the well, the subterranean watercourse with its fairy legends, the hurling-field, the cairns, circles, pillar-stones, and other surrounding topographical features remained. The gallant soldier who laid down his life for his royal master was buried where he fell; and as the army (stated to have been thousands strong) passed by, each man—as was the custom of the day—threw a pebble on his grave, then called and still known as "The cairn of the one man." Not long ago, with the written legend in my hand, and possessing a full knowledge of the locality, and accompanied by a few stalwart Connaught men, I proceeded to the spot, told my incredulous auditory the tale of their ancestors, dug and lifted stone after stone until we came upon a small chamber under a large flag, wherein we found deposited a beautiful cinerary urn containing some black earth

"We do *not* know," he says, "where nor by whom these annals were first committed to writing, nor what means were taken to alter them; but we possess what cannot be falsified by the scribe; and although styled prehistoric, they are far more truthfully historic than the writing that, no doubt, was largely interfered with, and which, if old, now requires a gloss to interpret it. The grassy mound or circle, the stones erected into a cromleach, the great sepulchral mound, the cinerary urn, the stone weapon or tool, the grain-rubber for triturating cereal food, the harpoon for spearing fish, the copper and bronze tools and weapons, and the gold ornaments of the very early tribes—all now are, in their way, far more truthful than anything that could have been committed to writing, even if there were letters in that day. They are litanies in stone, dogmata in metal, and sermons preaching from the grassy mound."

The first migration under the Lady Kaiser, in Irish annals, is passed over.

---

and fragments of burnt human bones. The sepulchre, with its surrounding stone circle, still exists on the battle-field of Moytura Conga, and the decorated urn is in the Museum of the Royal Irish Academy.—*From the Address by Sir William R. Wilde, M.D., M.R.I.A.*

On the other hand: "Let us admit," says Professor Blackie, "that there is such a thing as historical forgery; nay, that fictitious history is a thing to which the human mind is so prone, that there does not exist a single instance of accredited national record that is not, to some extent, adulterated with this element. . . . . Certain Jews, in ancient times, sat down with the utmost gravity, and wrote a detailed life of Adam with as much minuteness as if they had been the personal friends of the first man. Suidas tells us of a certain Asclepiades who composed an Egyptian history, extending over a period of thirty thousand years."—*Homeric Dissertation, vol.* 1, *page* 65. Homer and the Iliad, by Blackie:—Edmonston, and Douglas, Edinburgh, 1866.

History, and philology, and paleontology knit together form, regarding any event, a triple cord which fiction cannot sunder.

The second: He describes the coming of the Grecian leader, Parthalon and his cohorts, who landed in Dublin Bay, and took possession of the country, from Ben-edair to Wicklow. The record of their existence, as a colony in Ireland, is preserved in the name of *Tallaght*, near Dublin. The name means "plague-monument," from "táṁ," *plague, sleep, rest*, a common Gaelic term in use to this day; and "leaċt" a *monument*. We say in Gaelic "ni'l taṁ air," *there is not a wink on him*; "tá se 'nna táṁ," *he is in a state of rest, or dozing*. Sir William says that "Kisharies" are in that district occasionally turned up, containing decorated urns, having within them incenerated bones. Several of these are still in existence.

The third, Fomorians; fourth, Nemedians and other minor invaders, have left nothing after them by which to track their footprints. These were descended direct from Japhet. They were not Cuthites.

Fifth, "I will now tell" to use Sir William's words "what has been the result of my own examination of the races that migrated to, or are said to have conquered Ireland."

A patriotic people called Firbolgs, said to be of Greek or Eastern origin, and probably a branch of that race that, having passed through Europe, or around its shores, arrived in Ireland. We call them Kelts, and I do not know much of the Phœnicians or Carthaginians. These Firbolgs had laws and social institutions and established a monarchical Government at the far-famed Hill of Tara, about which our early centres of civilization sprung. . . . . I cannot say that the Firbolg was a cultivated man. He was a shepherd and an agriculturist. . . . The Firbolgs were a small, straight-haired, swarthy race, who have left a portion of their descendants with us to this very day. A genealogist (their own countryman, resident in Galway about two hundred years ago) described them as dark-haired, talkative, guileful, strolling, unsteady, 'disturbers of every council and assembly, &c.' . . . To these physical and mental characters described by Duald MacFirbis let me add those of the unusual combination of blue, or blue-gray eyes, and dark eyelashes, with a swarthy complexion. This peculiarity I have remarked elsewhere, only in Greece;—the mouth and upper gum are not good, but the nose is usually straight."

SIXTH MIGRATION.

The next immigration we hear of in the 'Annals' is that of the *Tuatha-de-Dannans*, a large, fair-complexioned, and very remarkable race; warlike, energetic, progressive, skilled in metal work, musical, poetical, acquainted with the healing art, skilled in Druidism, and believed to be adepts in necromancy and magic, no doubt the result of the popular idea respecting their superior knowledge, especially in smelting and in the fabrication of tools, weapons, and ornaments. From these two races sprang the Fairy Mythology of Ireland.

The Dannan spoke *the same language as his predecessors*, the Firbolgs. They met and fought for the sovereignity. The "man of metal" conquered, and drove a great part of the others into the islands on the coast, where it is said the Firbolg or Belgic race (so called) took their last stand. Eventually, however, under the influence of a power hostile to them both, these two people coalesced, and have to a large extent done so up to the present day. They are the true old Irish peasant and small farming class.

Then, on the other hand, their physiognomy, their fair or reddish hair, their size, conjoined with other circumstances, incline one to believe that they came down from

Scandinavian regions after they had passed up as far as they thought advisable into North-western Europe. If the word Dane was known at the time of their arrival here, it would account for the designation of many of our Irish monuments as applied by Molyneux and others. Undoubtedly the Dannan tribes presented Scandinavian features, but did not bring anything but Grecian art.

I believe that these Tuatha-de-Dannans, no matter from whence they came, were, in addition to their other acquirements, great masons, although not acquainted with the value of cementing materials. I think they were the builders of the great stone Cahirs, Duns, Cashels, and Caves in Ireland; while their predecessors constructed the earthen works, the raths, circles, and forts that diversify the fields of Erinn. The Dannan anticipated Shakespeare's grave-digger, for they certainly made the more lasting sepulchral monuments that exist in Ireland, such, for example, as New Grange, Louth, Howth, and Slieve na Cailleagh and other great cemeteries. Within the interior and around these tombs were carved, on unhewn stones, certain archaic markings, spires, volutes, convolutes, lozenge-shaped devices, straight, zigzag, and curved lines, and incised indentations, and a variety of other insignia, which, although not expressing language, were symbolical, and had an occult meaning known only to the initiated,

The Seventh: The next, and last, of the pre-Christian migrations was the Milesian. This race was Keltic. The people were brave, chivalrous, skilled in war, good navigators, proud, boastful, superior in outer adornment as well as in mental culture, to their opponents. Being the conquering race, they assumed the sovereignty of the country, and became its landed proprietors, and aristocracy.

MacFirbis, the genealogist, writes of the Milesian, a race to which he himself belonged: "Every man who is white of skin, brown of hair, bold, honourable, daring, prosperous, bountiful in battle, or combat—they are the descendants of the sons of Milesians in Erinn."

All these different migrations had come forth from the Keltic family home; and all spoke the same language. All were Aryan. Thus the ancient annals of Ireland accord most wonderfully with the teaching of the science of comparative philology.

The Irish race is Eastern. So says Duald MacFirbis; so proves the science of Comparative Grammar; so, too, the Round Towers, scattered in such numbers over the face of Erinn, proclaim.

CHAPTER XIV.

The question of the Round Towers brought in the foregoing chapter to a close; not, however, finally settled. A fuller analysis would not produce more definite results. Conclusion arrived at morally certain. Why has the question of the Pillar Towers been introduced? The language of Ireland helps from the Keltic names, and from the unwritten page of ancient history, to clear up the question of Ireland's Ancient Towers. The Pillar Towers on the other hand strengthen the position of the Gaelic, show its Aryan character and its philologic value. (1) The *Brehon Laws* of ancient Ireland. (2) Rhyme in Europe. (3) Names of places in Ireland and in Scotland. (4) Keltic Terms full of rich suggestiveness of historic interest. (5) Etymology of European tongues finds sure primitive roots in Keltic. These reasons are calculated to stimulate scholars to study Gaelic. Further development of these subjects. First, the *Brehon Laws*: Opinion of Scotchmen and Englishmen on the people of Ireland, and on their ancient laws; How very unjust and cruel—and, of course, ignorant—were those views. What are really the Irish laws, and the Irish people? Irish laws Aryan. Therefore the same as the laws of the Etrurians; or the laws of the Twelve Tables; the laws of the Romans; the Saxons. Thus the Brehon Laws prove, like the language and the Round Towers, that the Irish nation are Aryan, and the laws were those taught at the Aryan school in the cradle-land of Persia.

The learned will ask is the question regarding the Round Towers closed? Has the great controversy which has been going on fully two hundred years, but especially for the past century, since the days of Vallencey, been in a hundred pages set at rest? Well, the subject regarding the Pillar Towers of Ireland has been introduced into this volume in relation only to the native language of the Irish race. That language aids considerably to elucidate the vexed subject of the Round Towers, and it is only so far as "these grey pillars" lean for historic support on the language of the Keltic race that they have been taken notice of at present. The Gaelic names by which the Round Towers have been known amongst the present people of Ireland demanded some notice; and then the character of the pillar towers, their origin and use, as far as can be fairly shewn, tend to confirm the formal truth of all the conclusions which the discoveries in the Keltic department of comparative philology have, within the past decade of years, developed, and furnished as scientific dogmata to the linguistic literary savants of Europe.

The national question of the pillar towers, hitherto so much discussed, especially from the year 1832 to 1845, has been put before the reader, not, of course, as a subject of special interest, and one resting solely within the domain of paleontology, but to aid, as it has done, the force of philology in developing through the language of the Irish race, the conclusions already arrived at, that the primitive people who came to Ireland had been Japhetic, their language Aryan.

The question just discussed in the foregoing pages has, in pushing forward the developing theories of Keltic philology, acted as a lever with a three-fold power—*linguistic*, inasmuch as Irish terms have been introduced, explained, and their value in the argument utilised; *architectural*, in the worth of the towers as standing specimens of primeval architecture, and *historic*, because the Round Towers have been the gnomon on the dial of Ireland's historic day. So far, therefore, the language of Ireland has afforded valuable aid, by a kind of philologic electric conductive process, in dissipating the clouds which have hung over the archaic pillar piles of the land; and the discussion of the subject of the Towers has, by a historic process, added to the moral electric force of the speech of the Gael.

A fuller discussion than that just closed regarding "the mystic temples of our own dear isle," could not have produced a higher degree of certainty, or results more reliable or truthful than those which have been attained.

Other reasons still remain to be presented to the reader, to show that the study of the ancient language of Ireland is not only useful, but necessary, for men who aim at acquiring a knowledge of the archaic manners of the Irish race in the pre-Christian period—a knowledge of the laws by which they were governed—a knowledge of the poems and stories they narrated, and of the songs they sung at the festive board of lover or lord. The study of the Gaelic tongue commends itself to all Irishmen who wish to be familiar with the topography of their own country; and to all Scotchmen who wish to know the real meaning of *Ben* and *Loch*, *Glen* and *Craig*, in the Highlands; nay, to all Englishmen who are in any way concerned with the historic meaning of *Albion*, *Avon*, *Cambridge*, *Kent*, *London*, *Malvern*; and, lastly, to every Continental scholar who cares to be correctly acquainted with the meaning of the ancient topography of Europe, and with Keltic names that command historic interest.

The reasons that are here presented to the enlightened reader, to excite his interest and to enlighten his views on the value, and the practical profit of the Gaelic language in modern scholarship, are seen at a glance under the titles: (1) "The Brehon Laws;" (2) "Rhyme in European Poetry;" (3) "Irish Names of Places;" (4) "Keltic Names, rich in Suggestiveness of Historic

Interest;" (5) "Gaelic Etymology of the Languages of Western Europe."

In the world of letters these respective subjects have been treated with ability and erudition by men who, in each department, have undertaken the literary labour involved in duties so important, and of such immense value to European literature.

First—The Brehon Law Commission, established twenty three years ago, by order of the English Government, have given to the world three volumes of the ancient laws of Ireland, with an introduction to the *Seanchus Mor*, and *Ath-Gabhail*, or *Law of Distress*, as contained in the Harleian manuscripts. *Brehon Laws*, Vol. I., published in Dublin, and London, 1865; Vol. II., in 1869; Vol., III., in 1874.

The subject of "Rhyme in the Poetry of Europe" is discussed in the fourth part, or Prosody of the College Irish Grammar, from the pen of the present writer, and published by Mullany, Dublin. Signor Nigra confirms the views of the author of the College Grammar. Matthew Arnold's *Keltic Literature* (Smith, London, 1867), resting on Zeuss' erudite work, lends to the discussion the sanction of Oxford learning.

A really splendid volume on the origin and history of Irish names of places has been published in 1869, and again in 1873, by P. W. Joyce, A.M., M.R.I.A. In the preface he writes:—"In our island there was scarcly any admixture of races till the introduction of an important English element—chiefly within the last three hundred years—for, the Danish interruptions produced no appreciable effect; and, accordingly, our place-names are purely Keltic, with the exception of about a thirteenth part, which are English, and mostly of recent introduction. This great name system, begun thousands of years ago by the first wave of population that reached our island was continued unceasingly from age to age, till it embraced the minutest features of the country in its intricate net-work; and such as it sprang forth from the minds of our ancestors, it exists almost unchanged to this day.—*Preface to First Edition*, p. 7.

Several pamphlets have been published on the names of places throughout Europe; allusion has, from time to time, been made to the derivation of many Continental names from the days of Dr. John O'Brien, Bishop of Cloyne, up to the time of Zeuss, and to the present hour. The best work, however, on the subject is that by Wilhelm Ober Müller—*Deutsch-Keltisches, Geschichtlich, Geographisches, Wörterbuch, zur Erklarung der Fluss, Berg, Orts, Gan, Völker, und Personen—namen Europos. Leipzig*, 1867.

Joseph Boult, F.R.I.B.A., of Liverpool, has written, on the Keltic character of old British names, two very useful tracts. The one is styled—*The Danish Intrusion into South Britain*; the other, *The Angles, Dutes, and Saxons.—Liverpool*, 1873.

The able work of Zeuss, *Grammatica Celtica*, Second Edition, is well known; and Ebel's *Keltic Studies*, edited by Dr. W. K. Sullivan. The work just now being published by Charles Mackay, L.L.D (Trubner, & Co., London), Fellow of the Royal Society of the Antiquarians of Denmark supplies what has not come within the scope of those subjects treated in the works written by either Joyce, in Ireland, or Ober Müller, in Germany. Mr. Mackay's work is to be published in the present year, and it is known by the title "*The Gaelic Etymology of the Languages of Western Europe*, and more especially of the English and Lowland Scotch and their cant, slang, and colloquial dialects.

Each of these departments of Keltic study is most useful and important, and wound up with the study and cultivation of the Irish language. By a singular and a fortunate combination of the Scotch and Irish schools of Keltic learning, each section of linguistic research has found its scholastic explorer and director.

ANCIENT IRISH LAWS.

Up to a recent period, which dates from the year 1840, Irishmen and their progenitors have been, by all Philo-anglians, ranked as savages of the wildest and most unenlightened kind.

Mr. John Pinkerton, a native of Edinburgh, remarkable in a certain degree as antiquarian, has written of "Clan na Gael" in these terms: "The majority of the resembled in all probability that of the Hottontots, or Keltic race, others, the rudest savages, as the Kelts anciently were, and are, indeed, little better at present, being incapable only of any progress in society." Mr. Pinkerton is one of a large school of political and religious zealots, who think that they cannot show their just appreciation for England, and English laws, and English institutions, and flaunt their love for the British people but by depreciating everything Gaelic, and showing their scorn and hate for the Gaels and their speech. Pinkerton and his school have been the worst enemies of Britain. Indeed they had received strong encouragement from the words of the statute of Kilkenny (passed A.D. 1367) which denounce the Irish people and their language, and style the Brehon Law "*wicked* and damnable." "It is the same law," says Sir Henry Sumner Maine in his late work, *Lectures on the Early History of Institutions*, just published (London Murray), that "Edmund Spencer in his *View of the State of Ireland*, describes as a rule of right unwritten, but delivered by tradition from one to another, in which oftentimes there appeareth a great show of equity, in determining the right between party and party, but in many things repugning quite both to God's law and man's." It is the same lewd and unreasonable custom which Sir John Davis contrasts with the just and honourable law of England, and to which he attributes such desolation and barbarism in Ireland "as the like was not seen in any country that professed the name of Christ."

The foregoing views of the Brehon Laws have been reproduced by English writers, and propagated in a thousand forms in England, Scotland, Ireland, and in America. Everything Irish has been decried—and the laws in the past pronounced on the authority of respected English authors, such as Spencer, to have been lewd, and barbarous, and "repugning to God's law and man's." Such, until lately, had been the opinion of the educated upper-classes—the *Saturday Review School*—regarding Irishmen and their national laws.

This strong repulsive bias in the Saxon and in the Scotch Philo-Saxon—Pinkerton and his class—against everything Keltic, has arisen from (1) ignorance; (2) prejudice; (3) political antagonism and religious hatred.

Matthew Arnold, Professor of Poetry in the University of Oxford (*Study of Keltic Literature, p.* 13, London Smith, Elder, & Co.), shows this truth very plainly.

"So far I go along with the stream of my brother Saxons; but here I imagine I part with them. They will have nothing to do with the Welsh language and literature on any terms; they would gladly make a clean sweep of it from the face of the earth. I, on certain terms, wish to make a great deal more of it than is made now; and, dropping the distinction between Welsh and Irish, Gaels and Kymris, let me say, Keltic literature, is an object of very great interest. My brother Saxons have, as is well known, a terrible way with them of wanting to improve everything but themselves. I have no such passion; I like variety to exist and to show itself to me; and I would not, for the world, have the lineaments of the Keltic genius lost." Again:—"It is not in the outward and visible world of material life that the Keltic genius of Wales or Ireland can at this day hope to count for much; it is in the *inward world of thought and of science.*"

Those are remarkable words of the Professor of Poetry in Oxford University. Next, he shows what prejudice and political bigotry can produce:

"When I was young I was taught to think of Kelt as separated by an impassable gulph from Teuton. My father, in particular, was never weary of contrasting them; and he insisted much oftener on the separation between us and them (Saxons and Kelts), than on the separation between us and any other race in the world. In the same way Lord Lyndhurst, in words long famous, called the Irish 'aliens in speech, in religion, and in blood.' This naturally created a profound sense of estrangement; it doubled the estrangement which political and religious differences had already made between us and the Irish people. It seemed to make this estrangement immense, incurable, fatal."

He says: "The Jew of ancient times seemed a thousand degrees nearer than the Kelt to us. Puritanism had so assimilated Bible ideas and phraseology, that the sense of affinity between the Teutonic and Hebrew nature was quite strong. A steady, middle-class Anglo-Saxon much more imagined himself Ehud's cousin than Ossian's."

The effect of religious antagonism is made manifest by what is stated in the foregoing paragraph, particularly when every body knows that Matthew Arnold writes what he is convinced is true. Philology and ethnology and antiquities proclaim Britains to be, like the Gaels, Aryan in origin, Keltic in race, and not at all Semitic. Yet, the Anglo-Saxon believed the Hebrew his cousin; the Kelt, a stranger. Such, as told in the words of British writers, had been the notions of Englishmen in the past, regarding Irishmen, their laws and institutions; and such is the opinion regarding them to this day amongst hundreds and thousands of Philo-anglians in Ireland, in Scotland, and in America. This settled notion is the offspring of ignorance, fostered by prejudice and nurtured in the lap of political and religious hate.

Have they not ere this been told the contrary? Certainly. More than a century ago, the Most Rev. John O'Brien, Catholic Bishop of Cloyne and Ross, published in the *Collectanea* of Vallancey a dissertation on the "Tanistic Law of Senior-Succession, illustrated in an historical and genealogical account of the Kings of Munster"—and to this was annexed "Part of the ancient Brehon Laws of Ireland"—(printed by Thomas Ewing, Dublin, 1774.) The "Manners, Customs, Commerce, and Laws of the Ancient Scots" (Irish), had been even before that period (1775) presented to the public by the Very Rev. Dr. Charles O'Conor, of Belanagare. Dr. Lanigan did not neglect to treat this important subject in his *Ecclesiastical History of Ireland* (Dublin, 1822.) And in 1824 Edward O'Reilly published an essay on "The nature and influence of the Brehon Laws."

Moore and other Irish historians, previous to the publication of the *Annals of the Kingdom of Ireland*, so ably translated and edited by Dr. John O'Donovan, had alluded to the Brehon Laws. The Brehon Law was known by Englishmen from the days of Henry II. to have been the

Irish code. In the sixteenth vol. of the *Transactions of the Royal Irish Academy* (Dublin, 1830) is found an essay by John D'Alton on the social and political state of the people of Ireland from the commencement of the Christian era to the twelfth century.

The renaissance of Irish antiquities, however, and the marvellous growth of Irish learning, together with the glorious revival of Gaelic literature, based on scientific principles, date from the day when the Government established the Ordnance Survey in this country. The gifted Dr. Petrie, M.R.I.A., and his staff, did in a few years immense work. They had plans laid, and had begun actually to re-erect from the *debris* of past times monuments of Gaelic knowledge, which, for the nation, would have, like a new dawn, shed a fresh radiance over the past; and for Gaelic students in the future, would have been a beacon-light to enlighten and to guide them on the road of home linguistic studies.

The Irish nation had not, perhaps, been prepared for so great a change. The literary labours of Petrie and his staff were stopped. The mere mechanical survey went on. O'Donovan, however, gave us the *Annals of the Four Masters*, in an English and in an Irish dress; O'Curry his manuscript materials of Irish history. The British Government ordered, some twenty-three years ago, the publication of the Brehon Laws. Three volumes were translated, and have now been edited and published.

Let us now see, from impartial witnesses, what is the real truth regarding this code of laws; what is their origin; what their legal value?

The Brehon Law is so called from the Gaelic term for judge (*Breitheamh*,) whose office was to explain the law and apply its meaning to the several cases that were brought before him for adjudication. "There are startling points of correspondence between the functions of the Druids, as described by Cæsar, and the office of the Brehon. The extensive literature of law just disinterred testifies to the authority of the Brehons in all legal matters, and raises a strong presumption that they were universal referees in dispute. The schools of literature and law appear to have been numerous in ancient Ireland. The course was twelve years."—*Maine*, *p*. 32. The term *breith*, of the same origin with the Greek, *phero;* Latin, *fero;* and the English *bear*, signifies to carry, to seize, to join; and applying the name to the operation of the mind, to catch the thoughts and to compare them, and thus to form a judgment in the philosophic sense; and in the judicial, to pronounce the decision arrived at, whenever one has applied the law to the case at issue. The Brehon Law was that code by which the Irish race, in pagan and in Christian times, had been governed. It is, as shall be shown, the twin sister of the Roman code, known as the Laws of the Twelve Tables. It is of Aryan origin. These laws came from the same parent stock as those which direct the political and social life of Europe; "for," says Sir Henry Sumner Maine (*Preface to Lectures on the Early History of Institutions*) "the Roman law has never ceased to be spoken of with deep respect; and it is, in fact, the source of the greatest part of the rules by which civil life is still governed in the western world."

The laws of England and of Scotland are, in a certain measure, founded on the Roman law, and therefore the Brehon Law and the English law have had, so far, a common origin. Yet, *these* are the laws which those who enacted the Statute of Kilkenny pronounced "wicked and damnable," and which Edmund Spencer styled "repugning both to God's law and man's;" and Sir John Davis coolly calls "lewd" and "unreasonable," and contrasts it with the "just and honorable law of England."

Are we certain that the Brehon Law is Aryan—that it is the same as the laws of the Twelve Tables? Yes; three volumes of the Brehon Law are now before the public. Each *savant* can read and judge. An English legal lecturer (Sir Henry Sumner Maine) has published a volume of four hundred pages, pointing out the historic, archaic, legal, and philologic value of this code of laws.

The Brehon Law had been written in old Irish. Hence the necessity and value of the Irish language, in order to know with accuracy and certainty those ancient laws. It is true that they have been translated; yet, a knowledge of the language is still, to a great extent, necessary.

Of the extent of the Brehon Law manuscripts, and their historic importance, O'Curry in his ninth lecture thus speaks (*MS. Materials, p.* 201-202):—"This collection is so immense in extent,* and the subjects dealt with throughout the whole of it, in the utmost detail, are so numerous, and so fully illustrated by exact definitions and minute descriptions, that, to enable us to fill up the outline supplied and genealogies, these books of laws alone would almost be found sufficient in competent hands. . . . . . Any one who has examined the body of Welsh Laws, now some years before the world, will at once be able to form a fair opinion of the interest and value, in historical and social points of view, of this far larger—this immense and hitherto unexplored mass of legal institutes. And these were the laws and institutes which regulated the political and social system of a people the most remarkable in Europe, from a period almost lost in the dark maze of antiquity, down to within

* O'Curry had transcribed at the time eight thousand *quarto pages* of matter, relating to the Brehon Laws; and this immense pile was only part of the code.—*Study of Keltic Literature, p.* 29.

about two hundred years, or seven generations, of our own time, and whose spirit and traditions, I may add, influence the feelings and actions of the native Irish, even to this day. To these laws, may we, indeed, justly apply the expressive remark of the poet Moore on the old MSS. in the Royal Irish Academy, that they were not written by a foolish people, nor for any foolish purpose. . . . Copious though the records are in which the action and every day life of our remote ancestors have come down to us, through the various documents of which I have been speaking, still, without these laws, our history would be necessarily barren, deficient, and uncertain in one of its most interesting and important essentials."

This wonderful code of laws has, like Pompeii or Herculaneum entombed in lava, been sealed up for over one thousand years in the language of the Keltic race. For this reason the Brehon Law has come forth at the present time, like those specimens of art and of science, in painting or sculpture or architecture, which have been found in the buried cities near Vesuvius; or, farther still, like the Etruscan vases and statues that had lain entombed in the cities of the dead for a thousand years before Romulus founded, on the banks of the Tiber, the city that was destined one day to rule the world.

A modern writer narrating the discoveries made of the cities of the dead in Etruria, says: "It is only in modern times a general interest in the ancient Etruscans has been revived; that the Truscans begin to remember, with pride, that on their territory in particular flourished this civilization of two thousand years ago; and that some Italian families have been led to trace in their names and genealogies indications of a connection with the first civilizers of their fatherland."

Among the cemeteries explored by modern antiquaries

or by modern lovers of gain, that of Vulci, which has furnished the Prince of Canino with the means of forming a most splendid collection of Etruscan antiquities, which has, besides, enriched many of the museums of Europe, and which still yields an annual harvest to the successors of the Prince, was utterly unknown until the year 1828, when it was discovered by chance. . . . . The tombs of Norchia and Castel d'Asso, which are remarkable for their sculptured façades, were brought to light only forty years ago by some sportsmen of Viterbo, who, in the pursuit of game, penetrated into the secluded glens in which they are situated. The magnificent city of tombs, at Orte, were discovered in 1837. Others, at Savona, were brought to light in 1843."

"That the word *necropolis*, or city of the dead, had not, amongst the ancients, been a mere figurative expression, is, indeed, proved by many of these rock-hewn cemeteries; for, not only do the porticos, the pediments, the house-like roofs, and whole internal arrangement of the tombs, recall to mind the habitations of the living, but in several places, such as at Bieda and Cervetri, it is evident that the cemeteries have been laid out in streets, and even in squares, the façades of the tombs occupying the place of those of the houses in the cities of the living.

"At Castel d'Asso, Norchia, Bieda, Falerii, Sutri, and Orte—all places of little note in Italy at present, but occupying the *sites of cities* which once held a high rank in the history of Etruria—the tombs, as regards their external character, surpass in majestic grandeur and architectural decorations all that have as yet been discovered."

The Brehon Law, like the rich vases and works of art that lay buried in the tombs of Etruria, had not only been sealed up in the Irish language, unseen by the eye of any scholar outside Ireland, but had been for a period, lost.

Now, at length, they have been discovered, and are open to the view of the whole literary world.

Thus, the present generation of enquirers are brought back, at a bound, to the time when they can behold the social and civil state of Ireland in the fifth century, and even at a period much more remote.

"Up to the early dawn of civilisation, the very causes," says Sir Henry Sumner Maine, "which have denied a modern history to the Brehon Law have given it a special interest of its own in our day, through the arrest of its developement."

It is this arrest of the developement of the Brehon Law in the past that causes their translation and publication to be so much prized at present. Like the Round Towers, like the family features of the Japhetic race, like the laws of linguistic science, the Brehon Law comes in and forms an arc in the circle of newly-discovered truths that point up to the primitive Aryan period, full of knowledge, of action, of cyclopean power and grandeur.

It is in no way surprising that the Brehon code should appear archaic to moderns. In the form in which it is now presented to the public—with translation by O'Donovan and O'Curry—it has been a literary fossil for over a thousand years.

This fossil condition of Ireland's ancient law, morally speaking, is owing to four causes—the insular position of Ireland, its freedom from Imperial Rome, the antagonism of Britain and of British law, the love of the Keltic race to preserve traditional usages.

VALUE OF THE LAW.

The words of the present writer may be regarded as favoring too much these cherished monuments of Ireland's ancient civilisation. It is well, then, to quote Sir Henry

Maine once more: "The value which the ancient laws of Ireland—the Brehon Laws—will possess, when they are completely published and interpreted, may, I think, be illustrated in this way. Let it be remembered that the Roman law, which, next to the Christian religion, is the most plentiful source of the rules governing actual conduct throughout Western Europe, is descended from a small body of Aryan customs, reduced to writing in the fifth century, before Christ, and known as the Twelve Tables of Rome."

It is founded on the natural law, and, in part, on the written law. Such is the Brehon Law, also; it is Aryan in origin; it is founded on the natural law, and composed, in part, of the written law.

"Let it farther be recollected that the Roman law was at first expanded and developed, not at all, or very slightly, by legislation, but by a process which we may perceive still in operation in various communities—the juridical interpretation of authoritative texts by successive generations of learned men. Now, the largest collection of Irish legal rules which has come down to us professes to be an ancient code, with an appendage of later glosses and commentaries. . . . . This ancient Irish code corresponds historically to the laws of the Twelve Tables, and to many similar bodies of written rules which appear in the early history of Aryan societies." . . .

"That a kernel, or some kernels, of written law existed is highly probable; and it is also probable that the whole of the Brehon law consists of them and of accumulations formed upon them. . . . . The Brehon Laws are in no sense a legislative construction, and thus they are not only an authentic monument of a very ancient group of Aryan institutions; they are also a collection of rules which have been gradually developed in a way highly favorable to the preservation of archaic peculiarities."

The Brehon law had been expanded by the juridical interpretation of authoritative texts, just like the laws of the Hebrew race, or like the code of the Spartan State. The Roman law became transformed and modified by legislation, to suit the altered times, the varied new forms of society, the changes connected with growing States and with diverse races.

" Two causes (says Maine) have done most to obscure the oldest institutions of the portion of the human race to which we belong. One, the formation throughout the west of strong centralised governments; the other has been the influence, direct and indirect, of the Roman Empire, drawing with it an activity in legislation unknown to the parts of the world which were never subjected to it."

Ireland had never been exposed to these influences—she never formed a part of the Roman empire; she had a central government, but never a strong one, capable of exercising—like Rome of old, or England at present—a special centralising, legislative power.

" Under these circumstances, it is not wonderful that the Brehon Law, growing together without legislation upon an original body of Aryan customs, and formed beyond the limit of that cloud of Roman juridical ideas which for many centuries overspread the whole continent, and even at its extremity, extended to England, should present some very strong analogies to another set of derivative Aryan usages, the Hindu law, which was similarly developed."

The Hindu law, therefore, and the Brehon Law, and the Roman law are developements of one primitive Aryan code.

The laws of Europe, divested of their legislative and

judicial accessory forms, and reduced to first principles, are found to be identical—one with the primitive Aryan. "Wherever (says Maine) we have a body of Aryan customs, either anterior to, or slightly affected by, the Roman Empire, it will be found to exhibit some strong points of resemblance to the institutions which are the basis of the Brehon Law."

To conclude, the Brehon Law is not what the Parliament of Kilkenny, or Edmund Spencer, or Sir John Davis pronounced it to be—either "wicked and damnable," "repugnant to God's law and man's," or "lewd and unreasonable." On the contrary, it has been shown to be, and scholars versed in law declare that it is, just and in accord with the natural law, and with the written law, which is from God. It comes down from the Aryan period. It is twin sister, in legal parentage, of the code known as the "Laws of the Twelve Tables." It is therefore kindred in its institution to European law, and especially to the laws of England. The Eastern or Hindoo law and itself flow from the same source, and have been in time enlarged and extended quite in the same fashion.

Irishmen governed, in days that are gone, by such a code must have, like other nations grown up, children of honor and truth, with a strong aptitude for religion. The men must have been, as they were, truthful, brave, chivalrous, noble; the women free, honored, devoted, as amongst the Etrurians and the primitive Aryans; learning was fostered and respected; the arts and sciences cultivated; works of civilization and material progress patronised. The good resulting from such a code was manifold, not alone in social life, and in the political, but in the religious and the literary. It was admirably suited to the times and to the people.

The study of the language and of the laws of Ireland; the study, as French *savants* style it, "of the science of origins," has produced good results—ethnological and philological, historic, social, legal; it has shewn Englishmen, that after all, the Irishman is not a stranger even to the British; that the peoples of the two countries had been originally one family—the Aryan.

"In the sphere of politics, (says Matthew Arnold) there has appeared an indirect practical result from the study of this science; the sense of antipathy to the Irish people, of radical estrangement from them, has visibly abated amongst all the better part of us; the remorse for ill-treatment of them; the wish to make amends, to do them justice, to fairly unite, if possible, in one people with them, has visibly increased; hardly a book on Ireland is now published, hardly a debate on Ireland now passes in Parliament without this appearing. I am inclined to think that the march of science—the science of origins—shewing that there is no such original chasm between the Kelt and the Saxon as we once popularly imagined; that they are not truly what Lord Lyndhurst called them—*aliens in blood* from us; but that they are our brothers in the great Indo-European family, has had a share, an appreciable share, in producing this changed state of feeling."

The same ready writer shows that there are no greater foes to England than those who, from want of science and from prejudice, disclaim, as had been done in times past, right against the Irish. From the study of the language, of the laws and history of Ireland, Englishmen begin to learn that they are nearer a-kin to Irishmen than they had supposed.

The sons of Ireland, on the other hand, knowing from the same course of study themselves better, and the noble race from whom they have sprung, will learn to negative the saying of Moore—

> "Unprized are her sons till they learn to betray;
> Undistinguished they live, if they shame not their sires;
> And the torch that should light them to liberty's way
> Must be caught from the pyre where their country expires.

They will learn that it is not treason to love, nor death to defend a country so ancient, once so renowned for arts, laws, learning, civilisation. Knowledge, like the sun-light, throws a shower of bright coloring of beauty and life over all; makes things be seen fully and known better; ignorance, like night, prevents perception, produces persecution; begets tyranny in rulers, hatred and revenge in the souls of the oppressed.

CHAPTER XV.

Gaelic poetry the casket of nearly all Gaelic literature. Wonderful ability in versifing possessed by the bards. From a Keltic source spring the style and natural magic of English poetry. The Keltic element was not banished out of Britain by the coming of the Saxon. Germans are singularly devoid of style. The Gaels possess it in an eminent degree; their quick feeling gives them style; their high sensibility and aesthetic sense give them a higher gift, a lucid power at description. The magic of Romance is surely Keltic. Rhyme. It has certainly come from a Keltic source; reasons; authority. Men ignorant of the true cause of effects invariably assign—like the old philosophers who stated that nature abhored a vacuum a feigned cause to suit the emergency and defect of knowledge. Even clever men, like Thomas Moore and Lord Macauley, have fallen into this mistake. Their presumed knowledge is the cause of error to thousands. Versification as practised by Irish bards. Its qualities. Perfect assonance one of the qualities. Perfect assonance, when found in the final syllable, constitutes rhyme. Druids of the Continent. Eire's Brehons. They directed the literary life of the youth of the nation. Youths flocked to their schools. Hymnology. Latin hymns of the Church composed like the Gaelic poems. The style of versification not Roman or Greek, but Irish. Hymns composed by Irishmen in the fifth century—Sedulius, Secundinus; and by St. Ambrose, who was a native Kelt of Gaul. Their school adopted that style, and not the Latin. The Early Church embodied those hymns in her liturgy.

Sir Henry Sumner Maine (*Lectures on the Early History of Institutions*) says: "The ancient laws of Ireland have come down to us as an assemblage of law tracts, each treating of some one subject, or a group of subjects." And having told what these law tracts were, he adds: "It is extremely likely that the most ancient law was preserved in rude verse, or rhythmical prose." Sir Henry appears, as he gets into his subject, to acquire a fuller knowledge of it, and accordingly further on in his lectures he writes: "In the olden Irish traditions, the lawyer is distinguished with difficulty from the poet; poetry from literature." He thus points out poetry as the casket that contains the most precious gems of Keltic literary value. And still further on in his lectures he identifies Gaelic literature with poetry: "All literature, including even law, seems to have been identified with poetry." To have stated this much on one's own authority would not be valued by the scholar or by those of the British people who read this volume. The writer has therefore deemed it wise to present Sir Henry Sumner Maine's words, as he is the latest, the safest, and the best legal authority on the three volumes of the Brehon Law, already published; and Sir Henry cannot be considered by the English student as partial to the law or to the language of the ancient Gael.

It is not necessary at this stage to quote either Zeuss, Nigra, O'Curry, or Dr. Sullivan on the knowledge of the ancient Irish in the art of composing in metrical strains; or, of committing and of reciting the poems and songs of the bards. No scholar at present denies the surprising powers of intellect, of imagination, and memory possessed by the ancient Irish.

FROM A KELTIC SOURCE SPRING THE STYLE AND NATURAL MAGIC OF ENGLISH POETRY.

Mathew Arnold says: "If I were asked where English poetry got these three things—its turn for style, its turn for melancholy, and its turn for natural magic, for catching and rendering the charm of nature in a wonderfully clear and vivid way—I should answer, with much doubt, that it got much of its turn for style from a Keltic source; with less doubt, that it got much of its melancholy from a Keltic source; with no doubt at all, that from a Keltic source it got nearly all its natural magic."

"It is in our poetry that the Keltic part in us (English) has left its trace clearest. The Keltic element was not banished out of Britain by the coming of the Angles or the Saxon."—*Study of Keltic Literature, p.* 135.

"The turn of style is perceptible all through English poetry, proving the genuine poetical gift of the race; this turn imparts to our poetry a stamp of high distinction, and sometimes it doubles the force of a poet not by nature of the very highest order, such as Gray, and raises him to a rank beyond what his natural richness and power seem to promise. Gœthe, with his fine critical perception, saw clearly enough both the power of style in itself and the lack of style in the literature of his own country. He had to try and create out of his own powers a style for German poetry, as well as to provide contents for this style to carry; and thus his labor as a poet was doubled. . . . Style, then, the Germans are singularly without. . . . . But the Kelts have it in a wonderful measure. Style is the most striking quality of their poetry. Keltic poetry seems to make up to itself for being unable to master the world and give an adequate interpretation of it, by throwing all its force into style, by bending language at any rate to its will, and expressing the ideas it has, with unsurpassable intensity, elevation, and effect."

"Take this epitaph of an Irish Kelt, Angus the Culdee, whose *Felire*, or festology at the end of the eighth or beginning of the ninth century, he collected from the countless hosts of the illuminated books of Erin, giving the festivals of the Irish saints, his poem having a stanza for every day in the year. The epitaph on Angus, who died at Cluain Eidhnech, in Queen's County, runs thus

> Angus in the assembly of heaven,
> Here are his tomb and his bed;
> It is from hence he went to death,
> In the Friday—to holy heaven.
>
> It was in Cluain Eidhnech he was reared;
> It was in Cluain Eidhnech he was buried;
> In Cluain Eidhnech of many crosses
> He first read his psalms.

"That (says the Professor of Poetry of Oxford University) is by no eminent hand; and yet a Greek epitaph could not show a finer perception of what constitutes propriety and felicity of style in compositions of this nature."

THE MAGIC OF ROMANCE—KELTIC.

"The Kelt's quick feeling for what is noble and distinguished gave his poetry style; his indomitable personality gave it pride and passion; his sensibility and nervous exaltation gave it a better gift still—the gift of rendering, with wonderful felicity, the magical charm of nature. The forest solitude, the bubbling spring, the wild flowers are everywhere in romance. They have a mysterious life and grace there; they are nature's own children, and utter her secret in a way which makes them something quite different from the woods, the waters, and plants of Greek and Latin poetry. Now, of this delicate magic, Keltic Romance is so pre-eminent a mistres, that it seems impossible to believe the power did not come into romance from the Kelts. Magic is just the word for it—the magic of nature, not merely the beauty of nature—that the Greeks and Latins had; not merely an honest smack of the soil, a faithful realism, that the Germans had; but the intimate life of nature, her weird power and her fairy charm." The troubadours and those who recorded the events of the holy wars were chiefly from France, Spain, Belgium, and Northern Italy—the Keltic garden of Europe! Their weird tales were only their bardic tales revived on a grander scale.

RHYME.

Amongst the many important results from the modern study of Gaelic, as a language and as a branch of philology, is the certainty that from the "dáns," or songs of the Kelts has come the use of rhyme in modern European poetry.

The human mind seeks for knowledge, which is the atmosphere that supports the vitality of truth. The greatest of philosophers and theologians tells us that truth is the expression of the mind, declaring that a thing is what in reality it is; and that it is not that which it is not. There must be an agreement between the object and the mind that forms a notion of it. If in reality an object does not exist, the mind forms one according to its own fancy. This process of mental action is plain, if one only reflect how he frames his thoughts and make them the messengers of objective science. For instance, fame tells us of some celebrated personage whom we have never seen. Instinctively the mind pictures to itself some definite image of the object—one of its own creation,—and clothes it with robes which the light of fancy gilds with choicest coloring.

In this way, English literary writers of the past—not those of the present, who have written within the past ten years—have acted regarding the subject of rhyme in modern poetry. They knew that rhyme is found at the present time in poetry of every language throughout Europe. Where did it come from? Not from Latin poetry as practised by the Romans; not from the Greek, because the Greeks never knew anything about rhyme; not from Germany, for the ancient Germans did not regard rhyme as a requisite of poetic composition. Men ignorant of the true cause of an effect, like the philosophers of old, who, not being able to account for the fact that a fluid ascended an exhausted tube, said that it was because nature abhored a vacuum, feign a cause rather than admit their want of knowledge. Hence, not knowing the origin of rhyme, sciolists and mere literateurs stated that it must have been borrowed from the Saracens. Those who made this statement did not know Keltic poetry. Even good, clever, and learned men make great blunders on subjects concerning which they have not had any scholarly knowledge. For instance, Thomas Moore, the poet and historian, spoke slightingly of the value, to the historian of Ireland, of the materials afforded by Irish manuscripts. It was only in 1839, when he saw the enormous pile of Irish MS.S. in the Royal Irish Academy, that he admitted such splendid works *were not composed by fools, or for any foolish purpose.* Lord Macaulay played a similar part, and declared to Sir Robert Peel that the invaluable collection of Irish manuscripts in the Stowe Library were not worth the purchase, when, in 1849, his opinion had been asked by the Conservative Chief regarding their worth for the British Museum. Lord Macaulay himself knew nothing of their value, and therefore did not care, and consequently advised Sir Robert Peel not to purchase them. The presumed knowledge of scholars undoubtedly great in other departments lead many astray.

Men who have studied Irish poetry express their opinion forcibly and favorably on the subject of rhyme ject of rhyme, and say, with strong reason, that it is to the Kelts of Gaul and Ireland, Europe owes the poetic property of rhyme in modern metrical composition.

What says Zeuss, the greatest of German Keltic scholars, and his authority alone is worth that of a thousand others?

"In ea assonantia, origo prima assonantiæ *finalis* est, cultæ præsertim a populis recentioribus Europæ quam dicunt rimum." And he shows in a note that the word *rimum* (rhyme) is of Irish origin: "Quamvis ea vox computationem poeticam indicans in vetustis libris Hibernicis non occurrat, frequentissimi tamen est usus. Simplex Hibernica substantiva *rim*, inde derivatur *rimire*, computator."

The authority of Mathew Arnold, Professor of Poetry in the University of Oxford, ought on a subject relating to English poetry to have great weight with the English reader, both because he is a man of great learning, especially in poetry, and is an impartial witness on this special subject of Gaelic learning; moreover he is a man of honour and truth. He declares that "Rhyme is the most striking characteristic of our modern poetry as distinguished from that of the ancients, and a main source to our poetry of its magic charm of what we call its *romantic element*: rhyme itself, all the weight of evidence tends to show, comes into our poetry from the Kelts."

VERSIFICATION AS PRACTISED BY IRISH BARDS.

Was their versification founded on quantity or on accent, on measure alone, on assonance, alliteration, or parallelism? It was founded on none of these exclusively; not on quantity, as practised by the Greeks and Latins, which any one skilled in Latin prosody may readily learn by analyzing an Irish quatrain; nor on accent only. Of course it is true that accent plays a part in all kinds of versification. Nor was the ancient Irish metre one merely of measure, of assonance, or parallelism. It embraced all these qualities, some one of which was considered by other people specially essential in constituting verse. It is no wonder, then, that it has been pronounced by O'Molloy "the most difficult kind of composition under the canopy of heaven."

In reading the poetry of the ancient bards, either published or still in MS., one cannot fail to perceive in Irish verse composition that the following requisites have been deemed either essential or necessary:

1. Each stanza is a quatrain of four lines.
2. In each line there are seven syllables generally.
3. Of these, some must necessarily be *alliterative.*
4. Assonance is indispensable.
5. Rhyme, therefore, if the assonance be perfect.
6. Rhythm, as well as rhyme, lends its symphony.
7. Parallelism of thought is often—of words, usually—employed.
8. Each line expresses a judgment. The same word in the same sense is never used twice in a stave.
9. Special kinds of verse require (1) a syllable to be annexed to the prescribed number; or that (2) the final term in the second and fourth lines, or first and second lines, consist of one syllable more than that of the other verse in the same couplet; or that (3) there exist a certain alliteration or assonance. These specialities Irish bards and grammarians have distinguished by specific names.

"Assonance is an essential quality of ancient Irish Bardic poetry; but assonance when full, or perfect, at the end of a verse or line is rhyme. Therefore, rhyme had, as perfect assonance been found in ancient Gaelic versification. In perfect assonance the same vowel-sound, and the same accent must be repeated. This repetition, if it happen in the closing syllable of a line, constitutes rhyme, provided the final consonant and the accent are of the same kind as those in the closing of the preceding line.

(See *College Irish Grammar* for a full account of the prosody of ancient Irish Bardic poetry.)

Versification with these requisites was practiced before the Christian period. If it was so then, of course the Kelts had learned this art from those who preceded them; and a knowledge of this kind can be traced up to the early Aryan period, to the time when the emigration from the cradle-land of the race in the East took place.

From those examples now furnished—drawn as they are from the best authenticated sources—it is evident, first, that in the second, third, and sixth and subsequent centuries, the Irish bards and *filidh* composed verses in which (1) *assonance*, (2) *alliteration*, (3) *rhyme*, (4) *parallelism*, were essential qualities; that versification without some of these essential requisites was never tolerated by the bards. And bearing in mind that the bardic laws and regulations were very binding, and that all the Keltic races have adhered to the traditions and teachings of their progenitors, as Zeuss remarks: "*Morum priscorum semper tenacissimi fuerunt Celtici populi*," we must infer, secondly, that the Irish bards and *filidh* who flourished several centuries before the Christian era practised, as our historical annals testify, the same kind of versification which was in use in the early Christian ages. And the third conclusion to be drawn is that which Zeuss attests—the Druids and bards of Wales and Gaul practised the same kind of versification in which the bards and *filidh* of Eire composed their hymns and elegies. . . . Another inference is this, that the Keltic inhabitants of Gaul, Cambria, and Eire knew enough about rhyme and its use; that Keltic bards of Eire and Gaul put that knowledge into practice 2,000 years before the Saracens came to enlighten Europe.

These views receive authoritative force from the words of the learned scholar and critic, Rev. Edward Davies, Chancellor, at one time, of Christ's Church, Brecon, Cambria. It is admitted in all quarters with S. Turner, the historian, and Matthew Arnold shows the fact clearly, that the Cambro-Britons have considerable remains of poetry preserved since the sixth century. "Whom, then," asks Davies, "should the bards of the sixth century have imitated but their predecessors, in their own country, and who had composed in their own language? What had they to do with the Saracens? Nothing. "And he adds: "Or with the monks of Italy?" Had he known the history of hymnology fully at that time, he would not ask this last question; for the monks of Italy had, at the time, actually acquired from the Kelts the knowledge and the style of writing those hymns sung by the Church from the time of St. Ambrose and St. Augustine. "Had not sufficient proofs been adduced," he asks again, "that *rhyme* was generally known in Europe as early as the first century of our era? Yet, it was specially known to the Kelts, among whom we find it in full establishment."

RHYME, NOT FROM ARABIA.

The conclusion to be drawn as certain from the facts now known is, that rhyme in modern European poetry has not had its origin in Arabic or Saracen literature; not in

Roman or Grecian versification, but radically in the phonetic force of Gaelic vowel assimilation (explained in chapter X of this volume), and directly and immediately, in those laws by which poetry amongst the Keltic nations, in Christian and pre-Christian times, had been brought to the highest state of literary cultivation. This view put forward by the present writer, some fifteen years ago, is confirmed by the authority of Signor Constantinus Nigra, Italian Ambassador, before the late Franco-German war, at the Court of the Tuileries,—"Origo enim rimæ Arabica, inter fabulas omnino rejicienda est." As if he said, the idea that rhyme has come from any Arabic source should be scouted. Long before Tarik ben Zaid, with his fearless Arab force, had (A.D. 711) conquered Murcia, Granada, and Andulacia; nay, long before the founder of Islamism had (A.D. 622) fled from Mecca to Medina, bards in Eire and Gaul had composed songs and poems in which rhyme was one of the most distinguishing characteristics.

Signor Nigra devotes to this most interesting subject a chapter in the late work, "*Glossæ Hibernicæ*," (published at Paris, 1869) on the Irish M.SS. found at Turin. The chapter is most interesting; it is written in Latin of the highest classical style and of the purest kind. He says, in plain terms, that rhyme could not possibly have sprung from a Latin source; and he is right. Neither in reality, nor in name had such a thing as rhyme been ever known of old in Latin poetry.

"Porro rimæ ex solo naturali processu Latinæ linguæ explicari nullo modo potest. Apud Latinos nec res existit nec nomen. Assonantiam finalem Latini poetæ nunquam quæsiverunt immo semper sedulo evitaverunt. Neque in incultis Romanæ plebis vel Romanorum militum cantilenis, quæ supersunt, etiam in illis in quibus metrica forma jam deficit, ullum rimæ deprehenditur vestigium."

I hesitate not to affirm that rhyme has had its rise from the laws which direct the use of assonance in the Keltic dialects:

"Rimam a legibus assonantiæ Celticæ originem ducere affirmare non dubito, says Nigra."

Accent and a uniform number of feet in a line may have been derived in part from Greek, or Latin, or German; but rhyme, never.

Again, in the same chapter in the *Glossæ Hibernicæ veteris codicis Taurinensis*, 1869, p. 32, he says: "Rimam seu assonantiam finalem a solis Celticæ phonologiæ legibus derivatam esse."

And this assonance in the syllables of a word, in the middle as well as at the close of a line of poetry, is peculiar to the Keltic dialects of the Aryan family of languages.

"Hæc regula quæ jam late obtinet in documentis Hibernicis et Britannicis septimi et octavi seculi et multo amplius in posterioribus, *assonantia Celtica* noncupari potest, *peculiaris est et propria* (inter ariani stipitis idiomata) solis Celticis linguis."

This law of assonance, so peculiar to Gaelic, has its origin in the same principle—vowel assimilation—from which the rule "slender with slender and broad with broad" has sprung.—See c. ix. supra.

"Eadem est utriusque assonantiæ genesis, eadem ratio, idem processus."

DRUIDS OF THE CONTINENT, AND EIRE'S BREHONS.

Sir Henry Maine's views on this point are corroborative of the relation between the Kelts of the Continent and Eire, and their practice of composing and of treasuring their compositions in the store-house of the memory.

"There are a few very important points of detail to be

noticed in Cæsar's description of what may be called the lay portion of Keltic society. . . . He tells us that the Druids were supreme judges in all public and private disputes, and that all questions were referred to them." The same tendencies which produced among the Kelts of the Continent the class called the *Druids*, produced among the Kelts of Ireland the class known to us as the Brehons, in this way.

The Tribe-Chief, or King, whom the earliest Aryan records show us standing by the side of the popular assembly, was Priest and Judge, as well as King, that is head or captain of the host. The later Aryan history shows us this blended authority distributing, or differentiating itself and passing either to the assembly or to a new class of depositories. Among the Acheans of Homer, the chief has ceased to be priest, but he is still judge. Among the Kelts, both of Gaul and of Ireland, he has ceased to be priest, and almost ceased to be judge. In Athenian history the institution of Kingship survived only in the name King Archon, or Judge-King, and in Roman history in priest-king—"Rex Sacrificulus."

The difference between the *Druids* and their successors, the *Brehons*, would then be mainly this: The Brehons would be no longer priests. Kings have delegated their authority to judge to the Brehons, or authors of judgment. But the literary character of the Druid and judge remained unchanged. The Druid on the Continent, and the judge or Brehon in Ireland presided over the national literary life of the country.

The Druids presided over schools of learning, to which the Keltic youth flocked eagerly for instruction, remaining, as Cæsar tells, "in their schools for twenty years." Pupils learned an enormous quantity of verses, which they never committed to writing, and the object of this, it seems, was not merely to prevent sacred knowledge from being popularised, but to strengthen the memory, and to fit the scholar for the post of Ollamh, or judge, or Druid. (Cæsar de Bello Gallico, liber vi., c. 13, 14.) In Cæsar's account of the Druids there is not a word, says Maine, that is not perfectly credible. The Kelts of the Continent were before all things remarkable for the literary class which their society included. Now, the schools of literature and law appear to have been numerous in ancient Ireland, and O'Curry gives the course of instruction in one of them, extending over the space of twelve years. The chief Druid of Cæsar meets us on the very threshold of the Senachus Mor, in the person of Dubhtach Mac ua Lugair, the Royal poet of Erinn—the Brehon who was chosen by St. Patrick to arbitrate in a question of homicide, and whose mouth the Saint blessed. The preface of the Senachus Mor actually contains disquisitions on all the matters which Cæsar declares the Druids to have been specially fond of arguing. It sets forth how God made the Heavens and the Earth. It goes off, as Cæsar's Druids did, into a number of extraordinary statements, "*de sideribus atque eorum motu; de mundi ac terrarum magnitudine.*" The Irish Brehon was, therefore, in the literary world, amongst the Gaels of Ireland, what the Druid was on the Continent of Europe. His style of teaching, and the instructions he imparted, and the form of language in which he required his pupils to commit these instructions to memory, were the same. And this conclusion is confirmed by the authority of Zeuss.

Further—Maine states, it is now generally agreed that the voluminous Sanscrit literature in verse which embraces the poetry and most of the religion of the Hindoos, and much of what stands to them in place of history and law, was originally preserved by recollection and published by recitation; and even now, in the Sanscrit schools which remain, the pupil is trained to exercises of memory which is little short of miraculous to an Englishman.

HYMNOLOGY.

And this brings the reader to another important question—the Hymnology of the Catholic Church. It must be borne in mind that the bards of Ireland and the Keltic bards of the Continent—in Gaul, in Helvetia, in the north of Italy—composed in the same style of versification.

The present writer claims to be the first who discovered that the Latin hymns sung in the divine office of the Church have been, as a rule, composed, not in the style of versification known amongst Greeks and Latins, but in that adopted by the Kelts of Ireland and of the Continent.

From the close of the fourth century Latin hymns have been composed and sung in the Catholic Church—seculo quarto obeunte, et quinto incipiente, (Nigra). Anterior to that period, even in the time of St. Paul, hymns were usually sung in the synagogues. On the very night of the Last Supper, our Divine Lord and the Apostles sang a hymn before they proceeded to Mount Olivet. The hymns, however, known to the Jews at the time, and to the Early Christians, were recited rather than sung, much in the same way as the Jews to this day read the Hebrew psalms, or clergymen and canons of the Catholic Church recite the divine office in choir; much in the way that the Greeks of Ionia, and of the islands, those of Athens, and Sparta sang the rhapsodies of Homer, in a recitative strain, prolonging the tone at the cæsura or break in each half-line.

There are for the past fourteen hundred years, about

one hundred and fifty Latin hymns in the books of devotion in use amongst the children of the Catholic Church. Nine out of ten of these hymns are written in the same style as that in which the Irish people of the early period wrote their native "dáns." Of these hymns (1) some are composed in the metre of the poetic prototypes according to which Horace and Terence wrote—(*a*) Iambic trimetre, (*b*) iambic tetrametre, (*c*) sapphic, with a closing adonic to complete the strophé. Others have been composed irrespective of the laws of Latin versification. . . . As a matter of fact, however, the whole of this latter class, and a great many of the former, are written in verses of the same number of syllables, and adorned with the same phonetic qualities in which the bards of Keltic Gaul, of Cambria, of Eire, composed. How account for this fact? The hymnologists must . . . have learned of the Keltic bards, or the Keltic bards learned of them. The latter part of this proposition cannot be admitted—chronology and facts are against it. Again, Zeuss says, this form of versifying was unknown and entirely foreign to poets of classical antiquity.

THE WRITERS OF THE LATIN HYMNS WERE IRISHMEN OR NATIVES OF KELTIC GAUL.

The hymns sung in the Church prior to the period in which Urbam VIII. flourished, were composed either by (1) Irishmen, such as Sedulius, Columbanus, Columba, Secundinus; or (2) by men of Keltic origin, as St. Ambrose; (3) or those who, like St. Augustine, were of the same metrical school with St. Ambrose; or lastly (4) those who flourished between the fourth century and the fourteenth, and followed in the composition of hymns the metre and melody of the great master of hymnology, St. Ambrose. With regard to the first, they, like St Fiach, Bishop of

Sletty, wrote in Irish "dán díreac," and in that species of it called séadna, which contained eight syllables. . . . For men who understood Latin so well, that in all the ancient manuscripts we find they wrote alternately in Latin and Irish, the transition from Irish to Latin versification was quite natural and easy. When, therefore, one finds such hymns as those which an Irishman, Sedulius, composed:

"A solis ortus cardine,"

and

"Hostis Herodes impie,"

written like the Irish odes of the time, the proof is complete that that manner of composing hymns was borrowed from the Irish bards.

St. Ambrose wrote at least six out of ten of the early hymns, so much so that hymns were styled Ambrosiani.

"Assonantia finalis vel rima, seculo quarto obeunto et quinto incipiente vulgaris ævi, primum occurrit in hymnis Latinis ecclesiæ modiolanensis qui Sancto Ambrosio et Sancto Augustino tribuuntur. Prima itaque rimæ certa exempla inveniuntur in solo Celtico, apud Celticas gentes, in carminibus conditis a poetis qui vel Celticæ originis sunt, vel apud Celticas gentes diu commoraverunt."

The conclusion is therefore certain that it is from the lessons of the Irish or Keltic bards that the early Latin hymnologists (natives of Ireland or Kelts of the Continent) imbibed the style of writing hymns and sacred poems. A great school of poets of this class sprung up in the fifth century, the sixth, seven, and eighth. The style of writing these hymns became wedded to the literature of the Church, just as the metrical songs in English were wedded, by Moore, to the genius of Irish melody. As the native Irish melodies are not lost, but are revived in a new phonology—English—surrounded with all the old "airs" of centuries; so the Keltic style of composing in verse was not lost, but wedded thus to the melody of the Catholic Church, it sprang anew into life and became the tuneful mother of sacred song, and of all the rhythmical effusions of modern Europe. Even Greece in her popular songs of to-day has given up poetry—according to the metrical mode of quantity—and (A.D. 500) has adopted accent, and the Gaelic grace, alliteration, assonance, rhyme. Learned men must conclude that Irish Gaelic had been, at one period, better cultivated than Sanskrit; and secondly, that in all that relates to the doctrine of phonology, alliteration, assonance, rhyme, &c., Irish Gaelic is infinitely superior.

In the nineteenth, and in the sixty-first volume *Patrologiæ Cursus Completus*, published in Paris by Abbe, J. P. Migne, the learned reader will find poems written by Sedulius and Secundinus, scholars of the fith century. Sedulius's poems, composed in the style known to the Irish bards of the period, fill two hundred and fifty pages.

Whoever has a taste for style, and the study of this kind of literature, hitherto much ignored by English readers; whoever wishes to learn the origin of European poetry will find a treasure in the two volumes of the *Leabar Imuinn, or Book of Hymns of the Ancient Church of Ireland*, edited from M.SS., with translation and notes, by Rev. James H. Todd, Fellow of Trinity College, Dublin, and published, the one in 1855, the other in 1869, for the Irish Archaeological Society. The preface to each hymn is a mixture of old Irish and Latin—according to the custom of Gaelic writers of the period—some few of the hymns are in Irish.

Two or three examples to illustrate the style in which the Irish bards wrote in Latin as well as in their native Gaelic are here given:

FOURTH CENTURY—Hymn, by *Caius Cœlius Sedulius*—He was an Irishman, of the name of "Siadal" (Shiel) *s* before *i* has in Irish the same sound that *sh* in English receives; *d*, aspirated in the middle of a word, is equal in sound to *y* (English). He left the shores of his native country before St. Patrick had come to preach the Gospel in Ireland. He was then a Pagan; he travelled through France and Italy, where he received the light of the Christian Faith—*ad fidem Catholicam conversus*—he travelled through Greece, and Asia; taught poetry in Achaia; was ordained priest; returned to Rome. St. Jerome gives a summary of his live: "Sedulius versificus, primo laicus, in Italia philosophiam didicit; inde ad fidem Catholicam conversus; postea cum aliis metrum heroicum, Macedonio consulente, docuit in Achaia. Libros suos scripsit tempore Valentiniani et Theodosii." From this it is clear he lived, at least in the early part of the fifth century, for St. Jerome died A.D. 420. He was remarkable for extraordinary ability, wonderful learning, and great piety. By some writers he is styled Bishop. Had he lived in Ireland, like many of her ablest sons, his fame as a scholar would never have been known. That he was Irish, there is no doubt; for in his Commentaries (14 books) on the Epistles of St. Paul, he gives his name—*Sedulii Scoti Hiberniensis in omnes Epistolas Pauli collectaneum.*

A solis ortus card*ine*,
Ad usque terræ limit*em*,
Christum canamus princip*em*,
Natum Maria Virg*ine*.

In this stanza all the qualities deemed by the bards essential for Irish versification are found—eight syllables, alliteration—as c of Christum and *c* of canamus show: assonance, as *ine* and *em* point out—*ine* in cardine, and *ine* in virgine.—*From p. 763, tom. xix. Patrologiæ, Cursus Completus.*

FIFTH CENTURY.—The hymn of St. Columba—*In te Domine.* This hymn consists of thirty-three double verses, or lines; it is very beautiful, abounding in alliteration, assonance, parallelism, and all the graces of Irish bardic versification. There are only six lines given here. St. Columba was a scholar, a bard, a prince, a priest, and the Apostle of the Highlands:

Deus formator omnium; Deus et judex judicum;
Deus et *princeps principum*, elementorum omnium;

Deus *l*argus, *l*onganimis; *D*eus Doctor *d*ocibilis;
Deus qui facit omnia, nova cuncta et vetera:

Christus redemptor gentium; Christus amator virginum;
Christus fons sapientium; Christus fides credentium.

The words *j*udex, *j*udicum, *p*rinceps, *p*rincipum, and *l*argus *l*ongaminis, *D*eus, *d*octor, *d*ocibilis, show that alliteration is not overlooked.

Omni*um*, judic*um*, princip*um*, are instances of assonance (*us*, and *or*, and *is*, final syllables in first part, Deu*s*, larg*us*, longanim*is*, makes a parallelism with *us*, and *or*, and *is*, in the second part.) So, too, the final syllables of Christ*us*, redemt*or*, genti*um*, with those of Christ*us* amat*or*, virgin*um*. Each line expresses a proposition. In each the sense is complete.

Again—Read these four lines from another hymn, *Noli Pater*, by St. Columba, p. 262, vol. ii., *Book of Hymns*, by Dr. Todd:

Te timemus terribilem,
Nullum credentes simi*lem*;
Te cuncta canunt car*mina*
Angelorum per ag*mina*.

Alliteration—*T* in *te*, in *t*imemus, *t*erribilem.
C in *c*uncta, *c*anunt, and *c*armina.

Assonance, Rhyme, } *Bilem*, of terribilem; *milem*, of similem; *mina*, of carmina and agmina.

These few instances must suffice.

The writer has in his possession some twenty-five hymns in Irish Gaelic M.SS. attributed to St. Columba.

CHAPTER XVI.

A thousand volumes of unpublished Irish Gaelic still extant. Testimonies. Composed chiefly in and adorned with graces of Irish verse. The amazing literary labor of the Christian and pre-Christian Irish. Superiority of Irish Gaelic over Sanscrit, especially in the beautics of versification. Historic suggestiveness of Gaelic words. European Keltic area. Names of persons, places, things. Historical doubts cleared up. Rome called from the color of the Tiber's waters. Romulus from Romo. How the Sabines and Romans were amalgamated. Meaning of Quirites. Brennus. The Etruscan Lucumo. The Sabines were Gaels. Romans composed of four races. The Sabines lost their Gaelic, but gave to Rome their phonesis, and many of their civil and religious customs. Astronomical Gaelic terms were never borrowed from Rome—for at the time, in the early pagan period, Ireland had no connexion with Pagan Rome. Adolphe Pictet's proof of the Aryan origin of the Irish Gaelic and of the Irish Race. Frazer's Magazine. Conclusion. Summary of points proved. Shall the Gaelic language die?

A thousand volumes of unpublished Irish Gaelic are still extant. The highest testimony that can be presented on the subject of Irish manuscripts, the written assurance of Professor O'Loony, M.R.I.A., of the Catholic University, Dublin, and that of Rev. Professor O'Mahony, M.R.I.A. of Trinity College, Dublin—is offered as sufficient motive to convince the reader that the statement is only the expression of a fact. The learned reader may well be surprised, that after all the drowning and burning of Irish MSS by Danes for several centuries, and by Saxons for a period still longer, any codices of value should at all survive. Yet, there are one thousand still left to tell the tale of the literary, the social, political, and religious life of a people powerful at all times in vindicating the principles of science and religion, and ever prolific in productions of the mind.

In a letter to the present writer, dated March 20th, 1875, Professor O'Mahony says: "With regard to the number of Irish MSS yet unpublished, I am inclined to agree with Mr. O'Looney's opinion, that in all they do not fall far short of his estimate—that of one thousand volumes."

To strengthen the testimony of the living public witnesses—one from each of the two Universities in Ireland, the following from the late Professor O'Curry is brought forward:—"Notwithstanding the irreparable loss of the before-named books, there still exists an immense quantity of Gaelic writing of great purity and of the highest value as regards the history of this country. And these MSS. comprise general and national history; civil and ecclesiastical records, and abundant materials of genealogy, besides poetry, romance, law, and medicine, and some fragments of tracts on mathematics and astronomy."

The collection in Trinity College consists of over one hundred and forty volumes, several of them on vellum, dated from the early part of the twelfth down to the middle of the last century. There are also in this fine collection beautiful copies of the Gospels.

"The next great collection is that in the Royal Irish Academy, which, though formed at a later period than that of Trinity, is far more extensive, and taken in connection with the unrivalled collection of antiquities secured to this country by the liberality of this body, forms a national monument, of which we may well be proud. It includes some noble old volumes written on vellum, abounding in history as well as poetry, ancient law and genealogy, science, grammar, and romance. There is also a great body of most important theological and ecclesiastical compositions of the highest antiquity, and in the purest style, perhaps, that the Gaelic language ever attained."

Passing over some collections of M.SS. in private hands at home, I may next notice that of the British Museum in London, which is very considerable, and which contains much valuable matter; and next, that of the Bodleinn Library, Oxford, which is enriched by some most precious books.

Next comes the Stowe collection, now in the possession of Lord Ashburnham, and which is tolerably well described in the Stowe catalogue by the late Rev. Charles O'Connor. There are also in England some other collections of Irish manuscripts in the hands of private individuals.

There is a goodly collection in the College of St. Patrick, Maynooth, and in the possession of many private persons in Ireland.

Passing over to the Continent, in the National or Imperial Library of Paris, there are found a few Gaedhlic volumes, and in Belgium, and particularly in the Burgundian Library at Brussels.

Lastly, should be noticed the Irish glosses of the Latin M.SS. from which Zeuss drew the materials for the Irish portion of his celebrated *Grammatica Celtica* (*Leipsiæ* 1853).

Those manuscripts which Zeuss consulted are to be found in the libraries of St. Gall, of Milan, Bobbio, and throughout Germany—Wurtzburg, Carlsruh, Ratisbon—

and are the glosses written in Irish Gaelic, sometimes in Latin, on the margin, or between the written lines of the body of the work: "Hiberni codices vetustæ linguæ monumenta, servantes in copiosis præsertim glossis, interlinearibus plurimum, sæpius etiam marginalibus, in terra continente extant plures a monachis scripti Hibernis, jam a sæculo sexto per Europam continentem ad propagandam fidem Christianam dispersis."—*Zeuss.*

For example, at St. Gall, Switzerland, he found a manuscript copy of Priscian's famous work on grammar. This codex had been manifestly a copy made use of by a professor in Ireland, or from Ireland, for the margin of each page of fourteen books of the codex is laden with comments in the Irish language : magnam glossarum molem prebens, quibus refertus est.

The names of those scholars who wrote the glosses are given in the work; and Zeuss's own view on the authenticity and value of these M.SS. are seen in the preface to the *Grammatica Celtica.* But that special view of the subject cannot here be allowed more than a passing allusion.

All the early ancient Irish writings are, speaking generally, composed in bardic verse. "Hoc solum annalium genus habebant quod in epicis carminibus et in narrationibus metrice compositis consistet."—Henry Leo. Preface to his commentary on St. Fiacc's hymn in praise of St. Patrick.—*Halis Saxonum,* 1845.

The difficulty of writing in that style of verse is already known to any one who has read the chapter just brought to a close; each verse should consist of seven syllables, at times of eight ; each line should express a judgment, and form complete sense; alliteration and assonance, and consequently rhyme, at times should grace the verse; and parallelism of terms and thoughts should not be forgotten in building up the poetic stave With these golden links binding the poetic fancy it was difficult to soar. Yet, notwithstanding all obstacles, what a vast number of M.SS. volumes of verse had been written by the pagan and Christian bards in ancient Ireland! These M.SS. are standing proofs of the fostering care bestowed on the art of poetry by the literary sons of Eire.*

SANSKRIT AND GAELIC POETRY CONTRASTED.

In Sanskrit song or poem there is not a trace of alliteration, of assonance or rhyme; all that is found is an equal number of syllables in each recurring verse. "Antiqui Indi pari syllabarum numero versum ligaverunt." These are the words of Nigra, that the ancient Indians moulded their poetic thoughts in verse of the same number of syllables. None of the metrical qualities which Gaelic bards require is found in old Indian poetry. Irish Gaelic is therefore immensely superior in metrical developement to Sanskrit.

Besides the splendid and varied literary developements just named, that have come before the learned reader's view in studying the subject of Irish bardic versification, which is only a single department in the school of Gaelic study; other features of an interesting and a striking character still remain to be presented.

The present volume has increased in size many pages beyond the number contemplated; and hence the reasons not yet adduced—favorable to the study of Irish Gaelic—must, however deserving of developement on account of the literary interest with which they are entwined, be summarised for the present.

---

* The fullest record of Irish M.SS. is that just published by Rev. John O'Hanlon in his learned introduction to *Lives of the Saints, Vol. 1., pp.* 136-160.

Not only the Irish Brehon Law, and the Gaelic poems in matter as well as in form, but the very terms of the Irish Gaelic language are full of rich suggestiveness of historic interest.

EUROPEAN KELTIC AREA.

The topography of Europe is a history in Gaelic of the migrations of the Keltic race.

From the classical researches of Latham, one sees at a glance the wide range of territory which a Gaelic speaking race at one time occupied. They spread over Helvetia (modern Savoy and Switzerland), Rhœtia, or the Tyrol; Styria, Carinthia, Illyria, Dalmatia, the lower Danube, the Bastarnæ, the Galetæ, Wurtemburg, Bavaria, Bohemia, Thracia, Macedonia, Græcia, Galatia (in Asia Minor), Belgium, middle Rhine, the Ligurians, the Spanish Peninsula, Italia, Gallia, Britannia, Hibernia, or Scotia Major, Caledonia or Scotia Minor, the Isle of Man, and the islands to the west and north.

The original Keltic area is one thing, the areas into which the Kelts intruded themselves is another. Germany is the original English area. England, and still more America, are areas into which the English have intruded.

The Keltic area, then, according to Dr. Latham (see supplementary chapter in new edition of Prichard's *Keltic Nations, by Dr. Latham*, published by Bernard Quaritch, London, 1857,) extends over the foregoing territories:

NAMES OF PERSONS.

"How interesting," says Geddes, "it is to know that the leader under whom the Gauls poured down upon Rome in 390 B.C., bore among the Romans the name *Brennus*, and that this is still the Gaelic name for *judge* and *judgment*, *Breitheanas*, proving that the Gauls were under a social organisation at the time when the office of a king was not so much to lead in war, as to dispense judgment and administer justice. It is strange to find the same name appearing also in the leader of the irruption into Greece a century later, down upon Delphi, a portion of which band afterwards became the occupants of Galatia in the heart of Asia Minor."

How interesting to know that the greatest of Roman Epic writers was a Kelt of Cisalpine Gaul, as Zeuss assures us—*nomen Gallicæ originis*, for it is certain that *Virgilius*, or Vergilius (Virgil), is derived from the Irish term "fear," *a man* (*Gen. and Voc. fir*); and "gil" (*Gen and Voc.* of "geal," *white*).

"It might be," says Geddes, "hazardous to say what the *gilius* (of *Virgilius*) signifies, but of the *Vir* there can be no doubt; and the assurance is made all the surer by the old form *Vergilius*, to which the critics are now returning, which suits admirably the singular of the Keltic "fear" *a man*."

Regarding this observation of Geddes, the present writer does not deem it hazardous to say what *gilius* signifies; it means *white* or *fair*. Take away the usual ending *us*, or *ius*, and there remains the term *gil*, which is either *voc.* (or *gen*) case of "geal," *white*; that is *Virgil*, means *fair-haired man!* *Vergel* is the form that the word should assume if it were derived from the uninflected terms "fear" and "geal."

Critics are now aware that *Vergel* is the correct form at least in spelling. *Vergel* has been actually found to have been in use at the very earliest period.

The name of the most illustrious Roman historian of the Augustan Age—a native of Padua, as his name Titus Livius Patavinus clearly shows—the name of Pliny (born at Como) the most distinguished philosopher and scholar of the age in which he flourished, or in any age, as a writer of natural history and as a botanist, worthy of honour next to the great Grecian who is the founder of the school of Natural History, Aristotle, are, in the opinion of Zeuss, of Keltic origin—" Addo et Livius et Plinius nomina Gallica Italiæ superioris."

INSTANCES OF THE GREAT VALUE OF GAELIC IN QUESTIONS OF HISTORY.

Irish Gaelic sets to rest the question how " Quirites," the old name for the Sabino-Roman people, and " Quirinus," and Quirinal, is derived. Some say the term sprang from the name " Cures," a town in Sabine territory, because many Sabines had come from that locality. But all Keltic scholars now know that the name is derived from a Sabine word *Curis*, or *Quiris, a spear*; Gaelic " cuir," *a spear*; hence " Curaıd" in Irish: warrior, a spearman, as " Curaıd an Craoıḃ ruaıd," the *Knights of the Royal Branch*. The warrior-god of the Sabines was " Quirinus," that is, the " spear-god;" the people who served him, " Quirites," meaning " warrior-race," from " curıd,' heroes, and " aos," a race, a class. Hence the Romans were addressed in the Senate House by that title, " Quirites" or warrior comrades; the Quirinal was the " aıl," an elevated site where the Sabine warriors had, close to the Romans, taken up their abode.

Thus the Gaelic language throws much light on these simple points of historic interest regarding the Romans, and the Gauls; the Romans and the Sabines. The view just presented is true; for it is confirmed by the known laws and habits of the Sabine population. They were divided into " clans," like the Gaels in Ireland; each clan was a separate power; it could make laws to regulate its own members; it had its own religious rites; could make war. Attus Clausus was the "Ceand" or *head* of a clan of five thousand fighting men of the Sabine people. They obtained land in Rome, and formed the nucleus of the Claudian Tribe. The term *client*, too, is Gaelic, borrowed by the Romans from the language of their warrior-citizens, "Claınd," old form for "Clann," children. Now, from "Claınd" comes *client*, who bears to a patron the same relation in a remote way that children do to a father, or head of a "clan."

THE SABINES WERE GAELS.

"One of the four stocks of population out of which the mixed Roman people was made up spoke a tongue so much akin to Welsh and Gaelic, that we are justified (says Newman) in extending the term Keltic to embrace this Italian tribe. The Sabines, too, used a vocabulary which was akin to Gaelic. In fact, of all the Indo-European tongues none has so near a likeness to the Latin as the Gaelic has. The similarities of Gaelic to Latin are more striking than those of Welsh, although "the Gaelic races were *at that time* in Ireland, and were *never attacked* by the Romans." The people of Latium were made up of five races—the Pelasgians, the Umbrians, and Oscans, the Sabines and the Siculians. Each of these spoke a Keltic dialect; the Sabine speech was that most like to Gaelic.

A few common terms out of hundreds are here presented from the Sabine or warrior race:

COMMON TERMS.

Gaelic.	Latin.
Arm,	Arma.
Baıle,	Villa.
Caṫaır,	Castrum.

Claideam,	Gladius.
Gort, an enclosed space,	Cohors.
a garden,	Hortus.
Cata-tabal, battle-engine	Catapulta.
Fal,	Vallum
Fion, wine,	Vinum
Luireac	Lorica
Muneal, neck,	Monile, necklace
Mur, old Irish (wall)	Murus
Ord,	Ordo.
Rig, king,	Rex.
Saigead	Sagitta
Sgiath	Scutum
Seanad	Senatus
Sean-aois,	Senex.
Torc,	Torquis.
Treib	Tribus
Tarb	Taurus

These few names are, as Newman observes, all native to Keltic, or to Gaelic, while very few of them bear marks of being native to Latin. A new language, the *Latin*, came forth from the depurating admixture. The Gaelic form was lost ; its strength and phonesis survived in the Latin.

NAMES OF PLACES.

The names of the Tyrol, Helvetia, Italia, Rhætia, of the rivers Rhine, Rhone, Garonne, Seine, Danube, and of towns throughout Europe, present a Keltic complexion. The reader must be asked to read Zeuss.—*Gram. Cel. B. I., Newman's Rome, Latham, Prichard.*

Rome, or Roma means *town on the Yellow River*; "ruad" *red*, or *rufus*, and "an," that is, "aban" river; for the Tiber had at first been called *Rumon*, again *Albula*, and finally

"*Thybris.*" The first name was that given by the earliest Gaelic speaking settlers—as is their wont—from the nature of the waters of that turbid stream. The names Romulus and Remus are evidently taken, as Newman thinks, from Roma itself; "nor is there a single fact concerning either of these personages which has the slightest pretence to be called historical." *Romulus*, then, means Hero-of-Rome, from "Roma," and "laoc," a hero; Laoċ is found in the Etruscan title of dignity, "Lucu-mo," hero-man; laoċ, hero; and "mo" a man, a person—found in "ne-mo," no-man; "ho-mo," *the* man. Remus is derived from the Gaelic "Reım," *power, sway*, for he is represented as one wishing to rule over Romulus and Rome.

The Tyrol, (tır and aıl), means hill-country; Helvetia, hill-land, or high-land; Rhodanus, the rapid river; from "ro" rapid, "an" for "aḃan," river; so, too, the Rhenus, the King (rıġ), river; or the splendid river. The term rıġ means, not only king, sovereign, supreme, but very excellent, even to this day; for one says in Gaelic "Tá se rıġ-ṁaiṫ," it is exceedingly good; "ta se ro-ṁaiṫ," it is over-good. Sequana (or Seine) is "seċ," separating, parting, and "ana" waters, for at Paris it is separated into two, or two rivers unite at that point: Garumna (Garonne) from "garḃ," rough, and "ana" waters, on account of its strong, billowy character, sadly exemplified just now in the destructive force of the rising floods of June that have devastated the south of France.

THE ASTRONOMICAL VALUE OF KELTIC.

"Dıa," is a term which under modified forms, *Deus, Theos, Zeus, Dios, Dio, Dieu, Jove*, the Indo-Europeans apply to the supreme Lord of Heaven and Earth.

The sun's light is regarded by them as the symbol of God. "Sub Dio" means either in the open day, or under

God. The Keltic races, regarding the sun-light as the sign of God's majestic presence, called the day by the same name as that by which they styled the supreme Being Himself—"Dıa." The name of *day* (Dıa) and the name of *God* (Dıa) are alike in Irish Gaelic. In Latin, which is a cousin of Gaelic, the names of God and of day differ very little—*Dies* (day) ; *Deus* (God.) "Luan," is the old Gaelic for moon, perhaps because that Satellite is quickly (luaṫ) changeable, and ever varying; "*Mart*" is the Irish of *Mars* (*Martis*); "Cedeın" is the Gaelic of Mercury (Latin); *Hermes* (Greek) of *Woden*, or *Oden* of the Germans; "*Tordan*," *thunderer*, the name in Gaelic of Jove, thundering, root "Toran;" Tonans, toran, noise, "toırneac," thunder ; *Thor* (German and English) ; "áın," beauty, the goddess or queen of beauty, hence the Irish Venus. "Saturn," Saturn ; "Sol," *Sol* (Latin) the sun ; "suıl," eye ; "saoıl," think, (that is, to see mentally.)

Irish, "Dıa luaın," Monday (moonday); French, *Lun-di*; Latin, *dies lunæ*.

Irish, "Dıa márt," Mars'-day ; Latin, *Dies Martis*; French, *mardi ;* German, *Tcut, i.e. Mars*; hence Teuton and Teutonic, meaning warlike ; English, *Tuesday*.

Irish, "Dıa cedeın," Wednesday, that is *Woden's day*, or *Odin's day*; Latin, *Dies Mercurii*; French, *mercredi ; Odin*, in Germany, is "Cedeın" of Ireland.

Irish, "Dıa Tordaın," that is, the thunderer's day—*Dies Jovis ;* French, *Jeudi*.

Irish, "Dıa aoıne," the day of "aıne," or the goddess of beauty ; Latin, *Dies Veneris ;* French, *vendredi*.

Irish, "Dıa Satuırn ;" Latin, *Dies Saturni ;* French *samedi*.

Irish, "Dıa Doṁnaıġ ;" Latin, *Dies Domini*; French, *Dimanche*, Lord's day ; anciently, "Dıa Soıl," or Sunday.

By these names the days of the week had been for a

number of past centuries known to scholars; yet, Ireland was free, all the time, from every inroad of Romans or foreigners. Therefore, she had taken these names from an earlier and a higher authority than from the hands of pagan Rome. Irishmen must, therefore, have had a knowledge of astronomy long before the nation received the light of faith from St. Patrick. The terms "bliadain," a year; and "belteine," the month of May, are also names that bring the reader back to pagan times, and connect the Irish race with that which had dwelt in the land to which Daniel had been conveyed into captivity, eastward of Jerusalem to the banks of the River Chobar. "Bliadain," year, is derived from "Bel"—the god-Bel, or sun, and "ain," a circle—that is, a circle of the sun through the twelve signs of the Zodiac. "Samhradh," Summer, means the warm season, from "samh," (pr. sáwv,) Latin, *suave;* "geimhradh," the sharp season; "fogar," Autumn, means the booty—(fog) of (ár) cultivation; "earrach," Spring, from "eirigh," arise. "Samhain," November, from "samh-fain," end of warm time. "Lugh-nósa," Louis' customs or plays, applied to August.

ADOLPHE PICTET'S PROOF.

It remains to point to another class of terms, regarding which Monsieur Adolphe Pictet has written four hundred pages octavo in his splendid work *Les Origines Indo-Europeennes ou les Aryas Primitifs.* Paris, 1859.

The names refer not only to the year and the seasons—Summer, Winter, Autumn, and Spring—but to snow, "sneacht;" frost, "sioc;" and ice, "oidir;" heat, "teas;" cold, "fuacht," the seas, "mara," mountains, "sleibhte," cliffs, "aill;" glens, "gleanta;" rocks, "corraig;" valleys, "fala;" the winds, "gaoth;" and waves, "tonna;" the waters, "uisge," and tides, "tuile;" the courses of waters; "sruṫ;" "aḃan," "an," "aḃ," "aw," and names of several rivers, lakes, and fountains. The natural history, too, of the minerals is not forgotten—gold, "ór;" silver, "airgead;" iron, "iaran;" brass, "prás;" copper, "uma;" tin, "stan;" lead "luaḋ." The trees and plants; the names of the different parts of tree, plant, flower; the different species and names of special kinds are analysed, and the philological value of each term compared with that by which in other languages the object is known, are contrasted. The animals, wild and tame, foreign and domestic; the reptiles—fish, mollusks, and insects—are brought before the readers's view, even as all kinds of creatures, the beasts of the earth, and all the fowls of the air were brought before the view of Adam in Paradise, who gave each a name according to its kind. This portion of Monsieur Pictet's work is full of interest, and adds immensely to the proof that the Irish Gaelic language and race are certainly of Aryan origin.

FRAZER'S MAGAZINE.

Just as this page is being prepared for the press, the July number of *Frazer's Magazine* comes into the hands of the writer. Casting a glance over its pages, the eye rests on an article headed, "The Ancient Irish," in which the following words occur:

"Happily we are not left to the dim and deceiving light of these legends as our only guide through the obscure maze of Irish ethnology. The dialect of the old Keltic language spoken by the Gaedel, studied in its relation to other Keltic dialects, and to the other languages of Europe; the pagan deities they worshipped, the weapons of war they employed, their habits of life and physical characteristics, all furnish valuable and conclusive evidence as to the real place of the nation among the peoples of old Europe." That is testimony in favor of the value of Keltic names as philological boulders of historic interest.

The writer of the article in *Frazer* so far reasons like one who has bestowed pains on the study of philology, and has begun to form an idea of its value in matters of historic research. Ethnology, too, as a science, he recognises as a twin sister, and palæology comes in for a fair share of praise. These three sciences are certainly cousins, perhaps sisters, for they mutually support and strengthen their respective discoveries. It is perfectly true, then, to say that the dialect of the old Keltic language, spoken by the Gaidel, and compared with the other languages of Europe; that the physical characteristics of the people, the weapons of war which they employed—all furnish valuable and conclusive evidence as to the real place of the Gael amongst the peoples of old Europe. What surprises one, then, very much is just a few sentences after that statement, that the immigration known as the *Tuatha de Dannan* to Eire some sixteen hundred years before the Christian era, is a myth; that the immigration of the Keltic race, known in Irish annals as "Fır Boılg," or men of rotund set form, or "bag-men," Belgæ, or men carrying "quivers," or devoted to the worship of (Bel) Beal, is a myth. That is a very strange statement from any one professing to be a scholar. The deduction is quite illogical from the reasoning and from the premises; for he reasons out the subject of Ireland's ancient race either from historical data, such as the annals of the people supply; or on scientific principles, such as those on which comparative grammar, ethnology, and antiquities rest; or on both these grounds.

If he treats the question scientifically, then he comes, according to his own statement, to the conclusion, that these sciences furnish valuable and conclusive evidence as to the real place of the Gaelic nation amongst the peoples of old Europe. From these sciences it is certain that a people came some four thousand years ago, at a period even before the time Abraham had left Ur of the Chaldeans, from the country between the Euphrates and the Hindus; it is certain that from time to time for centuries afterwards, migratory bands came westward from the same eastern lands and took up their abode in Southern and in Northern Europe, and some of the same people proceeded thence, by different routes, to Ireland. All this is certain. The landing of these migrations on the shores of Ierne is no mere conjecture ; it is a matter of scientific certainty. It is quite true, however, that the names of these migratory bodies of the Keltic family—Belgian, or Dannan, or anything else—is unknown from a scientific point of investigation. They may have been "Fırboılg," or men of any other kind or character, or *Tuatha de Dannans.* Science does not say by what name they were known. Science simply declares that there were such migrations. Objectively, therefore, they were not myths. It matters little by what name they are called.

If he treat the question as one of history—such history as our annals furnish regarding the early Irish race—he cannot assert that the Dannan race and the "Fırboılg" race are myths. Their reality is supported by strong historical tradition. It shall be seen farther on that such universal tradition is good testimony in favour of the substantial truth of great events. The names are probably of no value ; the expression of the writer in the *Fraser* is at best vague, and calculated to lead astray the growing minds of youthful scholars. In one word, then, both from science and from Irish history it is certain that there were migrations to Ireland—all Keltic—at very early periods: what these migrations were by name, Dannan or Belgic, or both, or neither, does not make much matter to the present race or to themselves.

Such scholars as Niebuhr and Frederick Augustus Wolf have done much good in the fields of Roman history and of Grecian literature. Their doubts, like the Apostle Thomas's disbelief, have benefited thousands, and have furnished a solid foundation for the certainty of the superstructure of knowledge. With some less learned, it is not unusual even in this country, to doubt of things that no sensible man could have any doubt about. A certain youth coming from the halls of those colleges where uncertainty is substituted for knowledge and doubt for faith, said at one time in the hearing of the present writer, that he would not believe anything but what he had seen. "Well, then," said some one in reply to him, "you cannot believe you have had a grandfather, for you have never seen the good man, and you certainly cannot believe that you have a soul, for you have never seen it. You must believe that you have no soul. You cannot believe that there is such a place as America or Australia, for you have never been in these countries." To believe is to rest conviction on the truthful authority of another. One believes that there is such a city as Rome, although he may never have seen it, because the amount of authority assuring him that there is such a city is so strong that he cannot refuse to be convinced of the truth proposed to him. Faith comes by hearing; knowledge comes from seeing with the eye of the body or of the mind. Human belief rests on human testimony; divine faith, on divine testimony—that of Christ, or the Holy Spirit.

The science of exegetics demands that due regard be paid to the times and places recorded, and the authors and compilers by whom the histories, annals, records, or even legends, had been penned. It is certain that the Kelts were wonderfully conservative of ancient rights and laws. It is certain that the written works, particularly of a historic character, were under strict supervision; and that customs, even such as are known in fairy mythology at present, have been handed down in the same form for two thousand years.

The most sensible writer, perhaps, because the most learned amongst moderns, is Professor Blackie. He writes in his *Homer and the Iliad, vol. i.*:—"To me it appears that in the present age there is a tendency to fling away honest old traditions of this stamp as utterly worthless, and to substitute ingenious speculations in their stead. But before we allow ourselves to be carried away by such a fashion of sweeping negation, it were wise to make a large and cautious survey of the character of the ground on which we stand. It may be, after all, that there is more solidity at the root of old, venerable, popular belief than in the ingenious theory of our recent speculator. The thinking of the multitude is not always wrong. When a man with a large display of reading rejects as a figment, what all other men for centuries had received as a fact, there is an air of knowledge about this, before which the man of less, or of no reading, is often willing to surrender without enquiry."

"The soul and substance of all popular tradition is true, and the facts also, for the most part—if not in all their limbs and flourishes, at least in their framework."

Again he writes:—"The ingenuity of those who revel in this extreme (of doubting) is admirable, but their wisdom is doubtful; and a sober historical estimate such as belongs peculiarly to the cultivated intellect, must bring us back to the point of view from which the great

Roman historian started, when he said, that while we willingly grant the privilege to antiquity of mingling human things with divine, we can in nowise allow the systematic subtraction of that human element for the glorification of which this confusion took place.

"Popular tradition embodies facts and persons of great national significance. All great social changes take place through the instrumentality of great men."

If the writer in the magazine takes away "Dannan" as a myth, and "fear-bolg," what name does he substitute for these mythical titles? for, as a fact, the migrations came to Ireland—call them by any name he pleases.

One other passage from Blackie's pages :—

"Common sense understands how much exaggerated embellishments are consistent with the most solid nucleus of fact; but there is a certain school of Germans not without imitators in this country who, when they meet with marvellous descriptions, deny the historical reality of the hero described, register him with myths, degrade him into a symbol, or elevate him into a god. Scotchmen need not travel abroad for illustrations of the important proposition that all tradition is founded on reality, and that all popular poetry and national epic is only national history moulded into rhymithical shape by the passion and imagination of the people. . . And even in the remote misty antiquity of our ancient Gaelic poetry, a region where some dogmatical critics asserted that only fictitious bards and heroes were floating, as bodiless and bloodless as the mists that trail their skirts round the grey granite cones of the West Highlands, even in that unclear element, the brawny forms of real men and women, fighting, and loving, and singing like ourselves, are now being distinctly recognised. Who the FEINN were, and on what ground, Irish or Scotch, or both, their famous exploits were performed may, indeed, be debated, because there is no authentic Iliad of these early times existing either in Irish or Gaelic; but that they were men no one doubts; and if Keltic men, it would be strange, indeed, if, in the very earliest times, those bloody encounters between the Gaels and the Scandinivians of the north-west coast of Europe, should have failed, which flare out in such wild flashes athwart the dark pages of Scottish history in the Middle Ages. And as for the venerable old Scald, to whom the rhymed records of those earliest pictures of the chase and the battle-field are ascribed; if one were so credulous as to set his seal to the title of the sixteenth century manuscript, in which this line occurs—"THE AUTHOR OF THIS IS OSSIAN; not less, in my judgment, were he to be accounted unreasonably sceptical who should believe that this and other such verses went forth to the world under the name of Ossian, if no such Keltic bard had ever existed. If there is a church of St. Paul in London, and in almost in every town of western Christendom, it is because there was a St. Paul, and because he was the great apostle of the European gentiles; if there is a church of St. Columba on one of the great treeless isles of the Keltic Hebrides, it is because an adventurous saint of kingly blood actually did cross over from the North of Ireland to this coast in the sixth century, and founded a school of love, and gentleness, and truth in the midst of the wild, lawless chieftains who ruled over these wild regions." So far Blackie. He reasons with sense, philosophy, and in accord with the truth of history.

If there were "Fir-bolg," or "Belgæ," men of rotund shape, men devoted to the god of day, named in Irish pagan annals; if the race of the *Tuatha de Danann* is named, there must have been a people in reality, to represent races to whom those titles were applied. History and science demonstrate that there were such, although they do not show that the people called themselves by that name. All that is certain is, that they were Keltic migrations. The Greeks were known amongst the Grecian States as Hellenes; as Greeks to those living in Italy and to the north of Europe. That there was a battle fought between two Keltic races on the plains of *Magh Turra Conga*, or the Plain of Towers, near Cong, in the county Galway, is a certainty, and not a myth. The mounds, the cinerary urn found by Sir William Wilde, the name of the locality, the written records, over six hundred years old, the tradition from age to age, combine to give sufficient satisfactory testimony to the substantial truth of the battle fought over a thousand years before the Christian era.

SUMMARY.

Guided by the rules of scientific research; treading on sure principles of knowledge, the archaic paths which have, by time, been embedded into the national language and the genius of the Irish race; comparing on the way the signs of certainty which archæology and palæology furnish in manifold forms—at one time in cyclopean architecture, the Round Towers; at another, in poetry, in painting, in law, and in the varied foot-prints of a bygone civilisation, the writer has furnished to every rational thinker, and to every scholar who wishes to steer the middle course between credulity, on the one side, and scepticism on the other, reasons abundant and convincing that the Gaelic language and people have come from the cradle-land of the Japhetic race.

Other important questions connected with the main subject of the volume have been introduced—subjects which have for centuries engaged the attention of some of the most learned men in Ireland; these, too, have had a full share of historical and æsthetical consideration bestowed upon them; and the conclusions drawn have been, in these pages, quite in conformity with the spirit of our national annals; with the dictates of sense and science.

The phonesis of Irish Gaelic at present and in pagan times, is a subject quite new to the public, but very important, for it comes in, to confirm the views already arrived at in England regarding the correct sounds of the vowels and consonants. Irish-Gaelic pronunciation is the fountain from which the classic languages of Europe have drawn the flood of full and open sounds which constitutes the beauty of Italian, and which gave to the national pronunciation its *ore rotundo*, fullness and power, amongst the Romans, *rerum dominos gentemque togatam.*

Irish phonetic laws are in accord with Jacob Grimm's law of lingual interchange; and the bardic beauties of Irish song are the source from which the poetic children of modern literary Europe have drawn the grace which gives to versification its charm—Rhyme.

Few persons care to admit that pagan Ireland was civilised; yet, it is a fact, that the Gaelic-speaking tribes of pagan times enjoyed in the western isle an advanced state of material civilisation long before Rome or Carthage, or Corinth, or Priam's city had been built. The first people who came to the "Island of Destiny" were descended of an enlightened and a highly civilised parent stock. The knowledge of the natives in the art of writing, of dyeing, painting, illuminating, smelting metals, of coining money, and making ornaments in gold and brass; of cyclopean architecture, of which the Round Towers are a standing, and to this hour an abiding proof, point out clearly the archaic civilisation and primitive refinement of the pagan Irish race.

A knowledge of philology as a science supports the truth of history. This branch of study is therefore especially useful, at the present time, to every intelligent believer of the Christian religion, and to Catholic clergymen, who in an age of growing infidelity, must necessarily meet from time to time those who will oppose not alone Catholic teaching, but Christian truth; and who therefore will be called upon to shew that the words of the mosaic narrative are truthful, and to point out from scientific data that man, in pagan times, had not been progressive, but that on the contrary he had been in mental power and in knowledge retrogressive, until the coming of Christ, who, as God-man, not alone redeemed mankind, but ennobled them, and raised human nature in dignity above the angelic.

For the historian the Irish-Gaelic is useful, showing the value and significancy of names of persons and places connected with ancient European history.

The Gaelic-language is, in the words of Geddes, for scholars, "a great field of investigation, as yet comparatively unexplored; and for Irishmen it is their own tongue lying before them at their doors, an *El-dorado* for the winning."

A thousand volumes of Irish-Gaelic lie still unpublished in manuscript.

There are at present only a few texts books—*the Easy Lessons in Irish*, composed and published by the writer; and the *College Grammar*. The writer has a Dictionary ready for press, but in the present state of public apathy, he is unwilling to risk publication; he cannot afford to lose money, and time, and labour. There is, at times, a spurt of patriotic spirit made manifest here and there, but there is nothing permanent or fixed—nothing calculated to support Irish publications. The Government is at times called upon, as it has, on a late occasion, been, by the hon. member for Louth, Mr. Alexander M. Sullivan; and then promises are made, and some little good effected, but nothing of a permanent character has yet been done to keep alive all that is still living of the Irish-Gaelic speech. Germans have established at Berlin what English Statesmen and Irishmen have not done in Dublin.

One young man from the metropolis has sent ten pounds to the present writer, with a promise of ten more, to pen an Irish First Book, or Primer, as an introduction to the *Easy Lessons.* He leaves, besides, the profits of the publication, when it shall have been issued, to the writer. Instances like this show the spirit of our young men; but they never can produce permanent results. The hierarchy of Ireland alone, including bishops and priests, can, if they wish, make Irish-Gaelic a success in Ireland.

It is not the business nor the duty of the present writer to offer any suggestions. However, it is certain that a slight encouragement to the teachers of the National Schools, who are most anxious to help the cause, would effect much good. They have lately petitioned some of the Irish Hierarchy—his Grace the Archbishop of Tuam—to encourage them in their earnest and practical endeavours to keep Gaelic alive in Connaught. Thus a great body of National Teachers, and many private literateurs, are ready to act; but there is no sound organisation for that end, and no one with the power to make it a success is found willing to make a beginning. As it is, each must only do all that time and circumstances enable him to achieve.

The words of the lamented Thomas Davis on the language of our fathers must not be forgotten. "The language of a nation's youth," he says, "is the only easy and full speech, for its manhood and for its age. And when the language of its cradle goes, itself craves a tomb. What business has a Russian for the rippling language of Italy and India? How could a Greek desert his organs, or his soul to speak Dutch upon the sides of Hymetus, or the beach of Salamis, or on the waste where once was Sparta? And is it befitting the fiery delicate-organed Kelt to abandon his beautiful tongue, docile and spirited as an Arab, 'Sweet as music, strong as the wave'; is it befitting in him to abandon this mild liquid speech for that mongrel of a hundred breeds called English, which, powerful though it be, creaks and bangs about the Kelt who tries to use it. Even should the effort to save it, as the national language fail by the attempt, we will rescue its old literature, and hand down to our descendants proofs that we had a language as fit for love, and war, and business, and pleasure, as the world ever knew, and that we had not the spirit and the nationality to preserve it." The answer given to a London citizen by Seán O'Neil's interpreter, expresses the opinion of many in days past, regarding the language of the stranger. When asked why the Prince O'Neil did not speak English. "Think you," was the reply, "it would become the O'Neil *to writhe his mouth* with such barbarous jargon." Irishmen glory in their Keltic names and origin, and why not hold the language dear, wound up as it is with the past glories of their race? The language of a nation is the exponent of people's antiquity, the index of their refinement, the mouthpiece of their history, the type of their freedom, the echo of their greatness and fame. Shall Irishmen, then, let Irish fade and perish? No, a thousand times No!

With a slight alteration in a few of the sentences taken from the lecture delivered in 1864, on the Gaelic language by Professor Blackie, of the University of Edinburgh, this volume is brought to a close.

"In conclusion I say that the death of the Gaelic language, whenever it may take place, will be a dead loss to (Scotland) Ireland, and therefore we ought to delay that catastrophe, by every means in our power, as long as we possibly can. Let us leave it to Prussian bureaucratists, Parisian imperialists, and Russian despots to advocate the flat monotony of a centralised civilisation. What the instincts of our British culture point to as the proper end of all social improvement, is local independence, local spirit, and provincial variety. The moment the Gaelic language dies, the Highland (say the Irish) people, die with it; for, no people survives the death of its language—and with the Highland (Irish) people dies all the glory of Keltic chivalry, and all the wealth of Keltic story which the genius of Scott was proud to sing. Our glens and our isles which now tell their own tale graphically in their own tongue* will baffle a corrupted jargon which no man understands, and be haunted by traditions for which no man cares. . . . The duty of all true Kelts, at least in this matter, seems to be quite plain. Though it were distinctly known on earth, as perhaps it is already registered in the counsels of heaven, that the last Gaelic-speaking man on Caledonian (Hibernian) ground shall die in the year 1964, as certainly as Cornish died with Mrs. Dorothy Pentreath in the year 1778, that would not alter in the least degree the duty of the existing Kelts to their venerable mother tongue. Men

* The Keltic dialects seem to excel in expressive names of a topographical kind. Their nomenclatures are pictures of the countries which they inhabit."—Jamieson.

do not sleep in coffins or turn their shawls into shrouds because they know their dust must return to the dust from which we all came. The Highland (Irish) students in our colleges should not, in their eagerness to acquire the elements of a few dead languages, forget to cultivate the living power of their own. Let some rich Irishman found in our colleges some burses to give free places to those students, who to the qualifications of respectable scholarship still add a scientific knowledge of the language of the Gaël, . . .

A Maynooth Student writes in 1862 :—

The Keltic tongue, then must it die? Say shall our language go?
No; by Ulfadha's kingly soul; by sainted Lawrence, No!
No! by the shades of saints and chiefs, of holy name on high,
Whose deeds, as they have lived with it, must die when it shall die.
No! by the memories of the past, that round our ruins twine,
No! by our evening hope of suns in coming days to shine,
It shall not go, it must not die, the language of our sires.
While Erin's glory glads our souls, or freedom's name inspires,
That lingering ray, from stars gone down, oh! let its light remain,
That last bright link with splendours flown, oh! snap it not in twain!
Ay, build ye up the Keltic tongue above O'Curry's grave;
Speed ye the good work, ye patriot souls, who long your land to save—
Who long to light the flame again on freedom's altar dead—
Who long to call the glories back, from hapless Erin fled—
Who long to gem her saddened brow with queenly wreath again
And raise a warrior people up, a nation in her train.

To build up the edifice of the Nation's language much is required. The people must be taught to cultivate it. The scholar must bestow his loving care on it. All must be in earnest. The causes which have led to its decay must be removed, and adequate means adopted for its restoration. If Government fail, as it will, to effect any permanent benefit for the living speech, it devolves on the great men of the Irish people to come to the rescue.

GENERAL INDEX.

In preparation, and just now nigh ready for press

The Life of St. Jarlath,

(FIFTH CENTURY,)

FOUNDER, AND FIRST BISHOP OF THE SEE OF TUAM.

LATIN & OLD IRISH MANUSCRIPTS

Have been consulted for years past by the author.

JULY 1876.

GENERAL LIST OF WORKS

PUBLISHED BY

MESSRS. LONGMANS, GREEN, AND CO.

PATERNOSTER ROW, LONDON.

History, Politics, Historical Memoirs, &c.

The HISTORY of ENGLAND from the Accession of James the Second. By Lord MACAULAY.

STUDENT'S EDITION, 2 vols. crown 8vo. 12*s.*
PEOPLE'S EDITION, 4 vols. crown 8vo. 16*s.*
CABINET EDITION, 8 vols. post 8vo. 48*s.*
LIBRARY EDITION, 5 vols. 8vo. £4.

LORD MACAULAY'S WORKS. Complete and Uniform Library Edition. Edited by his Sister, Lady TREVELYAN. 8 vols. 8vo. with Portrait price £5. 5*s.* cloth, or £8. 8*s.* bound in tree-calf by Rivière.

The HISTORY of ENGLAND from the Fall of Wolsey to the Defeat of the Spanish Armada. By JAMES ANTHONY FROUDE, M.A. late Fellow of Exeter College, Oxford.

LIBRARY EDITION, Twelve Volumes, 8vo. price £8. 18*s.*
CABINET EDITION, Twelve Volumes, crown 8vo. price 72*s.*

The ENGLISH in IRELAND in the EIGHTEENTH CENTURY. By JAMES ANTHONY FROUDE, M.A. late Fellow of Exeter College, Oxford. 3 vols. 8vo. price 48*s.*

JOURNAL of the REIGNS of KING GEORGE IV. and KING WILLIAM IV. By the late CHARLES C. F. GREVILLE, Esq. Edited by HENRY REEVE, Esq. Fifth Edition. 3 vols. 8vo. 36*s.*

RECOLLECTIONS and SUGGESTIONS, 1813–1873. By JOHN Earl RUSSELL, K.G. New Edition, revised and enlarged. 8vo. 16*s.*

On PARLIAMENTARY GOVERNMENT in ENGLAND; its Origin, Development, and Practical Operation. By ALPHEUS TODD, Librarian of the Legislative Assembly of Canada. 2 vols. 8vo. price £1. 17*s.*

The CONSTITUTIONAL HISTORY of ENGLAND, since the Accession of George III. 1760—1860. By Sir THOMAS ERSKINE MAY, K.C.B. D.C.L. The Fifth Edition, thoroughly revised. 3 vols. crown 8vo. price 18*s.*

DEMOCRACY in EUROPE; a History. By Sir THOMAS ERSKINE MAY, K.C.B. D.C.L. 2 vols. 8vo. [*In the press.*

The NEW REFORMATION, a Narrative of the Old Catholic Movement, from 1870 to the Present Time; with an Historical Introduction. By THEODORUS. 8vo. price 12*s.*

The OXFORD REFORMERS— John Colet, Erasmus, and Thomas More; being a History of their Fellow-work. By FREDERIC SEEBOHM. Second Edition, enlarged. 8vo. 14*s.*

LECTURES on the HISTORY of ENGLAND, from the Earliest Times to the Death of King Edward II. By WILLIAM LONGMAN, F.S.A. With Maps and Illustrations. 8vo. 15*s.*

The HISTORY of the LIFE and TIMES of EDWARD the THIRD. By WILLIAM LONGMAN, F.S.A. With 9 Maps, 8 Plates, and 16 Woodcuts. 2 vols. 8vo. 28*s.*

INTRODUCTORY LECTURES on MODERN HISTORY. Delivered in Lent Term, 1842; with the Inaugural Lecture delivered in December 1841. By the Rev. THOMAS ARNOLD, D.D. 8vo. price 7*s.* 6*d.*

WATERLOO LECTURES; a Study of the Campaign of 1815. By Colonel CHARLES C. CHESNEY, R.E. Third Edition. 8vo. with Map, 10*s.* 6*d.*

HISTORY of ENGLAND under the DUKE of BUCKINGHAM and CHARLES the FIRST, 1624-1628. By SAMUEL RAWSON GARDINER, late Student of Ch. Ch. 2 vols. 8vo. with two Maps, price 24*s.*

The SIXTH ORIENTAL MONARCHY; or, the Geography, History, and Antiquities of PARTHIA. By GEORGE RAWLINSON, M.A. Professor of Ancient History in the University of Oxford. Maps and Illustrations. 8vo. 16*s.*

The SEVENTH GREAT ORIENTAL MONARCHY; or, a History of the SASSANIANS: with Notices, Geographical and Antiquarian. By G. RAWLINSON, M.A. Map and numerous Illustrations. 8vo. price 28*s.*

A HISTORY of GREECE. By the Rev. GEORGE W. COX, M.A. late Scholar of Trinity College, Oxford. VOLS. I. & II. (to the Close of the Peloponnesian War). 8vo. with Maps and Plans, 36*s.*

GENERAL HISTORY of GREECE to the Death of Alexander the Great; with a Sketch of the Subsequent History to the Present Time. By the Rev. GEORGE W. COX, M.A. With 11 Maps. Crown 8vo. 7*s.* 6*d.*

The GREEKS and the PERSIANS. By the Rev. GEORGE W. COX, M.A. (*Epochs of Ancient History, I.*) With 4 Coloured Maps. Fcp. 8vo. price 2*s.* 6*d.*

The TALE of the GREAT PERSIAN WAR, from the Histories of Herodotus. By GEORGE W. COX, M.A. New Edition. Fcp. 3*s.* 6*d.*

The HISTORY of ROME. By WILLIAM IHNE. VOLS. I. and II. 8vo. price 30*s.* The Third Volume is in the press.

GENERAL HISTORY OF ROME from the Foundation of the City to the Fall of Augustulus, B.C. 753—A.D. 476. By the Very Rev. C. MERIVALE, D.D. Dean of Ely. With Five Maps. Crown 8vo. 7*s.* 6*d.*

HISTORY of the ROMANS under the EMPIRE. By the Very Rev. C. MERIVALE, D.D. Dean of Ely. 8 vols. post 8vo. 48*s.*

The FALL of the ROMAN REPUBLIC; a Short History of the Last Century of the Commonwealth. By the same Author. 12mo. 7*s.* 6*d.*

The STUDENT'S MANUAL of the HISTORY of INDIA, from the Earliest Period to the Present. By Colonel MEADOWS TAYLOR, M.R.A.S. M.R.I.A. Second Thousand. Crown 8vo. with Maps, 7*s.* 6*d.*

The HISTORY of INDIA, from the Earliest Period to the close of Lord Dalhousie's Administration. By J. C. MARSHMAN. 3 vols. crown 8vo. 22*s.* 6*d.*

The NATIVE STATES of INDIA in SUBSIDIARY ALLIANCE with the BRITISH GOVERNMENT; an Historical Sketch. By Colonel G. B. MALLESON, C.S.I. With 6 Coloured Maps. 8vo. 15s.

INDIAN POLITY; a View of the System of Administration in India. By Lieutenant-Colonel GEORGE CHESNEY, Fellow of the University of Calcutta. New Edition, revised; with Map. 8vo. price 21s.

The BRITISH ARMY in 1875; with Suggestions on its Administration and Organisation. By JOHN HOLMS, M.P. New and Enlarged Edition, with 4 Diagrams. Crown 8vo. price 4s. 6d.

The HISTORY of PRUSSIA, from the Earliest Times to the Present Day; tracing the Origin and Development of her Military Organisation. By Captain W. J. WYATT. Vols. I. and II. A.D. 700 to A.D. 1525. 8vo. 36s.

POPULAR HISTORY of FRANCE, from the Earliest Times to the Death of Louis XIV. By ELIZABETH M. SEWELL, Author of 'Amy Herbert' &c. With Coloured Maps. Crown 8vo. 7s. 6d.

STUDIES from GENOESE HISTORY. By Colonel G. B. MALLESON, C.S.I. Guardian to His Highness the Maharájá of Mysore. Crown 8vo. 10s. 6d.

LORD MACAULAY'S CRITICAL and HISTORICAL ESSAYS. CHEAP EDITION, authorised and complete. Crown 8vo. 3s. 6d.

CABINET EDITION, 4 vols. post 8vo. 24s.
PEOPLE'S EDITION, 2 vols. crown 8vo. 8s.
LIBRARY EDITION, 3 vols. 8vo. 36s.
STUDENT'S EDITION, 1 vol. cr. 8vo. 6s.

HISTORY of EUROPEAN MORALS, from Augustus to Charlemagne. By W. E. H. LECKY, M.A. Second Edition. 2 vols. 8vo. price 28s.

HISTORY of the RISE and INFLUENCE of the SPIRIT of RATIONALISM in EUROPE. By W. E. H. LECKY, M.A. Cabinet Edition, being the Fourth. 2 vols. crown 8vo. price 16s.

The HISTORY of PHILOSOPHY, from Thales to Comte. By GEORGE HENRY LEWES. Fourth Edition. 2 vols. 8vo. 32s.

The HISTORY of the PELOPONNESIAN WAR. By THUCYDIDES. Translated by R. CRAWLEY, Fellow of Worcester College, Oxford. 8vo. 10s. 6d.

The MYTHOLOGY of the ARYAN NATIONS. By GEORGE W. COX, M.A. late Scholar of Trinity College, Oxford, 2 vols. 8vo. 28s.

TALES of ANCIENT GREECE. By GEORGE W. COX, M.A. late Scholar of Trin. Coll. Oxon. Crown 8vo. price 6s. 6d.

HISTORY of CIVILISATION in England and France, Spain and Scotland. By HENRY THOMAS BUCKLE. New Edition of the entire Work, with a complete INDEX. 3 vols. crown 8vo. 24s.

SKETCH of the HISTORY of the CHURCH of ENGLAND to the Revolution of 1688. By the Right Rev. T. V. SHORT, D.D. Lord Bishop of St. Asaph. Eighth Edition. Crown 8vo. 7s. 6d.

MAUNDER'S HISTORICAL TREASURY; General Introductory Outlines of Universal History, and a series of Separate Histories. Latest Edition, revised by the Rev. G. W. COX, M.A. Fcp. 8vo. 6s. cloth, or 10s. 6d. calf.

CATES' and WOODWARD'S ENCYCLOPÆDIA of CHRONOLOGY, HISTORICAL and BIOGRAPHICAL. 8vo. price 42s.

The ERA of the PROTESTANT REVOLUTION. By F. SEEBOHM. With 4 Coloured Maps and 12 Diagrams on Wood. Fcp. 8vo. 2s. 6d.

The CRUSADES. By the Rev. G. W. Cox, M.A. late Scholar of Trinity College, Oxford. With Coloured Map. Fcp. 8vo. 2*s.* 6*d.*

The THIRTY YEARS' WAR, 1618–1648. By SAMUEL RAWSON GARDINER, late Student of Christ Church. With Coloured Map. Fcp. 8vo. 2*s.* 6*d.*

The HOUSES of LANCASTER and YORK; with the Conquest and Loss of France. By JAMES GAIRDNER, of the Public Record Office. With Five Coloured Maps. Fcp. 8vo. 2*s.* 6*d.*

EDWARD the THIRD. By the Rev. W. WARBURTON, M.A. late Fellow of All Souls College, Oxford. With 3 Coloured Maps and 3 Genealogical Tables. Fcp. 8vo. 2*s.* 6*d.*

The AGE of ELIZABETH. By the Rev. M. CREIGHTON, M.A. late Fellow and Tutor of Merton College, Oxford. With 5 Maps and 4 Genealogical Tables. Fcp. 8vo. 2*s.* 6*d.*

The FALL of the STUARTS; and Western Europe from 1678 to 1697. By the Rev. E. HALE, M.A. Assistant-Master, Eton. With 11 Maps and Plans. Fcp. 8vo. 2*s.* 6*d.*

The FIRST TWO STUARTS and the PURITAN REVOLUTION, 1603-1660. By SAMUEL RAWSON GARDINER, late Student of Christ Church. With 4 Coloured Maps. Fcp. 8vo. 2*s.* 6*d.*

The WAR of AMERICAN INDEPENDENCE, 1775–1783. By JOHN MALCOLM LUDLOW, Barrister-at-Law. With 4 Coloured Maps. Fcp. 8vo. 2*s.* 6*d.*

REALITIES of IRISH LIFE. By W. STEUART TRENCH, late Land Agent in Ireland to the Marquess of Lansdowne, the Marquess of Bath, and Lord Digby. Cheaper Edition. Crown 8vo. price 2*s.* 6*d.*

Biographical Works.

The LIFE and LETTERS of LORD MACAULAY. By his Nephew, G. OTTO TREVELYAN, M.P. 2 vols. 8vo. with Portrait, price 36*s.*

The LIFE of SIR WILLIAM FAIRBAIRN, Bart. F.R.S. Corresponding Member of the National Institute of France, &c. Partly written by himself; edited and completed by WILLIAM POLE, F.R.S. [*In the Press.*

ARTHUR SCHOPENHAUER, his LIFE and his PHILOSOPHY. By HELEN ZIMMERN. Post 8vo. with Portrait, 7*s.* 6*d.*

MEMOIRS of BARON STOCKMAR. By his SON, Baron E. VON STOCKMAR. Translated from the German by G. A. M. Edited by F. MAX MÜLLER, M.A. 2 vols. crown 8vo. 21*s.*

AUTOBIOGRAPHY. By JOHN STUART MILL. 8vo. price 7*s.* 6*d.*

The LIFE of NAPOLEON III. derived from State Records, Unpublished Family Correspondence, and Personal Testimony. By BLANCHARD JERROLD. 4 vols. 8vo. with numerous Portraits and Facsimiles. VOLS. I. and II. price 18*s.* each. The Third Volume is in the press.

LIFE and LETTERS of Sir GILBERT ELLIOT, First EARL of MINTO. Edited by the COUNTESS of MINTO. 3 vols. 8vo. 31*s.* 6*d.*

ESSAYS in MODERN MILITARY BIOGRAPHY. By CHARLES CORNWALLIS CHESNEY, Lieutenant-Colonel in the Royal Engineers. 8vo. 12*s.* 6*d.*

The MEMOIRS of SIR JOHN RERESBY, of Thrybergh, Bart. M.P. for York, &c. 1634—1689. Written by Himself. Edited from the Original Manuscript by JAMES J. CARTWRIGHT, M.A. 8vo. price 21*s.*

ISAAC CASAUBON, 1559–1614. By MARK PATTISON, Rector of Lincoln College, Oxford. 8vo. 18*s*.

LORD GEORGE BENTINCK; a Political Biography. By the Right Hon. BENJAMIN DISRAELI, M.P. Crown 8vo. price 6*s*.

LEADERS of PUBLIC OPINION in IRELAND; Swift, Flood, Grattan, and O'Connell. By W. E. H. LECKY, M.A. New Edition, revised and enlarged. Crown 8vo. price 7*s*. 6*d*.

DICTIONARY of GENERAL BIOGRAPHY; containing Concise Memoirs and Notices of the most Eminent Persons of all Countries, from the Earliest Ages. By W. L. R. CATES. New Edition, extended in a Supplement to the Year 1875. Medium 8vo. price 25*s*.

LIFE of the DUKE of WELLINGTON. By the Rev. G. R. GLEIG, M.A. Popular Edition, carefully revised; with copious Additions. Crown 8vo. with Portrait, 5*s*.

MEMOIRS of SIR HENRY HAVELOCK, K.C.B. By JOHN CLARK MARSHMAN. Cabinet Edition, with Portrait. Crown 8vo. price 3*s*. 6*d*.

VICISSITUDES of FAMILIES. By Sir J. BERNARD BURKE, C.B. Ulster King of Arms. New Edition, enlarged. 2 vols. crown 8vo. 21*s*.

The RISE of GREAT FAMILIES, other Essays and Stories. By Sir J. BERNARD BURKE, C.B. Ulster King of Arms. Crown 8vo. price 12*s*. 6*d*.

ESSAYS in ECCLESIASTICAL BIOGRAPHY. By the Right Hon. Sir J. STEPHEN, LL.D. Cabinet Edition. Crown 8vo. 7*s*. 6*d*.

MAUNDER'S BIOGRAPHICAL TREASURY. Latest Edition, reconstructed, thoroughly revised, and in great part rewritten; with 1,000 additional Memoirs and Notices, by W. L. R. CATES. Fcp. 8vo. 6*s*. cloth; 10*s*. 6*d*. calf.

LETTERS and LIFE of FRANCIS BACON, including all his Occasional Works. Collected and edited, with a Commentary, by J. SPEDDING, Trin. Coll. Cantab. Complete in 7 vols. 8vo. £4. 4*s*.

The LIFE, WORKS, and OPINIONS of HEINRICH HEINE. By WILLIAM STIGAND. 2 vols. 8vo. with Portrait of Heine, price 28*s*.

BIOGRAPHICAL and CRITICAL ESSAYS, reprinted from Reviews, with Additions and Corrections. Second Edition of the Second Series. By A. HAYWARD, Q.C. 2 vols. 8vo. price 28*s*. THIRD SERIES, in 1 vol. 8vo. price 14*s*.

Criticism, Philosophy, Polity, &c.

The LAW of NATIONS considered as INDEPENDENT POLITICAL COMMUNITIES; the Rights and Duties of Nations in Time of War. By Sir TRAVERS TWISS, D.C.L., F.R.S. New Edition, revised; with an Introductory Juridical Review of the Results of Recent Wars, and an Appendix of Treaties and other Documents. 8vo. 21*s*.

CHURCH and STATE: their relations Historically Developed. By T. HEINRICH GEFFCKEN, Professor of International Law at the University of Strasburg. Translated from the German by E. FAIRFAX TAYLOR. [*In the press.*

A SYSTEMATIC VIEW of the SCIENCE of JURISPRUDENCE. By SHELDON AMOS, M.A. Professor of Jurisprudence to the Inns of Court, London. 8vo. price 18*s*.

A PRIMER of the ENGLISH CONSTITUTION and GOVERNMENT. By SHELDON AMOS, M.A. Professor of Jurisprudence to the Inns of Court. Second Edition, revised. Crown 8vo. 6*s.*

OUTLINES of CIVIL PROCEDURE. Being a General View of the Supreme Court of Judicature and of the whole Practice in the Common Law and Chancery Divisions under all the Statutes now in force. By EDWARD STANLEY ROSCOE, Barrister-at-Law. 12mo. price 3*s.* 6*d.*

The INSTITUTES of JUSTINIAN; with English Introduction, Translation and Notes. By T. C. SANDARS, M.A. Sixth Edition. 8vo. 18*s.*

SOCRATES and the SOCRATIC SCHOOLS. Translated from the German of Dr. E. ZELLER, with the Author's approval, by the Rev. OSWALD J. REICHEL, M.A. Crown 8vo. 8*s.* 6*d.*

The STOICS, EPICUREANS, and SCEPTICS. Translated from the German of Dr. E. ZELLER, with the Author's approval, by OSWALD J. REICHEL, M.A. Crown 8vo. price 14*s.*

PLATO and the OLDER ACADEMY. Translated from the German of Dr. EDUARD ZELLER by S. FRANCES ALLEYNE and ALFRED GOODWIN, B.A. Fellow of Balliol College, Oxford. Crown 8vo. 18*s.*

The ETHICS of ARISTOTLE, with Essays and Notes. By Sir A. GRANT, Bart. M.A. LL.D. Third Edition. 2 vols. 8vo. 32*s.*

The POLITICS of ARISTOTLE; Greek Text, with English Notes. By RICHARD CONGREVE, M.A. New Edition, revised. 8vo. 18*s.*

The NICOMACHEAN ETHICS of ARISTOTLE newly translated into English. By R. WILLIAMS, B.A. Fellow and late Lecturer of Merton College, and sometime Student of Christ Church, Oxford. New Edition. 8vo. 7*s.* 6*d.*

PICTURE LOGIC; an Attempt to Popularise the Science of Reasoning by the combination of Humorous Pictures with Examples of Reasoning taken from Daily Life. By A. SWINBOURNE, B.A. With Woodcut Illustrations from Drawings by the Author. Second Edition. Fcp. 8vo. price 5*s.*

ELEMENTS of LOGIC. By R. WHATELY, D.D. late Archbishop of Dublin. New Edition. 8vo. 10*s.* 6*d.* crown 8vo. 4*s.* 6*d.*

Elements of Rhetoric. By the same Author. New Edition. 8vo. 10*s.* 6*d.* crown 8vo. 4*s.* 6*d.*

English Synonymes. By E. JANE WHATELY. Edited by Archbishop WHATELY. Fifth Edition. Fcp. 8vo. price 3*s.*

On the INFLUENCE of AUTHORITY in MATTERS of OPINION. By the late Sir GEORGE CORNEWALL LEWIS, Bart. New Edition. 8vo. 14*s.*

COMTE'S SYSTEM of POSITIVE POLITY, or TREATISE upon SOCIOLOGY. Translated from the Paris Edition of 1851–1854, and furnished with Analytical Tables of Contents. In Four Volumes, 8vo. each forming in some degree an independent Treatise :—

VOL. I. General View of Positivism and its Introductory Principles. Translated by J. H. BRIDGES, M.B. Price 21*s.*

VOL. II. Social Statics, or the Abstract Laws of Human Order. Translated by F. HARRISON, M.A. Price 14*s.*

VOL. III. Social Dynamics, or the General Laws of Human Progress (the Philosophy of History). Translated by Professor E. S. BEESLY, M.A. 8vo. 21*s.*

VOL. IV. Synthesis of the Future of Mankind. Translated by R. CONGREVE, M.D.; and an Appendix, containing the Author's Minor Treatises, translated by H. D. HUTTON, M.A. [*In the press.*

DEMOCRACY in AMERICA. By ALEXIS DE TOCQUEVILLE. Translated by HENRY REEVE, Esq. New Edition. 2 vols. crown 8vo. 16*s.*

ORDER and PROGRESS: Part I. Thoughts on Government; Part II. Studies of Political Crises. By FREDERIC HARRISON, M.A. of Lincoln's Inn. 8vo. price 14*s.*

BACON'S ESSAYS with ANNOTATIONS. By R. WHATELY, D.D. late Archbishop of Dublin. New Edition, 8vo. price 10*s.* 6*d.*

LORD BACON'S WORKS, collected and edited by J. SPEDDING, M.A. R. L. ELLIS, M.A. and D. D. HEATH. 7 vols. 8vo. price £3. 13*s.* 6*d.*

On REPRESENTATIVE GOVERNMENT. By JOHN STUART MILL Crown 8vo. price 2*s.*

On LIBERTY. By JOHN STUART MILL. New Edition. Post 8vo. 7*s.* 6*d.* Crown 8vo. price 1*s.* 4*d.*

PRINCIPLES of POLITICAL ECONOMY. By JOHN STUART MILL. Seventh Edition. 2 vols. 8vo. 30*s.* Or in 1 vol. crown 8vo. price 5*s.*

ESSAYS on SOME UNSETTLED QUESTIONS of POLITICAL ECONOMY. By JOHN STUART MILL. Second Edition. 8vo. 6*s.* 6*d.*

UTILITARIANISM. By JOHN STUART MILL. New Edition. 8vo. 5*s.*

DISSERTATIONS and DISCUSSIONS: Political, Philosophical, and Historical. By JOHN STUART MILL. New Editions. 4 vols. 8vo. price £2. 6*s.* 6*d.*

EXAMINATION of Sir. W. HAMILTON'S PHILOSOPHY, and of the Principal Philosophical Questions discussed in his Writings. By JOHN STUART MILL. Fourth Edition. 8vo. 16*s.*

An OUTLINE of the NECESSARY LAWS of THOUGHT; a Treatise on Pure and Applied Logic. By the Most Rev. W. THOMSON, Lord Archbishop of York, D.D. F.R.S. New Edition. Crown 8vo. price 6*s.*

PRINCIPLES of ECONOMICAL PHILOSOPHY. By HENRY DUNNING MACLEOD, M.A. Barrister-at-Law. Second Edition. In Two Volumes. VOL. I. 8vo. price 15*s.* VOL. II. PART I. price 12*s.* VOL. II. PART II. *just ready.*

A SYSTEM of LOGIC, RATIOCINATIVE and INDUCTIVE. By JOHN STUART MILL. Ninth Edition. Two vols. 8vo. 25*s.*

SPEECHES of the RIGHT HON. LORD MACAULAY, corrected by Himself. People's Edition, crown 8vo. 3*s.* 6*d.*

The ORATION of DEMOSTHENES on the CROWN. Translated by the Right Hon. Sir R. P. COLLIER. Crown 8vo. price 5*s.*

FAMILIES of SPEECH: Four Lectures delivered before the Royal Institution of Great Britain. By the Rev. F. W. FARRAR, D.D. F.R.S. New Edition. Crown 8vo. 3*s.* 6*d.*

CHAPTERS on LANGUAGE. By the Rev. F. W. FARRAR, D.D. F.R.S. New Edition. Crown 8vo. 5*s.*

HANDBOOK of the ENGLISH LANGUAGE. For the use of Students of the Universities and the Higher Classes in Schools. By R. G. LATHAM, M.A. M.D. The Ninth Edition. Crown 8vo. price 6*s.*

DICTIONARY of the ENGLISH LANGUAGE. By R. G. LATHAM, M.A. M.D. Abridged from Dr. Latham's Edition of Johnson's English Dictionary, and condensed into One Volume. Medium 8vo. price 24*s.*

A DICTIONARY of the ENGLISH LANGUAGE. By R. G. LATHAM, M.A. M.D. Founded on the Dictionary of Dr. SAMUEL JOHNSON, as edited by the Rev. H. J. TODD, with numerous Emendations and Additions. In Four Volumes, 4to. price £7.

THESAURUS of ENGLISH WORDS and PHRASES, classified and arranged so as to facilitate the Expression of Ideas, and assist in Literary Composition. By P. M. ROGET, M.D. New Edition. Crown 8vo. 10*s.* 6*d.*

LECTURES on the SCIENCE of LANGUAGE. By F. MAX MÜLLER, M.A. &c. The Eighth Edition. 2 vols. crown 8vo. 16*s.*

MANUAL of ENGLISH LITERATURE, Historical and Critical. By THOMAS ARNOLD, M.A. New Edition. Crown 8vo. 7*s.* 6*d.*

SOUTHEY'S DOCTOR, complete in One Volume. Edited by the Rev. J. W. WARTER, B.D. Square crown 8vo. 12*s.* 6*d.*

HISTORICAL and CRITICAL COMMENTARY on the OLD TESTAMENT; with a New Translation. By M. M. KALISCH, Ph.D. VOL. I. *Genesis*, 8vo. 18*s.* or adapted for the General Reader, 12*s.* VOL. II. *Exodus*, 15*s.* or adapted for the General Reader, 12*s.* VOL. III. *Leviticus*, PART I. 15*s.* or adapted for the General Reader, 8*s.* VOL. IV. *Leviticus*, PART II. 15*s.* or adapted for the General Reader, 8*s.*

A DICTIONARY of ROMAN and GREEK ANTIQUITIES, with about Two Thousand Engravings on Wood from Ancient Originals, illustrative of the Industrial Arts and Social Life of the Greeks and Romans. By A. RICH, B.A. Third Edition, revised and improved. Crown 8vo. price 7*s.* 6*d.*

A LATIN-ENGLISH DICTIONARY. By JOHN T. WHITE, D.D. Oxon. and J. E. RIDDLE, M.A. Oxon. Fifth Edition. 1 vol. 4to. 28*s.*

WHITE'S COLLEGE LATIN-ENGLISH DICTIONARY (Intermediate Size), abridged for the use of University Students from the Parent Work (as above). Medium 8vo. Third Edition, 15*s.*

WHITE'S JUNIOR STUDENT'S COMPLETE LATIN-ENGLISH and ENGLISH-LATIN DICTIONARY. New Edition. Square 12mo. price 12*s.*

Separately { The ENGLISH-LATIN DICTIONARY, price 5*s.* 6*d.*
The LATIN-ENGLISH DICTIONARY, price 7*s.* 6*d.*

A LATIN-ENGLISH DICTIONARY, adapted for the Use of Middle-Class Schools. By JOHN T. WHITE, D.D. Oxon. Square fcp. 8vo. price 3*s.*

An ENGLISH-GREEK LEXICON, containing all the Greek Words used by Writers of good authority. By C. D. YONGE, M.A. 4to. price 21*s.*

Mr. YONGE'S NEW LEXICON, English and Greek, abridged from his larger work (as above). Revised Edition. Square 12mo. price 8*s.* 6*d.*

A GREEK-ENGLISH LEXICON. Compiled by H. G. LIDDELL, D.D. Dean of Christ Church, and R. SCOTT, D.D. Dean of Rochester. Sixth Edition. Crown 4to. price 36*s.*

A LEXICON, GREEK and ENGLISH, abridged from LIDDELL and SCOTT'S *Greek-English Lexicon.* Fourteenth Edition. Square 12mo. 7*s.* 6*d.*

A PRACTICAL DICTIONARY of the FRENCH and ENGLISH LANGUAGES. By L. CONTANSEAU. Revised Edition. Post 8vo. 7*s.* 6*d.*

CONTANSEAU'S POCKET DICTIONARY, French and English, abridged from the above by the Author. New Edition. Square 18mo. 3*s.* 6*d.*

A NEW POCKET DICTIONARY of the GERMAN and ENGLISH LANGUAGES. By F. W. LONGMAN, Balliol College, Oxford. 18mo. 5*s.*

NEW PRACTICAL DICTIONARY of the GERMAN LANGUAGE; German-English and English-German. By the Rev. W. L. BLACKLEY, M.A. and Dr. CARL MARTIN FRIEDLÄNDER. Post 8vo. 7*s.* 6*d.*

The **MASTERY of LANGUAGES**; or, the Art of Speaking Foreign Tongues Idiomatically. By THOMAS PRENDERGAST. 8vo. 6*s.*

Miscellaneous Works and *Popular Metaphysics.*

LECTURES delivered in AMERICA in 1874. By CHARLES KINGSLEY, F.L.S. F.G.S. late Rector of Eversley. Crown 8vo. price 5*s.*

GERMAN HOME LIFE. Reprinted, with Revision and Additions, from *Fraser's Magazine.* Crown 8vo. 6*s.*

THE MISCELLANEOUS WORKS of THOMAS ARNOLD, D.D. Late Head Master of Rugby School and Regius Professor of Modern History in the University of Oxford, collected and republished. 8vo. 7*s.* 6*d.*

MISCELLANEOUS and POSTHUMOUS WORKS of the Late HENRY THOMAS BUCKLE. Edited, with a Biographical Notice, by HELEN TAYLOR. 3 vols. 8vo. price 52*s.* 6*d.*

MISCELLANEOUS WRITINGS of JOHN CONINGTON, M.A. late Corpus Professor of Latin in the University of Oxford. Edited by J. A. SYMONDS, M.A. With a Memoir by H. J. S. SMITH, M.A. 2 vols. 8vo. 28*s.*

ESSAYS, CRITICAL and BIOGRAPHICAL. Contributed to the *Edinburgh Review.* By HENRY ROGERS. New Edition, with Additions. 2 vols. crown 8vo. price 12*s.*

ESSAYS on some THEOLOGICAL CONTROVERSIES of the TIME. Contributed chiefly to the *Edinburgh Review.* By HENRY ROGERS. New Edition, with Additions. Crown 8vo. price 6*s.*

RECREATIONS of a COUNTRY PARSON. By A. K. H. B. FIRST and SECOND SERIES, crown 8vo. 3*s.* 6*d.* each.

The Common-place Philosopher in Town and Country. By A. K. H. B. Crown 8vo. price 3*s.* 6*d.*

Leisure Hours in Town; Essays Consolatory, Æsthetical, Moral, Social, and Domestic. By A. K. H. B. Crown 8vo. 3*s.* 6*d.*

The Autumn Holidays of a Country Parson; Essays contributed to *Fraser's Magazine,* &c. By A. K. H. B. Crown 8vo. 3*s.* 6*d.*

Seaside Musings on Sundays and Week-Days. By A. K. H. B. Crown 8vo. price 3*s.* 6*d.*

The Graver Thoughts of a Country Parson. By A. K. H. B. FIRST, SECOND, and THIRD SERIES, crown 8vo. 3*s.* 6*d.* each.

Critical Essays of a Country Parson, selected from Essays contributed to *Fraser's Magazine.* By A. K. H. B. Crown 8vo. 3*s.* 6*d.*

Sunday Afternoons at the Parish Church of a Scottish University City. By A. K. H. B. Crown 8vo. 3*s.* 6*d.*

Lessons of Middle Age; with some Account of various Cities and Men. By A. K. H. B. Crown 8vo. 3*s.* 6*d.*

Counsel and Comfort spoken from a City Pulpit. By A. K. H. B. Crown 8vo. price 3*s.* 6*d.*

Changed Aspects of Unchanged Truths; Memorials of St. Andrews Sundays. By A. K. H. B. Crown 8vo. 3*s.* 6*d.*

Present-day Thoughts; Memorials of St. Andrews Sundays. By A. K. H. B. Crown 8vo. 3*s.* 6*d.*

Landscapes, Churches, and Moralities. By A. K. H. B. Crown 8vo. price 3*s.* 6*d.*

SHORT STUDIES on GREAT SUBJECTS. By JAMES ANTHONY FROUDE, M.A. late Fellow of Exeter Coll. Oxford. 2 vols. crown 8vo. price 12*s.* or 2 vols. demy 8vo. price 24*s.*

SELECTIONS from the WRITINGS of LORD MACAULAY. Edited, with Occasional Explanatory Notes, by GEORGE OTTO TREVELYAN, M.P. 1 vol. crown 8vo. [*In the press.*

LORD MACAULAY'S MISCELLANEOUS WRITINGS:—

LIBRARY EDITION. 2 vols. 8vo. Portrait, 21*s.*
PEOPLE'S EDITION. 1 vol. crown 8vo. 4*s.* 6*d.*

LORD MACAULAY'S MISCELLANEOUS WRITINGS and SPEECHES.

STUDENT'S EDITION, in crown 8vo. price 6*s.*

The Rev. SYDNEY SMITH'S MISCELLANEOUS WORKS; including his Contributions to the *Edinburgh Review.* Crown 8vo. 6*s.*

The WIT and WISDOM of the Rev. SYDNEY SMITH; a Selection of the most memorable Passages in his Writings and Conversation. 16mo. 3*s.* 6*d.*

The ECLIPSE of FAITH; or, a Visit to a Religious Sceptic. By HENRY ROGERS. Latest Edition. Fcp. 8vo. price 5*s.*

Defence of the Eclipse of Faith, by its Author; a rejoinder to Dr. Newman's *Reply.* Latest Edition. Fcp 8vo. price 3*s.* 6*d.*

CHIPS from a GERMAN WORKSHOP; Essays on the Science of Religion, on Mythology, Traditions, and Customs, and on the Science of Language. By F. MAX MÜLLER, M.A. &c. 4 vols. 8vo. £2. 18*s.*

ANALYSIS of the PHENOMENA of the HUMAN MIND. By JAMES MILL. A New Edition, with Notes, Illustrative and Critical, by ALEXANDER BAIN, ANDREW FINDLATER, and GEORGE GROTE. Edited, with additional Notes, by JOHN STUART MILL. 2 vols. 8vo. price 28*s.*

An INTRODUCTION to MENTAL PHILOSOPHY, on the Inductive Method. By J. D. MORELL, M.A. LL.D. 8vo. 12*s.*

PHILOSOPHY WITHOUT ASSUMPTIONS. By the Rev. T. P. KIRKMAN, F.R.S. Rector of Croft, near Warrington. 8vo. 10*s.* 6*d.*

The SENSES and the INTELLECT. By ALEXANDER BAIN, M.D. Professor of Logic in the University of Aberdeen. Third Edition. 8vo. 15*s.*

The EMOTIONS and the WILL. By ALEXANDER BAIN, LL.D. Professor of Logic in the University of Aberdeen. Third Edition, thoroughly revised, and in great part re-written. 8vo. price 15*s.*

MENTAL and MORAL SCIENCE: a Compendium of Psychology and Ethics. By the same Author. Third Edition. Crown 8vo. 10*s.* 6*d.* Or separately: PART I. *Mental Science,* 6*s.* 6*d.* PART II. *Moral Science,* 4*s.* 6*d.*

LOGIC, DEDUCTIVE and INDUCTIVE. By ALEXANDER BAIN, LL.D. In TWO PARTS, crown 8vo. 10*s.* 6*d.* Each Part may be had separately:— PART I. *Deduction*, 4*s.* PART II. *Induction*, 6*s.* 6*d.*

A BUDGET of PARADOXES. By AUGUSTUS DE MORGAN, F.R.A.S. and C.P.S. 8vo. 15*s.*

APPARITIONS; a Narrative of Facts. By the Rev. B. W. SAVILE, M.A. Author of 'The Truth of the Bible' &c. Crown 8vo. price 4*s.* 6*d.*

A TREATISE of HUMAN NATURE, being an Attempt to Introduce the Experimental Method of Reasoning into Moral Subjects; followed by Dialogues concerning Natural Religion. By DAVID HUME. Edited, with Notes, &c. by T. H. GREEN, Fellow and Tutor, Ball. Coll. and T. H. GROSE, Fellow and Tutor, Queen's Coll. Oxford. 2 vols. 8vo. 28*s.*

ESSAYS MORAL, POLITICAL, and LITERARY. By DAVID HUME. By the same Editors. 2 vols. 8vo. price 28*s.*

The PHILOSOPHY of NECESSITY; or, Natural Law as applicable to Mental, Moral, and Social Science. By CHARLES BRAY. 8vo. 9*s.*

UEBERWEG'S SYSTEM of LOGIC and HISTORY of LOGICAL DOCTRINES. Translated, with Notes and Appendices, by T. M. LINDSAY, M.A. F.R.S.E. 8vo. price 16*s.*

FRAGMENTARY PAPERS on SCIENCE and other Subjects. By the late Sir H. HOLLAND, Bart. Edited by his Son, the Rev. F. HOLLAND. 8vo. price 14*s.*

Astronomy, Meteorology, Popular Geography, &c.

BRINKLEY'S ASTRONOMY. Revised and partly re-written, with Additional Chapters, and an Appendix of Questions for Examination. By J. W. STUBBS, D.D. Fellow and Tutor of Trinity College, Dublin, and F. BRUNNOW, Ph.D. Astronomer Royal of Ireland. Crown 8vo. price 6*s.*

OUTLINES of ASTRONOMY. By Sir J. F. W. HERSCHEL, Bart. M.A. Latest Edition, with Plates and Diagrams. Square crown 8vo. 12*s.*

ESSAYS on ASTRONOMY, a Series of Papers on Planets and Meteors, the Sun and Sun-surrounding Space, Stars and Star-Cloudlets; with a Dissertation on the Transit of Venus. By R. A. PROCTOR, B.A. With Plates and Woodcuts. 8vo. 12*s.*

THE TRANSITS of VENUS; a Popular Account of Past and Coming Transits, from the first observed by Horrocks A.D. 1639 to the Transit of A.D. 2012. By R. A. PROCTOR, B.A. Second Edition, with 20 Plates (12 coloured) and 38 Woodcuts. Crown 8vo. 8*s.* 6*d.*

The UNIVERSE and the COMING TRANSITS: Presenting Researches into and New Views respecting the Constitution of the Heavens; together with an Investigation of the Conditions of the Coming Transits of Venus. By R. A. PROCTOR, B.A. With 22 Charts and 22 Woodcuts. 8vo. 16*s.*

The MOON; her Motions, Aspect, Scenery, and Physical Condition. By R. A. PROCTOR, B.A. With Plates, Charts, Woodcuts, and Three Lunar Photographs. Crown 8vo. 15*s.*

The SUN; RULER, LIGHT, FIRE, and LIFE of the PLANETARY SYSTEM. By R. A. PROCTOR, B.A. Second Edition, with 10 Plates (7 coloured) and 107 Figures on Wood. Crown 8vo. 14*s.*

OTHER WORLDS THAN OURS; the Plurality of Worlds Studied under the Light of Recent Scientific Researches. By R. A. PROCTOR, B.A. Third Edition, with 14 Illustrations. Crown 8vo. 10*s.* 6*d.*

The **ORBS AROUND US**; Familiar Essays on the Moon and Planets, Meteors and Comets, the Sun and Coloured Pairs of Stars. By R. A. PROCTOR, B.A. Second Edition, with Charts and 4 Diagrams. Crown 8vo. price 7*s.* 6*d.*

SATURN and its SYSTEM. By R. A. PROCTOR, B.A. 8vo. with 14 Plates, 14*s.*

The **MOON**, and the Condition and Configurations of its Surface. By EDMUND NEISON, Fellow of the Royal Astronomical Society, &c. With 26 Maps and 5 Plates. Medium 8vo. 31*s.* 6*d.*

A NEW STAR ATLAS, for the Library, the School, and the Observatory, in Twelve Circular Maps (with Two Index Plates). Intended as a Companion to 'Webb's Celestial Objects for Common Telescopes.' With a Letterpress Introduction on the Study of the Stars, illustrated by 9 Diagrams. By R. A. PROCTOR, B.A. Crown 8vo. 5*s.*

SCHELLEN'S SPECTRUM ANALYSIS, in its application to Terrestrial Substances and the Physical Constitution of the Heavenly Bodies. Translated by JANE and C. LASSELL; edited, with Notes, by W. HUGGINS, LL.D. F.R.S. With 13 Plates (6 coloured) and 223 Woodcuts. 8vo. price 28*s.*

CELESTIAL OBJECTS for COMMON TELESCOPES. By the Rev. T. W. WEBB, M.A. F.R.A.S. Third Edition, revised and enlarged; with Maps, Plate, and Woodcuts. Crown 8vo. price 7*s.* 6*d.*

AIR and RAIN; the Beginnings of a Chemical Climatology. By ROBERT ANGUS SMITH, Ph.D. F.R.S. F.C.S. With 8 Illustrations. 8vo. 24*s.*

AIR and its RELATIONS to LIFE; being, with some Additions, the Substance of a Course of Lectures delivered at the Royal Institution of Great Britain. By W. N. HARTLEY, F.C.S. Demonstrator of Chemistry at King's College, London. Second Edition, with 66 Woodcuts. Small 8vo. 6*s.*

NAUTICAL SURVEYING, an INTRODUCTION to the PRACTICAL and THEORETICAL STUDY of. By J. K. LAUGHTON, M.A. Small 8vo. 6*s.*

DOVE'S LAW of STORMS, considered in connexion with the Ordinary Movements of the Atmosphere. Translated by R. H. SCOTT, M.A. 8vo. 10*s.* 6*d.*

KEITH JOHNSTON'S GENERAL DICTIONARY of GEOGRAPHY, Descriptive, Physical, Statistical, and Historical; forming a complete Gazetteer of the World. New Edition, revised and corrected. 1 vol. 8vo. [*Nearly ready.*

The **PUBLIC SCHOOLS ATLAS of MODERN GEOGRAPHY.** In 31 Coloured Maps, exhibiting clearly the more important Physical Features of the Countries delineated, and Noting all the Chief Places of Historical, Commercial, or Social Interest. Edited, with an Introduction, by the Rev. G. BUTLER, M.A. Imperial 8vo. or imperial 4to. 5*s.* cloth.

The **PUBLIC SCHOOLS MANUAL of MODERN GEOGRAPHY.** By the Rev. GEORGE BUTLER, M.A. Principal of Liverpool College; Editor of 'The Public Schools Atlas of Modern Geography.' [*In preparation.*

The **PUBLIC SCHOOLS ATLAS of ANCIENT GEOGRAPHY**, in 25 Coloured Maps. Edited by the Rev. GEORGE BUTLER, M.A. Principal of Liverpool College. Imperial 8vo. or imperial 4to. 7*s.* 6*d.* cloth.

MAUNDER'S TREASURY of GEOGRAPHY, Physical, Historical, Descriptive, and Political. Edited by W. HUGHES, F.R.G.S. Revised Edition, with 7 Maps and 16 Plates. Fcp. 6*s.* cloth, or 10*s.* 6*d.* bound in calf.

Natural History and *Popular Science.*

TEXT-BOOKS of SCIENCE, MECHANICAL and PHYSICAL, adapted for the use of Artisans and of Students in Public and Science Schools.

The following Text-Books in this Series may now be had:—

- ANDERSON'S Strength of Materials, small 8vo. 3*s*. 6*d*.
- ARMSTRONG'S Organic Chemistry, 3*s*. 6*d*.
- BARRY'S Railway Appliances, 3s. 6d.
- BLOXAM'S Metals, 3*s*. 6*d*.
- GOODEVE'S Elements of Mechanism, 3*s*. 6*d*.
- ——— Principles of Mechanics, 3*s*. 6*d*.
- GRIFFIN'S Algebra and Trigonometry, 3*s*. 6*d*. Notes, 3*s*.6*d*.
- JENKIN'S Electricity and Magnetism, 3*s*. 6*d*.
- MAXWELL'S Theory of Heat, 3*s*. 6*d*.
- MERRIFIELD'S Technical Arithmetic and Mensuration, 3*s*. 6*d*. Key, 3*s*. 6*d*.
- MILLER'S Inorganic Chemistry. 3*s*. 6*d*.
- PREECE & SIVEWRIGHT'S Telegraphy, 3*s*. 6*d*.
- SHELLEY'S Workshop Appliances, 3*s*. 6*d*.
- THORPE'S Quantitative Chemical Analysis, 4*s*. 6*d*.
- THORPE & MUIR'S Qualitative Analysis, 3*s*. 6*d*.
- TILDEN'S Chemical Philosophy, 3*s*. 6*d*.
- WATSON'S Plane and Solid Geometry, 3*s*. 6*d*.

*** Other Text-Books in extension of this Series are in active preparation.

ELEMENTARY TREATISE on PHYSICS, Experimental and Applied. Translated and edited from GANOT'S *Éléments de Physique* by E. ATKINSON, Ph.D. F.C.S. Seventh Edition, revised and enlarged; with 4 Coloured Plates and 758 Woodcuts. Post 8vo. 15*s*.

NATURAL PHILOSOPHY for GENERAL READERS and YOUNG PERSONS; being a Course of Physics divested of Mathematical Formulæ expressed in the language of daily life. Translated from GANOT'S *Cours de Physique* and by E. ATKINSON, Ph.D. F.C.S. Second Edition, with 2 Plates and 429 Woodcuts. Crown 8vo. price 7*s*. 6*d*.

HELMHOLTZ'S POPULAR LECTURES on SCIENTIFIC SUBJECTS. Translated by E. ATKINSON, Ph.D. F.C.S. Professor of Experimental Science, Staff College. With an Introduction by Professor TYNDALL. 8vo. with numerous Woodcuts, price 12*s*. 6*d*.

On the SENSATIONS of TONE as a Physiological Basis for the Theory of Music. By HERMANN L. F. HELMHOLTZ, M.D. Professor of Physics in the University of Berlin. Translated, with the Author's sanction, from the Third German Edition, with Additional Notes and an Additional Appendix, by ALEXANDER J. ELLIS, F.R.S. &c. 8vo. price 36*s*.

The HISTORY of MODERN MUSIC, a Course of Lectures delivered at the Royal Institution of Great Britain. By JOHN HULLAH, Professor of Vocal Music in Queen's College and Bedford College, and Organist of Charterhouse. New Edition. 8vo. 8*s*. 6*d*.

The TRANSITION PERIOD of MUSICAL HISTORY; a Second Course of Lectures on the History of Music from the Beginning of the Seventeenth to the Middle of the Eighteenth Century, delivered at the Royal Institution. By JOHN HULLAH. New Edition. 8vo. 10*s*. 6*d*.

SOUND. By JOHN TYNDALL, LL.D. D.C.L. F.R.S. Third Edition, including Recent Researches on Fog-Signalling; Portrait and Woodcuts. Crown 8vo. 10*s*. 6*d*.

HEAT a MODE of MOTION. By JOHN TYNDALL, LL.D. D.C.L. F.R.S. Fifth Edition. Plate and Woodcuts. Crown 8vo. 10*s*. 6*d*.

CONTRIBUTIONS to MOLECULAR PHYSICS in the DOMAIN of RADIANT HEAT. By J. TYNDALL, LL.D. D.C.L. F.R.S. With 2 Plates and 31 Woodcuts. 8vo. 16*s.*

RESEARCHES on DIAMAGNETISM and MAGNE-CRYSTALLIC ACTION; including the Question of Diamagnetic Polarity. By J. TYNDALL, M.D. D.C.L. F.R.S. With 6 plates and many Woodcuts. 8vo. 14*s.*

NOTES of a COURSE of SEVEN LECTURES on ELECTRICAL PHENOMENA and THEORIES, delivered at the Royal Institution, A.D. 1870. By JOHN TYNDALL, LL.D., D.C.L., F.R.S. Crown 8vo. 1*s.* sewed; 1*s.* 6*d.* cloth.

SIX LECTURES on LIGHT delivered in America in 1872 and 1873. By JOHN TYNDALL, LL.D. D.C.L. F.R.S. Second Edition, with Portrait, Plate, and 59 Diagrams. Crown 8vo. 7*s.* 6*d.*

NOTES of a COURSE of NINE LECTURES on LIGHT delivered at the Royal Institution, A.D. 1869. By JOHN TYNDALL, LL.D. D.C.L. F.R.S. Crown 8vo. price 1*s.* sewed, or 1*s.* 6*d.* cloth.

FRAGMENTS of SCIENCE. By JOHN TYNDALL, LL.D. D.C.L. F.R.S. Third Edition, with a New Introduction. Crown 8vo. 10*s.* 6*d.*

LIGHT SCIENCE for LEISURE HOURS; a Series of Familiar Essays on Scientific Subjects, Natural Phenomena, &c. By R. A. PROCTOR, B.A. First and Second Series. Crown 8vo. 7*s.* 6*d.* each.

A TREATISE on MAGNETISM, General and Terrestrial. By HUMPHREY LLOYD, D.D. D.C.L., Provost of Trinity College, Dublin. 8vo. 10*s.* 6*d.*

ELEMENTARY TREATISE on the WAVE-THEORY of LIGHT. By HUMPHREY LLOYD, D.D. D.C.L. Provost of Trinity College, Dublin. Third Edition, revised and enlarged. 8vo. price 10*s.* 6*d.*

The CORRELATION of PHYSICAL FORCES. By the Hon. Sir W. R. GROVE, M.A. F.R.S. one of the Judges of the Court of Common Pleas. Sixth Edition, with other Contributions to Science. 8vo. price 15*s.*

The COMPARATIVE ANATOMY and PHYSIOLOGY of the VERTEBRATE ANIMALS. By RICHARD OWEN, F.R.S. D.C.L. With 1,472 Woodcuts. 3 vols. 8vo. £3. 13*s.* 6*d.*

PRINCIPLES of ANIMAL MECHANICS. By the Rev. S. HAUGHTON, F.R.S. Fellow of Trin. Coll. Dubl. M.D. Dubl. and D.C.L. Oxon. Second Edition, with 111 Figures on Wood. 8vo. 21*s.*

ROCKS CLASSIFIED and DESCRIBED. By BERNHARD VON COTTA. English Edition, by P. H. LAWRENCE; with English, German, and French Synonymes. Post 8vo. 14*s.*

The ANCIENT STONE IMPLEMENTS, WEAPONS, and ORNAMENTS of GREAT BRITAIN. By JOHN EVANS, F.R.S. F.S.A. With 2 Plates and 476 Woodcuts. 8vo. price 28*s.*

The NATIVE RACES of the PACIFIC STATES of NORTH AMERICA. By HUBERT HOWE BANCROFT. 5 vols. 8vo. with Maps, £6. 5*s.*

The ORIGIN of CIVILISATION and the PRIMITIVE CONDITION of MAN; Mental and Social Condition of Savages. By Sir JOHN LUBBOCK, Bart. M.P. F.R.S. Third Edition, with 25 Woodcuts. 8vo. 18*s.*

BIBLE ANIMALS; being a Description of every Living Creature mentioned in the Scriptures, from the Ape to the Coral. By the Rev. J. G. WOOD, M.A. F.L.S. With about 112 Vignettes on Wood. 8vo. 14*s.*

HOMES WITHOUT HANDS; a Description of the Habitations of Animals, classed according to their Principle of Construction. By the Rev. J. G. Wood, M.A. F.L.S. With about 140 Vignettes on Wood. 8vo. 14*s.*

INSECTS AT HOME; a Popular Account of British Insects, their Structure, Habits, and Transformations. By the Rev. J. G. Wood, M.A. F.L.S. With upwards of 700 Illustrations. 8vo. price 14*s.*

INSECTS ABROAD; a Popular Account of Foreign Insects, their Structure, Habits, and Transformations. By J. G. Wood, M.A. F.L.S. Printed and illustrated uniformly with 'Insects at Home.' 8vo. price 21*s.*

STRANGE DWELLINGS; a description of the Habitations of Animals, abridged from 'Homes without Hands.' By the Rev. J. G. Wood, M.A. F.L.S. With about 60 Woodcut Illustrations. Crown 8vo. price 7*s.* 6*d.*

OUT of DOORS; a Selection of original Articles on Practical Natural History. By the Rev. J. G. Wood, M.A. F.L.S. With Eleven Illustrations from Original Designs engraved on Wood by G. Pearson. Crown 8vo. price 7*s.* 6*d.*

A FAMILIAR HISTORY of BIRDS. By E. Stanley, D.D. F.R.S. late Lord Bishop of Norwich. Seventh Edition, with Woodcuts. Fcp. 3*s.* 6*d.*

The SEA and its LIVING WONDERS. By Dr. George Hartwig. Latest revised Edition. 8vo. with many Illustrations, 10*s.* 6*d.*

The TROPICAL WORLD. By Dr. George Hartwig. With above 160 Illustrations. Latest revised Edition. 8vo. price 10*s.* 6*d.*

The SUBTERRANEAN WORLD. By Dr. George Hartwig. With 3 Maps and about 80 Woodcuts, including 8 full size of page. 8vo. price 10*s.* 6*d.*

The POLAR WORLD, a Popular Description of Man and Nature in the Arctic and Antarctic Regions of the Globe. By Dr. George Hartwig. With 8 Chromoxylographs, 3 Maps, and 85 Woodcuts. 8vo. 10*s.* 6*d.*

THE AERIAL WORLD. By Dr. G. Hartwig. New Edition, with 8 Chromoxylographs and 60 Woodcut Illustrations. 8vo. price 21*s.*

KIRBY and SPENCE'S INTRODUCTION to ENTOMOLOGY, or Elements of the Natural History of Insects. 7th Edition. Crown 8vo. 5*s.*

MAUNDER'S TREASURY of NATURAL HISTORY, or Popular Dictionary of Birds, Beasts, Fishes, Reptiles, Insects, and Creeping Things. With above 900 Woodcuts. Fcp. 8vo. price 6*s.* cloth, or 10*s.* 6*d.* bound in calf.

MAUNDER'S SCIENTIFIC and LITERARY TREASURY. New Edition, thoroughly revised and in great part rewritten, with above 1,000 new Articles, by J. Y. Johnson. Fcp. 8vo. 6*s.* cloth, or 10*s.* 6*d.* calf.

BRANDE'S DICTIONARY of SCIENCE, LITERATURE, and ART. Re-edited by the Rev. George W. Cox, M.A. late Scholar of Trinity College, Oxford; assisted by Contributors of eminent Scientific and Literary Acquirements. New Edition, revised. 3 vols. medium 8vo. 63*s.*

HANDBOOK of HARDY TREES, SHRUBS, and HERBACEOUS PLANTS, containing Descriptions, Native Countries, &c. of a Selection of the Best Species in Cultivation; together with Cultural Details, Comparative Hardiness, Suitability for Particular Positions, &c. By W. B. Hemsley. Based on Decaisne and Naudin's *Manuel de l'Amateur des Jardins*, and including the 264 Original Woodcuts. Medium 8vo. 21*s.*

A GENERAL SYSTEM of BOTANY DESCRIPTIVE and ANALYTICAL. By E. LE MAOUT, and J. DECAISNE, Members of the Institute of France. Translated by MRS. HOOKER. The Orders arranged after the Method followed in the Universities and Schools of Great Britain, its Colonies, America, and India; with an Appendix on the Natural Method, and other Additions, by J. D. HOOKER, F.R.S. &c. Second Thousand, with 5,500 Woodcuts. Imperial 8vo. 31*s*. 6*d*.

The TREASURY of BOTANY, or Popular Dictionary of the Vegetable Kingdom; including a Glossary of Botanical Terms. Edited by J. LINDLEY, F.R.S. and T. MOORE, F.L.S. assisted by eminent Contributors. With 274 Woodcuts and 20 Steel Plates. Two Parts, fcp. 8vo. 12*s*. cloth, or 21*s*. calf.

The ELEMENTS of BOTANY for FAMILIES and SCHOOLS. Tenth Edition, revised by THOMAS MOORE, F.L.S. Fcp. 8vo. with 154 Woodcuts, 2*s*. 6*d*.

The ROSE AMATEUR'S GUIDE. By THOMAS RIVERS. Fourteenth Edition. Fcp. 8vo. 4*s*.

LOUDON'S ENCYCLOPÆDIA of PLANTS; comprising the Specific Character, Description, Culture, History, &c. of all the Plants found in Great Britain. With upwards of 12,000 Woodcuts. 8vo. 42*s*.

FOREST TREES and WOODLAND SCENERY, as described in Ancient and Modern Poets. By WILLIAM MENZIES, Deputy Surveyor of Windsor Forest and Parks, &c. With Twenty Chromo-lithographic Plates. Folio, price £5 5*s*.

Chemistry and *Physiology*.

A DICTIONARY of CHEMISTRY and the Allied Branches of other Sciences. By HENRY WATTS, F.R.S. assisted by eminent Contributors. Seven Volumes, medium 8vo. price £10. 16*s*. 6*d*.

ELEMENTS of CHEMISTRY, Theoretical and Practical. By W. ALLEN MILLER, M.D. late Prof. of Chemistry, King's Coll. London. New Edition. 3 vols. 8vo. PART I. CHEMICAL PHYSICS, 15*s*. PART II. INORGANIC CHEMISTRY, 21*s*. PART III. ORGANIC CHEMISTRY, New Edition in the press.

SELECT METHODS in CHEMICAL ANALYSIS, chiefly INORGANIC. By WILLIAM CROOKES, F.R.S. With 22 Woodcuts. Crown 8vo. price 12*s*. 6*d*.

A PRACTICAL HANDBOOK of DYEING and CALICO PRINTING. By WILLIAM CROOKES, F.R.S. With 11 Page Plates, 49 Specimens of Dyed and Printed Fabrics, and 36 Woodcuts. 8vo. 42*s*.

OUTLINES of PHYSIOLOGY, Human and Comparative. By JOHN MARSHALL, F.R.C.S. Surgeon to the University College Hospital. 2 vols. crown 8vo. with 122 Woodcuts, 32*s*.

HEALTH in the HOUSE; a Series of Lectures on Elementary Physiology in its application to the Daily Wants of Man and Animals, delivered to the Wives and Children of Working Men in Leeds and Saltaire. By CATHERINE M. BUCKTON. New Edition, revised. Small 8vo. Woodcuts, 2*s*.

The Fine Arts, and *Illustrated Editions.*

A DICTIONARY of ARTISTS of the ENGLISH SCHOOL: Painters, Sculptors, Architects, Engravers, and Ornamentists; with Notices of their Lives and Works. By S. REDGRAVE. 8vo. 16*s.*

MOORE'S IRISH MELODIES, with 161 Steel Plates from Original Drawings by D. MACLISE, R.A. Super-royal 8vo. 21*s.*

LORD MACAULAY'S LAYS of ANCIENT ROME. With 90 Illustrations on Wood, from the Antique, from Drawings by G. SCHARF. Fcp. 4to. 21*s.*

Miniature Edition of Lord Macaulay's Lays of Ancient Rome, with the Illustrations (as above) reduced in Lithography. Imp. 16mo. 10*s.* 6*d.*

POEMS. By WILLIAM B. SCOTT. I. Ballads and Tales. II. Studies from Nature. III. Sonnets &c. Illustrated by 17 Etchings by W. B. SCOTT (the Author) and L. ALMA TADEMA. Crown 8vo. price 15*s.*

HALF-HOUR LECTURES on the HISTORY and PRACTICE of the FINE and ORNAMENTAL ARTS. By WILLIAM B. SCOTT. Third Edition, with 50 Woodcuts. Crown 8vo. 8*s.* 6*d.*

The THREE CATHEDRALS DEDICATED to ST. PAUL, in LONDON; their History from the Foundation of the First Building in the Sixth Century to the Proposals for the Adornment of the Present Cathedral. By WILLIAM LONGMAN, F.A.S. With numerous Illustrations. Square crown 8vo. 21*s.*

IN FAIRYLAND; Pictures from the Elf-World. By RICHARD DOYLE. With a Poem by W. ALLINGHAM. With Sixteen Plates, containing Thirty-six Designs printed in Colours. Second Edition. Folio, price 15*s.*

The NEW TESTAMENT, illustrated with Wood Engravings after the Early Masters, chiefly of the Italian School. Crown 4to. 63*s.* cloth, gilt top; or £5 5*s.* elegantly bound in morocco.

SACRED and LEGENDARY ART. By MRS. JAMESON.

Legends of the Saints and Martyrs. New Edition, with 19 Etchings and 187 Woodcuts. 2 vols. square crown 8vo. 31*s.* 6*d.*

Legends of the Monastic Orders. New Edition, with 11 Etchings and 88 Woodcuts. 1 vol. square crown 8vo. 21*s.*

Legends of the Madonna. New Edition, with 27 Etchings and 165 Woodcuts. 1 vol. square crown 8vo. 21*s.*

The History of Our Lord, with that of his Types and Precursors. Completed by Lady EASTLAKE. Revised Edition, with 31 Etchings and 281 Woodcuts. 2 vols. square crown 8vo. 42*s.*

The Useful Arts, Manufactures, &c.

GWILT'S ENCYCLOPÆDIA of ARCHITECTURE, with above 1,600 Engravings on Wood. New Edition, revised and enlarged by WYATT PAPWORTH. 8vo. 52*s.* 6*d.*

HINTS on HOUSEHOLD TASTE in FURNITURE, UPHOLSTERY, and other Details. By CHARLES L. EASTLAKE, Architect. New Edition, with about 90 Illustrations. Square crown 8vo. 14*s.*

INDUSTRIAL CHEMISTRY; a Manual for Manufacturers and for use in Colleges or Technical Schools. Being a Translation of Professors Stohmann and Engler's German Edition of PAYEN'S *Précis de Chimie Industrielle*, by Dr. J. D. BARRY. Edited and supplemented by B. H. PAUL, Ph.D. 8vo. with Plates and Woodcuts. [*In the press.*

URE'S DICTIONARY of ARTS, MANUFACTURES, and MINES. Seventh Edition, rewritten and enlarged by ROBERT HUNT, F.R.S. assisted by numerous Contributors eminent in Science and the Arts, and familiar with Manufactures. With above 2,100 Woodcuts. 3 vols. medium 8vo. £5 5*s.*

HANDBOOK of PRACTICAL TELEGRAPHY. By R. S. CULLEY Memb. Inst. C.E. Engineer-in-Chief of Telegraphs to the Post Office. Sixth Edition, with 144 Woodcuts and 5 Plates. 8vo. price 16*s.*

TELEGRAPHY. By W. H. PREECE, C.E. Divisional Engineer, P.O. Telegraphs; and J. SIVEWRIGHT, M.A. Superintendent (Engineering Department) P.O. Telegraphs. Small 8vo. with 160 Woodcuts, 3*s.* 6*d.*

RAILWAY APPLIANCES; a Description of Details of Railway Construction subsequent to the completion of the Earthworks and Masonry, including a short Notice of Railway Rolling Stock. By J. W. BARRY, Member of the Institution of Civil Engineers. Small 8vo. with 207 Woodcuts, 3*s.* 6*d.*

ENCYCLOPÆDIA of CIVIL ENGINEERING, Historical, Theoretical, and Practical. By E. CRESY, C.E. With above 3,000 Woodcuts. 8vo. 42*s.*

OCCASIONAL PAPERS on SUBJECTS connected with CIVIL ENGINEERING, GUNNERY, and Naval Architecture. By MICHAEL SCOTT, Memb. Inst. C.E. & of Inst. N.A. 2 vols. 8vo. with Plates, 42*s.*

NAVAL POWERS and their POLICY, with Tabular Statements of British and Foreign Ironclad Navies, giving Dimensions, Armour, Details of Armament, Engines, Speed, &c. By JOHN C. PAGET. 8vo. 10*s.* 6*d.*

TREATISE on MILLS and MILLWORK. By Sir W. FAIRBAIRN, Bart. F.R.S. New Edition, with 18 Plates and 322 Woodcuts, 2 vols. 8vo. 32*s.*

USEFUL INFORMATION for ENGINEERS. By Sir W. FAIRBAIRN, Bart. F.R.S. Revised Edition, with Illustrations. 3 vols. crown 8vo. price 31*s.* 6*d.*

The APPLICATION of CAST and WROUGHT IRON to Building Purposes. By Sir W. FAIRBAIRN, Bart. F.R.S. Fourth Edition, enlarged; with 6 Plates and 118 Woodcuts. 8vo. price 16*s.*

The THEORY of STRAINS in GIRDERS and similar Structures, with Observations on the application of Theory to Practice, and Tables of the Strength and other Properties of Materials. By BINDON B. STONEY, M.A. M. Inst. C.E. New Edition, royal 8vo. with 5 Plates and 123 Woodcuts, 36*s.*

A TREATISE on the STEAM ENGINE, in its various Applications to Mines, Mills, Steam Navigation, Railways, and Agriculture. By J. BOURNE, C.E. Eighth Edition; with Portrait, 37 Plates, and 546 Woodcuts. 4to. 42*s.*

CATECHISM of the STEAM ENGINE, in its various Applications to Mines, Mills, Steam Navigation, Railways, and Agriculture. By the same Author. With 89 Woodcuts. Fcp. 8vo. 6*s.*

HANDBOOK of the STEAM ENGINE. By the same Author, forming a KEY to the Catechism of the Steam Engine, with 67 Woodcuts. Fcp. 9*s.*

BOURNE'S RECENT IMPROVEMENTS in the STEAM ENGINE in its various applications to Mines, Mills, Steam Navigation, Railways, and Agriculture. By JOHN BOURNE, C.E. New Edition, with 124 Woodcuts. Fcp. 8vo. 6*s.*

PRACTICAL TREATISE on METALLURGY, adapted from the last German Edition of Professor KERL'S *Metallurgy* by W. CROOKES, F.R.S. &c. and E. RÖHRIG, Ph.D. M.E. With 625 Woodcuts. 3 vols. 8vo. price £4 19*s.*

MITCHELL'S MANUAL of PRACTICAL ASSAYING. Fourth Edition, for the most part rewritten, with all the recent Discoveries incorporated, by W. CROOKES, F.R.S. With 199 Woodcuts. 8vo. 31*s.* 6*d.*

LOUDON'S ENCYCLOPÆDIA of AGRICULTURE: comprising the Laying-out, Improvement, and Management of Landed Property, and the Cultivation and Economy of Agricultural Produce. With 1,100 Woodcuts. 8vo. 21*s.*

Loudon's Encyclopædia of Gardening: comprising the Theory and Practice of Horticulture, Floriculture, Arboriculture, and Landscape Gardening. With 1,000 Woodcuts. 8vo. 21*s.*

REMINISCENCES of FEN and MERE. By J. M. HEATHCOTE. With 27 Illustrations and 3 Maps. Square crown 8vo. price 28*s.*

Religious and *Moral Works.*

CHRISTIAN LIFE, its COURSE, its HINDRANCES, and its HELPS; Sermons preached mostly in the Chapel of Rugby School. By the late Rev. THOMAS ARNOLD, D.D. 8vo. 7*s.* 6*d.*

CHRISTIAN LIFE, its HOPES, its FEARS, and its CLOSE; Sermons preached mostly in the Chapel of Rugby School. By the late Rev. THOMAS ARNOLD, D.D. 8vo. 7*s.* 6*d.*

SERMONS chiefly on the INTERPRETATION of SCRIPTURE. By the late Rev. THOMAS ARNOLD, D.D. 8vo. price 7*s.* 6*d.*

SERMONS preached in the Chapel of Rugby School; with an Address before Confirmation. By the late Rev. THOMAS ARNOLD, D.D. Fcp. 8vo. 3*s.* 6*d.*

THREE ESSAYS on RELIGION: Nature; the Utility of Religion; Theism. By JOHN STUART MILL. 8vo. price 10*s.* 6*d.*

INTRODUCTION to the SCIENCE of RELIGION. Four Lectures delivered at the Royal Institution; with Two Essays on False Analogies and the Philosophy of Mythology. By F. MAX MÜLLER, M.A. Crown 8vo. 10*s.* 6*d.*

SUPERNATURAL RELIGION; an Inquiry into the Reality of Divine Revelation. Sixth Edition, carefully revised, with Eighty Pages of New Preface. 2 vols. 8vo. 24*s.*

NOTES on the EARLIER HEBREW SCRIPTURES. By Sir G. B. AIRY, K.C.B. 8vo. price 6*s.*

ISLAM under the ARABS. By ROBERT DRURIE OSBORN, Major in the Bengal Staff Corps. 8vo. 12*s.*

RELIGION and SCIENCE, their Relations to each other at the Present Day; Three Essays on the Grounds of Religious Beliefs. By STANLEY T. GIBSON, B.D., late Fellow of Queen's College, Cambridge. 8vo. 10*s.* 6*d.*

The PRIMITIVE and CATHOLIC FAITH in Relation to the Church of England. Dy the Rev. B. W. SAVILE, M.A. Rector of Shillingford, Exeter, Author of 'Truth of the Bible' &c. 8vo. price 7*s.*

SYNONYMS of the OLD TESTAMENT, their BEARING on CHRISTIAN FAITH and PRACTICE. By the Rev. R. B. GIRDLESTONE, M.A. 8vo. 15*s.*

An INTRODUCTION to the THEOLOGY of the CHURCH of ENGLAND, in an Exposition of the Thirty-nine Articles. By the Rev. T. P. BOULTBEE, LL.D. New Edition, Fcp. 8vo. price 6*s.*

An EXPOSITION of the 39 ARTICLES, Historical and Doctrinal. By E. HAROLD BROWNE, D.D. Lord Bishop of Winchester. New Edit. 8vo. 16*s.*

The LIFE and EPISTLES of ST. PAUL. By the Rev. W. J. CONYBEARE, M.A., and the Very Rev. J. S. HOWSON, D.D. Dean of Chester:—

LIBRARY EDITION, with all the Original Illustrations, Maps, Landscapes on Steel, Woodcuts, &c. 2 vols. 4to. 42*s.*

INTERMEDIATE EDITION, with a Selection of Maps, Plates, and Woodcuts. 2 vols. square crown 8vo. 21*s.*

STUDENT'S EDITION, revised and condensed, with 46 Illustrations and Maps. 1 vol. crown 8vo. price 9*s.*

HISTORY of the REFORMATION in EUROPE in the TIME of CALVIN. By the Rev. J. H. MERLE D'AUBIGNÉ, D.D. Translated by W. L. R. CATES. 7 vols. 8vo. price £5. 11*s.*

*** Vol. VIII. completing the Work, is preparing for publication.

NEW TESTAMENT COMMENTARIES. By the Rev. W. A. O'CONOR. B.A. Rector of St. Simon and St. Jude, Manchester. Crown 8vo.

Epistle to the Romans, price 3*s.* 6*d.*
Epistle to the Hebrews, 4*s.* 6*d.*
St. John's Gospel, 10*s.* 6*d.*

A CRITICAL and GRAMMATICAL COMMENTARY on ST. PAUL'S Epistles. By C. J. ELLICOTT, D.D. Lord Bishop of Gloucester and Bristol. 8vo.

Galatians, Fourth Edition, 8*s.* 6*d.*
Ephesians, Fourth Edition, 8*s.* 6*d.*
Pastoral Epistles, Fourth Edition, 10*s.* 6*d.*
Philippians, Colossians, and Philemon, Third Edition, 10*s.* 6*d.*
Thessalonians, Third Edition, 7*s.* 6*d.*

HISTORICAL LECTURES on the LIFE of OUR LORD. By C. J. ELLICOTT, D.D. Bishop of Gloucester and Bristol. Sixth Edition. 8vo. 12*s.*

EVIDENCE of the TRUTH of the CHRISTIAN RELIGION derived from the Literal Fulfilment of Prophecy. By ALEXANDER KEITH, D.D. 37th Edition, with Plates, in square 8vo. 12*s.* 6*d.*; 39th Edition, in post 8vo. 6*s.*

HISTORY of ISRAEL. By H. EWALD, late Professor of the Univ. of Göttingen. Translated by J. E. CARPENTER, M.A., with a Preface by RUSSELL MARTINEAU, M.A. 5 vols. 8vo. 63s.

The ANTIQUITIES of ISRAEL. By HEINRICH EWALD, late Professor of the University of Göttingen. Translated from the German by HENRY SHAEN SOLLY, M.A. 8vo. price 12*s.* 6*d.*

The TREASURY of BIBLE KNOWLEDGE; being a Dictionary of the Books, Persons, Places, Events, and other matters of which mention is made in Holy Scripture. By Rev. J. AYRE, M.A. With Maps, 16 Plates, and numerous Woodcuts. Fcp. 8vo. price 6*s.* cloth, or 10*s.* 6*d.* neatly bound in calf.

LECTURES on the PENTATEUCH and the MOABITE STONE. By the Right Rev. J. W. COLENSO, D.D. Bishop of Natal. 8vo. 12*s.*

The PENTATEUCH and BOOK of JOSHUA CRITICALLY EXAMINED. By the Right Rev. J. W. COLENSO, D.D. Bishop of Natal. Crown 8vo. 6*s.*

An INTRODUCTION to the STUDY of the NEW TESTAMENT, Critical, Exegetical, and Theological. By the Rev. S. DAVIDSON, D.D. LL.D. 2 vols. 8vo. price 30*s.*

SOME QUESTIONS of the DAY. By the Author of 'Amy Herbert.' Crown 8vo. price 2*s.* 6*d.*

THOUGHTS for the AGE. By the Author of 'Amy Herbert,' &c. New Edition, revised. Fcp. 8vo. price 3*s.* 6*d.*

The DOCTRINE and PRACTICE of CONFESSION in the CHURCH of ENGLAND. By the Rev. W. E. JELF, B.D. 8vo. price 7*s.* 6*d.*

PREPARATION for the HOLY COMMUNION; the Devotions chiefly from the Works of JEREMY TAYLOR. By Miss SEWELL. 32mo. 3*s.*

LYRA GERMANICA, Hymns translated from the German by Miss C. WINKWORTH. Fcp. 8vo. price 5*s.*

SPIRITUAL SONGS for the SUNDAYS and HOLIDAYS throughout the Year. By J. S. B. MONSELL, LL.D. Ninth Thousand. Fcp. 8vo. 5*s.* 18mo. 2*s.*

ENDEAVOURS after the CHRISTIAN LIFE: Discourses. By the Rev. J. MARTINEAU, LL.D. Fifth Edition, carefully revised. Crown 8vo. 7*s.* 6*d.*

HYMNS of PRAISE and PRAYER, collected and edited by the Rev. J. MARTINEAU, LL.D. Crown 8vo. 4*s.* 6*d.* 32mo. 1*s.* 6*d.*

The TYPES of GENESIS, briefly considered as revealing the Development of Human Nature. By ANDREW JUKES. Third Edition. Crown 8vo. 7*s.* 6*d.*

The SECOND DEATH and the RESTITUTION of ALL THINGS; with some Preliminary Remarks on the Nature and Inspiration of Holy Scripture. By ANDREW JUKES. Fourth Edition. Crown 8vo. 3*s.* 6*d.*

WHATELY'S INTRODUCTORY LESSONS on the CHRISTIAN Evidences. 18mo. 6*d.*

BISHOP JEREMY TAYLOR'S ENTIRE WORKS. With Life by BISHOP HEBER. Revised and corrected by the Rev. C. P. EDEN. Complete in Ten Volumes, 8vo. cloth, price £5. 5*s.*

Travels, Voyages, &c.

The INDIAN ALPS, and How we Crossed them: being a Narrative of Two Years' Residence in the Eastern Himalayas, and Two Months' Tour into the Interior, towards Kinchinjunga and Mount Everest. By a Lady PIONEER. With Illustrations from Original Drawings made on the spot by the Authoress. Imperial 8vo. 42*s.*

TYROL and the TYROLESE; being an Account of the People and the Land, in their Social, Sporting, and Mountaineering Aspects. By W. A. BAILLIE GROHMAN. With numerous Illustrations from Sketches by the Author. Crown 8vo. 14*s*.

'The FROSTY CAUCASUS;' An Account of a Walk through Part of the Range, and of an Ascent of Elbruz in the Summer of 1874. By F. C. GROVE. With Eight Illustrations engraved on Wood by E. Whymper, from Photographs taken during the Journey, and a Map. Crown 8vo. price 15*s*.

A JOURNEY of 1,000 MILES through EGYPT and NUBIA to the SECOND CATARACT of the NILE. By AMELIA B. EDWARDS. With numerous Illustrations from Drawings by the Authoress, Map, Plans, Facsimiles, &c. Imperial 8vo. [*In the Autumn.*

OVER the SEA and FAR AWAY; being a Narrative of a Ramble round the World. By THOMAS WOODBINE HINCHLIFF, M.A. F.R.G.S. President of the Alpine Club, Author of 'Summer Months among the Alps.' With 14 full-page Illustrations, engraved on Wood from Photographs and Sketches. Medium 8vo. 21*s*.

THROUGH BOSNIA and the HERZEGOVINA on FOOT during the INSURRECTION, August and September 1875; with an Historical Review of Bosnia, and a Glimpse at the Croats, Slavonians, and the Ancient Republic of Ragusa. By A. J. EVANS, B.A. F.S.A. With Map and 58 Wood Engravings from Photographs and Sketches by the Author. 8vo. 18*s*.

DISCOVERIES at EPHESUS, including the Site and Remains of the Great Temple of Diana. By J. T. WOOD, F.S.A. 1 vol. Imperial 8vo. copiously illustrated. [*In the press.*

MEMORIALS of the DISCOVERY and EARLY SETTLEMENT of the BERMUDAS or SOMERS ISLANDS, from 1615 to 1685. Compiled from the Colonial Records and other original sources. By Major-General J. H. LEFROY, R.A. C.B. F.R.S. &c. Governor of the Bermudas. 8vo. with Map. [*In the press.*

ITALIAN ALPS; Sketches in the Mountains of Ticino, Lombardy, the Trentino, and Venetia. By DOUGLAS W. FRESHFIELD, Editor of 'The Alpine Journal.' Square crown 8vo. with Maps and Illustrations, price 15*s*.

The RIFLE and the HOUND in CEYLON. By Sir SAMUEL W. BAKER, M.A. F.R.G.S. New Edition, with Illustrations engraved on Wood by G. Pearson. Crown 8vo. 7*s*. 6*d*.

EIGHT YEARS in CEYLON. By Sir SAMUEL W. BAKER, M.A. F.R.G.S. New Edition, with Illustrations engraved on Wood, by G. Pearson. Crown 8vo. 7*s*. 6*d*.

TWO YEARS IN FIJI, a Descriptive Narrative of a Residence in the Fijian Group of Islands; with some Account of the Fortunes of Foreign Settlers and Colonists up to the Time of the British Annexation. By LITTON FORBES, M.D. F.R.G.S. Crown 8vo. 8*s*. 6*d*.

MEETING the SUN; a Journey all round the World through Egypt, China, Japan, and California. By WILLIAM SIMPSON, F.R.G.S. With 48 Heliotypes and Wood Engravings from Drawings by the Author. Medium 8vo. 24*s*.

UNTRODDEN PEAKS and UNFREQUENTED VALLEYS; a Midsummer Ramble among the Dolomites. By AMELIA B. EDWARDS. With a Map and 27 Wood Engravings. Medium 8vo. 21*s*.

The DOLOMITE MOUNTAINS; Excursions through Tyrol, Carinthia, Carniola, and Friuli, 1861-1863. By J. GILBERT and G. C. CHURCHILL, F.R.G.S. With numerous Illustrations. Square crown 8vo. 21*s.*

The ALPINE CLUB MAP of SWITZERLAND, with parts of the Neighbouring Countries, on the Scale of Four Miles to an Inch. Edited by R. C. NICHOLS, F.S.A. F.R.G.S. In Four Sheets, price 42*s.* or mounted in a case, 52*s.* 6*d.* Each Sheet may be had separately, price 12*s.* or mounted in a case, 15*s.*

MAP of the CHAIN of MONT BLANC, from an Actual Survey in 1863-1864. By ADAMS-REILLY, F.R.G.S. M.A.C. Published under the Authority of the Alpine Club. In Chromolithography on extra stout drawing-paper 28in. × 17in. price 10*s.* or mounted on canvas in a folding case, 12*s.* 6*d.*

HOW to SEE NORWAY. By Captain J. R. CAMPBELL. With Map and 5 Woodcuts. Fcp. 8vo. price 5*s.*

GUIDE to the PYRENEES, for the use of Mountaineers. By CHARLES PACKE. With Map and Illustrations. Crown 8vo. 7*s.* 6*d.*

The ALPINE GUIDE. By JOHN BALL, M.R.I.A. late President of the Alpine Club. 3 vols. post 8vo. Thoroughly Revised Editions, with Maps and Illustrations:—I. *Western Alps*, 6*s.* 6*d.* II. *Central Alps*, 7*s.* 6*d.* III. *Eastern Alps*, 10*s.* 6*d.* Or in Ten Parts, price 2*s.* 6*d.* each.

Introduction on Alpine Travelling in General, and on the Geology of the Alps, price 1*s.* Each of the Three Volumes or Parts of the *Alpine Guide* may be had with this INTRODUCTION prefixed, price 1*s.* extra.

Works of *Fiction.*

HIGGLEDY-PIGGLEDY; or, Stories for Everybody and Everybody's Children. By the Right Hon. E. H. KNATCHBULL-HUGESSEN, M.P. With Nine Illustrations from Original Designs by R. Doyle, engraved on Wood by G. Pearson. Crown 8vo. price 6*s.*

WHISPERS from FAIRYLAND. By the Right Hon. E. H. KNATCHBULL-HUGESSEN, M.P. With Nine Illustrations from Original Designs engraved on Wood by G. Pearson. Crown 8vo. price 6*s.*

NOVELS and TALES. By the Right Hon. B. DISRAELI, M.P. Cabinet Edition, complete in Ten Volumes, crown 8vo. price £3.

LOTHAIR, 6*s.*
CONINGSBY, 6*s.*
SYBIL, 6*s.*
TANCRED, 6*s.*
VENETIA, 6*s.*
HENRIETTA TEMPLE, 6*s.*
CONTARINI FLEMING, &c. 6*s.*
ALROY, IXION, &c. 6*s.*
The YOUNG DUKE, &c. 6*s.*
VIVIAN GREY 6*s.*

CABINET EDITION of STORIES and TALES by Miss SEWELL:—

AMY HERBERT, 2*s.* 6*d.*
GERTRUDE, 2*s.* 6*d.*
The EARL'S DAUGHTER, 2*s.* 6*d.*
EXPERIENCE *of* LIFE, 2*s.* 6*d.*
CLEVE HALL, 2*s.* 6*d.*
IVORS, 2*s.* 6*d.*
KATHARINE ASHTON, 2*s.* 6*d*
MARGARET PERCIVAL, 3*s.* 6*d.*
LANETON PARSONAGE, 3*s.* 6*d.*
URSULA, 3*s.* 6*d.*

BECKER'S GALLUS; or, Roman Scenes of the Time of Augustus: with Notes and Excursuses. New Edition. Post 8vo. 7*s.* 6*d.*

BECKER'S CHARICLES; a Tale illustrative of Private Life among the Ancient Greeks: with Notes and Excursuses. New Edition. Post 8vo. 7*s.* 6*d.*

The MODERN NOVELIST'S LIBRARY. Each Work, in crown 8vo. complete in a Single Volume:—

Atherstone Priory, 2*s.* boards; 2*s.* 6*d.* cloth.
Mademoiselle Mori, 2*s.* boards; 2*s.* 6*d.* cloth.
Melville's Gladiators, 2*s* boards; 2*s.* 6*d.* cloth.
——— Good for Nothing, 2*s.* boards; 2*s.* 6*d.* cloth.
——— Holmby House, 2*s.* boards; 2*s.* 6*d.* cloth.
——— Interpreter, 2*s.* boards; 2*s.* 6*d.* cloth.
——— Kate Coventry, 2*s.* boards; 2*s.* 6*d.* cloth.
——— Queen's Maries, 2*s.* boards; 2*s.* 6*d.* cloth.
——— Digby Grand, 2*s.* boards; 2*s.* 6*d.* cloth.
——— General Bounce, 2*s.* boards; 2*s.* 6*d.* cloth.
Trollope's Warden, 1*s.* 6*d.* boards; 2*s.* cloth.
———Barchester Towers, 2*s.* boards; 2*s.* 6*d.* cloth.
Bramley-Moore's Six Sisters *of the* Valleys, 2*s.* boards; 2*s.* 6*d.* cloth.
The Burgomaster's Family, 2*s.* boards; 2*s.* 6*d.* cloth.
Elsa, a Tale of the Tyrolean Alps. Translated from the German of Wilhelmine Von Hillern by Lady Wallace. 2*s.* boards; 2*s.* 6*d.* cloth.

Poetry and *The Drama.*

POEMS. By William B. Scott. I. Ballads and Tales. II. Studies from Nature. III. Sonnets &c. Illustrated by 17 Etchings by L. Alma Tadema and William B. Scott. Crown 8vo. price 15*s.*

MOORE'S IRISH MELODIES, with 161 Steel Plates from Original Drawings by D. Maclise, R.A. New Edition. Super-royal 8vo. 21*s.*

The LONDON SERIES of FRENCH CLASSICS. Edited by Ch. Cassal, LL.D. T. Karcher, LL.B. and Léonce Stièvenard. In course of publication, in fcp. 8vo. volumes. The following Plays, in the Division of the Drama in this Series, are now ready:—

Corneille's Le Cid, 1*s.* 6*d.*
Corneille's Polyeucte, 1*s.* 6*d.*
Racine's Iphigénie, 1*s.* 6*d.*
Voltaire's Zaïre, 1*s.* 6*d.*
Voltaire's Alzire, 1*s.* 6*d.*
Lamartine's Toussaint Louverture 2*s.* 6*d.*
De Vigny's Chatterton, 1*s.* 6*d.*

BALLADS and LYRICS of OLD FRANCE; with other Poems. By A. Lang, M.A. Late fellow of Merton College, Oxford. Square fcp. 8vo. 5*s.*

SOUTHEY'S POETICAL WORKS, with the Author's last Corrections and copyright Additions. Medium 8vo. with Portrait and Vignette, 14*s.*

LAYS of ANCIENT ROME; with IVRY and the ARMADA. By the Right Hon. Lord Macaulay. 16mo. 3*s.* 6*d.*

LORD MACAULAY'S LAYS of ANCIENT ROME. With 90 Illustrations on Wood, from the Antique, from Drawings by G. Scharf. Fcp. 4to. 21*s.*

Miniature Edition of Lord Macaulay's Lays of Ancient Rome, with the Illustrations (as above) reduced in Lithography. Imp. 16mo. 10*s.* 6*d.*

The ÆNEID of VIRGIL Translated into English Verse. By John Conington, M.A. New Edition. Crown 8vo. 9*s.*

HORATII OPERA. Library Edition, with Marginal References and English Notes. Edited by the Rev. J. E. YONGE, M.A. 8vo. 21*s.*

The LYCIDAS and EPITAPHIUM DAMONIS of MILTON. Edited, with Notes and Introduction (including a Reprint of the rare Latin Version of the Lycidas, by W. Hogg, 1694), by C. S. JERRAM, M.A. Crown 8vo. 2*s.* 6*d.*

BOWDLER'S FAMILY SHAKSPEARE, cheaper Genuine Editions. Medium 8vo. large type, with 36 WOODCUTS, price 14*s.* Cabinet Edition, with the same ILLUSTRATIONS, 6 vols. fcp. 8vo. price 21*s.*

POEMS. By JEAN INGELOW. 2 vols. fcp. 8vo. price 10*s.*
FIRST SERIES, containing 'DIVIDED,' 'The STAR'S MONUMENT,' &c. Sixteenth Thousand. Fcp. 8vo. price 5*s.*
SECOND SERIES, 'A STORY of DOOM,' 'GLADYS and her ISLAND,' &c. Fifth Thousand. Fcp. 8vo. price 5*s.*

POEMS by **Jean Ingelow.** FIRST SERIES, with nearly 100 Illustrations, engraved on Wood by Dalziel Brothers. Fcp. 4to. 21*s.*

Rural Sports, &c.

DOWN the ROAD; Or, Reminiscences of a Gentleman Coachman. By C. T. S. BIRCH REYNARDSON. Second Edition, with Twelve Coloured Illustrations from Paintings by H. Alken. Medium 8vo. 21*s.*

ANNALS of the ROAD; Or, Notes on Mail and Stage Coaching in Great Britain. By CAPTAIN MALET, 18th Hussars. To which are added, Essays on the Road, by NIMROD. With 3 Woodcuts and 10 Illustrations in Chromolithography. Medium 8vo. 21*s.*

ENCYCLOPÆDIA of RURAL SPORTS; a complete Account, Historical, Practical, and Descriptive, of Hunting, Shooting, Fishing, Racing, and all other Rural and Athletic Sports and Pastimes. By D. P. BLAINE. With above 600 Woodcuts (20 from Designs by JOHN LEECH). 8vo. 21*s.*

The FLY-FISHER'S ENTOMOLOGY. By ALFRED RONALDS. With coloured Representations of the Natural and Artificial Insect. Sixth Edition, with 20 coloured Plates. 8vo. 14*s.*

A BOOK on ANGLING; a complete Treatise on the Art of Angling in every branch. By FRANCIS FRANCIS. New Edition, with Portrait and 15 other Plates, plain and coloured. Post 8vo. 15*s.*

WILCOCKS'S SEA-FISHERMAN; comprising the Chief Methods of Hook and Line Fishing, a Glance at Nets, and Remarks on Boats and Boating. New Edition, with 80 Woodcuts. Post 8vo. 12*s.* 6*d.*

HORSES and STABLES. By Colonel F. FITZWYGRAM, XV. the King's Hussars. With Twenty-four Plates of Illustrations, containing very numerous Figures engraved on Wood. 8vo. 10*s.* 6*d.*

The HORSE'S FOOT, and HOW to KEEP it SOUND. By W. MILES, Esq. Ninth Edition, with Illustrations. Imperial 8vo. 12*s.* 6*d.*

A PLAIN TREATISE on HORSE-SHOEING. By W. MILES, Esq. Sixth Edition. Post 8vo. with Illustrations, 2*s.* 6*d.*

STABLES and STABLE-FITTINGS. By W. MILES, Esq. Imp. 8vo. with 13 Plates, 15*s*.

REMARKS on HORSES' TEETH, addressed to Purchasers. By W. MILES, Esq. Post 8vo. 1*s*. 6*d*.

The **HORSE:** with a Treatise on Draught. By WILLIAM YOUATT. New Edition, revised and enlarged. 8vo. with numerous Woodcuts, 12*s*. 6*d*.

The **DOG.** By WILLIAM YOUATT. 8vo. with numerous Woodcuts, 6*s*.

The **DOG in HEALTH and DISEASE.** By STONEHENGE. With 70 Wood Engravings. Square crown 8vo. 7*s*. 6*d*.

The **GREYHOUND.** By STONEHENGE. Revised Edition, with 25 Portraits of Greyhounds. Square crown 8vo. 15*s*.

The **OX;** his Diseases and their Treatment: with an Essay on Parturition in the Cow. By J. R. DOBSON. Crown 8vo. with Illustrations, 7*s*. 6*d*.

Works of *Utility* and *General Information.*

The **THEORY and PRACTICE of BANKING.** By H. D. MACLEOD, M.A. Barrister-at-Law. Third Edition, thoroughly revised. 2 vols. 8vo. price 26*s*.

The **ELEMENTS of BANKING.** By HENRY DUNNING MACLEOD, Esq. M.A. of Trinity College, Cambridge, and the Inner Temple, Barrister-at-Law. Crown 8vo. price 7*s*. 6*d*.

M'CULLOCH'S DICTIONARY, Practical, Theoretical, and Historical, of Commerce and Commercial Navigation. New and revised Edition. 8vo. 63*s*. Supplement, price 5*s*.

The **CABINET LAWYER;** a Popular Digest of the Laws of England, Civil, Criminal, and Constitutional: intended for Practical Use and General Information. Twenty-fifth Edition. Fcp. 8vo. price 9*s*.

BLACKSTONE ECONOMISED, a Compendium of the Laws of England to the Present time, in Four Books, each embracing the Legal Principles and Practical Information contained in their respective volumes of Blackstone, supplemented by Subsequent Statutory Enactments, Important Legal Decisions, &c. By D. M. AIRD, Barrister-at-Law. Revised Edition. Post 8vo. 7*s*. 6*d*.

PEWTNER'S COMPREHENSIVE SPECIFIER; a Guide to the Practical Specification of every kind of Building-Artificers' Work, with Forms of Conditions and Agreements. Edited by W. YOUNG. Crown 8vo. 6*s*.

WILLICH'S POPULAR TABLES for ascertaining according to the Carlisle Table of Mortality the Value of Lifehold, Leasehold, and Church Property, Renewal Fines, Reversions, &c.; also Interest, Legacy, Succession Duty, and various other useful Tables. Eighth Edition. Post 8vo. 10*s*.

HINTS to MOTHERS on the MANAGEMENT of their HEALTH during the Period of Pregnancy and in the Lying-in Room. By the late THOMAS BULL, M.D. Fcp. 8vo. 5*s*.

The MATERNAL MANAGEMENT of CHILDREN in HEALTH and Disease. By the late THOMAS BULL, M.D. Fcp. 8vo. 5*s*.

The THEORY of the MODERN SCIENTIFIC GAME of WHIST. By WILLIAM POLE, F.R.S. Seventh Edition, enlarged. Fcp. 8vo. 2*s*. 6*d*.

The CORRECT CARD; or, How to Play at Whist: a Whist Catechism. By Captain A. CAMPBELL-WALKER, F.R.G.S. late 79th Highlanders; Author of 'The Rifle, its Theory and Practice.' 32mo. 2*s*. 6*d*.

CHESS OPENINGS. By F. W. LONGMAN, Balliol College, Oxford. Second Edition revised. Fcp. 8vo. 2*s*. 6*d*.

THREE HUNDRED ORIGINAL CHESS PROBLEMS and STUDIES. By JAMES PIERCE, M.A. and W. T. PIERCE. With numerous Diagrams. Square fcp. 8vo. 7*s*. 6*d*. SUPPLEMENT, price 2*s*. 6*d*.

A SKETCH of the HISTORY of TAXES in ENGLAND from the Earliest Times to the Present Day. By STEPHEN DOWELL. Vol. I. to the Civil War 1642. 8vo. 10*s*. 6*d*.

The NEW CODE of the Education Department, with Notes, Analysis, Appendix, and Index, and a Sketch of the Administration of the Grants for Public Elementary Education (1839–1876). By H. J. GIBBS, and J. W. EDWARDS, Barrister-at-Law. Second Edition, revised and adapted to the New Code, 1876. Crown 8vo. 3*s*. 6*d*.

A PRACTICAL TREATISE on BREWING; with Formulæ for Public Brewers, and Instructions for Private Families. By W. BLACK. 8vo. 10*s*. 6*d*.

MODERN COOKERY for PRIVATE FAMILIES, reduced to a System of Easy Practice in a Series of carefully-tested Receipts. By ELIZA ACTON. Newly revised and enlarged; with 8 Plates and 150 Woodcuts. Fcp. 8vo. 6*s*.

MAUNDER'S TREASURY of KNOWLEDGE and LIBRARY of Reference; comprising an English Dictionary and Grammar, Universal Gazetteer, Classical Dictionary, Chronology, Law Dictionary, a synopsis of the Peerage useful Tables, &c. Revised Edition. Fcp. 8vo. 6*s*. cloth, or 10*s*. 6*d*. calf.

Knowledge for the *Young.*

The STEPPING-STONE to KNOWLEDGE; or upwards of 700 Questions and Answers on Miscellaneous Subjects, adapted to the capacity of Infant minds. New Edition, revised. 18mo. 1*s*.

SECOND SERIES of the STEPPING-STONE to KNOWLEDGE: Containing upwards of 800 Questions and Answers on Miscellaneous Subjects not contained in the FIRST SERIES. 18mo. 1*s*.

The STEPPING-STONE to GEOGRAPHY: Containing several Hundred Questions and Answers on Geographical Subjects. 18mo. 1*s*.

The STEPPING-STONE to ENGLISH HISTORY; Questions and Answers on the History of England. 18mo. 1*s*.

The **STEPPING-STONE to BIBLE KNOWLEDGE**; Questions and Answers on the Old and New Testaments. 18mo. 1*s.*

The **STEPPING-STONE to BIOGRAPHY**; Questions and Answers on the Lives of Eminent Men and Women. 18mo. 1*s.*

The **STEPPING-STONE to IRISH HISTORY**: Containing several Hundred Questions and Answers on the History of Ireland. 18mo. 1*s.*

The **STEPPING-STONE to FRENCH HISTORY**: Containing several Hundred Questions and Answers on the History of France. 18mo. 1*s.*

The **STEPPING-STONE to ROMAN HISTORY**: Containing several Hundred Questions and Answers on the History of Rome. 18mo. 1*s.*

The **STEPPING-STONE to GRECIAN HISTORY**: Containing several Hundred Questions and Answers on the History of Greece. 18mo. 1*s.*

The **STEPPING-STONE to ENGLISH GRAMMAR**: Containing several Hundred Questions and Answers on English Grammar. 18mo. 1*s.*

The **STEPPING-STONE to FRENCH PRONUNCIATION and CONVERSATION**: Containing several Hundred Questions and Answers. 18mo. 1*s.*

The **STEPPING-STONE to ASTRONOMY**: Containing several Hundred familiar Questions and Answers on the Earth and the Solar and Stellar Systems. 18mo. 1*s.*

The **STEPPING-STONE to MUSIC**: Containing several Hundred Questions on the Science; also a short History of Music. 18mo. 1*s.*

The **STEPPING-STONE to NATURAL HISTORY**: VERTEBRATE OR BACK-BONED ANIMALS. PART I. *Mammalia*; PART II. *Birds, Reptiles, and Fishes.* 18mo. 1*s.* each Part.

THE **STEPPING-STONE to ARCHITECTURE**; Questions and Answers explaining the Principles and Progress of Architecture from the Earliest Times. With 100 Woodcuts. 18mo. 1*s.*

INDEX.

Spottiswoode & Co., Printers, New-street Square, London.

OPINIONS OF THE PRESS

ON

"The Aryan Origin

OF THE

Gaelic Race & Language,"

Showing the present and past Literary Position of Irish Gaelic; its Phonesis the Fountain of Classic Pronunciation; its Laws accord with Grimm's Laws; its Bardic Beauties the Source of Rhyme: the Civilization of Pagan Ireland; Early Knowledge of Letters; the art of Illuminating; Ancient Architecture.

THE ROUND TOWERS.

Four Opinions regarding them.

THE BREHON LAW.

THE IRISH RACE NOT PHŒNICIAN

TRUTH OF THE PENTATEUCH.

Knowledge in Pagan Times Retrogressive, not Progressive; the Inductive Sciences; Philology and Ethnology confirm the truth of Irish History; Gaelic names of Persons and Places full of Historic Suggestiveness; in this respect and in poetic power,

IRISH GAELIC SUPERIOR TO SANSKRIT.

ONE THOUSAND UNPUBLISHED IRISH MANUSCRIPTS

BY THE

VERY REV. ULICK J. BOURKE, M.R.I.A.,

Canon of Tuam Cathedral and President of St. Jarlath's College,

---

LONDON:

LONGMANS, GREEN & COMPANY, PATERNOSTER ROW.

1875.

(*From the Freemans Journal*)

The consumate skill with which the Very Rev· Author has utilized his ponderous materials, the acumen with which he states and supports his own views, the dexterity with which he aids a concurrent or combats an opponent —these, joined to great force of expression, signal illustrative faculty, and a wonderful range of learning, make this book altogether out of the ordinary category. Its perusal offers the most conclusive answer to those who question the advantage of exploration in the language, literature, and antiquities of Ireland. From this book the sceptical or the ignorant will learn to look with new sentiments upon what is the fashion to contemn or to neglect; to the scientific it will be a welcome auxilary, and no reader, we venture to predict, but will own that he has never spent his time to better purpose than in gathering from the rich stores here provided for him.

(*From the Morning Mail*)

Neither can we do more than indicate the popular reasons for the cultivation of Irish which he deduces from the literature and architecture of Ireland, the extant evidences of high artistic culture among the ancient Irish, and the Keltic laws, all of which, he demonstrates prove the "Aryan Origin of the Irish Race." Canon Bourke treats all these subjects exhaustively, and with extraordinary erudition and laborious research. In such an investigation the vexed question of the origin of the Round Towers could not be overlooked, and the author presents us with an able summary of all that has been written on the subject for the past seven centuries, reviewing the arguments in support of each theory, and supporting his own opinions by reasons of a very convincing character . . . . . The work is a most valuable contribution to philological literature; it displays immense erudition and research, combined with a judicial impartiality not always found in the works of enthusiastic writers on controverted questions of race and language. In style, it can be compared for clearness, energy, and aptness of illustration with any work in the English language; and we should be glad if we could see more works of the kind as the result of the learned leasure of the higher dignitaries of the Roman Catholic Church.

(From the Irish Times)

CANON BOURKE shows with admirable skill how, to men learned in the science of languages, a knowledge of the Keltic is a necessary element in their investigation, and he brings a blush to the cheek of Irishmen when he informs them that in France and in Germany that language which they are fast abandoning is studied with much interest and zeal by the great philologists of the day. In his researches, the author shows that there is a great similarity between the Latin and Gaelic letters. The depth of thought displayed in this work must raise it above the level of the ephemeral productions which too frequently in latter times have issued from the press . . . . . . Canon Bourke devotes an interesting chapter to the consideration of the Round Towers, and who built them? The three well-known theories he rejects, viz., 1st that they are the work of Danish hands; 2nd, of the early Christians; and 3rd, that they are not of remote Pagan origin. His own opinion is, that they were built by the early settlers of the Aryan race, many, centuries before the coming of Christ. That the Danes built them he looks on as absurd, for why, he pertinently remarks, had not the Danes built similar towers in Denmark, England, Norway and Belgium, where their power was more firmly established than in Ireland? That they were of Christian origin he denies, seeing that from the time of St. Patrick to the Danish invasion no ecclesiastical structure of massive proportions was built; that the stones in no instance are of the same character as the adjoining churches, neither is the mortar of the same chemical composition, nor is their erection noticed in any of the many lives of the Irish saints.

(*From the Celtic Magazine* Inverness, Scotland)

The book is in every respet a wonderful and interesting volume to the Kelt, at home and abroad, whether he be Scotch or Irish. . . . . . It is a Keltic repository—the writers Keltic reading for many years being appearantly thrown into a crucible, and having undergone a certain process there, are forged into the handsome and bulky volume before us. The Keltic student will find it valuable, and no one who takes an interest in Keltic philology, antiquity, manners and customs should be without a copy, for it is a perfect store of Keltic learning.

[*From the Literary World.*]

The author enters upon an elaborate argument to show that the language of the Gael is Aryan, and came down the stream of migration that had begun to flow westward from the high country between the Tigris and the Indus before Abraham went forth out of his country. His object is to revive an interest in the study of the Gaelic language in Ireland. "Through the eastern origin of language in Ireland," he writes, "one reaches the habitat of the people who spoke a common mother tongue in the hilly country of Persia and Armenia, and all along the fertile valleys watered by the Oxus, the Araxes, and the Euphrates, once, as many learned men suppose, the blissful site of Paradise. The phonesis of this primitive Aryan tongue did not rest on chance, but had been wedded, like music, to principles of science. These principles were handed down to the oldest daughter of the mother tongue—Gaelic—the phonetic developements of which show forth as this day the truth of Jacob Grimm's laws.

[From Nature.]

"The Aryan Origin of the Gaelic Race" is one of those books which a few years back would have teemed with the wildest vagaries. A diligent study of works like those of Zeuss and Max Muller has kept the author in the right path, and though he startles us now and then with such assertions as that the Aryan is "the primeval language of man," or that "there had been only seventeen letters in the Greek at the earliest period," his views are in general just and sound. We may doubt whether his theory of the Pagan origin of the Round Towers will be widely accepted. The book is a striking example of the extent to which a knowledge of Comparative Philology has spread, and the wholesome influence its principles have exerted.

[*From the Athenæum.*]

Canon Bourke has long been an earnest and active labourer in the field of Celtic literature. "The College Irish Grammar" and "Easy Lessons in Irish" are works which possess considerable merit, and are, we believe, extensively used by students of the Irish language at home and abroad. The present publication is of a far more ambitious character, a treats of and great variety of topics more or less closely related to the question of the Aryan Origin of the Gaelic Race and Language. The author appears to have read many of the best writers on these subjects. The work brings within reach of the general reader, and of the tyro in philosophy, many of the most striking results achieved by the comparatively new Science of Language.

[*From the Liverpool United Irishman.*]

Canon Bourke's book on the Aryan Origin of the Gael is replete with deep thought and profound erudition Its conclusions as to the Aryan Origin of the Keltic race and tongue based on philological analogies will deeply interest all lovers of archaic lore—but in nothing will it more deeply interest the Irish reader than in the decision at which he arrives as to the origin of those mysterious mile-stones of the ages that have withstood the teeth of time, only to remain as a permanent puzzle to the learned —"The Pillar Towers of Ireland."

[*From the Belfast Newsletter*—second notice.]

Our attention has been called to a communication from the Very Rev. Canon Bourke, President of St. Jarlath's College, Tuam, addressed to the *Athenæum*, in reference to that gentleman's recent valuable work on the Aryan Origin of the Gaelic Race and Language. The reviewer stumbled, as a matter of course, at the Round Towers of Ireland, the subject of so much controversy, but now by almost universal consent settling down fast to Pagan period. Canon Bourke has shown that the writer in the *Athenæum* had very imperfect knowledge of the question; but the President of St. Jarlath's ought to have known that, in many cases, the want of knowledge is a qualification of this class of literary work. The reviewer has not only misquoted the work, he has displayed much of what might be called stilty performance in dealing with an Irish subject.

[*From the Belfast News-letter.*]

The Round Towers of Ireland have been a puzzle for our archæologists. When, by whom, and for what purpose they were built, are questions which have given rise almost to as many theories as there are structures of this class remaining. On the one hand very able men have contended for their Christian origin; and one, not the main, argument in support of this view is derived from the fact that a great number of them are found in connection with leading ecclesiastical establishments. If it were possible to connect the building of these "old majestic temples of our own dear isle" with the Christian period no one would be more willing to do so than Canon Bourke, who is a distinguished archæologist, and evidently anxious to bring all he can into the service of his own Church; at the same time that he writes in a liberal spirit which has given us much pleasure; but he cannot make them Christian in their origin. His study of the science of comparative philology has enabled him to identify the early Irish with the Aryan race, which he proves was possessed of sufficient skill and power to erect these Towers. In this respect his argument is very interesting.

Canon Bourke, a Roman Catholic priest, says we are all children of the great Aryan family, be our modern name what it may; and this fact of common brotherhood between the peoples of the United Kingdom ought to make it the more easy to reconcile these peoples and induce them to work harmoniously for the promotion of our common good.

[*Galway Vindicator—Second Notice.*]

We have now given our opinion, whatever may be its value, of the book before us, gladly acknowledging its merits, such as they appeared to us, and in all honesty expressing our censure where we thought it deserved. We believe, firmly, that Canon Bourke has produced a work superior to anything that can be accomplished with the same end in view, by any other writer of the day. If we are to judge them by their works we can have no hesitation in placing Canon Bourke at the head of the living Irish scholars, and, with general philological attainments, we may safely predict that the European reputation which he must certainly earn, will endure long after more showy names of contemporary worthies shall have lost the narrow notority, gained by political turbulence that seems the chief spring of present Irish fame.

[*From the Galway Vindicator*]

Canon Bourke has shown the people of Ireland from the researches of previous writers, that they have descended in common with the other European nations from that ancient stock that we call Aryans, who once inhabited a broad region of Asia, spreading southward and eastward from the Caspian sea. The line of poof lies in the affinities of languages, for history is silent on the subject, and even tradition gives no aid to this truth. The work must be considered a valuable acquisition to our national literature. The theme is fascinating and important and it is discussed with all the force that, in the present state of knowledge, can be brought to bear on it. At a time, too, when there are signal efforts to subvert Faith by science, there is a peculiar pleasure in seeing it adduced as the friend of piety; and in his various scientific allusions, Canon Bourke takes care to bring vividly before us the goodness and greatness of the Creator.

Full of valuable learning, and teeming with religion, and with that now rare patriotism which is closely allied to it, the book before us must command the admiration of every reader who holds learning, religion, and patriotism as matters of any account.

[*From the Tyrone Constitution*]

The Very Rev. Canon Bourke, President of St. Jarlath's Roman Catholic College, Tuam, is admittedly learned, and fearlessly and truly Irish. Men may disagree with him but they must admit that what he states he believes or knows; and if a matter in doubt, that he has patiently examined it with all the light of great learning and acuteness of mind before giving his decision. Overruling authorities may escape the best judge and render his labours of no avail, but before a solemn judgment in law or scholarship can be moved the adverse authority must be recited, and the superior principle laid down clearly and distinctly. A few months back, the Messrs. Longmans and Co., London, published a work from the pen of Canon Bourke, entitled "Aryan Origin of the Gaelic Race and Language." The book is the result of learning, natural ability, and patriotic earnestness; in short, such a book as Irishmen should buy, study, and circulate for their own advantage and honour. There is nothing under ordinary circumstances so easy as to make flippant remarks regarding the labours of a scholar. Persons altogether incapable of performing such labours can cry them down, and earn a false notority by pretending to a superior knowledge on any subject. Criticism of this nature, dishonest at every stage, is current in literature. These tricks of the magazines and journals sometimes provoke authors and scholars, and when they do, the result is a retort not always courteous, and an exposure of the malpractice which does an immense amount of good for truth and learning at the time and in various directions. Canon Bourke's book challenges criticism; the subject he dealt with is debatable, but only deep thinkers and persons of wide and general information in antiquities, and accustomed to balance the niceties of language, the origin and structure of words, the evidences of the migration of races, can be heard pro or con with advantage. Proofs are called for on both sides; authorities must be recited; nothing can be taken for granted; all and everything advanced must be submitted to argument, proof and authority. One of Canon

Bourke's critics, a gentleman of the flippant tribe, has incurred his hostility, and comes in for a pounding which he is not likely to forget. The *Athenæum* has tried a rough-and-tumble with the Canon, and the Canon has clearly and cleverly got the upper hand of the critic—a man announced by the editor of that journal of more than ordinary grasp and depth of intellect, and of general scholarship. All these qualities have not saved him from blundering, and misrepresenting, and misquoting, and the Canon detects him and exposes him without pity.

[*From the New York Irish World*]

The Very Rev. Ulick J. Canon Bourke, of St Jarlath's College, Tuam, has published a book of 530 pages, full of learning, full of patriotism, full of suggestion and hope, all devoted to the instruction of the present generation, concerning the generations that have long ago peopled Ireland, England, Scotland and Wales. We must draw to a close to-day, our review of this most valuable contribution to Irish history and Irish literature, which should be in the library of every Irish priest and every Irish scholar in the whole world.

(*From the London Daily Standard*)

"The Aryan Origin of the Gaelic Race and Language." By the Very Rev. U. J. Bourke. London, Longmans, and Co., 1875.

The thoughtful and learned Work before us is one after Matthew Arnold's own heart, abounding as it does in historical evidences of the hereditary genius of the Keltic race in arts, science, and letters. With pardonable pride and partiality, as a true Irish patriot, Canon Bourke looks upon the Irish Branch of the Keltic race as the purest and most perfect type. . . . . The historical and ethnological value of this writer's researches cannot be well over-rated. He brings a vast amount of historic truth to light, and dissipates many errors. He refutes, for example, beyond all question, the common myth that the Pagan Irish were barbarians, and that civilisation only came to them by the preaching of St. Patrick; and yet a thousand years before "the saint of saints" landed on "the melancholy shores" of Ireland, a highly civilised race of Kelts lived in that kingdom, skilled in architecture, in painting, in music, in sculpture, in glass-making, in enamelling, in dying, in the workmanship of brass, silver, gold and iron, in the knowledge of reading and writing, and in the arts of colouring glass and metals which were not unknown, with laws of social life of the highest type of civilisation, and with a Constitutional Government partly Monarchical and partly Republican.

[*From the Globe.*]

The work contains a great deal of sound philological knowledge. Canon Bourke is familiar with the established laws of philology, and expounds them with reference to his subject in a lively and clear style. It is to be hoped his counsel will have some effect in rousing the learned class in Ireland to a sense of their duty in a matter in which they ought long ago to have distinguished themselves.

[*From the Derry Standard*]

This is a work of first-class merit, which every Irish scholar will peruse with satisfaction, as placing Irish Ethnology, and the ancient Language of Ireland, upon a rational, and withal a strictly critical basis, in conformity with the laws of Comparative Philology, as determined by the results of the latest modern researches.

(*From the Derry Sentinel*)

The author's universal reputation as one of the greatest living masters of the Gaelic language, his intimate knowledge of the history, traditions, and people of this country and the able and unbiassed manner in which he treats every branch of literature he handles, are sufficient credentials of his competency to explore a field where so many archæologists, historians, and philologists have floundered We cannot be expected to do justice in a small compass to this splendid volume of erudition and research, which we may, without fear of contradiction, say is a remarkable scholarly production. . . . . . "The Aryan Origin of the Gaelic Race and language" helps to settle this much-vexed question, irrespective entirely of the wonderful philological erudition in the volume, he will indeed deserve thanks from the Royal Irish Academy and sustain his claim for national recognition of the importance of education by means of the Gaelic language.

(*From the Scotsman*)

CANON BOURKE gives a deplorable account of the decay of the Gaelic Language in Ireland; and, although he is probably fighting a loosing battle, it is impossible not to sympathize with him in his desire to prolong the existance of Gaelic as a spoken tongue. His thorough knowledge of the grammatical structure of this ancient language has enabled him to give contributions to linguistic science in the shape of etymological notes respecting its inflections and its relationship to other tongues. This is a field in which very important results may yet be wrought out.

(*Limerick Reporter and Tipperary Vindicator.*)

Ireland really owes a debt of gratitude, and that no inconsiderable one. to the very reverend and very learned President of St. Jarlath's College, for this truly valuable and exceedingly interesting contribution to the knowledge of the language, literature, and antiquities of that "Isle of ancient fame." . . . . . Father Bourke, wielding his pen, as if it were the wand of Prospero, has brought us, whom he has shown to be the noblest Kelts of the noble Aryan race, back to our old home in the East; has worked language, and traditions, and legends most effectively with a view to this end, and has unquestionably succeeded in the grand object of his most interesting publication. The author's history of the Round Towers is that they are of Pagan (Eastern) Origin, built by the first Aryan Kelt settlers in Ireland, but have been utilised by the early Christians.

[*From the Roscommon Messenger.*]

We scarcely know which to admire most—its learned and solid matter, or its charming and felicitous style. It is easy to see at a glance that Canon Bourke is no novice at composition. He writes with great care and elegance, displaying at every page the riches of a well-stored and highly-cultivated mind. His sentences flow with an easy grace, while his power of illustration is admirably and skilfully displayed. His work is a splendid contribution to what he himself styles linguistic lore. . . . . It is for the general and intelligent reader a delightful and instructive work. . . . . We may liken Canon Bourke's new work to an Exhibition Palace, in every department of which we meet objects of great interest and attraction.

[*From the Academy.*]

The volume gives a good insight into the present state of the Gaelic Language in Ireland. Moreover the Aryan origin will not be disputed by the students of comparative philology.

[*From the Belfast News-Letter.*]

We want to show that, relatively to Englishmen, we are not what Lord Lyndhurst was accustomed to describe us, "alien in speech, in language, and in blood," and for this purpose we mean to rely on the valuable labours of the Very Rev. U. J. Canon Bourke, M.R.I.A., President of St. Jarlath's College, who has just published a most interesting work on the subject, and who generously acknowledges the efforts, in the same field, of Mathew Arnold, Professor of Poetry in the University of Oxford, and of John Stuart Blackie, Professor of Greek in the University of Edinburgh. Thus it is that great minds in Ireland, England, and Scotland, released from the restraints of prejudice, have been working in different parts; travelling, perhaps, in different routes.

[*From the London Morning Post.*]

The main value of the work lies in its store of comparative philology; but, to the curious in archæological lore, there will be found even more attractive matter in the able dissertation on the Round Towers and the Brehon Laws. . . . . The account of Gaelic poetry is also very good, as are the descriptions of early Irish art, which is shown to have been highly advanced, as all antiquarians knew that it was. . . . . . And altogether Canon Bourke has produced a book which is an honour alike to his country, his sacred profession, and to his own scholarship, and which is sure to obtain the respect it deserves.

[*From the Hour.*]

We believe Canon Bourke to be a favorable specimen of a clever, genial, patriotic Irish priest. Though of Norman race, he belongs to a country which has had a sad history. Critical honesty compels us to say that the

Canon's book contains much interesting matter, and several capital stories. Canon Bourke is scandalized—and we frankly go with him—that Irishmen are so ill-informed and apathetic about the language and archæology of their own land, while an Arnold in England, and a Blackie in Scotland, are lecturing and writing about Keltic literature. The Canon shows that the Gaelic language is Aryan or Indo-Earopean. Roman Catholicism he holds to be the only true variety of Christianity.

[*From Notes on Books, by Longmans, Green, & Co.*]

It has been the object of the author in the present work to subject to a systematic examination the language, the the national history, the laws, and the arts of the Gaelic population of Ireland.

His conclusion is that the Gaelic people is strictly Aryan —Sanskrit, Gealic, Latin, and Umbrian pointing to a primeval low Aryan type; while Zend, and British and Welsh, Greek and Oscan have sprung from a high Aryan source.

Reviewing the ancient Irish jurisprudence, the author endeavours to shew that the social and civil habits of the people evinced a highly-developed civilization in the pre-Christian period; and that their policy rested on the same foundation with that of the Hindus and Romans.

(*From the Belfast Eveniny Telegraph*).

While differing from many of the conclusions of the learned writer, we do not hesitate to say that the subject has been treated of in a manner which evidences a vast amount of original and painstaking research into a most interesting study, and is the most masterly work upon that subject we have ever perused. We would recommend its careful study not only by the philologist, but by those interested in the early history of their country.

From the Londonderry Standard.

This is a work of first-class merit, which every Irish scholar will peruse with satisfaction, as placing Irish ethnology, and the ancient language of Ireland, upon a rational, and withal a strictly critical basis, in conformity with the laws of Comparative Philology, as determined by the results of the latest modern researches. . . . But it is time that we should endeavour to give our readers some idea of the contents of Canon Bourke's admirable volume, whose appearance, as we have already said, every genuine Irish scholar will hail with delight not only as delivering our national literature, and archæology, from the ridicule and burlesque entailed upon both by the reveries of Vallancy, but as placing the whole subject upon the high vantage ground of science as now developed and elaborated by European scholarships in its highest department. . . . We commend this truly learned and critical work on the Gaelic Language, and Gaelic Antiquities, to all classes of educated readers.

[*From the Connaught Telegraph.*]

There is scarcely one of our readers to whom the name of the erudite President of St. Jarlath's College is not familiar as a household word. His varied attainments profound knowledge, and passionate devotion to the language of the Gael have won for him honor and esteem at home, appreciative recognition and respect in other lands. From his earliest youth, Canon Bourke has devoted himself with a missionary zeal, in the brief hours he could snatch from his many and engrossing avocations to the study and investigation of the history and the language of a race which was mature in all the noblest arts of civilization, long ages before the desecrating footsteps of the Danish invader first polluted our shores.

. . . . We heartily commend the "Aryan Origin of the Gaelic Race and Language" to the attention and perusal of our readers. It is written in a style at once clear and forcible, logical and eloquent. Is there a question to be proved, a doubt to be solved, the author invariably arrays his arguments in the convincing form of a syllogism. Is the imagination had to be pressed, are the feelings to be appealed to? Canon Bourke rises at once to the lofty height of descriptive eloquence, and his glowing words reproduce to the mind of the reader the ancient glories of Carnac and Luxor. . . . The publication of Canon Bourke's last and most successful effort ought to stimulate Irishmen to a proper appreciation of the value of the language of their fathers.

[*From the Northern Whig.*]

This learned and elaborate work shows the importanc of an exhaustive study of the ancient Irish language as a contributiou to the science of comparative philology. It is only recently that this science has attained to an independent position and dignity in the rich domain of analytic knowledge; and Canon Bourke has, we believe, successfully shown what a large place the Keltic tongue holds in any truly scientific inquiry into the relation of the early languages of the human race to each other. . . We must refer our more learned readers to the book itself for a thorough elucidatiou of the linguistic problems involved in the study of Irish. We have also several chapters on the Round Towers; and on the ample store of of ancient Keltic MSS. which lie nursed till the genius or patriotism of some future O'Curry or O'Donovan, or Joyce shall take them in hand, and let forth their light to the world. Canon Bourke is evidently a solid linguist and his work is a notable contribution to our national literature.

(*From the Nation.*)

We regard with pleasure the appearance of the present work of Father Bourke in conjunction with some recent and very satisfactory movements in favour of Ireland's ancient tongue; they wear to our eye something like the air of cause and effect. If our conjecture be correct, the fact must be eminently gratifying to the able and zealous President of St. Jarlath's, who has the cause of Irish Gaelic so truly at heart.

In concluding this brief and very inadequate notice of Canon Bourke's remarkable work, it is right to say that notwithstanding the number and the variety of the matters brought into its pages, its hold on the reader's interest is very persistent. Were we to indicate any divergent tendency, we should point to the too great amplitude with which the author has developed some of the analogies he employs. Though the title-page bears the imprint of a London publishing house, the book has been printed at home—an example which some other Irish authors might follow with benefit to themselves and their country.

(*From the Cork Examiner.*)

The author of this book is well known among Gaelic scholars for his very excellent "Irish Grammar," and "Easy Lessons in Irish." The present work exhibits all that one acquainted with his great linguistic acquirements might expect from his pen. How few, even among highly-educated Englishmen, or Irishmen either, know anything about the history of the Irish language, its Aryan relationship, or its vast importance in philological research. To the shame of Ireland, those long undiscovered facts have been established by no son of hers, but rather by Englishmen and foreigners, chiefly Germans, such as Pritchard, Grimm, Zeuss, Bopp, Ebel, Schleicher,

Max Muller, &c. Canon Bourke is the first Irishman who has followed up the work of those great philologists; and he now presents us with the fruits of his own industry in utilizing and adding to the explorations of his predecessors. His proofs in favour of the Aryan origin of the Gaelic race and language are drawn from comparative grammatical analysis with dialects which are well known as off-shoots of the primitive Aryan speech; from Gaelic phonesis; from names of Gaelic origin—extending all along from the Tigris to the Tagus and the Shannon; from the wonderful knowledge which the ancient Gaels had of painting and poetry; of law and architecture.

He devotes several chapters to an account of the decline of the Gaelic language in Ireland, where it was first made illegal, and then unfashionable. He taunts his fellow-countrymen and the Catholic Clergy with their apathy in "preserving!" (neglecting) the old tongue, and foretells that even in the most Irish-speaking counties, like Galway and Mayo, it must become extinct in another hundred years.

(*From the Ulster Daily Examiner.*)

Not to go outside "the Northern Athens," we were glad to note how cordially those, from whom no partiality for the clerical and national author might be expected, welcomed while reviewing the publication. The *News-letter* and the *Whig* were amongst the loudest in praise of the book, which the most hostile cannot deny to be a monument to the industry of an Irish priest who occupies the time which he can spare in discharge of his presidential duties in really painstaking investigation in the highest departments of learning, and who gives evidence that in the far West of Ireland pace is kept with the progress of the English Universities. A Catholic priest who gains words of praise and honour in the world of science from his Protestant fellow-workers elevates his creed and his cloth in the estimation of all, and is a virtual worker in the field of religion while he seems only to labour in the domain of science.